Consuming China

In the post-Mao era, China is often noted for its burgeoning consumer society in the train of economic reform. Consuming China explores the notion of Chinese consumption, refocusing attention on broader processes of social and cultural change in Greater China. Interrogating the concept of consumption in a Chinese context, the book suggests that it is not simply a symptom of economic reform. Rather, consumption has to be seen as a fundamental component of contemporary Chinese cultural practices, taking into account both the continuities and the ruptures between different contexts in Greater China and beyond.

In a departure from previous literature, the contributors extend their focus to incorporate a discussion of consumption outside mainland China, including case studies from Taiwan and Hong Kong. By considering these comparable transnational contexts, *Consuming China* affords a greater understanding of the practice of Chinese consumption and will appeal to China scholars and anthropologists, and to those with an interest in cultural studies.

Kevin Latham is a lecturer in Social Anthropology at the School of Oriental and African Studies, University of London.
Stuart Thompson is formerly lecturer in the department of Anthropology and Sociology at the School of Oriental and African Studies, University of London.
Jakob Klein is a lecturer in Social Anthropology at the School of Oriental and African Studies, University of London.

ConsumAsiaN Book Series
Edited by Brian Moeran and Lise Skov

The ConsumAsiaN book series examines the way in which things – and ideas about things – are consumed in Asia, the role of consumption in the formation of attitudes, experiences, lifestyles and social relations, and the way in which consumption relates to the broader cultures and societies of which it is a part. The series consists of both single-authored monographs and edited selections of essays, and is interdisciplinary in approach. While seeking to map current and recent consumer trends in various aspects of Asian cultures, the series pays special attention to the interactions and influences among the countries concerned, as well as to the region as a whole in a global context. The volumes in the series apply up-to-date theoretical arguments frequently developed in Europe and America to non-Western societies – both in order to analyse how consumption practices in Asia compared to those found elsewhere, and to develop new theories that match a specific Asian context.

Women, Media and Consumption in Japan
Edited by Lise Skov and Brian Moeran

A Japanese Advertising Agency: An Anthropology of Media and Markets
Brian Moeran

Contemporary Japan and Popular Culture
Edited by John Whittier Treat

Packaged Japaneseness: Weddings, Business and Brides
Ofra Goldstein-Gidoni

Australia and Asia: Cultural Transactions
Edited by Maryanne Dever

Staging Hong Kong
Rozanna Lilley

Asian Department Stores
Edited by Kerrie L. MacPherson

Consuming Ethnicity and Nationalism
Edited by Kosaku Yoshino

The Commercialized Crafts of Thailand: Hill Tribes and Lowland Villages
Erik Cohen

Japanese Consumer Behaviour: From Worker Bees to Wary Shoppers
John L. McCreery

Adult Manga: Culture and Power in Contemporary Japanese Society
Sharon Kinsella

Illustrating Asia: Comics, Humour Magazines, and Picture Books
Edited by John A. Lent

Asian Media Productions
Edited by Brian Moeran

Asian Food: The Global and the Local
Edited by Katarzyna Cwiertka and Boudewijn Walraven

Refashioning Pop Music in Asia: Cosmopolitan Flows, Political Tempos, and Aesthetic Industries
Edited by Allen Chun, Ned Rossiter and Brian Shoesmith

Consuming China

Approaches to cultural change in contemporary China

Edited by Kevin Latham, Stuart Thompson and Jakob Klein

Routledge
Taylor & Francis Group
LONDON AND NEW YORK

First published 2006 by Routledge
2 Park Square, Milton Park, Abingdon, Oxon OX14 4RN

Simultaneously published in the USA and Canada
by Routledge
270 Madison Ave, New York, NY 10016

Routledge is an imprint of the Taylor & Francis Group, an informa business

Transferred to Digital Printing 2009

Typeset in Times New Roman by Taylor & Francis Books

British Library Cataloguing in Publication Data
A catalogue record for this book is available from the British Library

Library of Congress Cataloging-in-Publication Data
A catalog record for this book has been requested

ISBN10: 0–700–71402–2 (hbk)
ISBN10: 0–415–54686–9 (pbk)
ISBN10: 0–203–64184–1 (ebk)

ISBN13: 978–0–7007–1402–5 (hbk)
ISBN13: 978–0–415–54686–7 (pbk)
ISBN13: 978–0–203–64184–2 (ebk)

Contents

Figures

Contributors

John Bayne is a freelance writer and trainer in intercultural communications, and part-facilitator in Intercultural Communications for the University of British Columbia, Vancouver, Canada.

Elisabeth J. Croll is Professor of Chinese Anthropology in the Department of Development Studies, School of Oriental and African Studies, University of London.

Harriet Evans is Professor in the Centre for the Study of Democracy, University of Westminster.

Jakob Klein is Temporary Lecturer in the Department of Anthropology and Sociology, School of Oriental and African Studies, University of London.

Kevin Latham is Lecturer in the Department of Anthropology and Sociology, School of Oriental and African Studies, University of London.

Michael Palmer is Professor in the Department of Law, School of Oriental and African Studies, University of London.

Luke Robinson is a doctoral candidate in the Centre for Media and Film Studies, School of Oriental and African Studies, University of London.

Charles Stafford is Professor in the Department of Anthropology, London School of Economics and Political Science, University of London.

Nicholas Tapp is Senior Fellow in the Department of Anthropology, Research School of Pacific and Asian Studies, Australian National University.

Stuart Thompson is Lecturer in the Department of Anthropology and Sociology, School of Oriental and African Studies, University of London.

Acknowledgements

The chapter entitled 'The consuming or the consumed? Virtual Hmong in China', by Nicholas Tapp, has previously appeared in *The Asia Pacific Journal of Anthropology* 1 (2), 2000, 73–101 (available online at www.tandf.co.uk/). Reproduced with permission of the publisher.

1 Introduction

Consumption and cultural change in contemporary China

Kevin Latham

Introduction

In the period of reform since the death of Chairman Mao and the fall of the Gang of Four, the People's Republic of China (PRC) has been consumed by the practices and rhetorics of consumption. On the one hand, from the early 1980s on, market reforms gave a new place in Chinese society to practices of consumption, with far-reaching social consequences (Link *et al.* 1989, 2002; Davis and Vogel 1990; Davis and Harrell 1993; Li 1998; Davis 2000; Huot 2000). Starting in the countryside with the introduction of the household responsibility system, Deng Xiaoping's economic reforms enabled Chinese families to accumulate new wealth and develop a new spending power not seen for decades. Between 1978 and 1985 alone, both rural income and rural consumption more than doubled. Urban income and consumption increased more slowly through the 1980s (61 per cent and 47 per cent respectively for the same period) but soared in the 1990s as rural rises slowed (Chao and Myers 1998: 353–4). The asceticism of revolution was replaced by the economic driving force of consumerism. Throughout the 1980s the Chinese population strived to buy the 'four goods': colour television sets, stereo cassette players, washing machines, and fridges. In the 1990s these were supplemented by motorbikes, cars, karaoke video-disc players, pagers, faxes and much more. In the first five years of the 1990s alone, the number of mobile phones in China grew from 20,000 to 3.4 million (Erwin 2000) and by early 2005 there were more than 350 million mobile subscribers (MII 2005).

At the same time as this massive growth in consumer spending on household, entertainment and electronic goods, there were accompanying increases in expenditure on food and leisure activities (Chao and Myers 1998; Davis 2000: 3–12) and people saw their leisure time transformed in the reform period (Wang 1995). Under Mao, time not spent working was generally taken up with household chores, political meetings and collective activities organized by the work unit. In the reform period, by contrast, domestic appliances such as washing machines and fridges reduced the time spent on housework, even if they simultaneously reinforced patriarchal attitudes (Robinson 1985), while political meetings became far fewer and more relaxed. Television provided entertainment without the need to leave home, and there was an explosion of opportunities for individual or family, rather than collective, leisure activities such as cinema or theatre-going, snooker, dancing, restaurant dining, bowling or other sports.

By the early 2000s, at least in urban areas, consumerism and its trappings had become regular features of everyday life, whether through consumer practices or media imagery. Consumerism has also contributed to the spatial transformation of Chinese cities, self-perceptions and social interactions in ways similar to what Lui has called the 'malling' of Hong Kong in the 1960s and 1970s (Lui 2001). Some of China's historic cities have relaunched themselves as the playgrounds of China's super-rich. Hangzhou, for instance, partly exploiting the historic resonances of its time as an Imperial capital and centre of affluence, has seen its famous West Lake revitalized as a relatively tranquil retreat for eastern China's multi-millionaires, with villas selling at 50,000 yuan per square metre and shopping malls filled with names like Armani, Dolce & Gabbana, Zegna, Louis Vuitton, Rolex and Dior (O'Neill 2005a). Indeed, international luxury goods makers have started to see China as a major market for conspicuous consumption, with an estimated 4.5 million Chinese having annual disposable income in excess of US$30,000 in 2005 (O'Neil 2005b).

These consumer practices, ranging from domestic spending to conspicuous consumption, constitute the tangible features of what has been characteristically described by scholars and journalists as China's 'consumer revolution' (see e.g. Davis 2000; Wu 1999; Li 1998; Chao and Myers 1998). Scholars and observers of China have also gorged themselves on the greater openness and access to China that has been brought by the reform period, and on the massive social, cultural, political and economic changes that it has entailed. Just as the Party, intellectuals and others in China were finding new ways to indulge in 'fevers', whether in contradistinction to the new consumerism, as with the intellectuals' 'Cultural Fever' (Zhang 1997; Wang 1996: 38, 48–56) or intricately embroiled with it as with 'Mao fever', 'Hula Hoop fever', or even patriotic fevers (Barme 1999: 8; Dirlik 1996: 194–5), so, too, scholars of China throughout the world have participated in what we might call a 'consumption fever', for the social and cultural changes of the reform era have been almost unknowable outside the frames of reference of markets and consumption. We need only think of how the post-Mao period is generally characterized as the 'reform' period. Given that the reforms in question are on the whole 'market reforms', such characterization clearly forefronts the economic aspects of social change in the country.

However, the focus of this volume is different to other recent volumes that have given important and insightful overviews and examples of recent consumer practices in mainland China (e.g. Davis 2000; Link *et al.* 2002). It differs in two fundamental ways. First, the focus is on practices of consumption, understood more broadly than consumerism, and their relation to different manifestations of social and cultural change. This includes the ways in which practices of consumption contribute to broader Chinese social and cultural changes, and also the ways in which various different kinds of changes are culturally understood in and through practices of consumption. Hence, Palmer (Chapter 4), Latham (Chapter 5) and Klein (Chapter 6) chart the appearance of 'the consumer' as a social actor and legal entity in China, while Tapp (Chapter 11) investigates the way that technological changes have transformed the consumption of ethnicity and Thompson (Chapter 7) considers the relationship between food consumption, death rituals and the transition from parent to ancestor.

Second, the focus of this volume is not restricted to mainland China and includes chapters on consumption in Taiwan (Stafford's Chapter 3), Hong Kong (Robinson's Chapter 10), and a transnational virtual context (Tapp's Chapter 11). In the light of recent work undermining unitary notions of Chineseness (e.g. Sun 2002; Chow 2000; Dirlik and Zhang 1997), the juxtaposition of different Chinese contexts is not intended to postulate broader underlying 'cultural Chineseness' of the kind often seen in the past (see, e.g., Johnson *et al.* 1985; Link *et al.* 1989; Sangren 1987). Rather, it offers a number of alternative starting points for the pursuit and understanding of both similarities or continuities as well as disjunctures and differences between Chinese practices of consumption. The emphasis in this volume is on cultural perspectives on Chinese consumption, broadly understood, and the identification of different kinds of change that can be viewed through the prism of consumption in Chinese contexts.

Several chapters in this volume do deal with consumption in post-Mao mainland China, but they also carry with them this underlying interest in social and cultural change. This is broadly pursued in one of two ways. One is through historical reflection over several decades. So, for instance, Croll (Chapter 2) offers an anthropological reflection on the cultural changes accompanying China's consumer revolution in the 1980s and 1990s, while Evans (Chapter 9) shows the importance of considering how forms of consumption in the reform period may be informed by practices dating back to the Mao period. The other way that cultural change is dealt with is by focusing on different key moments of change or transition. I have argued elsewhere (Latham 2002) that, although China's reform period has been dominated by 'rhetorics of transition', there is none the less a great deal of ambiguity as to what kind of transition is taking place. Different people may have quite different formulations of what China's transition is either from or to. Seen in this light, several chapters in this volume can be seen as detailing specific moments of transition that have helped make up the kaleidoscopic picture of China's changing social landscape. Bayne (Chapter 8), for instance, in a specifically historically situated paper, traces the emergence of practices of photography in early-1990s Hangzhou. Latham plots the emergence of the imagined consumer as a driving force in Chinese media production at a time when the newspaper group where he conducted research was launching a new, commercially-driven expansion strategy.

Klein, meanwhile, identifies a series of changes in the mediated consumption of food in Guangzhou accompanying the transformation of the city's restaurant scene by the arrival of ethnic and regional cuisines.

However, the idea of moments of transition can be extended to several of the other chapters in the volume dealing with other non-mainland contexts. Robinson, for instance, deals with the relation between mediated consumption in and of the films of Wong Kar-wai, against the backdrop of Hong Kong's 1997 handover and changes in global modernity more generally. Meanwhile, Tapp plots the transition of Hmong identity with the arrival of the internet, and Thompson considers the complex interrelationship between ritual, myth and consumption in the physical and symbolic transformations accompanying death. In all of these examples we find an underlying theme of cultural change related to consumption.

Characterizing Chinese consumption

This volume emerged from responses to a fairly straightforward-looking, but deliberately problematic question: what, if anything, is distinctive about or particularly characteristic of Chinese consumption? Considering the amount of scholarly attention devoted to China in the era of market reforms, and the commonplace observations of the consumerism, materialism and commodification that now characterize everyday life throughout Greater China, this is a surprisingly little-asked question. Indeed, consumption and consumerism have on the whole been taken for granted as already known and unproblematic categories of social behaviour, which do not require further elaboration.[1]

This question was one of the main starting points of a series of seminars organized and chaired by Stuart Thompson and Kevin Latham for the London China Seminar held at London University's School of Oriental and African Studies (SOAS) between October 1998 and June 1999, and earlier versions of several chapters in this volume were given at that time. The seminar set out to investigate the question of the 'Chineseness' of consumption in China and the issues that it raises. However, though the question may initially appear straightforward, contemporary China's economic, political and social contexts reveal a diverse range of complexities and contradictions, which make the answers to it complex.[2]

Since the publication of Galbraith's *The Affluent Society* in 1958 there has been a growing interest in consumption and consumerism in the social sciences, and there have been numerous calls to reappraise our understandings of contemporary society forefronting consumption rather than production which had previously occupied centre stage (see, e.g., Miller 1987, 1995; Parkin 1993; Appadurai 1986; Campbell 1987; Featherstone 1991; Douglas and Isherwood 1979; Bourdieu 1984; du Gay 1996).[3] Such theories also often link consumption to globalization and post-modernity. Several of the chapters in this volume also therefore consider the usefulness of these theories in Chinese contexts (e.g. those by Robinson, Bayne, Evans, Tapp). However, such theories of consumption have been worked out almost entirely in terms of European, American and other 'Western' experiences and, on the whole, in ways that assume a homogeneity to those experiences. There is a danger here of falling into the traps of exoticization through the use of the 'ethnic qualifier' (Chow 2000, 2004), contrasting 'Chinese consumption' with 'Western' consumption or consumption in general. However, this volume should be seen as an attempt not to instantiate essentialism but to problematize it, while simultaneously resisting the opposing tendency to homogenize through generalization or Eurocentrism. In this vein, the chapters refer to and apply Western theories of consumption in a range of different ways – some appreciative and some critical – without attempting to set up rigid delineations of what is 'Chinese' and what is 'Western'. At the same time we find several chapters in this volume identifying alternative issues that arise given quite different Chinese cultural, economic, political and historical contexts.

We might consider, for instance, how Chinese consumption may, in part at least, itself constitute a quite different *kind* of economy to those elsewhere. Hence, Charles Stafford argues that one cannot properly understand the development of so-called free markets in China without considering their imbrication in pre-existing but shifting relations of exchange. This is what he calls the Chinese 'ritual economy', which 'may be said to encompass not only traditional patterns of gift-giving during festivals and ritual occasions, but also the reciprocal provision of financial and practical support within networks of kin and friends, and . . . as a kind of "tribute" to the powerful'. Although analysts may be tempted to separate such a realm of cultural practices from conventionally conceived economic activity, Stafford argues that such a separation is problematic. It is not simply that there are particular culturally defined ways in which Chinese people come to conceive of their economic affairs, but rather that this ritual economy, in many instances, is precisely the economic activity about which they are thinking. At the same time, he argues that the emergence of free markets in China has to be understood in terms of a moral negotiation about changing relationships of exchange (cf. also Li 1998: 13–14).

Over the last decade, the academic study of what Stafford refers to as the ritual economy has been centred around the related activities of gift exchange and the cultivation of personal networks, or the 'art of *guanxi*' (e.g. Yang 1994; Yan 1998). Croll considers these emerging forms of social interaction when she investigates the relationship between China's new consumerism, the rising importance of *guanxi*, and political rhetorics which appeal to the 'traditional' values of a reformulated Confucianism in the 1980s and 1990s. Croll, like Stafford, deals with the complex intermingling of China's 'three economies': the State redistributive economy, the commodity economy and the gift economy. She argues that the increasing levels of consumption in China and the demise of Maoist political certainties fostered a revived interest in or nostalgia for the moral economy of Confucian social relationships. Contrary to the Weberian thesis that Confucianism held back the development of capitalism in China, Croll therefore argues that in fact a rehabilitated Confucianism provided some consolation in a new disconcertingly materialist and individualist social context.

However, the problematization of consumption with Chinese characteristics also demands questioning the homogenizing implications or tendencies that come with thinking of consumption in relation to national or cultural characteristics. Notions of Chineseness are no longer necessarily centred around the geo-politically defined area of China (Sun 2002; Lee, G. P. 2003; Lee, C. C. 2003; Tu 1994; Chun 1996) and it is widely accepted that there is an increasing disjuncture between the 'nation-form' presupposed by the Marxist–Maoist modernist project of the Chinese Communist Party, with its multiple manifestations, and the possibility of any longer conceiving of that nation as the coherent, unitary entity that that project requires (see, e.g., Dirlik and Zhang 1997: 3; Anagnost 1997; Rofel 1999). The reform period has brought with it, not least through differential access to consumption, new or increasing social and economic divisions between urban and rural areas, between the coastal provinces and the hinterland, between rich and poor, between men and women, young and old; and between entrepreneurs and state employees. With China's uniquely 'intranational transnational' character, which sees Hong Kong, Taiwan and the mainland all operate as distinct but closely intertwined political, social, cultural and economic entities, while at the same time, in theory at least, all being parts of thc same country, the issue of intra-cultural disjunctures cannot be avoided. Several chapters in this volume therefore attempt to gauge the relationships between specific local practices of consumption and broader national or transnational frames of reference (e.g. those of Robinson, Stafford, Tapp, Bayne), while others pay attention to socially differentiating factors such as gender (Evans, Croll), local identity or ethnicity (Klein, Tapp), family and kinship relations (Thompson), notions of modernity (Robinson) or access to technology (Tapp). All of these issues and chapters warn us against the dangers of homogenizing notions of Chineseness. They also suggest the importance of historically situating Chinese consumption, as we shall see in the next section.

The past in the present: how revolutionary is China's 'consumer revolution'?

The history of China in the twentieth century is scattered with significant watershed dates, such as 1911 and 1949, which each marked the revolutionary end to one era and the start of a new one. The year 1978 may be another such watershed, marking the moment of change between the Mao and the reform periods, following the Third Plenary Session of the Eleventh

National Party Congress in that year, when the projects of economic reform and the 'open door' policy were first publicly aired. Book titles give away the new periodization with their oft-repeated delineations of post-Mao, reform-era or reform-period China as their scope of inquiry.[4] Marked by consumption and consumerism, this new, post-Mao period of market reforms has come to be seen as radically different from the revolutionary period, and it is certainly important to recognize the substantial changes that have taken place. For instance, the renunciation of class struggle and collectivization as the driving forces of economic and social development, the decollectivization of agriculture, the acceptance of private entrepreneurship and the introduction of market-oriented rhetorics, cannot be seen as anything but totally radical reorientations from the past. However, at the same time it is important to historically contextualize these changes:

> While China disengages from its revolutionary past, as a postrevolutionary and postsocialist society, it still bears strong traces of that past, which serve as reminders of an earlier challenge to the capitalist world-system. The contradictions are most evident in the anomalous situation of a state that still claims socialism to legitimize itself, but must nevertheless demonstrate that legitimacy by being more successful at capitalism than capitalist societies (Dirlik and Zhang 1997: 8).

Even if one can find radical breaks, as Dirlik and Zhang suggest, it is crucial also not to overlook important continuities: the continuation of Party rule, the continuation of large-scale state enterprises as a unit of social organization (for a further twenty years at least), the continuation of strong, unquestionable political control of the media and the continuation of many rhetorics and practices of socialism. Hence, trying best to understand reform period China is often about identifying both the radical breaks and the continuities, as well as the contradictions, tensions, disjunctures and readjustments that result from their often awkward juxtaposition (cf. Anagnost 1997; Rofel 1999). In the context of consumption, consumerism and market reform we have to think not only of present practices but also in terms of what came before them, what has persisted from that past and how the present has always borne and continues to bear the marks of that past, even if at the same time it is often something radically new.

Ci Jiwei (1994), for instance, has characterized the reform period in terms of an emerging hedonism, associated with consumption and consumerism, contrasting the utopianism of the Maoist period. Yet, importantly, he does not characterize this as a simple historical transition, a step from one failed ideology to another. He argues, rather, that in fact hedonism was at the heart of the Maoist utopian project in the first place. The asceticism it invoked for the present was always seen in terms of the deferred satisfaction of material needs and desires to be enjoyed in the future. This offers a whole new perspective on the characterization of the reform period as something radically different, as something new, imported or liberated; as the replacement of a defunct political dogma. It also calls for consumption and consumerism in China in the 1980s and 1990s to be understood not only in terms of the present but also in relation to what went before it.

In a similar vein, the burgeoning consumerism under reform has been characterized by some scholars as a kind of palliative to relieve the pain of ideological nihilism (e.g. Croll 1994; Ci 1994; Liu 1997; Tang 1996). As Tang explains:

> A direct function of the rising consumerism is to contain and dissolve the anxiety of everyday life, to translate collective concerns into consumer desires (Tang 1996: 113).

However, palliative consumerism needs to be understood in terms of its specific historical situation.[5] As Tang argues, this new materialism has to be seen in relation to the earlier transcendence of the everyday through utopianism, under Mao, which it replaces (Tang 1996). Similarly, Liu (1997) has argued that, as the rhetorics and imagery of Mao's utopianism slipped away from the everyday experiences of Chinese citizens, so they 'failed to provide a stabilizing and enduring point of reference' (1997: 120) as they had been envisaged to do. Consequently, the social relevance of everyday life has come to be affirmed through the contemporary culture industries and the rise of commercial popular culture (Liu 1997: 120). In this respect, consumption in China has to be understood in relation to the recent political history of the nation and its shifting discourses of utopia, satisfaction and aspiration over the last five decades.

The government's conception of its own regulatory role in relation to consumption is a clear example of how the present needs to be seen in terms of the past. The Chinese authorities have always seen market regulation as being one of their key responsibilities in the new economy. So, for instance, in 1989 they introduced measures to slow the economy in the face of slowly spiralling inflation, while in 1999 they felt the need to promote consumption and discourage saving when economic growth seemed more sluggish. The Chinese government was becoming increasingly concerned about the preference of Chinese families to save rather than spend their money, and was keen to stimulate consumption through a number of devices, such as facilitating access to bank loans and introducing a new weighty tax on savings interest (Roberts *et al.* 1999; see also Latham 2002, footnote 16). Once again, in 2005, they saw themselves promoting consumption in order to reduce the nation's trade surplus and relieve the pressure on the yuan to drop its long-standing peg to the US dollar (*China Daily* 2005).

Palmer's chapter takes up the issue of the government regulation of consumption and also reveals the juxtaposition of conceptual frameworks from the past alongside radically new legal formulations. He charts the emergence of 'the consumer' as a legal entity in the 1980s and 1990s, through the extension of administrative measures, criminal penalties and civil law. Yet, though the idea that 'the consumer' should benefit from special legal protection is fairly new in China, Palmer concludes that the Chinese government's approaches to consumer welfare have remained ambiguous. Although substantial effort has been made to put in place a legal framework to protect the consumer, this effort none the less 'continues to bear the imprint of a strong state interest and to rely heavily on old-style campaigns, administrative controls, criminal law and mediation'. The radically new in the present is thoroughly imbued with the conceptualization and practices of the past.

In her chapter on images of women in Chinese media, Evans also questions whether or not what appears to be a radically different representation of women in the reform era compared to the Maoist era, should in fact be seen as quite so radically different. Through a close analysis of representations of women over recent decades, she argues that, despite the undeniable and eye-catching differences between reform and pre-reform imagery, in fact the underlying assumptions about gender have remained remarkably constant. She demonstrates that at the level of expectations of appropriate feminine behaviour there is no radical rupture occurring with the onset of reform. What has changed, rather, is the public and official affirmation of consumption and, with it, the acceptance of the notion of women's naturalized character as consumers of beauty. She points out how the assumptions about women as natural consumers, in fact, spans the two periods, but what has led to the marked differences in representations of women is the shift in the political constructions of consumption.

What emerges from an examination of reform-period China is, therefore, a fragmented picture of tensions, contradictions and divergent tendencies. Though the period is defined and named in relation to the radical political and economic breaks that have marked it, there remain none the less persistent imperatives which come from the past. The reform period, named as such principally because of the economic reforms which it has instantiated, has none the less been characterized by continuations with the preceding period even in the realm of the economy. Similarly, the rising consumerism of the 1980s and 1990s in China has to be seen as carrying with it in the post-revolutionary period the marks of its previous absence.

It is also important to situate consumption historically in relation to Taiwan and Hong Kong (cf. Mathews and Lui 2001; Bosco 1994; Gold 1996; Tu 1996). Hence, Stafford in this volume argues that contemporary Chinese consumption in both Taiwan and northern China has to be historically situated in relation to China's longstanding, but constantly shifting, ritual economy and conceptualizations of moral relationships. Meanwhile Thompson historically situates both the practices of death ritual and their representation in ethnography. In relation to Hong Kong, Robinson resists readings of Wong Kar-wai's films that centre around the 1997 watershed handover and, through an investigation of the continuities from one film to another, situates the consumption of Wong's films in relation to broader historical experiences of modernity. In so doing, he also draws our attention to the importance of broader global contexts of Chinese consumption.

China's consumption in global contexts

In recent years China has become an increasingly significant player on the global economic stage, metonymically symbolized by the country's entry into the World Trade Organization (WTO) in 2002. Consequently, China's various practices of consumption are also now embroiled in complex configurations of global practices and have to be understood sometimes as much in relation to global contexts as to Chinese ones. This raises the question of how to theorize Chinese consumption in global contexts, or how these contexts impact upon our understandings of Chinese consumption.

Some authors have taken consumption and consumerism in China to be merely the Chinese manifestation of global practices. So Dirlik, for instance, asserts that anything particularly Chinese about Chinese consumerism is merely nationalist Party rhetoric:

> For all the claims to 'Chineseness,' neither in motivation nor in form is there anything particularly 'Chinese' about the new cultural products, which are recognizable only as very contemporary products, on a local terrain, of a global consumer culture that erases the distinctiveness of the local by commodifying it. Claims to 'Chineseness' appear at best as efforts to contain the corrosive effects of commodification in a society where the present betrays no visible links to a past or an imagined future – except in the assertions of future power (Dirlik 1996: 195).

For Dirlik, in this passage, commodification is a universal process and the commodity form of goods is unitary and, indeed, corrosive.[6] Over recent decades, however, anthropological approaches to material culture have suggested that goods are not best thought of simply as goods in themselves but have to be understood in relation to the social contexts of their circulation and the way in which they move in and out of social relationships of different kinds (Appadurai 1986; Miller 1987; Parkin 1993). By such an understanding, the notion of indistinct products of 'global consumer culture' rapidly dissolves and consumption becomes always locally and historically situated (cf. also Watson 1999).

Several chapters in this volume (those of Tapp, Bayne, Stafford, Robinson) deal with issues of China's consumption, understood specifically in relation to either global or transnational contexts. Tapp, for instance, in his theoretically engaged chapter dealing with transnational practices of Hmong identity formation, shows how the notion of consumption with Chinese characteristics involves distinct discourses of local specificity, national heritage and transnational ethnic representation. On the one hand, he shows, there are particular Han Chinese ways of appropriating or reinventing minority nationality identities. On the other hand, any such identity formation takes place in the context of the geo-political state of China. However, Tapp's account makes it abundantly clear how neither of these contexts of Chineseness is adequate for understanding a 'Hmongness' which is virtually produced on the internet and negotiated, invented, imagined and misunderstood through the practices of diasporic living and travel. Hmong identity in the late twentieth century was negotiated as much in the virtual realm of the internet, in the imaginations of overseas Hmong in the United States or Taiwan, and in other regional contexts of Southeast Asia, as it was in the 'homelands' of western China.

Bayne is less concerned with transnational practices but addresses the issues of global homogenization and cultural interconnectedness associated with spreading practices of consumerism. He argues that it is perhaps more appropriate that we should consider not 'Chinese characteristics of consumption' so much as 'characteristics of consumption in or in relation to China'. Through a detailed and historically situated ethnographic account of photographic practices in Hangzhou in the 1990s, ranging from professional photographers to family snapshots, Bayne argues that, even though the technical and material forms of technology may be identical in different parts of the world, this does not bring about identical practices in their usage. However, at the same time, he argues that this does not mean that local practices of photography in Hangzhou should be considered inherently 'Chinese', or for that matter 'Hangzhounese'. Rather, they should be considered to be particular characteristics of consumption *in* China, a point which, following Parkin (1993) avoids the necessity to exoticize difference.

Viewed in this way it seems problematic, therefore, to simply construe consumption in China in terms of just one more manifestation of a global consumer society. Indeed, such characterizations are also heavily theoretically implicated, and observations such as Dirlik's that the world is being homogenized and 'corroded' by universal consumer culture are based upon a series of theories and presuppositions about the workings of global capitalism and the nature of commodified culture that should not be left unproblematized. These theories commonly associate the production of desire with the machinations of late capitalism, a formula which not only assumes a homogeneous global economic infrastructure but also denies people's agency in the making of their own histories (see, e.g., Baudrillard 1988: 5).

Baudrillard's early formulation of the position has been influential. He suggested that in 'consumer society' the workings of capitalist logic have transformed. Objects are no longer objects in and for themselves tied to a particular function or defined need (1988: 44) but have come to function as substitutable signifiers whose consumption therefore comes not to meet needs but to signify differences (1988: 45). By such accounts consumption is to be understood as part of the larger framework of productive forces. The capitalist system has come to produce desire such that production and consumption are one and the same thing (1988: 50). With theories of post-modernity, we see Baudrillard's assertions about substitutable signs, the production of desire and the identity of production and consumption mapped onto a global stage (see, e.g., Harvey 1990: 285–7; Jameson 1991, 1994; Ferguson 1990).[7] The relevant point here is that the notion of a global market is not a neutral space but one that is intricately constructed through numerous theoretical formulations and metaphors. Consequently, the appeal to a 'global consumer culture' cannot be treated as theoretically neutral either. This forces us to recognize that the incessantly produced consummation of desires understood in terms of the machinations of a global system is quite different from the satisfaction of material needs understood in relation to a previously unachieved and deferred utopianism. In this sense, it must be remembered that the social, historical and political contexts of capitalism in China have a certain specificity of their own.

We might think, for instance, of how consumption in China in the 1980s and 1990s found itself following a set of imperatives, derived from the persistence of bureaucratic control and ownership of large sectors of production, quite different from those typically associated with capitalism elsewhere. Chinese consumption is not always best thought of in terms of the individual private consumers on whom most theories of consumption are usually based. In the first decade of reform and to varying degrees in the second and third, the new 'socialist entrepreneurs' often worked not, as planned, according to capitalist principles but according to the hybrid logic of the unique economic situation in which they found themselves. State factory managers pursued policies of blind expansion and production involving alternative forms of consumption. Hence:

> Instead of seeking to maximize profits, managers sought to maximize enterprise wealth by maximizing inputs including raw materials and means of production, labour, wages, and state-supplied capital – with little concern for efficiency (productivity) or demand (the market). Instead of plowing surpluses back into production, to increase their competitive edge, they systematically sought to divert profits toward consumption (especially to build housing, recreational facilities, cultural and educational facilities, to purchase vehicles and consumer durables etc.) even when this threatened the financial health of the enterprise and/or caused it to fall into debt (Smith 1993: 65–6).

Such consumption expenditure was made precisely because of the continued existence of bureaucratic collective ownership and the welfare and cultural responsibilities that State enterprises continued to bear, even if decreasingly, through the reform period.[8] Furthermore, tackling these kinds of problem has figured prominently in Chinese economics and politics since the 1980s. Throughout the 1990s there were repeated campaigns against corruption and excessive expenditure by State-employed cadres, and it is precisely the problems caused by contradictions in the system that were being faced in the late 1990s and early 2000s by those embroiled in state enterprise reforms (cf. Cao and Chen 1997; Jin 1997). These peculiarities of Chinese capitalism and consumption are undoubtedly linked to the incorporation of Chinese manufacturing into the global market. However, they also show the importance of recognising the outcome of a complex configuration of economic, social and political forces that do not all derive from the Western-centred notion of the global expansion of late capitalism that is assumed in universalizing theories of consumption and globalization.

Foreign media products are also increasingly part of China's globalized consumption. Morris (2002), for instance, has argued that the mediated consumption of US basketball has not only been transformed in the process of consumption in China into something other than a representation of 'global culture', but has also given young Chinese people the chance to 'understand or shape their identities and communities' in different ways (2002: 11). As China becomes increasingly embroiled in international global politics and economics, it is therefore also important to consider how Chinese increasingly consume in global contexts and how this consumption often entails a negotiation of different internal and external influences.

China, consumption and representation

China's incorporation into the global economy has not only entailed consumption of global products, but also entailed reconceptualizations of Chinese society and the Chinese population, in terms both of academic understandings and representations of China and of China's representations of itself to itself. Hence, mass campaigns of the 1980s and 1990s promoting 'spiritual civilization' (*jingshen wenming*) were thoroughly embroiled in efforts by Chinese authorities at all levels to incorporate the nation's huge workforce into the global market economy (Anagnost 1997: 76). Similarly, discourses of population 'quality' (*suzhi*) have become important features in the public imagination of China's relation to global contexts (see, e.g., Greenhalgh 2005; Murphy 2004; Kipnis 2001; Bakken 2000; cf. also Fong 2004). This is one sense in which the reform period and the open door policy has led not only to consumption within China but also to consumption *of* China in a global context. However, this raises the question of representation more generally.

Considering academic and journalistic representations of China and the reform period we find, for instance, that the 1980s and 1990s have been almost inextricable from economic backdrops of consumption and market reforms. Some Chinese scholars, for instance, have been concerned about the threat that the marketization of cultural production poses to traditional Chinese high culture (e.g. Meng 1997: 67). Meanwhile, in scholarship on China more generally, the understanding of social relationships and changes to them in the reform era have often been characterized in terms of commodification, individualism, self-interest and utility (see, e.g., Gold 1985; Yang 1994; King 1994; Yan 1998) – terms either directly or indirectly derived from economic discourses. By contrast, the chapters in this volume take broadly cultural approaches to understanding consumption in Chinese contexts, including those situated outside post-Mao China. In this vein Thompson, for instance, revisits some of his own earlier ethnography to allow a consideration of how China, death and Taiwan are, have been, or ought to be consumed ethnographically. His chapter reveals the interplay of 'consuming' at three levels. There is the issue of consuming, or more accurately, not consuming, the dead in the rites, myths and narratives which constitute the focus of the chapter witnessed through fieldwork. Then there is also a re-working or 're-consuming' of that ethnography for a changed interpretive anthropological community (cf. Fardon 1991). Finally, this further relates to a context in which anthropologists are 'consuming China' through the specificity of particular death rituals in Western Taiwan.

The other way in which representation comes to play a crucial role in understanding consumption and cultural change in contemporary China is through practices of media production and consumption. The media and consumerism have together played a crucial part in the remoulding of contemporary China in a global context of market capitalism (Lee 2003; Rawnsley and Rawnsley 2002; Hemelryk Donald *et al.* 2002; Dirlik and Zhang 1997: 9). The proliferation of media over the last two decades, in the PRC in particular but also in Hong Kong and Taiwan, has been breathtaking. Since the early 1980s the vast majority of the Chinese population has gained access to television, and newspapers, magazines, radio stations and more recently websites, internet bulletin boards, chat-rooms and SMS text messaging services have all proliferated to a degree that the China of 2005 would have been unrecognizable to Chinese in 1980. At the same time advertising, which had no part to play in the media under Mao, has become part of everyday life and, often following Hong Kong and Taiwanese precedents, has become an ever more sophisticated feature of Chinese public communication and interaction.[9]

This media explosion in China has not only been an important part of the new consumer-oriented lifestyles, but it has also presented China-watchers with a plethora of new resources for seeking to understand the changes going on in Chinese society. We might note, for instance, the increasing attention to Chinese cinemas in recent years (see, e.g., Berry 1991; Browne *et al.* 1994; Lu 1997; Zhang 2004; Kuoshu 2002; Silbergeld 1999; Teo 1998; Bordwell 2000; Yau 2001; Fu and Desser 2000; Chu 2003) and how it is often taken as a route to understanding contemporary China, even as 'ethnography' (Chow 1995). Media consumption is therefore vital for understanding the changing profiles of China's 'imagined communities' (see Anderson 1983) with all their disjunctures and divisions. Consequently several chapters in this volume deal with both media representations themselves (those of Evans, Klein, Latham) and the changing nature of commodification and consumption that they may entail (those of Bayne, Tapp, Robinson).

Picking up on the relationship between China, representation, cinema and consumption, Robinson offers a detailed analysis of the films of Hong Kong director Wong Kar-wai. He pursues the question of whether or not the theme of consumption and the relationships between people and commoditized objects, which runs through Wong's films, is best understood in terms of Hong Kong's political economy and post-modernity, as many authors have tended to suggest. Robinson therefore resists standard 'national allegorical' interpretations of Wong's films that would correlate Hong Kong's oft-noted consumer culture with the consumption in Wong's films. However, Robinson concludes, on the contrary, that Wong's depiction of people's interactions with objects owes less to the fact that Hong Kong is a consumer society and more to an experience of modernity and the global market that is not in itself confined to Hong Kong. He resists the temptation to subsume Wong's treatment of consumption simplistically into a depiction of a world devoured by the passion for consumption. Rather, he suggests, these films revel in the passions *of* consumption and their significance in the making and experiencing of the worlds around us and that Wong's films themselves take on such a role.

Latham and Klein both return the discussion to the PRC and the interrelationship between different kinds of consumption and media representations. Latham, like Palmer, considers how China's consumerism has led to further reimaginings of the Chinese populace. His paper looks at China's media revolution of recent decades, focusing on newspaper production in Guangzhou and the Pearl River Delta. Through an ethnography of journalists, he investigates how the notion of the consumer figures broadly in journalists' everyday conceptions of their work and their products in two ways. On the one hand, the imagined consumer as the reader of their newspapers plays a vital role in daily editorial decision-making. The new emphasis, in a highly commercialized newspaper industry, is on pleasing readers in order to sell newspapers and hence also advertising space. On the other hand, this imagined reader is also often conceived of as the consumer of other products in a thoroughly consumerist world. Latham argues that the imagined consumer-reader is one of the key ways in which journalists have come to deal with the intense commercial pressures they now find themselves under. At the same time, it has provided an important mechanism by means of which journalists in the 1990s found themselves confronting and sometimes challenging the Party's long-standing control of media content.

As Latham points out, this situation can only be understood in relation to the specificities of China's media industries, which work simultaneously with notions of the consumer and the importance of advertising revenue, but also with the Party's conception of the instructive, educational or propaganda roles of the media as its 'mouthpiece'. This is a situation also dealt with by Klein (Chapter 6) in his close analysis of mediated gastronomy in Guangzhou's newspapers. He outlines how food pages and columns in newspapers in the later 1990s were not only practical guides to consumption but also enabled the vicarious consumption of expensive and exotic cuisines through the writings of journalists. However, Klein also shows how writings such as these simultaneously served the educational function attributed to Chinese media by the Party. These accounts served a double purpose by attracting Latham's reader-consumers to buy the newspapers, while also fulfilling journalistic responsibilities to 'civilize' the population.

All of these chapters remind us of the complex interaction between different representations and practices of representation within global contexts of both representation and consumption. They also remind us of the complexities involved in answering questions about Chinese characteristics of consumption, for we are faced with a dual imperative to consider both what may be particular to China, or parts of China, and what can only be understood in terms of broader political, economic, cultural and historical contexts. The challenge is clearly how to do this without reducing answers to the simplicity of either one or the other. As multiple representations come to compete as accounts of Chinese identity, and in our case, more specifically, as the characterization of China's consumerism, so we are increasingly faced with 'serious challenges to narrativizing China as a historical entity' (Dirlik and Zhang 1997: 7). This volume seeks to rise to such challenges.

Notes

1 Hence Madsen, for example, in his analysis of spiritual crisis among reform-era intellectuals, notes that 'Economic reforms have stimulated desires for more individual self-expression through the acquisition of consumer goods' (1990: 243). Yet he does not see it as necessary to either justify or question the assumption, common though it is in Western theorizing, that consumption is about self-expression. Madsen is but one example of this very common practice. As further examples consider for instance Davis (1995: 12, 18), Davis and Harrell (1993: 3), Siu (1993: 165), Vogel (1989: 76), Tang (1996: 107), Dirlik and Zhang (1997: 9), Liu (1997: 106), Croll (1994). This does not constitute a failing in these works or the many others that could be added to them, but highlights a largely unasked question.

2 On the complexity and contradictions of the contemporary PRC with attention to consumerism see, e.g., Barme (1999), Dutton (1998), Dirlik and Zhang (1997), Anagnost (1997). On Hong Kong see, e.g., Abbas (1997), Teo (1998), Leung (1995), Mathews *et al.* (2001). On Taiwan see, e.g., Harrell *et al.* (1994), Rubinstein (1994), Tu (1996), Gold (1996).

3 For useful critical overviews of such theorizing in different disciplines over this period of time, including anthropology, economics, sociology and media studies, see the contributions to Miller (1995).

4 Consider, e.g., Davis *et al.* (1995); Davis and Harrell (1993); Chen (1995); Rosenbaum (1992); Davis & Vogel (1990); Zhang (1997); Vogel (1989).

5 Elsewhere I have argued that, although such palliative arguments have validity in the Chinese context, they none the less fail adequately to address the question of Party legitimacy (Latham 2002).

6 Writing in 1997 with Zhang Xudong, Dirlik offers a more nuanced understanding of consumption in China, placing much more emphasis on the particular historical circumstances pertaining to recent Chinese consumption. It

might be argued, none the less, that consumption and consumerism are not problematized in themselves by Dirlik and Zhang (1997), or by others in that volume (e.g. Liu 1997).

7 The argument is neatly summarized by Ferguson (1990: 253): 'The "absolute" dimensionality of the market and its independence from the commodities exchanged upon it turned out to be illusory. The market is itself an aspect of production, locally "deformed" by the mass of commodities in it and directly expandable, perhaps infinitely so, through the creation of new exchange-values . . . It is not simply a matter, then, of large corporations monopolizing production and, by ideological means, manipulating the "need" for a particular commodity. Modern commodities are no longer subservient to the market; they are not tied "rationally" to needs or desires. The wishfulness they might satisfy is intrinsically renewable and unlimited. The "space" for their exchange is created in the same moment that the commodity is produced.'

8 In Smith's (1993) terms this is also why, in the 1980s and early 1990s at least, the reform-era economy in China could not be thought of as a market economy conventionally conceived (i.e. in terms of an outright capitalist system). This argument still holds true in the early 2000s.

9 Geremie Barme (1999), for instance, has argued that, with the technical and technological possibilities that commercialism has brought, the new era has nurtured mutual exploitation between a flourishing Hong Kong- and Taiwan-influenced advertising culture and the Party with its eye on the moving ball of power. Hence on the one hand the Party has adapted to ever more commercially and technically sophisticated ways of promoting itself in contrast to the stodgy propaganda of old, and has sought to appropriate both Kong-Tai culture and the local avant-garde. On the other hand advertisers have sometimes found it in their interests to exploit Maoist or Party imagery or symbolism for commercial purposes (see, e.g., Barme (1999), Dirlik (1996: 194–5), Tang (1996), Liu (1997: 108–9)).

References

Abbas, A. (1997) *Hong Kong: Culture and the Politics of Disappearance*. Hong Kong: Hong Kong University Press.

Anagnost, A. (1997) *National Past-times: Narrative, Representation and Power in Modern China*. Durham, N.C.: Duke University Press.

Anderson, B. (1983) *Imagined Communities: Reflections on the origins and spread of nationalism*. London: Verso.

Appadurai, A. (ed.) (1986) *The Social Life of Things: Commodities in Cultural Perspective*. Cambridge: Cambridge University Press.

Bakken, B. (2000) *The exemplary society: human improvement, social control, and the dangers of modernity in China*. Oxford: Oxford University Press.

Barme, G. R. (1999) *In the Red: On Contemporary Chinese Culture*. New York: Columbia University Press.

Baudrillard, J. (1988) 'Consumer Society', in M. Poster (ed.), *Jean Baudrillard: Selected Writings*. Cambridge: Polity.

Berry, C. (ed.) (1991)*Perspectives on Chinese Cinema*. London: British Film Institute.

Bordwell, D. (2000) *Planet Hong Kong: Popular cinema and the art of entertainment*. Cambridge, MA: Harvard University Press.

Bosco, Joseph (1994) 'The Emergence of a Taiwanese Popular Culture', in M. A. Rubenstein (ed.), *The Other Taiwan: (1945 to the Present)*. New York: M. E. Sharpe.

Bourdieu, P. (1984) *Distinction: A social critique of the judgement of taste*. London: Routledge.

Browne, N., Pickowicz, P. G., Sobchack, V. and Yau, E. (eds) (1994) *New Chinese Cinema: forms, identities, politics*. Cambridge: Cambridge University Press.

Campbell, C. (1987) *The Romantic Ethic and the Spirit of Modern Consumerism*. Oxford: Blackwell.

Cao, J. Q. and Chen, Z. Y. (1997) *Walk Out the Ideal Castle: the research about the phenomenon 'Chinese living in units'* (Zouchu 'lixiang' chengbao: zhongguo 'danwei' xianxiang yanjiu). Shenzhen: Haitian chubanshe.

Chen, Xiaomei (1995) *Occidentalism: the theory of counter-discourse in Post-Mao China*. Oxford: Oxford University Press.

Chao, L. and Myers, R. H. (1998) 'China's consumer revolution: the (1990s and beyond', *Journal of Contemporary China*, 7 (18), 351–68.

China Daily (2005) 'Spur consumption, eliminating trade gap', *China Daily*, 7 June 2005. Available online at www.chinadaily.com.cn (accessed 15 June 2005, source: Bloomberg).

Chow, R. (1995) *Primitive Passions: visuality, sexuality, ethnography and contemporary Chinese cinema*. New York: Columbia University Press.

—— (2000) 'Introduction: On Chineseness as a Theoretical Problem', in Chow, R. (ed.), *Modern Chinese Literary and Cultural Studies in the Age of Theory*. Durham, NC, and London: Duke University Press.

—— (2004) 'The old/new question of comparison in literary studies: a post-European perspective', *ELH*, Summer 2004, 71:2, 289–311.

Chu Yingchi (2003) *Hong Kong Cinema: Coloniser, motherland and self*. London: RoutledgeCurzon.

Chun, Allen (1996) 'Discourses of identity in the changing spaces of public culture in Taiwan, Hong Kong and Singapore', *Theory, Culture & Society*, 13:1, Feb., 51–76.

Ci Jiwei (1994) *Dialectic of the Chinese Revolution: From Utopianism to Hedonism*. Stanford: Stanford University Press.

Croll, E. (1994) *From Heaven to Earth: Images and Experiences of Development in China*. London: Routledge.

Davis, D. S. (1995) 'Introduction', in D. S. Davis *et al.*, *Urban Spaces in Contemporary China: The Potential for Autonomy and Community in Post-Mao China*. Woodrow Wilson Center Series. Cambridge: Cambridge University Press.

—— (2000) (ed.) *The Consumer Revolution in Urban China*. Berkeley: University of California Press.

Davis, D. S. and Harrell, S. (eds) (1993) *Chinese Families in the Post-Mao Era*. Berkeley: University of California Press.

Davis, D. S., Kraus, R., Naughton, B. and Perry. E. J. (1995) *Urban Spaces in Contemporary China: The Potential for Autonomy and Community in Post-Mao China*. Woodrow Wilson Center Series. Cambridge: Cambridge University Press.

Davis, D. S. and Vogel, E. (eds) (1990) *Chinese Society on the Eve of Tiananmen: The impact of reform*. Cambridge, MA: Harvard University Press.

Dirlik, A. (1996) '*Looking Backward* in the age of global capital: thoughts on history in Third World Cultural Criticism', in Tang Xiaobing and Stephen Snyder (eds), *In Pursuit of Contemporary East Asian Culture*. Boulder: Westview Press.

Dirlik, A. and Zhang, X. (1997) 'Introduction: Postmodernism and China', *Boundary 2*, 24:3 (Fall), 1–18.

Douglas, M. and Isherwood, B. (1979) *The World of Goods*. London: Penguin.

Du Gay, P. (1996) *Consumption and Identity at Work*. London: Sage.

Dutton, M. (1998) *Streetlife China*. Cambridge: Cambridge University Press.

Erwin, K. (2000) 'Heart-to-Heart, Phone-to-Phone: Family Values, Sexuality, and the Politics of Shanghai's Advice Hotlines', in D. S. Davis (ed.), *The Consumer Revolution in Urban China*, Berkeley: University of California Press.

Fardon, R. (1991) 'Introduction', in R. Fardon (ed.), *Localising Strategies*. Edinburgh: Scottish Universities Press.

Featherstone, M. (1991) *Consumer Culture and Postmodernism*. London: Sage.
Ferguson, H. (1990) *The Science of Pleasure: Cosmos and psyche in the bourgeois world view*. London: Routledge.
Fong, V. L. (2004) 'Filial Nationalism among Chinese Youth with Global Identities', *American Ethnologist* 31(4): 629–46.
Fu, P. and Desser, D. (2000) *The Cinema of Hong Kong: history, arts, identity*. Cambridge and New York: Cambridge University Press.
Gold, T. (1985) 'After comradeship: personal relations in China since the Cultural Revolution', *China Quarterly*, 104, Dec., 657–65.
—— (1996) 'Taiwan Society at the *fin de siecle*', *China Quarterly*, No. 148. Special Issue: Contemporary Taiwan.
Greenhalgh, S. (2005) 'Globalization and Population Governance in China', in A. Ong and S. J. Collier (eds), *Global Assemblages: Technology, Politics, and Ethics as Anthropological Problems*. Malden: Blackwell.
Harrell, Stephan and Huang Chun-chieh (eds) (1994) *Cultural Change in Postwar Taiwan*. Boulder: Westview Press.
Harvey, D. (1990) *The Condition of Postmodernity*. Oxford: Blackwell.
Hemelryk Donald, S., Keane, M. and Liu, H. (eds) (2002) *Media in China: consumption, content and crisis*. London: RoutledgeCurzon.
Huot, Claire (2000) *China's New Cultural Scene: a Handbook of Changes*. Durham, NC, and London: Duke University Press.
Jameson, F. (1991) *Postmodernism or, the cultural logic of late capitalism*. London: Verso.
—— (1994) 'Remapping Taipei', in N. Browne *et al.* (eds), *New Chinese Cinemas: forms, identities, politics*. Cambridge: Cambridge University Press.
Jin, Pei (1997) *Where to and where from: the current problems of China's state-owned enterprises* (Hequ hecong: dangdai zhongguo de guoyou qiye wenti). China's Problems series. Beijing: Jinri zhongguo chubanshe.
Johnson, D., Nathan, A. J. and Rawski, E. S. (eds) (1985) *Popular Culture in Late Imperial China*. Berkeley: University of California Press.
King, A. Y. (1994) 'Kuan-his and Network Building: a sociological interpretation', in W. Tu (ed.), *The Living Tree: the Changing Meaning of Being Chinese Today*. Stanford: Stanford University Press.
Kipnis, A. B. (2001) 'The Disturbing Education Discipline of "Peasants"', *The China Journal* (46), 1–24.
—— (2005) 'Suzhi and Post-Mao Socialist Governance', paper presented for the conference *Trajectories of Socialism in Contemporary Asia: Anthropological Perspectives*, St Anne's College, Oxford, 29 June–1 July 2005.
Kuoshu, H. H. (ed.) (2002) *Celluloid China: Cinematic Encounters with Culture and Society*. Carbondale and Edwardsville: Southern Illinois University Press.
Latham, K. (2002) 'Rethinking Chinese consumption: social palliatives and the rhetorics of transition in postsocialist China', in C. M. Hann (ed.), *Postsocialism: Ideals, Ideologies and Practices in Eurasia*. London: Routledge.
Lee, C. C. (ed.) (2003) *Chinese Media, Global Contexts*. London: RoutledgeCurzon.
Lee, G. P. (2003) *China's Unlimited: making the imaginaries of China and Chineseness*. London: RoutledgeCurzon.
Leung Ping-kwan (1995) *Hong Kong Culture*. Hong Kong: Urban Council.
Li, Conghua (1998) *China: the Consumer Revolution*. Singapore: John Wiley.
Link, P., Madsen, R. and Pickowicz, P. G. (eds) (1989) *Unofficial China: Popular Culture and Thought in the People's Republic*. Boulder: Westview Press.
—— (2002) *Popular China: Unofficial Culture in a Globalizing Society*. Lanham: Rowman and Littlefield.
Liu, Kang (1997) 'Popular Culture and the Culture of the Masses in Contemporary China', *Boundary 2*, 24(3) (Fall), 1–18.

Lu, S. H. (1997) *Transnational Chinese Cinemas: Identity, Nationhood, Gender*. Honolulu: Hawaii University Press.
Lui, T. L. (2001) 'The Malling of Hong Kong', in G. Mathews and T. L. Lui (eds), *Consuming Hong Kong*. Hong Kong: Hong Kong University Press.
Madsen, R. (1990) 'The spiritual crisis of China's intellectuals', in D. Davis and E. Vogel (eds), *Chinese Society on the Eve of Tiananmen: The impact of reform*. Cambridge, MA: Harvard University Press.
Mathews, G. and Lui, T. L. (eds) (2001) *Consuming Hong Kong*. Hong Kong: Hong Kong University Press.
Meng, F. H. (1997) *Madness and Joy of the Spirit of the People: the problem of cultural conflict in contemporary China* (Zhongshen kuangxi: dangdai zhongguo de wenhua chongtu wenti). China's Problems series. Beijing: Jinri zhongguo chubanshe.
MII (Ministry of Information Industries) (2005) MII website www.mii.gov.cn (accessed 15 February 2006; note: website text in Chinese).
Miller, D. (1987) *Material Culture and Mass Consumption*. Oxford: Blackwell.
—— (ed.) (1995) *Acknowledging Consumption: a review of new studies*. London: Routledge.
Morris, A. (2002) '"I believe you can fly": Basketball Culture in Postsocialist China', in P. Link *et al.* (eds), *Popular China: unofficial culture in a globalizing society*. Lanham: Rowman and Littlefield.
Murphy, R. (2004) 'Turning Peasants into Modern Chinese Citizens: "Population Quality" Discourse, Demographic Transition and Primary Education', *China Quarterly* 177: 1–20.
O'Neill, M. (2005a) 'Hangzhou remains a city of consuming passions', *South China Morning Post*, 23 May 2005. Available online at www.scmp.com (accessed 23 May 2005).
—— (2005b) 'Mainland taste for the expensive grows', *South China Morning Post*, 23 May 2005. Available online at www.scmp.com (accessed 23 May 2005).
Parkin, D. (1993) 'Nemi in the modern world: return of the exotic?', *Man* 28/l: 79–99.
Rawnsley, G. D. and Rawnsley, M. Y. T. (2003) *Political Communications in Greater China: The Construction and Reflection of Identity*. London: RoutledgeCurzon.
Roberts, D., Clifford, M. and Brady, D. (1999) 'Playing the credit card: China is urging consumers to take on debt', *Business Week* 5 July, 20–1.
Robinson, J. (1985) 'Of Women and Washing Machines: employment, housework and the reproduction of motherhood in socialist China', *China Quarterly*, 101, 32–57.
Rofel, L. (1999) *Other Modernities: Gendered Yearnings in China after Socialism*. Berkeley: University of California Press.
Rosenbaum, A. L. (ed.) (1992) *State and Society in China: The Consequences of Reform*. Boulder: Westview Press.
Rubenstein, M.A. (ed.) (1994) *The Other Taiwan: (1945 to the Present)*. New York: M. E. Sharpe.
Sangren, P. S. (1987) *History and Magical Power in a Chinese Community*. Stanford: Stanford University Press.
Silbergeld, Jerome (1999) *China into Film: Frames of reference in contemporary Chinese Cinema*. London: Reaktion Books.
Siu, H. (1993) 'Reconstituting Dowry and Brideprice in South China', in D. S. Davis and S. Harrell (eds), *Chinese Families in the Post-Mao Era*, Berkeley: University of California Press.
Smith, R. (1993) 'The Chinese road to capitalism', *New Left Review*, No. 199, May–June, 55–99.
Sun, W. (2002) *Leaving China: media, migration, and transnational Imagination*. Lanham: Rowman and Littlefield.

Tang Xiaobing (1996) 'New Urban Culture and Everyday-Life Anxiety in China', in Tang Xiaobing and Stephen Snyder (eds), *In Pursuit of Contemporary East Asian Culture*. Boulder: Westview Press.

Teo, S. (1998) 'Postmodernism and the end of Hong Kong cinema', in *Hong Kong Cinema: the Extra Dimensions*. London: British Film Institute.

Tu Wei-ming (1994) 'Cultural China: the periphery as the center', in Tu Wei-ming (ed.), *The Living Tree: the changing meaning of being Chinese today*. Stanford: Stanford University Press.

—— (1996) 'Cultural Identity and the Politics of Recognition in Contemporary Taiwan', *China Quarterly*, No. 148. Special Issue: Contemporary Taiwan.

Vogel, E. (1989) *One Step Ahead in China: Guangdong Under Reform*. Cambridge, MA: Harvard University Press.

Wang, Jing (1996) *High Culture Fever: Politics, Aesthetics, and Ideology in Deng's China*. Berkeley: University of California Press.

Wang Shaoguang (1995) 'The politics of private time: changing leisure patterns in urban China', in D. S. Davis *et al.* (eds), *Urban Spaces in Contemporary China: The Potential for Autonomy and Community in Post-Mao China*, Woodrow Wilson Center Series, Cambridge: Cambridge University Press.

Watson, J. L. (ed.) (1999) *Golden Arches East: McDonald's in East Asia*. Stanford: Stanford University Press.

Wu Yanrui (1999) *China's Consumer Revolution: the emerging patterns of wealth and expenditure*. Cheltenham: Edward Elgar.

Yan Yunxiang (1998) *The Flow of Gifts: Reciprocity and Social Networks in a Chinese Village*. Stanford: Stanford University Press.

Yang, Mayfair (1996) 'Travelling Theory and Modernity in China', in H. L. Moore (ed.), *The Future of Anthropological Knowledge*. London: Routledge.

Yang, M. (1989) 'The Gift Economy and State Power in China', *Comparative Studies in Society and History*, 31 (1): 25–54.

—— (1994) Gifts, Favors and Banquets: The Art of Social Relationships in China. Ithaca: Cornell University Press.

Yau, E. (ed.) (2001) *At Full Speed: Hong Kong Cinema in a Borderless World*. Minneapolis: University of Minnesota Press.

Zhang Xudong (1997) *Chinese Modernism in the Era of Reforms: Cultural Fever, Avant-garde Fiction and the New Chinese Cinema*. Durham, NC: Duke University Press.

Zhang, Y. (2004) *Chinese National Cinema*. London: Routledge.

2 Conjuring goods, identities and cultures

Elisabeth J. Croll

In the 1980s and 1990s, both casual observation and field investigations in China's cities and villages confirmed that there was a rapid growth in profusion of goods or things alongside a sharp rise of interest in consumption, the spread and scale of which amounted to a revolution – and not only in the flow of material goods.[1] In this new world of things, both images and ideas about goods generated new languages, new desires, new socio-economic relationships and new individual, gendered and collective identities, including that of China itself. This chapter explores the powerful connection between consumption and culturalism or the ways in which cultures too can be imagined, invented and asserted via things, images and ideas about goods. In China, the historical legacies of both Confucian and Communist ideals shaped understandings and responses to the explosion of goods and commoditization in ways which gave rise not only to socialism with Chinese characteristics but also to consumption with Chinese characteristics.

In exploring the language and discourse of everyday practice, anthropologists have focused on the social life of persons and things (Appadurai 1986), and this chapter also centres on the social representations of and everyday linkages between persons and things within the contexts of consumption and Confucianism which constituted two of the most conspicuous social movements in China in the mid-1990s.[2] Indeed the introduction and rapid profusion of things or goods from the early 1980s, and changes in the relations between persons and goods, underlay the ensuing and shifting transitions between socialism and capitalism, production and consumption, the local and global, Chinese and cosmopolitan or Western, and tradition and modernity. These constituted the dualities that were incorporated into contemporary and conscious processes of self-definition or quests for new individual, gendered and collective identities which underlay perceptions of everyday desires and destinies or event and discourse in China in the 1990s.

Goods

One of the major differentiating factors distinguishing the period of reform from the previous thirty years of revolution was the shift in emphasis from production, work and the comrade-worker to consumption, lifestyle and the consumer. Formerly and officially, revolutionary economic policy and rhetoric were almost exclusively centred on production as both a means and an end, while, informally and unofficially, village field work revealed the importance of shared work as the symbolic medium for the affirmation of everyday relationships: 'We Chinese show our feelings for one another in our work, not with words' (Potter and Potter 1990: 194). Primarily, comrades did not conspicuously consume and, if they did, it was in secret and centred around food, that most impermanent of possessions. As to everyday consumption, in some places and at some times it was a feat of some magnitude just to fill the family rice bowl (Croll 1983). Much of this was to change dramatically and at the behest of the reform government, for it was to rising expectations and spiralling consumption that the government turned in its bid for legitimacy, for socialist modernization and for compensatory popularity following unpopular policies such as the single-child family or unpopular events such as Tiananmen. The late Deng Xiaoping repeatedly referred to consumption as the motor of production and, in his words, 'to get rich was glorious'. Indeed, consumption symbolized the new freedom after years of controlled scarcity and the ensuing reduction in the defining features of work, occupation, class origins or class labels, as the major socio-economic and political classifications gave rise to an important shift in perceptions and self-perceptions – from comrades to consumers. This shift not only differentiated reform from revolution within China, but also constituted an important difference between the recent histories of China and the former Soviet Union. If in the latter there had been an earlier move from an almost exclusive emphasis on production to a concern with consumption, then what began as a dream might not have ended as a stampede for scarce foods and goods in the shops, as headlines of the time had it.

A consumer revolution amounts to more than the introduction and profusion of material goods. For Western Europe and America, historians have recently argued that the profundity of the consumer revolution as a process is often ignored or at least under-emphasized compared to the attention given to the industrial revolution. That consumer revolution constituted: new categories of goods, new times, places and patterns of purchase, new marketing techniques, new ideas about possessions and materialism, changes in reference groups and life styles, diffusion patterns, product symbolism, patterns of decision-making and the creation of demand. The sum of these phenomena, historians claim, perhaps passed unnoticed because of their gradual, seeping nature – over four centuries (Campbell 1987). In China the onset of these processes was so fast, so highly visible that they could not escape unnoticed. Indeed it might be argued that, in China, the industrial and consumer revolutions were so collapsed into one decade that it is arguable which came first. Within the first few years of reform, observers spoke of 'a consumer rush', 'a headlong rush into consumerism', 'a consumer fever', 'consumer madness' – the scale and scope of which could be seen to give new meaning to the term 'mass consumption'. If, in the West, China was again primarily thought of as a potential mass market, now the Chinese began so to perceive themselves. In the mid-1990s, I came across this graffiti inscribed in a taxi, which had perhaps been written with a hint of Orientalist irony: 'China is the biggest market in the world, we are all Chinese, we must help this market'. China's new consumer temples, the large plate-glass department stores and shopping malls, fast became the new cardinal points replacing North, South, East and West in giving city directions, and with the introduction of a new maxim for department-store workers – the consumer is god (*guke shi shangdi*) – consumption was elevated to the status of a religion.

At the centre of this consumer boom in the early 1980s lay the profusion of consumer goods, the novel and exaggerated arrival of which, after years of absence or minimal presence, assumed the status of a cargo cult. The speed and intensity of expansion and the all-pervasive interest in goods, style, colour, material and, above all, brand, together generated 'a new world of goods' (Douglas and Isherwood 1979) which increasingly was evident in both village and city, on coast and in remote interior, and in domestic and public spaces. In conditions in which all consumption was newly conspicuous, some phenomena were more conspicuous than others. First, and most visible, there was a change from blue garb to a dress of colour, variety and style, with constantly shifting fashions or crazes, often changing from one week to the next, so that in the early years of reform neither the fashion conscious nor production lines could keep pace. Another conspicuous change was the advent of fast street and restaurant food, so that 'eating something interesting' became synonymous with eating Kentucky Fried Chicken and McDonalds' hamburgers, although the proud boast of the latter on their billboards in Beijing to 'serve a billion customers' was still something of an exaggeration. Another visible change was the city celebration of new Western festivals. At Christmas, urban shops were inundated with Christmas lights and cards of conspicuous flamboyance and, at Easter, live rabbits jostled with chickens to inhabit large chocolate hutches or Easter eggs. Very conspicuous too were the new forms of entertainment, including the ubiquitous karaoke early established in city, town and village which perhaps, I often think, owed much to the new democratization of the microphone. New spaces for consumption ranged from dance halls to new restaurants such as the Hard Rock Cafe. This first temple of rock in Beijing had its stained glass windows etched with an overarching 'Hail Hail Rock and Roll' and featured Elvis in the middle, with a crown poised high above his head and 'The King' inscribed above and 'Love me Tender' below. The scripture on the menu read 'Love All Serve All', while, shrine-like, the cafe displayed 314 rock and roll relics, had a vault-like central dome painted in the style of the Sistine chapel so that the Beatles and the Rolling Stones looked benignly down upon brass rails, dark-stained wood and an electric organ. Opened in the early 1990s as a temple of rock, or of the 'modern other', it is still land-marked outside with tall, scrolled pillars reaching upwards to a suspended red Cadillac.

Lastly, and more widespread, the selling and purchasing of goods became one of the most common of economic activities. Even university campus walls were converted into shops and restaurants, with professors and students hustling goods in an effort to supplement institutional and individual funds. As a form of recreation, shopping too became both a means and an end in itself with visits to up-market department-store displays, tableaux or dream worlds visited and gazed upon. These were the new museums, not so much of past record and achievements as of future lifestyles arousing curiosity, desire and anticipation – and perhaps even constituting the first opportunities for retail therapy in uncertain times. The answer to the riddle of why, despite thousands upon thousands of daily visitors to department stores, consumer spending was less than expected and caused Japanese and Western retailers such as Yaoshan, Lane Crawford, Kmart, Galeries Lafayette and our own Marks and Spencer to withdraw, slow down their plans for expansion or delay entry into China (*The Economist* 1996, 1997), can perhaps be found in the musings of a young women shopper:

> I like to go window shopping and always go to several stores – luxury department stores or small shops that sell particular products. I seldom go shopping with a particular need to buy something; rather if I am melancholy or distressed, I tend to go shopping. Walking slowly before a beautiful collection of goods, I gradually calm down. Therefore, for me, shopping is often good medicine to treat emotional qualms.
>
> (Ying Hong 1993: 36)

Some of these changes might be less than everyday examples and drawn from the cities, suburbs and coastal regions, but even small county and township settlements burgeoned within ten to fifteen years into city centres of exchange, while a migrant population upwards of 60, 70 or 80 million persons moved goods between city and countryside. In the poorer and more remote villages, too, clothes brightened, food was more plentiful, markets were revived and new goods treasured, including the television set which alone permitted 80 to 90 per cent of the population to consume vicariously. Even in circumstances of non-electrification, a memorable sight was the television sitting in waiting on the family altar, or powered by yards of batteries intricately tied together and stretching across whole tabletops. If consumers were elevated to gods, goods too were elevated to become important or significant others. On Chinese television, advertised goods such as washing machines were personalized and given tongues or even mobile phones to talk to one other or to potential customers. Objects were commonly given legs, so that one's house possessions or wedding dowries were reckoned or tabulated by the number of durable legs – giving rise to a 30-leg house or 20-leg dowry. Some years ago, in order to investigate the child's perception of the family, I asked children in kindergartens and schools to draw their 'families'. Many not only featured televisions and fashionably bright-green refrigerators prominently placed, life-sized but also life-like, these goods were given their own faces and legs, suggesting that, perhaps in the absence of siblings, significant things vied with significant persons in defining the single-child's sense of self or family.

Identities

Anthropologists and sociologists are long used to recognizing the significance of goods as means of social communication, and analysing their semiotics or the language, signs and symbols of goods. In recent decades, anthropologists have turned their attention to shopping as an under-researched mass activity or everyday practice in which the consumer engages in an on-going process of self-creation so that goods become agents of change in perception (Miller 1987, 1994, 1995). In China, too, it was via goods that individuals, the female gender and communities first all rethought themselves. Take, for example, the introduction of blue jeans, the individual adoption of which was highly symbolic as a proudly fashionable moment combining difference and defiance. As one young student explained to his teacher:

> Jeans are the symbol of the new fashion, and are still novel for some in China. But it's more than that. The [person who wore the] older garment, the . . . Mao suit was well-balanced, right-thinking and stable, someone who conforms. But jeans would make you feel independent, just like cowboys from America – wearing them would make you feel like a real individual. Its an utterly different feeling from the sense of dependence we used to have . . . all in those Mao suits . . . real conformists. So you see what jeans can mean to us.
>
> (Rice 1992: 88–9)

Others emphasized the daring shaping and contouring of the body outline that jeans afforded. Similarly the rehabilitation of the category 'female' via the appropriation of fashion, jewellery and cosmetics was a widely-observed example of the use of goods or things to recraft or fashion a new identity. The new emphasis on fashions, cosmetics and accessories by women who 'know how to be women' was a reversal of past practice. It took place against a background of the perceived loss of female-specific identity during the revolution, when the image of Iron Girls, the language of comrades, the unisex blue garb and exhortations to enter half of heaven or a 'yang' or male space to become 'men of women' had inscribed androgyny. In later interviews, women recognized that their coming out into society had been an important legacy of the revolution, but it had been at the cost of losing 'something of their female selves' or 'the difference between themselves and men' (Li 1994). The ensuing use of goods or things 'to become women' constituted an explicit and conscious rejection of the 'masculinization of the female', the 'female man' or 'super-women's masculinization'.

Just as for the individual and for gender, so collectively the acquisition of goods and associated lifestyles was instrumental in signifying difference from or rejection of a revolutionary past in favour of exciting new claims to be advanced, modern, developed, progressive or capturing of the Western, cosmopolitan or global. In this process material culture became cultural material, perhaps giving new meaning to the term 'designer culture'. Indeed it was via consumption that strategies of appropriation or localization of the global were most advanced and cultural identity most conspicuously constructed and reconstructed. In this respect the important point about the rapid profusion of new things or goods in the early years of reform was that they were associated with the outside, the global, the cosmopolitan or the 'West'. In other words new goods were perceived as imports from North America or Europe, whether or not they were produced or rather reproduced within China.

During the first years of reform it was predominantly via its goods or material culture that the 'West' came to be known or imagined in China. Of course, the presence of the 'Western other' in China was not a new phenomenon given the previous century of contact prior to 1949, but in retrospect that presence, significant though it was, was very much more limited and bounded, mediated as it was by treaty port, missionary and merchant. Without the benefit of an increasingly common English language (now taught widely in China), fast media communication and a mass market, previous contact had been conducted largely in person terms with less in the way of goods and not much beyond the largest cities and communication routes. Now it is much more than a Western person-presence which constitutes points of encounter; it is screens and counters of material contact which have reduced the distance between Chinese culture and the Western 'other'. A prevalent theme within anthropology has been a concern with the process of 'othering', or an awareness or consciousness of an 'other' with which to compare, contrast or rethink the self (Cohen 1994). In China it was the profusion of things 'originating' in the West that brought with them new images of this Western 'other'.

Recent works by anthropologists and others have drawn attention to Occidentalism or the construction and derivation of images of the West, which, like its counterpart, Orientalism, is at best an imagined West, and one that often obscures areas which sit uneasily or conflict with the desired attributes of a highly essentialized image or selected vision (Carrier 1995; Chen 1995). In China there was and still is no one construction of the West, but as interesting as the range of images constructed and imagined was the process or politics of construction and the uses to which these imagined images were put. In anthropology, Foucault's writings have changed forever the way the discipline associates the construction of knowledge or discursive practices (and by implication the generation of ignorance), with definitions of and the will to power (Parkin 1993; Fardon 1985; Hobart 1993). In China there is a clear sequence in which representations of the Western other, based on 'things', have variously influenced the ongoing process of self-definition or quest for identity in China. First, and almost overnight, the previously negative image of the West as capitalist and exploitative was transformed into an image of a desired destination, a process fostered by the new reform government's bid to modernize and 'catch up with the West'.

Cultural seduction

Interviews with young persons during the first ten years of the Reform era show there to have been a shattering 'loss of confidence', 'loss of faith', or 'despair beyond words' as 'the door swung open' and they became aware of a different West from that previously portrayed. As one young man said, 'when we became open and turned to the world outside we found we had got the wrong image of ourselves and of the world. We felt cheated' (Rice 1992: 116). The ideological disillusionment and depression that followed had the appearance of a visible gap into which images and things 'Western' could conveniently step with a seduction enhanced by the former prohibitions and critiques. With increased goods, what seemed like colour, variety, texture and style were splashed on a retrospectively dull blue-grey canvas so that these dramatically absent goods suddenly came to constitute not only claims to the global and the modern but the missing ingredients of the thirty years of revolution. At the time it was interesting to observe the ways in which everyday knowledge of the West was first constituted out of new objects, Western billboards or advertisements for new and novel objects, and how entire lifestyles came to centre on goods featured in imported Western magazines, television series or soap operas. The main attraction of new foreign television series such as 'Starsky and Hutch' centred on the images and lifestyles featured in each weekly episode. The West, a new desired destiny, was initially imagined as a seductive repository of all good things. In interviews and conversations with young students, the West was represented as a land of plenty, of profusion, of good things, of the good life and of high earnings 'where there are no taxes, no poor, a freedom to do anything, earn anything, spend everything and own anything' (Rice 1992: 83–122, 158–82).

With a millenarian or utopian flavour, the image of the West served as a foil deployed to illustrate all that China was not. This criticism of things Chinese reached its apogee in what has become known as the Heshang phenomenon which refers to the debates surrounding a six-part television series shown twice in 1988. The very title of the series, 'Heshang', gives a clue to the content. 'He' refers to the Yellow River, the cradle of Chinese civilization, and 'shang' means dying before coming of age. The television programme juxtaposed the shadowed yellow river culture of China and the bright ocean culture of the West, negated the achievements of Chinese culture and catalogued a history of previously lost opportunities to learn from a superior West (Chen 1992). In this initial mood of cultural abandonment or rejection, there was a pivotal rush by the urban and the young to become Western, global and cosmopolitan. However, such was the rush that its unanticipated consequences led to new fears in the 1990s that China might be destined for cultural oblivion. There was much official and intellectual concern that what was culturally-specific or distinctively Chinese would be consigned to history, the museum or a tourist attraction, leading to an ensuing loss of culturally-specific identity. Residents of large cities, such as Beijing, felt that they needed to look no further than their own cityscape where the old was disappearing at a rapid pace. Anthropologists of the landscape, exploring the sites of spatial forms and fantasies through which culture declares its presence and tensions (Hirsch and O'Hanlon 1995), would have had a field-day in this capital city as section by section was razed to the ground. The pace and style of reconstruction was such that jostling for space and emphasis were tall Greek and Roman columns, half-timbered dormer windows, medieval knights on armoured horses, Rodin's 'Thinker' in both male and female forms, a Chinese Wall Street, Las Vegas-lit night palaces, Greek gods, and James Bond or Playboy billboards, all visually exemplifying a post-modernist landscape or a Levi-Straussian 'bricolage'. The older Chinese style was relegated to the odd roof, a wall, a left-over *hutong* and a few famed temples, palaces and gardens or theme parks packaging China's history for tourists. Several years ago the juxtaposition of three neon signs prominent one above the other at a central interchange in Beijing seemed to me to symbolize this substitution: 'Californian Beef King Noodle USA', 'Karaoke and Seafood from around the World' and 'Oriental Civilization Garden'. Many city dwellers often said that they felt abroad in their own country. Indeed at the centre of the ways in which global and cosmopolitan fast foods, fashions and furnishings were deployed or localized to construct new socially or culturally differentiated lifestyles lay a paradox – that a new identity had to be embraced using the very same materials or goods which placed the previous, culturally specific identity most at risk.

It was the fear of loss of centuries of culture which sparked the pursuit of a selective rather than promiscuous cultural borrowing in which the West became primarily a resource for acquiring some but not all of the attributes of Western wealth and power. In a timely conversation discussing attitudes towards and utilization of things Western, an elderly professional woman in Beijing quickly retorted that these were being adopted 'without discrimination'. This new plea for discrimination was echoed in another interview on the theme of blue jeans, this time with a different young man:

> We allowed jeans in . . . and they didn't do any harm. I think we should allow in religion and the God, and other Western things, and see how they fit too. Generally in China we've been told the God is a bad thing, but most people don't know much about it, so how can we judge? I

> think these things should be imported, and examined carefully, and then accepted or rejected. As we did with jeans.
>
> (Rice 1992: 116)

Not all would equate the respective importance of jeans and God, but the principle of selectivity is well expressed. This view of the West, as a repository not so much of all but of some things desirable, was not new.

Selective borrowing

Just over one hundred years ago, in the last decade of the nineteenth century, when the wealth and power of the West similarly attracted attention, a succinct new formula encapsulated the prevailing mood: Western learning and knowledge for practical or technical application or for the material and the outside, and Chinese knowledge for the base, the spiritual, the social or the inside. What underlay this division was the observation that Western societies were beset by 'money worship', 'the pursuit of profit', and 'social confusion', which were surely all qualities to be avoided in China's own development (Teng and Fairbank 1967). At an equivalent moment at the end of the twentieth century, the image of the West was seen similarly by intellectuals and older generations to incorporate selfishness, egoism, permissiveness, materialism, decadence and money worship; lands where people look out for themselves and, motivated as they are by money and possessions, have a 'cold face'. Gradually the West became as much a source of spiritual pollution as of good things. In an equivalent movement towards selectivity, there was the same ontological separation of *ti* (substance or spirit) from *yong* (form) in the definition of Western things or goods, and a determined attempt to borrow one and not the other. In this attempt, the separation of ideas from their ontological structure either left a landscape of fragments and bricolage without substance, or, in the process of consumption, spirit proved to be inseparable from form and thus threatened the Chinese 'spirit' or *ti*. The dilemmas of selective borrowing along the *ti–yong* formula were heightened by two very significant factors which differentiated the selective borrowing of contemporary times from that of one hundred years previously.

The first was the spread of a new kind of knowledge – comparative knowledge. During previous years, spaces or spatial images beyond the local, and inclusive of abroad, became important new frames of popular reference making for another major contrast with the revolutionary years when frames of reference or mythical geographies were more temporal than spatial. Then, time had been the predominant frame of reference, made up of a past that was bitter or semi-colonial, reducing China to its knees, with the present as a liminal or transitional phase en route but subordinated to a glorious communist future, represented as the site of postponed desires and destiny (Croll 1994). In the 1990s attention was focused increasingly on the present with a new spatial curiosity and comparison that was fostered by new media, markets and mobility and characteristic of everyday conversation from village to the capital city and remote to coastal regions. One of my prevailing memories from fieldwork in the 1970s was the intricacy and boundedness of local knowledge with an emphasis on what we are doing, when and how we do it, where we are coming from and where we are going, while the only comparative yardstick available was sanitized national models designed for emulation. There was a marked ignorance of how others, even in the next village, town or city and abroad, were going about their everyday business. Twenty years later it was very different, as events and lifestyles elsewhere gleaned from television, hearsay and direct observation elicited an enormous amount of everyday interest. As anthropologists well know, it is comparative knowledge that underpins the cognitive process of othering and thus definitions of the self, and many in China have come to know, compare and judge their own country and culture via this process. However, many of those in China who came to know the West better or at first hand complained that those who adopted the ways of the West made no effort to understand Western ideas and appropriated symbols without any knowledge of their contexts or the thought, production, hard work or striving that they themselves had also observed in the West. Moreover, as more was known about the West it became common in conversation to be told that it was all the more important that China retain its own *ti* or spirit in the face of an unwelcome invasion of Western form and spirit.

The second significant factor differentiating selective borrowing in the 1990s was the coincidence of this perceived new threat to Chinese *ti* with a crisis of confidence in what constituted 'Chineseness' or a feeling that the characteristics which had long distinguished Chinese culture could not be taken for granted (*Wenshi Zhishi* 1987a, 1987b). What lent urgency to the 'rescue of China's body and soul' was that it took place against a background of perceived loss of cultural identity due to socialism and the Cultural Revolution. Anthropologists and historians, in their recent interest in the role of memory in the interpretation and construction of the past or how images of the past are conveyed and sustained, have turned their attention to memory as a cultural or social rather than individual faculty (Connerton 1989; Fentress and Wickham 1992). In looking at how societies remember, it has become fashionable to speak of lapses of cultural memory or cultural amnesia to refer to loss of identity or social memory during and after periods of colonialism. In China it was possible to identify a similar cultural lacuna, due not so much to its former semi-colonial status as to the dislocation caused by the Cultural Revolution which 'trampled on our own culture and on our ancient civilization'. In its aftermath, it became customary to talk of being left with 'a big mess', 'a wound', 'a scar', 'a lost generation' or 'a loss of who we were', and it is in anticipation of another loss of self or culture due to an onslaught of cosmopolitan goods and things that the new search for culturally-specific Chinese characteristics could be understood. In the 1990s, it was not so much the definitions of socialism or capitalism in Deng Xiaoping's memorable phrases about back and white cats or 'socialism with Chinese characteristics' that were the focus of attention, but definitions of 'Chinese characteristics', and this was so in both official and everyday discourse. I can still remember the urgency in the voice of a young man who, in an ordinary conversation about another matter, inadvertently suddenly exclaimed that 'what we want is an identity, but first we need to find out what our identity is!'

Chinese characteristics

In this search for an identity or 'Chinese characteristics', culture itself became an object of analysis, both official and popular. In the self-conscious culturalism or strategic assertion of culture of the 1990s, 'Chinese characteristics' were also referred to as the 'Chinese Way', the 'Chinese tradition' or simply 'Chineseness', the centrepiece of which was invariably a looking back to Confucius in what could be seen as an urgent search for cultural roots. There is a popular saying in China that 'a fallen leaf returns to its roots', and it was an uprooting of Confucian precepts that was seen to underlie loss of uniqueness and continuity. It became common to talk of a recently broken past or narrative and to hear that Confucianism had a history of two thousand years, socialism a history of thirty years and contact with the West a past of fifteen or at most one hundred and fifty years. In terms of sheer longevity, the Confucian inheritance was seen to have served China well and was therefore more than capable of healing any scar or rupture. To this end Confucius himself was rehabilitated. A symbolic moment for myself in the mid-1990s occurred in an old school in a poor Anhui village on the banks of a Yangtze tributary that habitually flooded. At the end of a rather tiring day of fieldwork I suddenly looked up, and there for the first time saw that Confucius and Sun Yat-sen had taken their place alongside the old Gang of Four (Marx, Lenin, Stalin and Mao). There have been many such moments since. However, the rehabilitation of the person of Confucius still begged the question of what lay at the centre of a willed and conscious search for what is authentically 'Chinese'.

In talk about invention or reinvention of tradition, it is helpful to think of Confucianism as a repository of myths, symbols, heroes, art forms, customs, values, symbols, rites, artefacts, festivals and institutions, which all acted as cultural markers collectively defining the Chinese 'way' or 'tradition'. In this reassertion of Confucianism, or more accurately of Confucian and neo-Confucian influences, state leaders made offerings to Confucius on the occasion of his birthday, people flocked to the newly renovated Confucian temples and to his birthplace, countless books on the life and sayings of Confucius were published in textual and cartoon form, and national civilizing campaigns were held in support of his precepts. Most of these efforts at rehabilitation were dismissed by foreign academics and journalists, either as a Chinese promotion of an Orientalist image derived from a discourse invented by the Jesuits or as the basis of a burgeoning tourist industry, a new nationalism, or official attempts to support an ailing communist government. What these interpretations suggested was that the new movement to rehabilitate Confucius was separate, and implied little support, from the population at large.

These interpretations ignore evidence from everyday social life and discourse which featured a set of precepts that pervade the very definition of persons and sociality and which made up a diffuse and living Confucianism of everyday practice; a Confucianism that was evident in conversation and interview whether it be that of an official or a Tiananmen dissident, an urban intellectual or a villager, or members of the younger or older generation. This discourse of everyday activity centred around the strategic assertion of distinctive person-to-person relations, including those both within and outside of family and kin. Underlying both the practice and the discourse of this personalism were two concepts which were Confucian in origin and are still regarded as such. The first was that to be fully a person or human involved a lifelong process of self-cultivation, the destiny or outcome of which is *ren* – a state of supreme virtue (Dawson 1981; Tu 1979; Lu 1983). It is commonly agreed among sinologists that English translations of such ethical terms are not entirely satisfactory. Translations attempting to capture both the centrality and breadth of *ren* include notions of benevolence, altruism, reciprocity, compassion and the humane. I myself prefer the latter designation denoting humanity and humaneness, given the ways in which phrases such as 'less than human' or 'less than a person' and about 'being a person or human in relation to others' are common and still punctuate everyday speech in China. But the important point here is not so much the meaning as the belief that this state, *ren*, is entirely cultivated within inter-personal relations or a social context, and indeed can only be manifested in the context of human relatedness. Indeed the very orthographic character for *ren* is made up of an ideograph of 'a person plus two', constituting human relations and signifying the centrality of human relatedness to self-cultivation. Dependent on others, the 'self' that is cultivated is not reclusive, isolated or even self-sufficient, but is a 'self' unceasingly engaged in everyday actions so that the ability to relate to others reflects one's level of self-cultivation, which in turn both embraces and reproduces sociality.

Self-cultivation, however, is not just about the achievement of *ren*, for it is also about a process of self-transformation, the guide to which is *li*. *Li* is usually translated as ritual or protocol, and refers not only to elaborate or ceremonial occasions but more importantly to the more diffuse qualities of propriety, politeness, reverence or respect. *Li* commonly signifies proper conduct in obligation, duty and loyalty, ideally regulating all human relationships in everyday contexts. It rests on two qualities: the tempering of desires such as those of greed; and an awareness of or respect for the needs and desires of others incorporated into the famous precept: 'do unto others as you would have others do unto you'. Here again, importance is placed on *li* as a process of becoming humanized via participation in social relationships. Of course not all everyday conversations go into such nuanced elaborations, but conversations commonly refer to 'a falling short of personhood or humanity', to 'the three principles' inclusive of *ren* and *li*, and to 'the five relationships' which embrace all relations between the individual or self and others.

This emphasis on person-to-person, or *guanxi*, relations has led to an everyday focus on particularistic individual ties, connections or relations and networks, rather than on structures, institutions or groups, so that Chinese society is often described as uniquely *guanxi*-based (Sun 1983). Much attention is given to the importance of familial ties in Confucian or Asian values, but they are also important as the template for all other networked relations in which individuals are equally expected to conform to particular role definitions. In the 1990s, these too remained carefully graded in terms of obligation, loyalty or sincerity, degrees of which differed according to each relationship category, and it is this particularism which had given rise to a number of very distinctive tendencies characterizing inter-personal, or *guanxi*, relations in China (Yang 1994; Yan 1996). First, the primary social contract remains that which exists between designated individuals rather than individual and society or state, informal relationships rather than formal contracts are negotiated (as businesses soon learn), and social relationships are primarily personalized between known individuals rather than between an individual and collective or generalized others. Hence a much commented upon Chinese mistrust of strangers and their own surprise at the very different welcome that they themselves may receive as strangers abroad (Sun 1983; Wang 1995). Distinctive too are the devices immediately familiarizing the stranger with which relations have to be had and the importance of known intermediaries or go-betweens in these introductions and negotiations. As the stranger anthropologist, I have always been struck by the way in which, on only a second meeting, one is recategorized as an old friend, or *lao pengyou*. Similarly the importance attached to the necessity of a go-between at each administrative level that has on occasions resulted in a convoy of several jeeps collected between capital city and village which it took every ounce of ingenuity to lose before embarking on the serious side of fieldwork. Nevertheless, I recognized long ago that much of the initial cooperation in a new field site is at first dependent on the presence and status of intermediaries. It is this emphasis on the go-between and the particularistic forms of personal as opposed to universalistic trust that has led to the categorization of Chinese societies as 'low on trust', first by Weber (1968) and more recently by Fukuyama (1995: 29). In writing about trust as a form of social capital, Fukuyama cited China as an example of a low-trust society less able to generate large-scale complex institutions and organizations.

In respect of the centrality and nature of everyday social relationships, it can be argued that the onset of revolution in 1949 did not make for a major break. The idea of self-cultivation via relationships with others was continued in manuals on 'how to be a good communist', in the Maoist precepts on how to live everyday life reiterated in the Little Red Book and the ideal of 'serving the people'. The Communist Party also placed social relationships at the core of its socio-political theory and practice and it can be argued that the bounded restrictions on movement, media and market during the revolution localized and intensified particularistic inter-personal relations even though they were criticised as politically incorrect at the time. In these circumstances the Cultural Revolution marked more of a break. Much of the retrospective venom reserved for this event derives not only from the legacy of disorder, but also from wounds and scars originating in the disruption of person-to-person relations when, in a reversal of Confucian and communist norms, members of family and other local networks felt that they had to turn on each other to save themselves. However it is something of an anthropological truism that rituals of reversal in extraordinary times can reinforce the more common rituals of ordinary times. Whatever the degree to which this was so in the Cultural Revolution, it was certainly the onset of reform in 1979 which signified an important rupture as two major changes began profoundly to affect the extent and qualities of inter-personal relations.

New characteristics

Firstly, the importance of '*guanxi*', or networks of personal connections, spiralled after the introduction of reforms in 1979 to become essential, pervasive and even rampant in all new facets of social, political and economic life. Economically, the demands of the market economy, alongside new forms of individual and institutional entrepreneurial responsibility for procuring raw materials, credit, expertise and markets, widened the circles of strangers to be necessarily incorporated into personalized networks with relationships sub-contracted and lengthened by chains of intermediaries. In the absence or under-development of formal horizontal mechanisms across government departments and administrative units, almost all individual and institutional linkages or business and organizational transactions in job recruitment, protection from predation, access to resources or in the procuration of almost any service became dependent upon negotiated personalized connections and networked mutual obligations. *Guanxi*, previously and largely limited to the bureaucracy of latticed patron–client cadres and political favours, now extended to include all other socio-economic relations as connections were accumulated and patrons became local bosses while simultaneously themselves becoming go-betweens and clients in an expanding edifice or elongated chains of simultaneous and deferred obligations. In the near absence of public-sector financing even the simplest service became dependent not just on who you know, but who you know who knows whom. If the modal person was the hustler, and direct-selling more successful than department store, so also the mobile phone with its by-line 'connecting people' or a 'one-to-one connection' proved tailor-made for negotiating *guanxi* relations, the number and type of which became the most valuable of operational assets and an important source of status and security. Indeed these networks were such an important part of everyday life for all but the poorest and the 'bare sticks' of society that they generated their own vocabulary. For example, *guanxixue*, translated as the art or study of personal connections, was not the specialized study of social scientists but the everyday study of everyday relations which also came to require especially designated resources. Listed alongside other expenses in all households and public units of government from one end of the country to another was a new budget item made up of '*guanxi* costs' or '*renqing* costs', which were increasingly necessary as *guanxi* relations not only expanded but became commodified, with goods, things and money playing an increasing role.

In a second major difference after 1979, the passage of goods and money became such new and conspicuous adjuncts facilitating and maintaining inter-personal relations and *guanxi* connections that it was commonly argued that there were now three economies in China – made up of the state redistributive, the commodity, and the gift economies, each relying on the passage of goods, of things or increasingly of money to procure favours, deals and ordinary everyday public services. Following the revolutionary period in which such monetarization and material exchanges were minimized, money and monetary relations acquired unprecedented importance in everyday life as they became a central feature of the new market and political economy. If words were the coinage of exchange in the revolution, money quickly became the new language of value. Although it is common to attribute to money a powerful agency in effecting social and cultural transformations, anthropologists have also emphasized the cultural variations in the ways in which money is perceived and symbolized. They have argued that the meanings with which money is invested are quite as much a product of a cultural matrix as of its economic function as a means of exchange, unit of account or store of value (Parry and Bloch 1986). Ethnographic studies in China suggested that money was perceived to have newly distorted notions of mutual obligation or reciprocity. For example, it was often said that money transactions represented the closure of obligation 'in just one hammer blow', and thus acted as both a depersonalizing agent diminishing bonds of personal inter-dependence and an individuating agent permitting – if not encouraging – the detachment of individuals from kin and other personal bonds (Ku 1998).

Equally, the commodification of inter-personal relations and the creation of a market in which connections were bought and sold underlay charges of cadre and party privilege, nepotism and inflationary corruption which, before, during and following Tiananmen, became a most important source of criticism and unrest in China. By highlighting the linkages between material objects, things or money and persons, a person's face or standing and motivation were now said to have less to do with means of self-cultivation than with accumulation or appropriation of material possessions. The result of the emphasis on possessions and, above all, 'money worship', which according to Confucius was the mark of an inferior or small man, was a new ambivalence reflected in both everyday and official language. For many, the resulting 'spiritual pollution' was thought to have derived from the import of foreign-devil capital and capitalist relations from the West, where social relations increasingly were reported to be impersonal, calculating and profit-focused or devoid of moral and affective content – as if the mere presence of money cancelled out affectivity and extinguished any of the solidary bonds of kinship, community and society that were most widely thought in China to distinguish the Chinese Way. Hence the onset of an officially-sponsored series of civilizing spiritual and morality campaigns which, although not especially effective, did represent a popular wish to revive an older and more Chinese or Confucian ideal of self- and moral-cultivation via 'proper' inter-personal relations that would exist alongside monetization or a market economy.

These recent attempts to establish a morally-embedded economy in China might be seen as a localized version of the global debates about the role of Asian values in the then miracle economic development of East and Southeast Asia, or of conflictual economic cultures as mooted by Huntington (1996). However, in China it was because of the sequence of interest in consumption followed by the rise of interest in Confucianism that there was a new interest in the relationship between ideology and economic development, perhaps reminiscent of Weber's (1930) 'Protestant Ethic and the Spirit of Capitalism'. Although for centuries past it was argued by Weber himself that Confucian precepts in China had inhibited capitalist economic growth (Weber 1968, 1978), it was now posited by many that Confucianism had done for China, East and Southeast Asia what the Protestant ethic did for Europe. However this chapter questions both these sequential arguments and instead suggests that it is the everyday commodification of personal relations which has encouraged the rehabilitation or rise of Confucianism, rather than vice versa. This chapter also suggests that, in everyday practice, it was consumption or the profusion and increasingly exclusive interest in goods and money that led to a simultaneous nostalgia for Confucian and, by implication, socialist ways of relating. To dismiss the new interest in Maoism in the latter half of the 1990s, and the floods of Mao emblems on the market from t-shirts to cigarette lighters, as mere commodification was to separate symbol from substance, miss a selective nostalgia and ignore the attempt to evolve a new everyday identity syncretically embracing of the opening dichotomies of capitalist/socialist, traditional/modern and Western/Chinese. This selective everyday rehabilitation of

Maoism attempted harmoniously to balance both inherited and imported characteristics in everyday practice and perhaps give new meaning to *Zhongguo* (China) as 'middle kingdom' or, in its broadest meaning, 'middle civilization'.

Several everyday metaphors can be said to reflect an everyday desire for the adaptive and selective notion of the hybrid or 'the middle'. First, newer models for emulation came to lie not so much in the West as in the dragons or tigers of East and Southeast Asia which were seen then to have successfully combined rising consumption and Confucianism. The term *rushang* or 'Confucian businessman' made a reappearance, while the little yellow locust taxis that scurried around Beijing displayed a Mao equivalent of St Christopher at the front and a Confucian slogan at the back: 'When you take a guest/stranger somewhere, do it with a piece of your heart.' Small peasant houses combined a family altar, socialist posters and Western girlie calendars, new Western buildings had Chinese-style roofs, and a McDonald's New Year hanging was inscribed with '*fu*' or good fortune. New feminal definitions of womanhood incorporated both the feminine softness of Confucian demeanour and deportment without its dependence on fathers, husbands and sons, and the independence of Western feminism without its perceived hardness and shoulder-pads (Croll 1995). Lastly, fashion shows attempted to blend eye-catching Western and Chinese stylistic features 'seamlessly in a single garment', which perhaps more than any other metaphor provided a concluding ideal for a middle destiny which is of a civilization that is both syncretic and seamless or consumption with Chinese characteristics.

Giving new meanings to Chinese characteristics requires the painting of a broad canvas, and only a very few of its constituent stitches and patterns can be touched on in this chapter, but it is the movement between stitch and canvas which is the hallmark not only of the holistic and layered approach of the anthropologist but also of the degree of everyday reflexivity which characterized both official discourse and casual conversation in both the public and the domestic spaces of 1990s China. It was the self-conscious way in which, by 'touching stones to cross the river', the larger changes emanating both from outside and from the top were negotiated mindfully and localized in an everyday pragmatic and creative crafting of identity, be it of individual, gender, family, local community or society-wide and in ways that were inclusive of China's legacy of socialism and Confucianism. It would be easy to dismiss many of the juxtapositions or bricolage of the mid-1990s as cultural dissonances or deterioration, but this ignores the self-conscious reflexive agency of, first Revolution, then Reform, and of the more recent phase of Readjustment (*tiaozheng*) as a succession of innovative and engaged attempts to debate and explore the modernizing dilemmas of identity and culture that were so evident in city and rural fieldwork during the last decade of the twentieth century.

Towards the close of the twentieth century it became evident that, although the quest for China's cultural identity and modernity would proceed, the appropriation of new goods and lifestyles would be less the focus of everyday practice and discourse than savings, securing services and ensuring security. The process of economic reform, with rising costs, unemployment and bankruptcy, has altered socio-economic environments and values at the turn of the millennium, generating new and mounting demands for social welfare, increased concerns about income, pension and service, and the greater pursuit of security. Thus it was welfare demand, service supply and security support within and outside of China that then became the common topics of everyday conversation from capital city to village, and one of the most common yardsticks defining good governance. The consequent diminution in consumer spending and the reduction in retail purchase at the turn of the century were telling signs that individuals and their families increasingly worried about their ability to meet the rising costs of estate and services, and short- and long-term welfare responsibilities, in uncertain times. Nevertheless it is also in uncertain times that cultures continue to be not only imagined, invented and conjured, but also asserted via consumption and the flow of goods and ideas about goods.

Notes

1 Some of the ideas for this chapter were first outlined in an Inaugural Lecture entitled 'Desires and Destinies: Consumption and the Spirit of Confucianism', presented at the School of Oriental and African Studies, University of London, on 19 March 1997.

2 Much of this chapter is based on my own interviews and an accumulation of observations and insights based on over twenty years of documentary and fieldwork on China.

References

Appadurai, A. (ed.) (1986) *The Social Life of Things: Commodities and the Politics of Value*, Cambridge: Cambridge University Press.

Campbell, C. (1987) *The Romantic Ethic and the Spirit of Modern Consumerism*, Oxford: Basil Blackwell.

Carrier, J. (ed.) (1995) *Occidentalism*, Oxford: Clarendon Press.

Chen Xiaomei (1992) 'Occidentalism as Counterdiscourse: "He Shang" in Post-Mao China', *Critical Enquiry*, 18: 686–712.

—— (1995) *Occidentalism: A Theory of Counter Discourse in Post-Mao China*, New York: Oxford University Press.

Cohen, A. (1994) *Self-Consciousness: An Alternative Anthropology of Identity*, London: Routledge.

Connerton, P. (1989) *How Societies Remember*, Cambridge: Cambridge University Press.

Croll, E. (1983) *The Family Rice Bowl: Food and the Domestic Economy in China*, London: Zed Press.

—— (1994) *From Heaven to Earth: Images and Experiences of Development in China*, London: Routledge.

—— (1995) *Changing Identities of Chinese Women: Rhetoric, Experience and Self-Perception in Twentieth Century China*, London: Zed Press; Hong Kong: University of Hong Kong Press.
Dawson, R. (1981) *Confucius*, Oxford: Oxford University Press.
Douglas, M. and Isherwood, B. (1979) *The World of Goods*, London: Allen Lane.
The Economist (1996) 'The Lessons the Locals Learnt Too Quickly', Business Section, 28 September.
—— (1997) 'Window Shopping in Shanghai', Business Section, 25 January.
Fardon, R. (ed.) (1985) *Power and Knowledge: Anthropological and Sociological Approaches*, Edinburgh: Scottish Academic Press.
Fentress, J. and Wickham, C. (1992) *Social Memory*, Oxford: Blackwell.
Fukuyama, F. (1995) *Trust: The Social Virtues and the Creation of Prosperity*, New York: Free Press.
Hirsch, E. and O'Hanlon, M. (eds) (1995) *The Anthropology of Landscape: Perspectives on Time and Place*, Oxford: Clarendon Press.
Hobart, M. (ed.) (1993) *An Anthropological Critique of Development: The Growth of Ignorance*, London: Routledge.
Huntington, S. (1996) *The Clash of Civilization and the Remaking of the World Order*, New York: Simon and Schuster.
Ku Hok-Bun (1998) 'Defining Zeren: Cultural Politics in a Chinese village', unpublished PhD thesis, University of London.
Li Xiaojiang (1994) '*Gaige Yu Zhongguo Nüxing Qunti Yishi De Juexing*' (Economic Reform and the Awakening of Women's Consciousness), *Shehui Kexue Zhanxian* (Social Science Battlefront), 4: 300–10. Translated in C. Gilmartin *et al.* (eds) (1994) *Engendering China: Women, Culture, and the State*, Cambridge, MA: Harvard University Press.
Lu, M. (1983) *Confucianism: Its Relevance to Modern Society*, Singapore: Federation Publications.
Miller, D. (1987) *Material Culture and Mass Consumption*, Oxford: Basil Blackwell.
—— (1994) *Modernity: An Ethnographic Approach*, Oxford: Berg.
—— (ed.) (1995) *Acknowledging Consumption*, London: Routledge.
Parkin, D. (1993) 'Nemi in the modern world: return of the exotic?' *Man (N.S.)*, 28: 79–99.
Parry, J. and Bloch, M. (eds) (1986) *Money and the Morality of Exchange*, Cambridge. Cambridge University Press.
Potter, S. H. and Potter, J. M. (1990) *China's Peasants: The Anthropology of a Revolution*, Cambridge: Cambridge University Press.
Rice, D. (1992) *The Dragon's Brood: Conversations with Young Chinese*, London: Harper Collins.
Sun Longji (1983) *The Deep Structure of Chinese Culture*, Hong Kong: Yishan.
Teng Ssu-yu and Fairbank, J. K. (1967) *China's Response to the West: A Documentary Survey, 1839–1923*, Cambridge, MA: Harvard University Press.
Tu Wei-ming (ed.) (1979) *Humanity and Self-cultivation: Essays in Confucian Thought*, Berkeley: Asian Humanities Press.
Wang Jinguang (1995) *Westerners through Chinese Eyes*, Beijing: Foreign Languages Press.
Weber, M. (1930) *The Protestant Ethic and the Spirit of Capitalism*, London: Allen and Unwin.
—— (1968) *The Religion of China*, trans. Hans Gerth, New York: Free Press.
—— (1978) *Economy and Society*, Berkeley: University of California Press
Wenshi Zhishi (Knowledge of Culture and History) (1987a) 1, 'Whither Shall Chinese Culture go?'
—— (Knowledge of Culture and History) (1987b), 1, 'Chinese and Western Cultural Exchange'.

Yan Yunxiang (1996) *The Flow of Gifts: Reciprocity and Social Networks in a Chinese Village*, Stanford: Stanford University Press.
Yang, M. (1994) *Gifts, Favors, and Banquets: The Art of Social Relationships in China*, Ithaca: Cornell University Press.
Ying Hong (1993) 'The Pleasures of Shopping', *Zhongguo Funü* (Women of China), Beijing, 1 August.

3 Deception, corruption and the Chinese ritual economy

Charles Stafford

In this chapter, I will focus on three phenomena which have had a significant impact on the Chinese economy in recent years. The first is widespread popular concern about 'deception' (*pian*) in the course of economic transactions. Anxiety about deception informs the buying and selling of goods and services in China in a number of interesting ways. The second is widespread concern with 'corruption' (*fubai*), an increase in which is held to have seriously complicated modern economic life, and to have helped undermine traditional values and ethics. The third is the persistence of what might be called a 'ritual economy' in China – and possibly even its growth and intensification. Depending on definitions, this ritual economy may be said to encompass not only traditional patterns of gift-giving during festivals and ritual occasions, but also the reciprocal provision of financial and practical support within networks of kin and friends, and – last but not least – the handing over of direct and indirect bribes as a kind of 'tribute' to the powerful. By its broadest definition the ritual economy is huge, and a significant proportion of the goods and services purchased in China today are destined for circulation and consumption within it.

What brings these three things – deception, corruption and the ritual economy – together is their link to popular ideas about the morality of exchange. For this reason, I would like to start by drawing attention to two rather different perspectives on the moral landscape of post-Mao economic life.

One perspective is seen in the fascinating work of Mayfair Mei-hui Yang, an anthropologist who carefully examined the exchange of gifts, favours and banquets, and in particular the ways in which such exchanges – integral to the art of 'cultivating *guanxi*' (relatedness) – help to solidify ties between persons (Yang 1989, 1994). Much of Yang's material came from cities, but such practices are perhaps especially visible in the Chinese countryside, where families are linked together in extensive networks of reciprocity. They help each other not only with costly life-cycle rituals such as weddings and funerals, but also with practical activities such as harvesting and house-building (Yan 1996). To participate in such exchanges is to 'follow *li*' (*suili*), that is, to abide by the precepts of conventional moral etiquette. However, while on the surface this may seem the exact opposite of acting in immoral or 'corrupt' (*fubai*) ways, everyone knows that similar (sometimes identical) practices and idioms of gift-giving and reciprocity are used to cultivate relationships which may indeed be corrupt, including those with important people such as government officials.

In analysing the highly complex business of Chinese reciprocity, and noting in particular the apparent intensification of the explicit 'art of *guanxi*' in the post-Mao era, Mayfair Yang avoids drawing simple conclusions. However, she does suggest that the ritual economy (or 'gift economy', as she refers to it) *may* have the potential to be subversive of the power of the state for two interconnected reasons. First, because the cultivation of relatedness through gift-giving and other means, including the outright giving of bribes, undermines the administrative effectiveness of the state and its mechanisms of control. Second, on a more abstract level, because the popular ethics which underpin the ritual economy (and which may be said to be 'relational') are contrary to those of Chinese communism (which may be said to be 'universalist'). Yang suggests that by undermining both the mechanisms and the ethics of state control, the ritual economy may even contribute to 'the development of civil society' in China (Yang 1994: 295).

However, the Chinese economist He Qinglian, in her critique of the post-Mao reform process – which was written, as I should stress, about ten years after Yang's original article on gift-exchange and the state – puts forward a rather different hypothesis. (I rely here on the detailed review of He's book, *Zhongguo De Xianjing* [*China's Pitfall*], by Liu Binyan and Perry Link (1998) in the *New York Review of Books*.) To put it bluntly, she suggests that the reform process in China has been a fraud, and that it is having extremely negative social and economic consequences. The rapid rise in average incomes, she argues, has largely been the product of transfers of wealth from the public sector into the private hands of 'power-holders and their hangers-on' (quoted in Liu and Link 1998: 19). This she calls 'the marketization of power' (1998: 20), a process in which illegal ways of making money are simultaneously the most profitable. For this reason, she suggests, the process will *not* produce a healthy civil society, nor will it produce a market economy in the normal sense. Inequality and corruption are increasing.

In order to illustrate the relationship between He's thesis and that of Mayfair Yang, allow me to quote from the review article by Liu and Link:

> Some have argued that in any transition from a planned to a market economy, corruption and inequality are necessary, or perhaps even useful. He Qinglian acknowledges that when a society and economy are stultified by political terror, as China's were during the late Mao years, the unofficial trading of favors can indeed have a part in loosening up the system. But she argues that this stage has long passed in China, and that the effects of the corruption of the 1980s and 1990s have badly hurt the economy.
>
> (Liu and Link 1998: 22)

He calculates that, of the money diverted in recent years to private use, less than 25 per cent has actually made its way back to the economy as private capital, whereas over 75 per cent has been spent on the 'bribes, entertainment, and favors that are necessary to divert the money and to cover it up', thus leading to staggering inefficiencies (1998: 22).

What concerns her most, however, is the effect of this process on public ethics and morality. At a time when people in China speak of 'slaughtering' each other (*zai*) in economic transactions, Liu and Link observe:

> Probably in no other society today has economic good faith been compromised to the extent that it has in China. Contracts are not kept; debts are ignored, whether between individuals or between state enterprises; individuals, families, and sometimes whole towns have gotten rich on deceitful schemes. He Qinglian sees the overall situation as unprecedented. 'The championing of money as a value,' she writes, 'has never before reached the point of holding all moral rules in such contempt.' She finds the collapse of ethics – not growth of the economy – to be the most dramatic change in China during the Deng Xiaoping era.
>
> (Liu and Link 1998: 22)

The arguments of Yang and He might be said – hopefully without doing too much damage to the authors' original intentions – to move in roughly opposite directions. Yang suggests that the morality which is found among ordinary people has the capacity to 'trickle up', undermining the state, transforming China into a more rather than a less ethical place, and creating the potential for a Chinese civil society. By contrast, He suggests that corruption at the highest levels has the capacity to 'trickle down' to the masses, undermining the ethical foundation of all social relationships, and destroying the potential for a Chinese civil society. The possibility that *both* of these arguments could be right rests in part on a conundrum found at the heart of Chinese ways of conceptualizing social relationships. This is, briefly, that the *most* moral relationships, notably those between closest kin and friends – which in some contexts are portrayed as being above economic interest – are in fact intensely economic, and often quite oppressive and exploitative as well. Meanwhile, some of the *least* moral relationships, specifically those which are portrayed as 'corrupt' (*fubai*), are able to share idioms of gift-giving, commensality and reciprocity with those which are portrayed as highly moral. The ritual economy can therefore be said to encompass relations of both kinds, and this arguably means that the upward-morality-transfer suggested by Yang and the downward-immorality-transfer suggested by He are both equally plausible outcomes of the system. In any case, both arguments highlight the possible connections between everyday Chinese morality – with all of its ambiguities – and the national politics of economic reform in contemporary China.

But now let me focus on this everyday morality in a bit more detail. I want to sketch out some highly selective ethnography from two Han Chinese localities where I have conducted fieldwork in the past: the farming community of Dragon-head, in northeastern mainland China, and the fishing community of Angang, in southeastern Taiwan. The conflation of material from Taiwan and China is of course very problematic; but the ritual economies of Angang and Dragon-head operate in a reasonably similar fashion, and I hope that in this case the conflation of material will not be entirely misleading. I should also stress that my examples are drawn from the countryside. One could argue that material from villages is irrelevant to the urban-based, large-scale, and often institutionalized corruption which, in the view of many, is undermining the process of economic reform in China. But the popular moralities which I will here describe are not simply rural, nor are they esoteric: they arguably have a deep influence at all levels of Chinese society.

I will start with ideas about deception. During my fieldwork in Angang (in Taiwan in the 1980s), and even more so in Dragon-head (in China in the 1990s), one of the notably frequent topics of conversation was the possibility of being 'deceived' or 'swindled', *pian*, by others, and especially by strangers. The Mandarin term *pian* covers a good deal of ground, and may include, for example, the selling of faulty goods (such as a radio which stops working after several weeks); or the selling of goods at inflated prices. It also means, more generally, to 'take people for a ride', for example by telling lies or tall tales (*huangyan*). If someone talks rubbish, a bystander may comment *pianren!* – meaning 'fraud!'. While living in Angang and Dragon-head, I heard many people say that increasing numbers of 'deceitful operators' (*pianzi*) were about in those days, due to a general decline in public morality. One should therefore always be on one's guard, or be cautious – *xiaoxin*, literally 'little-hearted' – where money is concerned. Such warnings are significant, because a person who is cheated in a transaction is often said to have only themselves to blame. They can expect to be laughed at by others (*gei ren xiao*), and to be cheated (*pian*) is thus to 'lose face' (*diu mianzi*).

As one might expect, the chances of this happening are seen to be especially great when one's counterparts in a transaction are unfamiliar, *bu shuxi*, literally 'not cooked'. Let me give one brief example of this. In China and Taiwan there is a roaring trade in traditional Chinese medicines (*zhongyao*), as well as 'strengthening tonics' (*buyao*) and various over-the-counter remedies. Because such medicines tend to be expensive, and because it is difficult for non-specialists to assess the quality of what they buy, this field is seen to be especially rife with fraudsters. It happens that people in Angang (the Taiwanese fishing community) raise deer (*meihualu*) from which they produce two popular traditional remedies: deer antler wine (*lurongjiu*), and chopped deer penis (*lubian*). Both of these are said to be 'hot' (*re*) and to therefore help to 'strengthen the body-person' (*bushen*) against the effects of cold and illness. In the 1980s, the price of *lurongjiu* and *lubian* collapsed because of oversupply and, according to my informants in Angang, because the market was flooded with fakes. However, people from outside continued to travel to Angang in order to buy supplies from their relatives, friends and 'old acquaintances' (*shuren*) there. This was, obviously, a way of guaranteeing the 'authenticity' (*zhen*) of the medicines they bought, and ensuring that the goods were not 'fake' (*jia*) – in other words, a way of avoiding being 'ripped off', *pian*.

Not surprisingly, given anxieties about *pian*, the question of believability or 'trust' (*xinyong*, *qinxin* or *xinren*) is central to the conceptualization in Angang, as elsewhere in Taiwan and China, of good trading relations between persons (cf. Gates 1996: 31ff; DeGlopper 1995: 29–55). For this reason, anonymity, exactly the thing which free markets supposedly love, at first appears deeply problematic. It might even be tempting to call this the birth of Chinese cronyism, because it encourages a mindset in which one does business with relatives, friends and acquaintances because strangers are not reliable. However, things are not so simple. At this stage, let me note that among the common Chinese translations for the English phrase 'crony capitalism' is *qinxin zibenzhuyi*: literally 'trust capitalism', or 'trusted-confidante capitalism'. However, the first character in this expression, *qin*, which can mean 'close' or 'intimate', is most often used to indicate a *kinship* connection. Another of the translations for 'crony capitalism', *qundai zhuyi*, makes this link to kinship even more explicit. *Qundai*, literally 'apron strings', indicates the useful connections a man has through his wife's relatives, i.e. through his affines, and by extension *all* useful connections. But this is very interesting terminology because affinal, or 'apron-string', connections have been viewed, almost by definition, with considerable ambivalence in patrilineal China. They are not necessarily a good thing.

So: *do* people in Angang and Dragon-head prefer to do business with their relatives, friends, acquaintances in order to avoid deception (*pian*)? Perhaps. But it is striking that in Angang, at least, almost all of the local shop-keepers are 'outsiders' in some way, mostly people who have moved to the community from elsewhere. Although they have, in every case, quite a few friends and acquaintances among their fellow-villagers, what they normally do *not* have is many relatives. One shop-keeper explained to me that kinship ties, and even ties of friendship, would make selling things very difficult. With too many relatives and friends walking through the door of his shop, he would feel obliged to 'give everything away to them' (*dou song gei tamen*). I should point out that his observation was somewhat misleading, because people in Angang do in fact sell things to relatives and friends. But the *idea* that to do so is in some way problematic is very widely held.

To put all of this differently: if it is true that *buyers* sometimes desire familiarity, as a form of protection against deceit, it is equally true that *sellers* sometimes desire anonymity, as a form of protection against kinship. But in order to explain why this should be so, we must shift from transactions in which deception is high on the agenda (including, for example, the notoriously risky buying of medicinal remedies) to transactions in which trust is normally taken for granted, starting inside of families.

As is well known, in China the moral logic of the relationship between parents and their children is redundantly addressed through the Confucian idiom of *xiao*, 'filial obedience'. *Xiao* implies a reciprocal relationship, one in which the care and support of parents for their children must be repaid to them in old age. Repayment normally comes through the provision of grandchildren (that is, through continuation of the family line), through the provision of financial and emotional support in old age, and through the provision of ongoing ritual inclusion after death by means of ancestor worship. The extent to which any or all of this repayment, and the support which compels it in the first place, should be characterized as 'economic' is rather hard to assess. On the one hand, Confucian ideology condemns those who simply 'care for' (*yang*) their elderly parents in the way that one might 'care for' (*yang*) a pig or a horse – that is, in the absence of warm sentiments and respect. But on the other hand, the folk model of parent–child reciprocity – something which I have characterized elsewhere as 'the cycle of *yang*' – is very clear about its strictly economic dimensions and normally does not seek to deny or devalue them. It costs a great deal of money to raise a child, and if children have obligations it is due in large part to the economic sacrifices which their parents have made (Stafford 1995; 2000a; 2000b).

Both the support and the cultivation of children by their parents (*yang*), and the 'respectful support' of ageing parents by their children (*fengyang*), are significantly focused on the provision of food and money, in what might be called both 'real' and 'symbolic' forms. For example, while parents give 'symbolic' gifts of actual money (*yasuiqian*) to a child on lunar new year's eve (*chuxi*), they also provide the child with 'real' housing, clothing, food, education, money, etc. As children get older, not only do they transfer 'symbolic' food and money back to their parents (for example, by means of gifts of actual food and money during calendrical festivals), they also normally transfer significant amounts of 'real' wealth – in many cases, a high proportion of their total income, and sometimes all of it. Such contributions may give old-age security to parents, but they also typically underwrite the establishment of independent households (as children marry), and eventually become part of a divisible family estate.

All of this is perfectly well known, but I want to underline the important point that parent–child reciprocity in China is not simply a matter of symbols and sentiments; it simultaneously organizes a vast amount of economic activity, including the accumulation and distribution of wealth within families. And to the extent to which virtually *all* wealth in China is conceived of in familial rather than individual terms, the Chinese economy takes the economy of family units as its starting point. In any case, the moral logic of parent–child reciprocity – found in the cycle of *yang* – is at the core of the Chinese ritual economy; that is, it is the model from which all other types of reciprocity flow.

What other types of reciprocity? Here let me focus on Dragon-head, the farming village in rural northeastern China. In this community, as in Angang, one clearly sees the extension of the principal of parent–child reciprocity, and more generally of family-based reciprocity, out towards expanding networks of social relations. In other words, the ritual economy, which starts within household units around the 'cycle of *yang*', expands out from them to encompass not only members of the local community, but also many people from neighbouring communities, and from further afield as well. Systems of this kind – which may be said to be constructed around 'cycles of *laiwang*' (an expression which literally describes the 'back-and-forth' movements between visiting neighbours) – are very familiar from the ethnographic literature on China, and are perhaps most obviously and publicly seen in the provision of mutual ritual support.

For example, in the mid-1990s a wedding in Dragon-head cost the 'groom's side' (*nanfang*) about 20,000 renminbi, over £1600 (Stafford 2000a). This represented anything from roughly two to ten years' income for a rural family (schoolteachers, for instance, made about 2400 renminbi per year at that time, but some wealthy farmers made much more). For all families, regardless of their wealth, the marriage of sons is a very expensive undertaking. The expense relates not only to ritual *per se*, but also to the setting up of the bride and groom in a 'new room' (*xinfang*), or even a new house, preferably one filled with new furniture, new appliances, and so on. As the groom on one occasion explained to me, in order to attract a bride to the countryside these days even 'a poor groom's side still has to spend a lot of money – and if they're rich they must spend even more!' Part of this crippling cost is, however, offset by the contributions of relatives and friends. Everyone who attends a wedding banquet in Dragon-head arrives with a gift of cash which is duly registered in a wedding book. In some cases, the amounts given will be quite small, but the groom's father's closest patrilineal relatives, for example, will often dig very deeply into their pockets to ensure that this entire marriage transaction – and not just the wedding banquet which marks it – is not a collective embarrassment. Every family in Dragon-head spends a great deal of money, year in, year out, underwriting the collective ritual expenses of the community.

But just as the line between symbolic and practical assistance is blurred within the family 'cycle of *yang*', so it is within this broader system of collective support, the 'cycle of *laiwang*'. This is not simply a 'cultural' add-on to the economy proper, nor does the economics of reciprocity simply balance out. On the contrary, a great deal of wealth is redistributed in this way, and the networks generated and sustained through such circulations have highly significant economic effects. The anthropologist Yan Yunxiang has illustrated this beautifully in his comprehensive study of gift-giving in one village in Heilongjiang. Yan calculates that fully one-fifth of household net income is used for gift exchange (1996: 77), and he stresses that the flow of gifts is directly tied to concrete mutual assistance in numerous forms, including not only support for expensive life-cycle rituals, but also agricultural cooperation, the raising of personal finance, and help during disasters such as famines (1996: 89–95ff). There is therefore little question that this kind of reciprocity is 'economic' by any definition: it is a *direct* source of collective financing to take advantage of opportunities, and of social insurance against economic hardship.

But here we get to the crucial point: while reciprocity within expanding networks of kin, friends and neighbours is explicitly acknowledged to have an economic dimension, and in some cases to be economically beneficial, it is also meant to be non-exploitative. As I have noted, this is why it may be desirable to do business in contexts of familiarity, that is, alongside those with whom one shares mutual support, as a protection against exploitation and fraud. But at the same time it is frequently acknowledged that actually *providing* this support to others is very demanding and places considerable burdens on many families, including the obligation to give things away rather than sell them, to underwrite the lavish life-cycle expenses of other families, and so on. These obligations are arguably themselves exploitative, albeit sometimes in indirect ways. For instance, one teacher in Dragon-head complained to me that his modest annual income *would* be sufficient, were it not for the burden of 'rushing to the rituals', *ganli*, as it is called colloquially. Every time someone has a wedding, a funeral, a house-building, a birth celebration, or an old-age celebration, there is no question but they will 'grab some money' from him (*naqian*). But let me cite a very different illustration of the same principle. Rubie Watson has shown, in her study of a powerful lineage in the New Territories of Hong Kong, that kinship-based ideals of equality and brotherly reciprocity are often in fact the pretext for sustaining *inequalities* among lineage brothers (Watson 1985). In short, the economic burdens imposed by familiarity are often as irksome as the economic burdens imposed by anonymity, and this is one source of the considerable ambivalence towards kinship, and towards relatedness in general, which one constantly encounters in rural China.

Now I will turn to the issue of 'corruption' (*fubai*), which by my definition falls within the sphere of the Chinese ritual economy because, as I have already said, when people in China 'cultivate relationships' (*yang guanxi*) with the powerful or the useful, this is often done through familiar idioms of gift-giving and reciprocity rather than through outright bribery. Notably, engaging in commensality – that is, sharing meals with others, an act which takes its meaning explicitly from family-based commensality – is an extremely common way of establishing relationships of a primarily utilitarian, or self-interested, kind. Not surprisingly, the cultivation of the powerful in this or other ways is not *necessarily* portrayed as corrupt (*fubai*); it can simply be portrayed as the nurturance of useful friendships. Let us call this the attempt to make strangers familiar, or, in other words, the attempt to extend the cycle of *laiwang* to its outer limits, because once this is achieved the problem of corruption is partly diminished. Helping one's friends, as a sign of one's loyalty to them, is of course a highly moral thing to do (*you daoli*). Note, however, that just as the disinterested cultivation (*yang*) of ties within families is often more economic than it at first seems, the interested cultivation (*yang*) of ties with the powerful is often less friendly than it at first seems. As Yan illustrates, for example, the giving of gifts to superiors is often done under at least implicit coercion, and is reflective of political hierarchies and the distribution of power in Chinese society (1996: 147–75).

As you might expect, people in China often make clear, and sometimes even absolute, distinctions between good and bad kinds of utilitarian reciprocity; that is, they do *not* necessarily confuse such matters. When brothers-in-law give each other financial and practical support in the normal ways, for example, very few people would say that they are doing anything bad, whereas most people would recognize as corrupt (*fubai*) and rotten (*huai*) the taking by officials of cash in return for special favours. But distinguishing between obviously good and obviously bad reciprocity is not always such an easy task. For instance, in her analysis of gift-exchange, Mayfair Yang pointed out that a distinction is normally drawn between 'the art of cultivating relationships' (*guanxixue*), and outright 'bribery' (*shou hui*). But she also observes that people sometimes find it difficult to say precisely what this distinction consists in. They tend to suggest that outright bribery is less 'reasonable' (*heli*), less subtle, more selfish, and more strategically 'self-contained' than is the long-term cultivation of *guanxi* (1994: 62–3). It is, however, easy to imagine a large number of examples which would fall somewhere between outright bribery and the more subtle cultivation of *guanxi* for 'reasonable' purposes – thus the moral ambiguities with which people must deal.

Some of these ambiguities may be illustrated with two relatively minor, but I think informative, examples drawn from my research in China and Taiwan. The first example is drawn from when I first moved to Angang in the late 1980s. I lived for a while in the teacher's dormitory of the local middle school (*zhongxue*) and, as I befriended the young teachers there, I discovered that in order to be posted to particular locations in Taiwan teachers often had to pay bribes – in the local idiom to 'give red envelopes' (*song hongbao*) – to officials. This was reportedly most often paid to the principal of the school to which they hoped to be assigned, and the amounts of money involved were often substantial. The point was to initiate in this way what would hopefully become an ongoing friendly relationship with a potential employer. Here the receivers of red envelopes might be characterized as corrupt (*fubai*), but the givers of them – young teachers – were normally seen to be motivated by high ideals. Most often they simply wished, quite 'reasonably' (*heli*), to move closer to their families, normally in order to fulfil their obligations towards ageing parents: in order to fulfil the requirements of the cycle of *yang*. So, while it is illegal for teachers to make bribes in order to live close to their ageing parents, most people would understand perfectly well the moral logic which compels them to do so, and they would *certainly* understand the cultural routine through which this is achieved.

Now this sounds suspiciously close to an admission that bribery in the service of kinship is in some ways permissible. This brings me to the second example, which is from rural northeastern China. Here I met a woman who was vociferous in her complaints about a local cadre. The problem arose because the cadre's dog had attacked and bitten the woman, but he had given her only a very small amount of money for medical treatment (100 renminbi) and no additional compensation. She felt that he had used his position to unfairly protect himself from criticism, by virtue of which he was 'corrupt' (*fubai*). But in her attempts to explain to me exactly what a bad man he was – I, for my part, thought he was the most stunning example of the 'good cadre' I had ever met – the woman gave a further, and quite interesting, example. She said that the cadre had once been in a position to help one of his own kinsmen (specifically, to help the son of a relative obtain a place in school), but that he had *refused* to do so. As far as she was concerned, this refusal to be corrupt in the service of kinship was very *huai*, rotten, and was evidence of moral failure in its own right. (I should perhaps point out that the cadre, for his part, criticised this woman in return because her aged mother-in-law, a relatively vigorous 87-year-old, was still made to go out to work.) Anyway, my point with this example is to illustrate that kinship morality did *not* compel this particular cadre to behave corruptly, but that his 'upright' behaviour meanwhile provoked condemnation on moral grounds.

The effect of these two examples is perhaps to further muddy the water by simply emphasizing the capacity of social realities to outrun cultural preconceptualizations. Is there a culture of loyalty in China which positively encourages corruption and fraud? Well, when teachers make bribes, when, that is, they participate in corruption (*fubai*) in order to fulfil the cycle of *yang*, it may be seen as a perfectly reasonable outcome of Chinese kinship, so here the answer might be yes. By contrast, even when there is considerable pressure for cadres to give special assistance to their kin and friends, they often simply decline to do so, in which case the answer might be no.

The fact is that, as soon as one begins to examine folk perspectives on things like 'deception' (*pian*) and 'corruption' (*fubai*), they turn out to be highly complex, and sometimes downright contradictory. As I have been saying, this is partly because morally questionable economic practices are not entirely disconnected from the morally elevated sphere of kinship, and from the operation of the Chinese ritual economy. This ritual economy – which starts in the family, and then sets the framework within which the moral value of all exchange relationships is ultimately evaluated – comprises a social field within which 'good' economic behaviour is sometimes rather like 'bad' economic behaviour, and vice versa.

This complicates very seriously any attempt to draw simple causal links between 'cultural values' and what has been happening recently with Chinese economic life. None the less, as everyone knows, the dramatic successes and failures of the East Asian economies in recent years have generated considerable discussion precisely about the relationship of culture to economic outcomes in the region. Confucian ethics have been praised for encouraging hard work, frugality and loyalty to the group, all of which are taken as constitutive of Chinese (and by extension East Asian) capitalism, and almost simultaneously damned for encouraging loyalty to the group, and therefore the corruption and cronyism which hinder the emergence of genuinely free markets. *The Economist* for its part suggested that the relative calm in China, Taiwan, Hong Kong and Singapore throughout the Asian reversal of fortune in the 1990s might have been the product of positive 'ethnic' (for which read 'cultural') traits, and even cited *approvingly* Sun Yat-sen's bitter lament that the Chinese were no more cohesive than grains of sand: 'Just the thing', enthused *The Economist*, 'to make free markets work smoothly.'[1] (Interestingly, this culturalist analysis of the downturn elides the fact that Chinese communities played a pivotal role in many of the worst-affected Southeast Asian economies, including Thailand. Perhaps they were more cohesive, there?)

Meanwhile, anthropologists – who used to be the only people with much to say about culture, but who have now lost control of this famously difficult concept – have been among the harshest critics of the new cultural determinism. Hill Gates, for one, has suggested that 'laundry lists' of culture traits, many of which may be said both to enable and to inhibit development, can only take us so far in understanding what has been happening in the various Chinese economies (1996: 14). One good Weberian reason for this (as anthropological research has repeatedly shown) is that any particular cultural characteristic – for example, placing a high moral value on frugality, or believing that moon-cakes symbolize reunion – is really only a potential: never something which leads, *on its own*, to any necessary conclusions, economic or otherwise.

The thrust of most anthropological work on China has therefore been to historicize and contextualize the interrelationship between given cultural forms (e.g., patrilineal ideologies) and economic life. Basu, for instance, has argued that, although one can specify characteristically 'Chinese' aspects of overseas Chinese enterprises in India, their actual success or failure may depend on very different kinds of external factors, including the emergence and disappearance of market opportunities (Basu 1991). It is well known that some south China lineages have been economic powerhouses; but the legal scholar Michael Palmer has shown that one New Territories lineage, far from being an entrepreneurial unit, proved to be 'an inadequate or inappropriate vehicle' for taking advantage of new development opportunities when these arose (Palmer 1991). Other work has stressed the economically exploitative potential, in certain historical contexts, of seemingly benign Chinese kinship ideals. As noted above, Watson has shown how the ideology of equality inherent to Chinese lineages may help produce the exploitation of poorer families within them (Watson 1985). Greenhalgh has meanwhile argued that the division of labour in Chinese family firms is not an ahistorical reflection of tradition, and that the success of the firms she studied was, in practice, highly dependent on the exploitation of women's labour (Greenhalgh 1994).

Given this inherent ambiguity – that is, given that culture never appears to 'cause' anything to happen in a simple way – it may be tempting simply to ignore culture altogether in our analyses of the Chinese economy. But this, I will suggest, would be mistaken on at least two grounds. First, because the 'emergence of free markets' in China – or more properly the emergence of institutions which make particular kinds of economic activities viable – is in part a protracted negotiation over the morality and immorality of different kinds of exchange. This negotiation, which doesn't have a pre-determined outcome, only makes sense in light of values which are inculcated, at all levels of Chinese society, through participation in the ritual economy. Second, because, even by the most restricted definition, the ritual economy comprises a vast arena of economic activity in its own right. It is not merely an exotic way Chinese people have of thinking about economic activity; to a remarkable extent it *is* the economic activity about which they think.

Now there are three possible versions of this second claim: weak, moderate and strong. The weak version simply notes that a significant amount of wealth in China circulates due to ritual activity, narrowly defined, for example in the form of wedding gifts. Here recall Yan Yunxiang's calculation that 20 per cent of household net income in one Heilongjiang village is used for gift exchange. If this is workable as an average expenditure for gift exchange proper in all of contemporary rural China, the total amount of wealth in ritual circulation is already very substantial indeed, and this would undoubtedly account for a significant proportion of total consumption (especially of food, alcohol and household goods) in the countryside. Also bear in mind that Chinese gift exchanges, again narrowly conceived, do not simply balance out. They may be defined as reciprocal, but they are often in fact asymmetrical, and therefore redistribute wealth in significant ways.

The moderate version of the claim takes this one step further, stressing the more extended economic effects, both proper and *improper*, of the ritual economy. On the proper side, as Yan makes clear, the idiom of ritual reciprocity is simultaneously a kind of banking activity, one which provides both investment capital and social insurance in rural China. It implies much more than simply 'rushing to the rituals' and giving people gifts. On the improper side, we might consider the implications of He Qinglian's estimate that over 75 per cent of the wealth taken from the state in reform-era China is actually absorbed in bribes, entertainment and favours. If the scale of corruption is anywhere near as great as He and others have suggested, if corruption is taken as part of the ritual economy, and if this is added to the extended economic implications of 'proper' ritual reciprocity, then the total amount of wealth in ritual circulation in China is even greater than might at first be assumed.

The strongest version of the claim goes one step beyond this. To the extent to which virtually all wealth in contemporary China is conceived of in familial or 'collective' terms, it could be argued that *all* wealth in China is ultimately located within the ritual economy – that is, within expanding cycles of *yang* and *laiwang* – and therefore is always at the service of reciprocity. I should mention that a different formulation of this strong version is found, at least implicitly, in the work of the anthropologist Hill Gates. In her ambitious and thought-provoking book, Gates suggests that the motor of Chinese history has for centuries been the tension between two very different modes of production (Gates 1996). These are, on the one hand, a 'tributary mode' (explicitly a ritual economy in which surplus is extracted as tribute by the state and redistributed among its officials), and a 'petty capitalist mode' (in which small, usually family-based, firms produce and exchange commodities amongst themselves, preferably just out of reach of state control). It is striking to me that *both* sides of Gates's equation – one in which surplus rises to the top as tribute, and another in which it circulates at the bottom – may be defined as ritual economies. Gates herself does not stress this singular fact very strongly, perhaps in part because her argument rests on the *discontinuities* between the two modes of production. But much of her evidence about Chinese petty capitalism would support such an interpretation.

In any case, these weak, moderate and strong claims about the status of the ritual economy have implications for our understanding of economic agency in China. As actors in economic transactions, Chinese people have to come from somewhere, and of course they come from the homes and communities in which they learn concepts which they deploy in economic life – concepts, for example, of exchange, of work, of money, of reciprocity, of trust, of deception, of corruption, and so on. This means that when people buy and sell, when they take risks or fail to do so, and when they praise or damn the economic initiatives of the state, they partly enact a morality, with all its ambiguities, learnt through participation in the ritual economy. To pretend that this is *not* the case is to indulge in the worst kind of economic formalism, and to risk a complete misunderstanding of recent Chinese economic history.

Note

1 *The Economist* (1998) 'In Praise of Paranoia: Survey of Taiwan', 7 November.

References

Basu, E. O. (1991) 'The Sexual Division of Labor and the Organization of Family and Firm in an Overseas Chinese Community', *American Ethnologist*, 18 (4): 700–18.

DeGlopper, D. (1995) *Lugang: Commerce and Community in a Chinese City*, Albany: State University of New York Press.
Gates, H. (1996) *China's Motor: A Thousand Years of Petty Capitalism*, Ithaca: Cornell University Press.
Greenhalgh, Susan (1994) 'De-Orientalizing the Chinese Family Firm', *American Ethnologist*, 21 (4): 746–75.
Liu Binyan and Link, P. (1998) 'A Great Leap Backward?', *New York Review of Books*, XLV (15): 19–23, 8 October. [Review of He Qinglian (1998), *Zhongguo De Xianjing* [*China's Pitfall*], Hong Kong: Mingjing Chubanshe.]
Palmer, M. (1991) 'Lineage and Urban Development in a New Territories Market Town', in H. Baker and S. Feuchtwang (eds), *An Old State in New Settings*, Oxford: Oxford University Press.
Stafford, C. (1995) *The Roads of Chinese Childhood: Learning and Identification in Angang*, Cambridge: Cambridge University Press.
—— (2000a) 'Chinese Patriliny and the Cycles of *Yang* and *Laiwang*', in J. Carsten (ed.), *Cultures of Relatedness*, Cambridge: Cambridge University Press.
—— (2000b) *Separation and Reunion in Modern China*, Cambridge: Cambridge University Press
Watson, R. (1985) *Inequality Among Brothers*, Cambridge: Cambridge University Press.
Yan Yunxiang (1996) *The Flow of Gifts: Reciprocity and Social Networks in a Chinese Village*, Stanford: Stanford University Press.
Yang, M. (1989) 'The Gift Economy and State Power in China', *Comparative Studies in Society and History*, 31 (1): 25–54.
—— (1994) *Gifts, Favors and Banquets: The Art of Social Relationships in China*, Ithaca: Cornell University Press.

4 The emergence of consumer rights

Legal protection of the consumer in the PRC

Michael Palmer

Introduction

This chapter examines the development and principal dimensions of consumer law in the People's Republic of China (hereinafter, the PRC) during the post-Mao era and assesses the significance of attempts to provide a protected legal status for the consumer (*xiaofeizhe*) in contemporary China. The official embrace of a 'socialist market economy' (*shehui zhuyi shichang jingji*) in the spring of 1993 – when Article 7 of the 1982 Constitution was amended so that the formal commitment to a state-planned economy based on public ownership was abandoned in favour of a more market oriented approach to economic development – was quickly followed by the introduction of a law for the protection of consumer rights and interests.[1] The idea that the consumer should be explicitly afforded special protection is thus relatively new in China's socialist legal system, although a limited form of consumer protection had long existed in the guise of trademark protection.[2] Moreover, the establishment of the China Consumers' Association (*Zhongguo Xiaofeizhe Xiehui*) in 1982 indicates that efforts had been made from the beginnings of the post-Mao economic reform process to develop institutional support for the interests and rights of consumers. The establishment of the national association foreshadowed the creation of many local consumer associations and consumer protection regulations later in the 1980s and early 1990s.

The PRC's economic reform programme was itself initiated in the late 1970s in large part to enhance the standard of living and level of consumer satisfaction for a Chinese population that had enjoyed little significant increase in disposable income since the late 1950s and which had become somewhat disillusioned by years of political turmoil and economic uncertainty. And although the human rights rhetoric of the PRC has for many years stressed the primary importance of the attainment of widespread enjoyment of the 'right to subsistence', attention has also been given increasingly to the importance of consumer demand and, in particular, to consumer rights and interests. The consumer or *xiaofeizhe* has emerged as a class of person to whom protection has steadily been extended by means not only of administration measures and criminal penalties but also of civil law. Such protection is in part necessary because of significant levels of consumer dissatisfaction with a wide range of quality, safety and other issues, relating to electrical appliances, agricultural goods such as seeds and fertilizers, computers, housing, motor vehicles, footwear and clothing, food hygiene, tourism, beauty parlours, jewellery and so on. The introduction in 1993 of the Consumer Protection Law, which firmly defines the consumer as a subject of civil law and which had its genesis in various provincial consumer regulations first introduced in the late 1980s and early 1990s, should be seen as a critically important step in safeguarding consumer concerns. Accordingly, that law forms the principal focus of this chapter. Nevertheless, the Consumer Protection Law was only one element in a range of new legislation put into force in 1993 and 1994 in order to strengthen the economic reform programme. Within this broader legislative framework, the 1993 Product Liability Law, the 1993 revised Trademark Law,[3] the 1993 Anti-unfair Competition Law,[4] the 1993 Decision of the Standing Committee of the National People's Congress on the Punishment of the Crimes of Production and Sale of Fake and Substandard Commodities,[5] and the 1994 Advertising Law[6] were particularly significant, and their relevance for the development of consumer protection will therefore also be considered.[7]

The emergence of the consumer

In the late 1970s, the Chinese leadership took the view that the People's Republic needed a new economic direction in order to overcome a wide range of serious problems that it considered to be hindering modernization. These difficulties included 'the faltering performance of agriculture, lack of industrial productivity growth and the inability and unwillingness of the Party to provide incentives and reasonable living standards' (Howe and Walker 1984: ii). One observer noted that 'gains in personal consumption between 1957 and the late 1970s were remarkably small' (Lardy 1984: 849). Old economic policies based on state planning, state monopolies and public ownership were to be supplanted by initiatives aimed at decollectivizing agriculture, introducing new rights in land, promoting private trade, encouraging foreign investment, and fostering the view that a 'few should get rich first'. The resulting rapid economic growth meant that by the early 1990s it was possible to conclude that 'since 1978 real per capita material consumption has risen at an average annual rate of 7 per cent and more than doubled the standard of living of the average citizen' (Chai 1996: 275). In addition, 'consumer satisfaction has significantly increased, thanks to much greater freedom of consumer choice, as well as improved distribution and allocation of consumer goods and services' (Chai 1996: 276). The higher priority accorded to personal consumption and living standards relative to investment allowed greater attention to be given to the production and import of consumer goods. In addition, it has contributed to a steady rise in the development of residential homes, schools, hospitals and other 'non-productive' construction efforts.

With the emergence of the consumer as a distinct social category, worthy of protection, official efforts have been made to justify the role of the consumer and to shape the conduct of the new consumers. The emphasis on the development of productive forces that dominated economic policy in the first few decades of Communist Party rule has given way to an acknowledgement that Marx himself considered that standards of consumption and the development of productive capacity are inextricably linked. Moreover, the creation of a social category of wealthy persons was characterized by the Chinese leadership as an indication that in due course prosperity would be attained by all. However, there is also a strand of official thinking that indicates a felt need to promote 'healthy consumption' and to avoid some of the worst excesses of consumerism – gift-giving is seen as creating social problems by encouraging an unhealthy reliance on personal connections (*guanxi*) and even leading to bribery and corruption.[8] Moreover, there have been from time to time efforts by the authorities to discourage certain forms of consumer purchases, such as colour televisions, by means of additional taxes (King and Gao 1991: 6–7).

More importantly, there are indications that the PRC leadership is concerned to retain a very restricted understanding of the nature of 'consumerism' in the Chinese context. Article 12 of the Consumer Protection Law provides that 'consumers have the right to form social organizations [*shehui tuanti*] for the maintenance of their own legitimate rights and interests in accordance with the law'. The various provincial regulations introduced in the late 1980s and early 1990s for the purpose of consumer protection assumed the existence of consumer associations but did not make the establishment of such bodies a consumer right. Despite this legislative change, however, there continues to be little official sympathy with the notion that consumers should actively combine in autonomous unions and associations in order to promote consumer interests through, *inter alia*, political lobbying and to protect consumers against such problems as unsafe products, qualitatively defective goods and services, fraudulent trading, lack of information necessary for appropriate purchasing decisions and lack of competition. Such forms of association carry considerable political potential in the context of the PRC because they are based on the premise that citizens should be active participants in shaping social policy rather than passive recipients of paternalistic government protection.

As a result, consumer associations in the PRC are quasi-official, and have as their general aims the exercise of what is called 'social supervision' (*shehui jiandu*) over the provision of goods and services, and the protection of the lawful rights and interests of consumers (Consumer Protection Law, 1993, Article 31). More specifically, they are expected to provide citizens with relevant consumer information and to offer advice to consumers through consultation services, to assist in the inspection of goods and services carried out by government departments (notably, the State Administration of Industry and Commerce, or SAIC),[9] to communicate with government departments on matters affecting consumer rights and interests to report on matters relating to goods and services to relevant administration bodies and to receive the investigative conclusions of such bodies, to hear consumer complaints and to investigate or mediate complaints or assist complainants to bring suit in a People's court, and to work with the mass media to expose conduct which infringes consumer rights and interests (Consumer Protection Law, 1993, Article 32). These wide-ranging responsibilities would not be ascribed to the consumer associations if they were not government-sponsored (Consumer Protection Law, 1993, Article 32[7]). The Consumer Protection Law at Article 33 prohibits consumer associations from engaging in profit-making activities such as recommending particular goods and services to the consumer. This restriction severely limits the capacity of consumer associations to break free from their dependence on government funding and thus traps them in the status of 'mass organizations' – similar to the All-China Women's Federation and the All-China Federation of Trade Unions – and thus may be characterized as 'governmentally-organized non-governmental organizations'. Indeed, in much of their work, the consumer associations operate closely with the State Administration of Industry and Commerce. Many members of the Council of the China Consumers' Association are serving members of the state bureaucracy. In 1990, the then Premier Li Peng characterized the China Consumers' Association as a bridge (*qiaoliang*) between the consumer and government (Shi *et al.* 1994: 91). This 'bridging' role is very characteristically a mass organization function in the PRC. The close link with the organs of the state is a double-edged sword. On the one hand, for example, it raises problems of divided loyalties when complaints are brought regarding the products of state-owned enterprises. On the other hand, there is little doubt that the consumer associations enjoy enhanced authority as a result of their close association with the state bureaucracy.

The China Consumers' Association (*Zhongguo Xiaofeizhe Xiehui*) was established upon receiving approval from the State Council on 26 December 1982. The Association's Council (*Lishi Hui*), comprising 134 member in 1994 (Shi *et al.* 1994: 91), is the governing body of this organization, and includes in its ranks senior figures from the National People's Congress, the government and the judiciary. It coordinates the efforts of local consumer associations and committees which, by 1997, numbered more than 3000 (Zhongguo Xiaofeizhe Zazhi Bianjibu 1998: 3). These are, in turn, subdivided into more than 300,000 branch consumer associations, 'liaison stations' (*lianluo zhan*) and supervision offices located in such bodies as urban wards, villages and townships, schools, government departments, market places (*zahuo shichang*) and medium and large scale industrial and commercial enterprises. Semi-official sources estimate that by the mid-1990s there were more than three million people working in these various forms of 'grass-roots' consumer protection body (Zhongguo Xiaofeizhe Zazhi Bianjibu 1998: 3). Since the late 1980s the China Consumers' Association has organized large-scale publicity campaigns to coincide with international consumers' day in mid-March, and includes in its publicity vivid accounts of ten major consumer harm cases occurring during the previous year.

Despite these laudable efforts, it is clear that an inherent limitation in the ability of consumer associations to adopt a broad, pro-active role in promoting the interests of consumers in the PRC is their lack of independence. In keeping with the official view that robust NGOs, autonomous trade unions and so on are of limited value in China, genuinely independent consumer protection associations are regarded as bodies that would seek to challenge the authorities on issues of fundamental concern if allowed to operate in China. Such bodies would be 'unsuitable' for China at its current level of development. In addition to this problem, however, there is the difficulty that arises from the particular orientation taken towards law and legal development in the post-Mao era. Thus, the reconstruction of the legal system has been prompted by not only a felt need to protect individual rights but also a concern to promote stability and order so that a repeat of the social unrest experienced during the Cultural Revolution might be avoided. Article 1 of the Consumer Protection Law 1993 provides: 'This law is formulated to protect the lawful rights and interests of consumers, to maintain social and economic order, and to promote the healthy development of the socialist market economy.' This suggests that the rights and interests of the individual consumer are only one part of the agenda of consumer protection law, and that there is also a strong concern with the interests of the party-state. Moreover, it should be remembered that the 1982 Constitution itself – despite the new commitment to the 'rule of law' introduced by the 1999 constitutional amendments[10] – places a strong emphasis on the limited nature of rights in contemporary China, as Article 51 indicates: 'Citizens of the PRC, in exercising their freedoms and rights, may not infringe the interests of the state, society or the collective, nor the lawful freedoms and rights of other citizens.' Given that, as I shall indicate, the easiest and cheapest mechanisms by which an aggrieved citizen may secure redress are often administrative in nature, this concern with state and collective interests is an inherent weakness in the structure of consumer rights.

The growing interest in consumer protection in the PRC during the 1990s to a significant extent also reflects international influences. Thus, since the early 1980s, the PRC has been a member of a number of international, multilateral bodies with a view to expanding foreign investment, trade and borrowing. In particular, the United Nations Development Programme has provided aid to the PRC since 1979, the World Bank and the International Monetary Fund both admitted China in 1980, in 1986 the People's Republic joined the Asian Development Bank, and much more recently China became a member of the World Trade Organization. Alongside these important developments, the PRC has of course also allowed greater foreign access to its domestic markets and encouraged direct foreign investment in China. This internationalization of China's economic relations has significantly affected thinking about consumer protection in the PRC. First, not unlike another area of law in which there is a clear 'precautionary' principle at work, namely environment law, there is a tendency to use consumer protection as a vehicle for harnessing 'anti-foreigner' sentiments. The Chinese consumer needs to be cushioned against unscrupulous foreign manufacturers intent on dumping substandard products in China. Certainly, some Western law firms now operating in China seem increasingly worried about the growing willingness of the Chinese consumer to sue foreign parties:

> . . . for western [companies], in particular, the impact could become explosive. 'China is a much more litigious society than it used to be,' says . . . an attorney [in a US law firm] in Shanghai. 'Western or foreign invested companies are viewed as having deeper pockets and are better targets.' Quips . . . a Beijing-based attorney [in another US firm]: 'It's payback time for the Opium Wars'.[11]
>
> (Saywell 1999: 42)

Second, however, if Chinese goods produced for the domestic market are to be able to withstand competition from high-quality imported products, their standard must be improved significantly, and consumer protection laws are one means of addressing this problem – Article 1 of the 1993 Consumer Protection Law declares that one of the aims of its is 'the healthy development of a socialist market economy'. Third, the view is taken that, if the PRC is to be a successful exporter to world markets, its goods must meet international standards. By the mid-1990s the PRC was probably the world's eighth largest exporter of manufactured goods. However, the share of this trade enjoyed by state owned enterprises – often regarded as the major culprits in the production of sub-standard and harmful goods – had slipped to only one fifth (Lardy 1995: 1075–7).

Enhancement of product quality is also seen as important because to some extent it symbolizes the virtues of the economic reform programme. Under the planned economy system, the relationship between product quality and the financial results of enterprises was very tenuous. The separation of consumer prices and producer prices, lack of consumer choice, and the limited degree of enterprise autonomy in decisions regarding output, meant that there was no economic pressure on producers to respond to consumer dissatisfaction with the quality of goods on sale. Fairly early on in the reform process serious attention was therefore given to the issue of product quality. As Epstein (1988: 285) has pointed out, a significant change occurred in 1978 when the Chinese Communist Party advised the State Council to prohibit official statistics on annual production output from including substandard products. Shortly thereafter, the PRC introduced national regulations for the administration of standardization. Moreover, since 1984 all industrial products must be licensed. The quality of licensed products is monitored and a licence will be revoked, and the product therefore withdrawn from the market, if quality standards are not maintained. (Epstein 1988; 288). In April 1986 the State Council promulgated the Regulations Concerning Liability for the Quality of Industrial Products.[12] These Regulations made manufacturers, retailers, transporters, bailees and even quality inspection authorities directly liable to end-users for substandard goods. Their introduction was followed by the promulgation of local legislation in varying forms designed to strengthen the administrative control of product quality. Thus, for example, the Beijing Municipal Regulations on the Supervision of the Quality of Industrial Products 1996 placed responsibility on the local Bureau of Standards and Measurements in Beijing for, *inter alia*, encouraging enterprises to improve the quality of products and protecting the rights and interests of the users and consumers of products (Article 1), and for exercising powers of supervision over a wide range of product quality controls as well as dealing with consumer disputes (Article 3).[13]

The development in consumer protection in the mid-1980s was significantly assisted by the introduction of the General Principles of the Civil Law, 1986.[14] This provided (and continues to provide) a broad corpus of rules that integrates various types of more specific regulations and laws, including the wide range of local consumer protection rules introduced from 1988 onwards. At Article 88 – and it should be noted that broadly similar wording is now to be found in the 1999 Contract Law at Article 61 and 62 – it is provided that, if the contractual terms of a sale are ambiguous on such matters as quality, time periods, price and so on, the intended meaning of the terms should – in the absence of an agreement between the parties – be performed in accordance with national or customary standards. As a result, unless the parties have reached their own agreement on the matter, sellers of products necessarily assure consumers that the quality of goods being sold conforms with known, objective standards. Failure of the products to meet these standards means that the vendor has failed to fulfil her or his obligations under the contract of sale, and the consumer has the right to demand performance or to secure other remedies and to claim damages. In addition, it is stipulated in the chapter on 'Civil Liability for Infringement of Rights' that sellers or manufacturers of substandard products bear civil liability for property damage or physical injury caused by such defective goods (Article 122). The General Principles also provide ten forms of civil remedy that remain important today. These include compensation, restoration of original condition, repair, and replacement, damages, elimination of ill effects and rehabilitation of reputation, and apology (Article 134). These remedies are sometimes directly appended to local consumer protection regulations. After the General Principles had been put into effect, various provinces and municipalities introduced local consumer protection regulations – these were in effect the experimental precursors of the national Consumer Protection

Law 1993. The local codes are somewhat briefer than the national law that they preceded. In addition, they are usually interpreted by the local Bureau for the Administration of Industry and Commerce rather than the particular local People's Congress that enacted them. In addition to this emphasis on administrative rather than legislative interpretation, there was some concern to stress not only the rights but also the duties of consumers. Thus, the Shanghai regulations at Article 6 imposed the following obligations on consumers: first, obedience to social morality (*shehui daode*), and respect for the labour and legal rights of manufacturers, sellers and servants; second, installation and maintenance of commodities in accordance with the contents of the instructions booklet, and adherence to the regulatory or agreed service systems; and third, reporting situations truly and submitting relevant evidence where a complaint about quality, price and so on is brought by a consumer.[15]

An additional factor promoting interest in consumer protection was a concern to enhance consumer access to relevant information regarding such matters as product quality, safety and similar issues. As we have seen, the China Consumers' Association was established in 1982, and one of its principal functions has been dissemination of consumer information. It has, for example, for more than a decade assumed responsibility for promoting and organising in China the local version of the international consumer day held on March 15 annually – these events include publishing the ten most important cases of infringement of consumer rights that year. The Consumer Protection Law 1993, made provision for liability for producers and sellers who omit to furnish valid information. Thus, at Article 8, the right is conferred on consumers to 'obtain true information' regarding the goods that they produce or the services they receive. The right, in formal terms at least, is very broad. Consumers may demand from sellers information regarding various aspects of the goods purchased. These include: price, origin, manufacturers, usage, functions, standards, grades, main ingredients, date of production, expiry date, certificate of inspection, operating instructions, and after-sales services or data. In addition, service providers are obliged to provide information regarding the nature, standards and costs of their services if the consumer so requests. Article 19 places on sellers the duty to provide consumers with authentic information regarding their goods and services, and prohibits the use of false and misleading advertising. Sellers must also answer consumer queries truthfully and mark prices clearly. Moreover, Article 24 of the same law prohibits the use in sales literature, public notices and so on of unfair or unreasonable terms, and characterizes as invalid those contract terms that are unfair or unreasonable for the consumer. These provisions in the Consumer Protection Law 1993 are supplemented by similar rights in several closely related area of law. Thus, the Law on Product Quality 1993 gives users and consumers the right to seek information from producers and sellers about product quality (Article 12) and requires producers and sellers to provide comprehensive package information on quality inspection, the name and address of the producer, expiry date, and warnings about the consequences of inappropriate use (Articles 15 and 24). In addition, the Advertising Law 1994 requires all advertising to be truthful (Article 3) and to exclude false information (Article 4), and advertisers and their agents and publishers to be fair, honest and credible (Article 5). Advertisements must be accurate, clear and explicit in their statements about such matters as a product's performance, place of origin, mode of use, quality, price, producer, as well as expiry date, and there are similar requirements for services (Article 9). Advertisers are prohibited from giving information that is false in an advertisement to the effect that a patent right in a product has been obtained when, in fact, no such right has been granted (Article 11). In addition, newspapers and other media outlets are not permitted to publish advertisements that take the form of news reports (Article 13). Advertisement for foods, alcoholic drinks and cosmetics may not use language that leads consumers to confuse these products with pharmaceuticals (Article 19). There are strict rules on tobacco advertising and where advertisements for tobacco are permitted they must carry the warning 'smoking is harmful to health' (*xiyan youhai jiankang*). In addition, it is specified at Article 30 that the publisher of an advertisement must provide advertisers and their agents with true information on such matters as media coverage, audience rate and circulation. The 2002 Shanghai Regulations, reflecting a growing concern with 'unethical selling',[16] place an even heavier burden on sellers to advise consumers of the relevant aspects of their products and services, and honestly to answer consumer queries (Articles 17, 19, 21, 22 and 23). The problem of dishonest dealing is exacerbated by the relatively recent development of a consumer market in the PRC – on the one hand sellers have little sense of business ethics, and on the other consumers have little sense of the need to protect their rights.

Consumer rights and sellers' duties under the Consumer Protection Law 1993

The 1993 Consumer Protection Law – unlike the earlier provincial regulations and drafts of the national law[17] – does not place duties on consumers. The 1993 Law also differs from the earlier regulations in that it places important, general obligations on the state – in particular, the State Administration of Industry and Commerce – to promote consumer interests through efficient administration, the use of punitive methods, and effective access to the civil courts (Articles 26–30). The Consumer Protection Law also, as we have seen, provides a role for consumer associations to assist consumers by providing relevant information, assisting in the supervision of products and services, dealing with consumer grievances by investigation, mediation and assisting disgruntled consumers in bringing suit in a people's court, and using the mass media to expose cases of consumer maltreatment.

The principal purpose of the Consumer Protection Law is, however, to define the rights of the consumer and the obligations of the seller. Certain of these rights and duties – those relating to the provision of information – have already been considered. In addition, the Law treats the consumer's right to buy goods that do not harm the personal safety and property of the consumer and the right to seek compensation if the consumer suffers personal injury or damage to property from her or his purchase or use of a product or service (Articles 7 and 12). Sellers have a corresponding duty to 'guarantee' (*baozheng*) that the goods and services they provide are not harmful to personal safety or property. If vendors should discover serious defects in a good or service that they supply, there is an obligation on them to make an immediate report to the relevant administrative departments, inform consumers, and take steps to prevent damage (Article 18). The Product Quality Law 1993 further provides that the seller should examine goods before accepting delivery, examine quality certificates, maintain products in good quality and refrain from selling goods that are out of date or which have deteriorated (Articles 21, 22, and 23). Under the Consumer Protection Law 1993, sellers bear civil liability in any the following circumstances: the product sold was defective, the product lacked properties that it ought to possess and this fact was not declared at the time of sale, the product failed to conform to the product description or samples, the product had been officially declared obsolete, the product sold was short of weight or quantity, the substance or cost of services did not conform to the agreement, deliberately delaying or refusing the consumers requests for repair, replacement, compensation and so on, and other infringements of the consumer's rights and interests (Article 40).

The Consumer Protection Law also adopts a firm position on contractual exclusion of contractual and tortious liability by means of exemption clauses. Thus, according to Article 24, 'Business operators may not, through standard contracts, notices, announcements, entrance hall bulletins and so on, make unfair or unreasonable rules regarding consumers or diminish or exempt themselves from civil liability for their infringement of the legitimate rights and interests of consumers.' The same article declares that contracts or notices which bear such terms are invalid.

The Consumer Protection Law appears, however, also to follow principles of strict civil liability envisaged by Article 106(3) of the General Principles: 'Civil liability shall still be borne even in the absence of fault, if the law so stipulates.' Thus, Article 41 of the Consumer Protection Law specifies that 'Business operators shall, if the commodities or services they supply have caused personal injury to consumers or other victims, pay the victims' medical expenses, nursing expenses during the period of medical treatment, reduced income for loss of working time and other expenses.' Similar liability rules apply under Article 44 where damage has been caused to a consumer's property: the seller is obliged to bear civil liability, regardless of fault, and is therefore responsible for repairing, replacing, providing a refund, returning goods, or making up any shortfall in goods sold. In addition, sellers are responsible for the repair, replacement or return of goods where this course of action is guaranteed by state regulation, or where it has been agreed between sellers and consumers. Replacement or return of goods is required if the products sold continues to malfunction after being repaired twice within the period for which the repair is guaranteed (Article 45).[18] Where the goods or services have caused disability, the unfortunate consumer is entitled to compensation and to reimbursement of expenditure on special equipment, living allowances and the living costs of persons who are supported by the disabled consumer (Article 41, paragraph 2). Should the commodity or services provided cause the death of the consumer or another user, the seller is liable for the funeral expenses, compensation for the death, and the living costs of the persons who had been supported by the deceased during her or his lifetime.

A long-standing issue in Chinese consumer protection law has been the respective liabilities of the seller and the manufacturer of a product that causes harm to the consumer. Many sellers, faced with consumer claims, have responded by refusing to admit liability and, instead, advising aggrieved consumers that they should contact the manufacturer. However, the producer has often proved difficult to locate or, if located, unwilling to respond to the complaint, especially if based in another province. In the mid-1980s, one official response to this problem was to introduce a system of national warranties for certain kinds of consumer goods (Epstein 1988: 286). In addition, local consumer protection regulations attempted to establish a system in which primary liability for resulting injury and loss was placed on the retailer, and the latter given the right then to recover compensation from the manufacturer or other operator actually responsible for the problem: 'When consumers legal rights and interests are infringed, the sellers or service providers shall compensate. If damage is caused by the manufacturers, warehouse, or transportation operators, the sellers or service providers may in turn seek compensation from them' (Beijing Municipal Regulations on the Protection of Consumers' Legal Rights and Interests, 1986).[19] This basic approach is confirmed at the national level by Article 35 of the Consumer Protection Law 1993 which stipulates that the aggrieved consumer should seek compensation from the seller of the suspect goods or the supplier of services that have infringed consumer rights and interests. If it is the manufacturer that is responsible for the problem, then the seller, after paying compensation to the aggrieved consumer, may seek to recover the compensation from the manufacturer. But where the consumer has suffered personal injury or damage to property as a result of the defects in a product, it is open to the consumer to pursue the complaint against either the seller or the manufacturer; however, if it shown that the particular defendant should not be liable and that responsibility lies with another provider – either the seller or producer, depending on the identity of the defendant – the defending party may recover the compensation from the other provider.

Nevertheless, failure of an 'innocent' seller to locate a supplier or producer who should bear liability in a product quality case is no longer a *de facto* barrier to consumer rights because 'where the seller can identify neither the producer nor the supplier of the defective product, the seller is liable for compensation' (Article 30). This affords the aggrieved consumer a broader range of opportunities for redress than was permitted under earlier local regulations.

One problem that has emerged on a significant scale since the introduction of the Consumer Protection Law in the early 1990s has been disclosure of consumers' personal details to third parties (Liu 2004).[20] The 1993 Law failed to address this privacy issue, and it has been left to provincial regulations to fill in the legislative gap. Thus, the 2002 Shanghai Regulations stipulate not only that business operators may not require consumers to provide personal information that is unconnected to their purchase but also that sellers may not for any reason divulge personal information of consumers to third parties without the consent of the consumers concerned. Such information includes name, sex, occupation, educational background, means of contact, marital status, income and property, finger prints, blood type, medical history, 'and any other information that is closely related to the individual consumer and her or his family' (Article 20). In addition, Article 14 makes provision for another problem that was also not directly dealt with in the Consumer Protection law 1993, namely personal rights such as name, portrait, reputation and honour, and Article 18 protects against over-robust responses by sellers to complaints by consumers:

> When providing goods or services, business operators shall not behave as follows:
> (1) insult or slander consumers;
> (2) search the bodies of consumers or things they carry on their person;
> (3) violate the personal freedom of consumers;
> (4) cause the permanent destruction or damage of specified mementos that are of symbolic personal significance to consumers.

Producers – but not sellers – are, however, offered a number of grounds by which they may avoid civil liability in product quality cases, and this is more consistent with the basis for liability provided in Article 106(2) of the General Principles of the Civil Law which makes fault (*guocuo*) a general standard of liability for torts. Thus, Article 29 of the Product Quality Law 1993 provides that a producer is not liable for compensation if she or he is able to demonstrate that the product concerned was not distributed (*touru liutong*, literally 'put into circulation'), the defect which caused the harm did not exist when the product was distributed, or scientific or technological knowledge was incapable of detecting the defect at the time the product was distributed. Nevertheless, the basic principle of strict liability appears to apply also to manufacturers – Article 24 of the Product Quality Law declares that 'a producer shall be liable for compensation if her or his defective product causes damage to human life or property other than the defective product itself'. However, it is significant that the defences available to the manufacturer are not also available to the seller, and this represents an attempt to deal with the vexed issue of the seller whose response to a consumer complaint about a product is to refer the unhappy customer to some distant and difficult-to-locate manufacturer.

Sellers and producers may also be liable for administrative penalties for infringing consumer rights and interests. In the PRC, administrative liability lies with civil and criminal liability as one of the three main types of legal liability for breaches of law. Thus, among the administrative offences stipulated in Article 50 are: the production or sale of substandard goods that endanger personal safety and may damage property, adulterating the contents of products, selling fake, defective or substandard or obsolete or out-of-date goods, forging particulars of the origin of goods, using fraudulently the marks of other products, selling commodities that require inspection or guarantees but which have neither been inspected nor subjected to guarantees, disseminating false information about the goods or services being sold, delaying or refusing consumers' justified demands for repair, replacement, refund, compensation for losses and so on, violating the 'human dignity' or personal freedom of consumers, and 'other circumstances in which punishment is imposed for infringement of consumer rights and interests as provided for in relevant laws and regulations'. The administrative measures that may be taken – either exclusively or concurrently – against a seller whose conduct falls within one or more of these categories include warnings and either confiscation of unlawful earnings or the imposition of a fine of up to five times the value of the unlawful earnings. If there have been no unlawful earnings, then a fine up to 10,000 *yuan* may be imposed – however, if the circumstances are nevertheless serious the seller's business activities may be suspended and her or his business licence revoked (Article 50). Moreover, if a seller hinders or obstructs administrative personnel in carrying out their duties, she or he may be subject to punishment under Regulations on the Administrative Penalties for Public Security.[21] Should the attempt to frustrate official business in this manner involve violent or threatening conduct, a criminal prosecution may be brought (Consumer Protection Law 1993, Article 52).

The most important offences are now contained in Chapter III of the 1997 Criminal Law.[22] This chapter deals with 'Crimes of Undermining the Order of the Socialist Market Economy'. The 1979 Criminal Law contained few provisions which dealt directly with consumer welfare, and the offences contained in Chapter III of the 1997 amended Criminal Law are based on the 1993 Decision on Punishment of the Crimes of Production and Sale of Fake or Substandard Products.[23] Thus, in the amended code it is an offence punishable by up to two years fixed-term imprisonment or criminal detention[24] to adulterate products, or pass off imitation goods as genuine, or sell seconds at best-quality price where proceeds from the sale are between

50,000 and 200,000 yuan. Additional punishment of a fine of between 50 per cent and 200 per cent of the proceeds of the sale may also be imposed. Heavier terms of imprisonment are to be applied if the proceeds are more than 200,000 yuan, and rise incrementally to a sentence of fifteen years fixed-term imprisonment or life imprisonment where sales exceed two million yuan (Article 140).

Fake medicines (*jiayao*) and poor-quality medicines (*lieyao*) have been persistent problems for Chinese consumers in the post-Mao era, and are a public health matter taken very seriously by the authorities. Thus, the sale or production of fake medicines which seriously endanger human health is, according to Article 141, punishable by up to three years fixed-term imprisonment or criminal detention, or by a fine of between 50 per cent and 200 per cent of the sales proceeds, or by both imprisonment and the fine. If the fake medicines cause serious harm to health the penalty of imprisonment is obligatory and the term is extended to between three and ten years. More significantly, should the fake medicines cause death or 'particularly serious harm' (*tebie yanzhong weihai*) to human health, the punishment is a sentence of not less than ten years, life imprisonment or execution. The production or sale of substandard medicines or medical equipment and clinical-use sanitary materials are punishable by imprisonment and fines – in serious circumstances (*houguo tebie yanzhong*) by not less than ten years fixed-term imprisonment and a substantial fine (Articles 142 and 145). Further, the production and sale of unhygienic cosmetics and the sale of such products knowing of the defect resulting in serious harm is punishable by a heavy fine and up to three years imprisonment or criminal detention (Article 148).

An additional significant problem for the Chinese consumer in recent times has been unhygienic foodstuffs. The consumption of inferior food products has from time to time caused either incidents of food poisoning or the spread of viruses such as hepatitis A. The production or sale of foodstuffs that cause serious harm to human health is an offence punishable by a substantial fine and a minimum term of imprisonment of seven years (Article 143). The penalties that apply when the defective food has been adulterated with harmful materials and then knowingly sold with such defects are more severe and include the death penalty (Article 144).

A further alarming problem facing the consumer in post-Mao China is the production and sale of electrical appliances or explosive or combustible materials that endanger human safety. Offences of this nature may be subject to a substantial fine and a sentence of not less than five years fixed-term imprisonment (Article 140).

In rural areas, an additional difficulty has been the supply of insecticides, fertilizers, seeds, veterinary medicines and so on that are either fake, out of date or substandard. The maximum penalty for the production or sale of such goods is between three and seven years fixed-term imprisonment and a heavy fine (Article 147).

Provincial regulations introduced subsequent to the 1993 national Consumer Protection Law – most notably those for Shanghai (Shanghai Regulations for the Protection of Consumers' Rights and Interests, 2002, Article 33) – have also imposed on sellers mandatory responsibility for product recall in certain circumstances.

> If business operators have identified serious defects in the goods or services they provide and such goods or services still endanger the personal and property safety of consumers even if used or received correctly, they shall immediately suspend or terminate the sale of such goods or the provision of such services. If the goods have already been sold, emergency measures shall be taken to inform the consumers thereof and such goods must be called back for repairs, replacement or destruction, and at the same time, reports thereof are to be submitted to relevant administrative departments and trade associations.
>
> If serious defects mentioned [above] are identified in the goods or services provided, and the business operators fail to take [the appropriate measures] . . . relevant administrative departments shall require according to law the business operators to suspend or stop at once the sale of such goods or the provision of such services, and to recall the goods already sold.
>
> When the Municipal Consumers' Association identifies serious defects in goods or services, it may make appropriate suggestions to relevant administrative departments.

This obligation was not provided for in the 1993 national provisions.

Consumer disputes and consumer justice

In the post-Mao era, serious efforts have been made in China to construct institutions and processes that facilitate the handling and resolution of civil disputes. To a significant extent the need for the revival of such institutions, following their suppression during the Cultural Revolution, has been created by the rapid development of commercial relations, the decollectivization of agriculture, and greater personal freedoms. The response to the resulting upsurge in civil and economic disputes has been to enhance institutional strength in three areas: mediation, adjudication, and arbitration. Thus, in 1989, revised organic rules for local mediation committees were introduced the better to regulate the work of local mediators in resolving minor disputes and promoting social stability. In addition, courts have been revived and reformed. Civil litigation has been allowed to expand significantly, and although inheritance and divorce cases still predominate, many other kinds of civil and commercial dispute have also increased in significance. A Civil Procedure Law was introduced experimentally in 1982, and then revised in 1991. In addition, since 1995 a nationwide system of local arbitration commissions has operated to deal with labour, economic contracts and similar disputes.

The Consumer Protection Law is an important element in this general institution building process,[25] and has as one of its major functions the provision of an effective and accessible means of resolving consumer disputes (*xiaofei zhengyi*) and enforcing the rights of consumers. The possibility of using such mechanisms to pursue a grievance enhances the position of the consumer in the early stages of a dispute – such as bringing a complaint, and negotiations between the parties – and such mechanisms may in fact have to be relied on to enforce substantive rights. In post-Mao China, as in a wide range of other jurisdictions, there are many difficulties that the individual, aggrieved consumer faces in attempting to secure redress by formal legal action. In many consumer cases the personal injury, damage, or loss is comparatively limited, and the financial realities of litigation mean that the civil process is too expensive and cumbersome to involve. Moreover, the aggrieved consumer is often a 'one-shot' party who seeks redress against an experienced seller or producer who is a 'repeat player', well versed in dealing with consumer complaints.

Moreover, there are the difficulties that result from the long-standing socio-political concerns with harmony and stability, the emphasis on the importance of moral duties and the disdain for pursuing private interests through lawsuits. Negotiation and mediation outside the court remain the preferred means of dispute processing, and even in court hearings, the judge is encouraged by the Civil Procedure Law 1991 (Article 9) to attempt to mediate the dispute in order to secure a settlement.[26] Popular social attitudes continue to favour mediation over litigation and adjudication processes, and simply putting up with a problem and 'yielding' (*rang*) ground is often seen as the most appropriate response to infringement of consumer rights, and those who have recourse to courts are often characterized as *diaomin* or 'cunning people'. It will be recalled that in our discussion of consumer rights we observed that early provincial regulations affording consumer protection placed on consumers the duty to be morally worthy and to tell the truth, to acknowledge their own unreasonable use of products, and to refrain from taking direct action in the form of reprisals or deliberately causing trouble for business operators. Although such provisions are absent from the 1993 Consumer Protection Law, this national legislation nevertheless places mutual obligations of 'voluntariness, equality, honesty and credibility' on both sellers and consumers (Article 40), and Article 6 of the 1999 Contract Law states that all parties to a contract 'must act in accordance with the principle of good faith, whether in exercising rights or in performing obligations'.

Articles 34 to 39 of the Consumer Protection Law 1993 specify the processes by means of which consumer disputes are handled, and stipulate the circumstances under which a second action may be brought in order that compensation might be obtained from the party who is in fact at fault. For the resolution of disputes the five processes identified in the Law are: negotiation with the seller, consumer association mediation, complaint to the relevant administrative department, arbitration in accordance with an agreement to arbitrate and legal proceedings in a people's court.

The process of negotiation between the aggrieved consumer and the seller (or manufacturer) is characterized in the Law as 'consultation and conciliation' (*xieshang hejie*) This is an officially encouraged form of dispute resolution and consumers themselves often say that they still prefer the 'realistic' process of negotiations because one of the main alternatives – litigation – is too time-consuming and costly. However, negotiation does not always seem to work effectively in practice for various reasons – these include the general difficulties faced by consumers in complaining to shopkeepers, such as power imbalances between the parties (Liu 2004) as well as the social values manifested in the earlier local legislation that placed an obligation on the consumer to be courteous and not to cause trouble nor to attempt reprisals. The continuing preference for yielding and refraining from asserting one's rights, and the loss of face that may result from an unsuccessful attempt to make a complaint and negotiate some form of recompense, also do not encourage reliance on this approach to consumer claims.

The most common approach to the resolution of consumer disputes is third party intervention through mediation (*tiaojie*). Mediation offers the consumer the possibility of a face-saving compromise rather than outright rejection of a complaint by an unresponsive seller or the uncertainty of litigation. In addition, many consumer problems are considered to be too small to be worth the bother of going to court, even if the consumer is sufficiently well informed to realize that her or his legal rights have been infringed. I have elsewhere described the early developments in specialized consumer mediation (Palmer 1988: 276–7). Suffice it to say here that by the late 1980s there had developed in China an awareness of the distinctive nature of consumer disputes, and that in some parts of the country at least 'payments by results' systems had been put in place in order to deal effectively and professionally with consumer complaints. Nevertheless, the principal motive for relying on extra-judicial mediation is often that the likely compensation does not justify the time and trouble of going to court.

As the Consumer Protection Law envisages, the mediation of consumer disputes is now often carried out by consumer associations – a process popularly referred to as '*xiaoxie tiaojie*' or 'consumer association mediation'. In one very recent case known to me,

> ... a young professional was involved in a dispute in which he successfully secured redress from a hospital in Guangzhou. His son, aged 12, went for a routine medical examination at the local hospital and was diagnosed as suffering from a particular illness and prescribed an expensive medicine that was to be purchased from the hospital.

> The young man and his wife (also a young professional) did not believe that the diagnosis was correct, and challenged the hospital. They criticised the medical staff and threatened to take the case to the Guangzhou Municipal Consumer Protection Committee. Indeed, one telephone call to the Committee, and one telephone call to a local newspaper produced results. The Committee immediately proceeded to mediate the dispute. As a result, the President of the Hospital came to the young man and his wife a few days later to apologize in person. In addition, the hospital published a public apology in the local newspaper, and agreed to pay any costs that the parents had incurred.

An aggrieved consumer may bring a complaint about a seller or a producer to a government department. In many cases, the departmental personnel will attempt to resolve the dispute through the processes of 'administrative mediation' (*xingzheng tiaojie*), but sterner action may follow in the form of administrative penalties (*xingzheng chufa*), if it is shown that there has been a breach of relevant administrative regulations or if a minor criminal offence has been committed. Some administrative penalties may be imposed on the spot by means of summary procedures, but more serious penalties will only be imposed after a comprehensive investigation carried out by at least two law enforcement officials from within the relevant administrative organ. In order to encourage such administrative intervention, the State Administration of Industry and Commerce introduced in 1999 a complaints system using the common telephone number '12315' by which consumers can report fraudulent sales and other consumer problems. A hearing may be held at which the investigator in effect acts as prosecutor and another person who has been appointed by the administrative organ as an adjudicator will hear and decide on the case (Law on Administrative Penalties, 1996, Article 42).[27] The offender is exempted from a penalty if the conduct complained of is minor or if the facts about the illegal act have not been established (Law on Administrative Penalties, 1996 Article 38). It is open to a party on whom an administrative penalty has been imposed either to seek administrative reconsideration (*xingzheng fuyi*) or to bring an administrative lawsuit.

Article 34(4) of the Consumer Protection Law also encourages consumers to settle their disputes with producers by means of arbitration between the parties if there is a prior arbitration agreement. The small-scale nature of many consumer disputes is probably the most important factor explaining the relatively limited use of arbitration procedures to deal with consumer complaints. Moreover, as we have just noted, there has to be an existing agreement to arbitrate, and this is relatively uncommon in relations between consumers and seller. A further complication is that Chinese understanding and practice of arbitration often involves a heavy emphasis on mediation, especially in the early stages of the proceedings, and therefore recourse to an arbitral body often seems unnecessary when local administrative or consumer association mediation is so readily at hand. Moreover, arbitration bodies are usually self-financing, and therefore not interested in the typical consumer dispute – which involves a small claim, and may present problems in determining the relevant expert evidence. Nevertheless, on 1 September 1995 the PRC introduced a new Arbitration Law with the intent of creating a nationwide, integrated system of arbitration, and this may in due course encourage greater consumer reliance on the arbitral process, especially when large-scale unified purchases of products are made – for example, where local farmers combine together to make bulk purchases of seeds and fertilizers. In addition, local consumer protection regulations continue to encourage recourse to arbitration – for example, Article 51 of the 2002 Shanghai Regulations specify that, 'in order to settle a consumer dispute, consumers may apply for arbitration under the arbitration agreement or bring suit according to law. After accepting the case the arbitration commission or the people's court should (*yingdang*) deal with the consumer dispute by means of summary procedure . . . '

We have indicated that the nature of consumer disputes in China often does not make it worthwhile for an aggrieved consumer to take a complaint to court. And courts in China are still not in general viewed in a positive light. They have for many years been associated with criminal law, and are not seen as independent bodies but, rather, as *fora* in which personal influence and political pressures are important factors in decision-making. These attitudes reinforce the traditional social antipathy to the assertion of claims through litigation. Lawyers are not particularly keen to involve themselves in consumer protection cases, *inter alia*, because they often feel that administrative intervention is a more effective way of dealing with the problem and they advise clients accordingly. Nevertheless, the social changes that have resulted from the process of economic reform have encouraged a stronger interest in individual rights, resulting in a greater willingness of aggrieved parties to have recourse to courts to secure redress. The growth in this reliance on litigation is reflected in the ever-increasing number of civil and economic cases brought before the courts. In 1996 the people's courts dealt with more than three million civil cases and 1,500,000 economic disputes, with an average increase in the case load in recent years of 15 per cent annually (Ren 1998: 30–1). By 2004 the number of civil cases handled in courts of first instance had further risen to more than 4,300,000 (Xiao 2005). Indeed, many of the provisions in the Consumer Protection Law are dependent on the aggrieved consumer taking action, and may be regarded as part of a more general policy in which the Party-State is concerned to encourage greater litigiousness amongst ordinary people in order to shift some of the burden of regulating society from the state to the private citizen. This is consistent with the general drift of the economic reform programme, in which the individual is given greater scope to engage in private commercial and civil activities, with the State to some extent withdrawing from its hitherto very dominant role. In the context of consumer disputes there are two developments in particular that reflect this growing propensity for litigation: collective actions, and the 'Wang Hai Phenomenon'.

Somewhat surprisingly for a society that has for so long discouraged litigation, the civil and administrative procedure laws of the PRC permit what is popularly referred to as *jituan susong* or 'group litigation' but which is provided for in the Civil Procedure Law (Article 53, 54, 55) and Administrative Procedure Law (Article 26) under the appellation *gongtong susong* or 'joint action'. Typically this involves a group of litigants whose rights have been adversely affected by the same problem joining together and electing representatives (*daibiaoren*) to act for the group in the litigation. The conduct of the representatives is characterized as being on behalf of the whole group, but if the representatives decide to modify their claim, or admit the claim of the defendant, or pursue settlement, the people's court should issue at the commencement of the case a public routine that not only states the particulars and the claims of the case but also informs those who feel entitled to bring suit to register their rights with the people's court within a fixed period of time. The judgement or written orders rendered by the court are valid for all those persons who have registered their rights with the court. Moreover, the outcome is binding on parties who did not register their rights at the time of the action but who subsequently instituted legal proceedings within the period of limitation of the action.

Collective litigation is not a type of civil proceeding provided for in many legal systems other than the United States. It is very likely that the US experience was an important factor encouraging what is, in effect, an experimental form of litigation in the PRC. It is also likely that a felt need to incorporate 'socialist' principles of local community representation into proceedings was also influential in the Chinese legislators' decision to adopt this type of action. There have been similar developments in the Chinese political process that lend support to this view, namely, the rapid growth since the mid-1980s of *jiti shangfang gaozhuang* or collective letters of complaint which, for the most part, are formal complaints signed (or thumb-printed) by a group of villagers to a township or county seat, detailing deviant conduct by a cadre or cadres, making specific charges of misconduct, and demanding certain responses from the authorities (O'Brien and Li 1995: 758). The initial development of collective litigation *per se* appears to have taken place in the mid-1980s when some 1,500 Sichuan farmers filed suit to enforce a contract for seed grain, the court deciding that the most appropriate way of dealing with the problem was to encourage the litigants to select a few representatives to carry out litigation on behalf of the whole group. In more recent times, successful collective litigation has included a suit brought by more than 80 airline passengers for losses stemming from a delayed flight, a case brought by students against the publisher and seller of low-quality textbooks, and an action brought against various Beijing department stores and watch wholesalers by aggrieved purchasers of watches sold in celebration of the one hundredth anniversary of Mao Zedong's birth – advertisements for the product claiming that the watches were manufactured from gold and diamonds were spurious because, in reality, the watches were made from low-quality substitute materials. In one high-profile case, some two to three thousand local people in Nantong, Jiangsu Province, were misled by dishonest advertising at the end of 1994 into purchasing small motorcycles which, they were assured, were exempt from the city's new regulations banning most kinds of motorcycles from travelling in the main streets in the urban area. When the bikes they had purchased – the 'Da Yang DY50III A' moped – was quickly found to infringe the new rules and was therefore quite unsuitable, a local law firm publicized the problem and then on behalf of 556 consumers successfully brought a collective action against the manufacturer of the moped and a number of local department stores, and secured substantial compensation (Zhou 1997: 29–31). In general, collective litigation appears to have been most common in disputes involving consumer fraud, environmental pollution, economic contracts, local government contracts, and poor product quality. In the countryside, peasants continue to bring frequently such actions for losses caused by low-quality seed grains, chemical fertilizers and pesticides.[28]

One of the benefits accruing from collective litigation is that even when a suit is unsuccessful the fact that such high-profile litigation has been attempted may well attract interest in the case from the media or from higher-level authorities. It is thus a very potent weapon for improving consumer welfare in China. Although it remains relatively under-used, collective action litigation represents a potentially fruitful avenue in which litigants can use the law both to pursue their own interests and to publicize infringements of consumer rights.

These benefits may also be found in another critically important civil procedure development, namely, the 'Wang Hai Phenomenon' (Wang Hai *xianxiang*).[29]

In 1995 newspapers in China began to publish accounts of the deeds of Wang Hai, a young man from Shandong Province who had worked for a while in the Beijing Dongan Market. Apparently worried about the widespread sale of counterfeit products, Wang decided to take advantage of the provisions in Article 49 of the Consumer Protection Law. These make sellers who engage in fraudulent activities liable for compensation payments twice the purchase price of the goods or service received. Wang carefully purchased counterfeit goods from various stores in Beijing, and then brought suit claiming compensation. He has been cast by the China Consumers' Association in heroic mould as a citizen battling against the status quo in an effort to enhance consumer welfare by strategic use of litigation, and now runs a consulting company for consumers.[30] Nevertheless, officials in the State Administration of Industry and Commerce are known to have disapproved of this action, arguing that Wang was not really a 'consumer' under the meaning of the Consumer Protection Law as he did not intend to use or consume the doubtful products that he purchased.[31] Not all courts have taken a sympathetic view of Wang's activities, and a number of suits brought by Wang and other disaffected consumers have been rejected. The 2002 Shanghai Regulations appear to reflect business pressures by adopting a restrictive view of the nature of a consumer, as Article 2 provides that a 'consumer' is only protected by the Regulations if she or he, for reasons of personal consumption, needs (*shenghuo xiaofei xuyao*) purchases or uses goods, or receives services. This wording appears not only to exclude purchases made for reasons other than genuine consumption but also throws in doubt the position of products or services purchased by an enterprise or similar body but then used by employees at their place of work.

Conclusions

The promotion of consumer welfare in post-Mao China has been closely related to the preservation of the Party-State, and in this chapter we have seen that imperfect but substantial efforts have been made, especially in the 1990s, to put in place a legal framework for consumer protection. As a result of these developments, there are now clearer definitions of consumer rights, sellers' and manufacturers' civil liabilities, an application of principle of strict liability, development of consumer associations with wide-ranging functions, and official support for a more litigious spirit on the part of the aggrieved consumer. The authorities' approach to consumer welfare is, however, deeply ambiguous. It continues to bear the imprint of a strong state interest and to rely heavily on old-style campaigns, administrative controls, criminal law and mediation. Moreover, the consumer protection system continues to overlap with intellectual property protection, especially for trademarks, and to characterize some kinds of producer as consumers – a feature of relatively embryonic systems of consumer protection. But the Consumer Protection Law 1993 is also part of an effort by the Party-State to promote the rule of law in post-Mao China – now enshrined in Article 5 of the Constitution following amendment in 1999 – and to that end it provides a language of rights and obligations that enables aggrieved consumers to pursue their interests. Moreover, there is a general drift towards enhancing the role of courts in the system of access to justice, and suggestions are now being made for the creation of consumer chambers in the people's courts.[32] Collective litigation is already producing an effect, and Wang Hai's enthusiastic use of courts to make claims under Article 49 of the Consumer Protection Law is now being emulated by other consumers. In this context we may see the Consumer Protection Law as laying the ground for the emergence of the pro-active aggrieved consumer who promotes general consumer welfare though aggressive use of the formal legal process.

The PRC is unable to draw upon firmly-established systems of democratic governance, civil society or the rule of law in its efforts to protect the consumer. However, given that continuing economic reforms provide the backdrop for legal developments, the likelihood is that attempts to promote consumer welfare will continue to strengthen. Moreover, China's willingness to sign the International Covenant on Economic, Social and Cultural Rights and the International Covenant on Civil and Political Rights, and to become a member of the WTO, suggest that the balance between the authoritarian dimension and the rights-creating aspect of modern Chinese law will continue to move in a direction favourable to consumer rights. The worry is that the deep-seated problems which have bedevilled the emerging post-Mao legal system will undermine such progress. These problems include local protectionism, corruption, and lack of institutional autonomy, all directly or indirectly reflective of the Party's dominant political and legal position.

Notes

1 In force 1 January 1994. See 'Xiaofeizhe Quanyi Baohu Fa' (Law for the Protection of Consumers' Rights and Interests), 1993, Zhongguo falü nianjian bianjibu, *Zhongguo falü nianjian 1994* (*Law Yearbook of China 1994*) (Beijing: Zhongguo falü nianjian chubanshe, 1994), pp. 321–4.

2 Trademark law survived the socialist transformation of property rights in the 1950s and was even strengthened prior to the Cultural Revolution by a requirement of mandatory registration. The trademark registration system helped to protect the consumer by providing a mark that could be used by the consumer to identify particular products and to gain some idea of the provenance and quality of the products to which the mark was attached.

3 See 'Shangbiao Fa' (Trademark Law), 1993, Zhongguo falü nianjian bianjibu, *Zhongguo falü nianjian 1994* (*Law Yearbook of China 1994*) (Beijing: Zhongguo falü nianjian chubanshe, 1994), pp. 283–5. See also 'Quanguo Renmin Daibiao Dahui Changwu Weiyuanhui Guanyu Chengzhi Jiamao Zhuce Shangbiao Fanzui de Chongbu Guiding' (Supplementary Rules of the Standing Committee of the National People's Congress on the Punishment of the Crimes of Counterfeiting Registered Trademarks), 1993, Zhongguo falü nianjian bianjibu, *Zhongguo falü nianjian 1994* (*Law Yearbook of China 1994*) (Beijing: Zhongguo falü nianjian chubanshe, 1994), p. 286.

4 See 'Fan Buzhengdang Jingzheng Fa' (Anti-unfair Competition Law), 1993, Zhongguo falü nianjian bianjibu, *Zhongguo falü nianjian 1994* (*Law Yearbook of China 1994*) (Beijing: Zhongguo falü nianjian chubanshe, 1994), pp. 319–21.

5 See 'Quanguo Renmin Daibiao Dahui Changwu Weiyuanhui Guanyu Chengzhi Shengchan Xiaoshou Wei Lie Shangpin Fanzui de Jueding' (Decision of the Standing Committee of the National People's Congress on the Punishment of the Crimes of Production and Sale of Fake and Substandard Commodities), 1993, Zhongguo falü nianjian bianjibu, *Zhongguo falü nianjian 1994* (*Law Yearbook of China 1994*) (Beijing: Zhongguo falü nianjian chubanshe, 1994), pp. 310–11.

6 See 'Guanggao Fa' (Advertising Law), 1994, Zhongguo falü nianjian bianjibu, *Zhongguo falü nianjian 1995* (*Law Yearbook of China 1995*) (Beijing: Zhongguo falü nianjian chubanshe, 1994), pp. 202–5.

7 The Contract Law, 1999, which unified a number of key aspects of the contract regime that had prevailed until its implementation on 1 October 1999, disappointed a number of analysts within China by its failure to provide a special chapter dealing with consumer contracts. 'Hetong Fa' (Contract Law), 1999, (Beijing: Zhongguo fazhi chubanshe, 1999).

8 See generally Chen, Xie, and Wang 1996.

9 The State Administration of Industry and Commerce was set up in 1953 in order to facilitate socialist economic transformation. It is a State Council

organ which supervises many aspects of the economy and bears responsibility for the registration of commercial and industrial enterprises in both the public and the private sectors, licensing and administering markets and enterprises as well as advertising, and registering trademarks. It includes special divisions with responsibility for dispute resolution and for investigatory work. According to one source, by the end of the 1980s there were over 30,000 SAIC offices in China, and these employed some 335,000 professional staff (Lubman 1994: 26–7).

10 Following amendment in March 1999, Article 5 of the Constitution now commits the PRC to a system of government based on the rule of law.

11 Legal System Daily, 'Xiaofeizhe jiaoban tiyu yongpin bazhu: Naike qidian xiebei su "wei kexue"' (Consumers challenge overlords of sports product: Nike trainers accused of 'false science'), *Fazhi Ribao*, no. 7144, 20 May 2005, p. 4

12 'Gongye Chanpin Zhiliang Zeren Tiaoli' (Regulations Concerning Liability for the Quality of Industrial Products), 1986, Zhongguo falü nianjian bianjibu, *Zhongguo falü nianjian 1987* (*Law Yearbook of China 1987*) (Beijing: Falü chubanshe, 1987), pp. 323–5.

13 'Beijing Shi Gongye Chanpin Zhiliang Jiandu Tiaoli' (Regulations on the Supervision of the Quality of Industrial Products of Beijing Municipality), 1986, Zhongguo falü nianjian bianjibu, *Zhongguo falü nianjian 1987* (*Law Yearbook of China 1987*) (Beijing: Falü chubanshe, 1987), pp. 419–20. See also King and Gao 1991: 43–4.

14 'Minfa Tongze' (General Principles of the Civil Law), 1986, Zhongguo falü nianjian bianjibu, *Zhongguo falü nianjian 1987* (*Law Yearbook of China 1987*) (Beijing: Falü chubanshe, 1987), pp. 68–76.

15 'Shanghai Shi Baohu Xiaofeizhe Hefa Quanyi Tiaoli' (Shanghai Municipal Regulations on the Protection of Consumer Legal Rights and Interests), in Wang and Xiao 1991: 1246–9. In the latest version of these Regulations, many of these requirements of proper conduct have been omitted – see 'Shanghai Shi Xiaofeizhe Quanyi Baohu Tiaoli' (Shanghai Municipal Regulations on the Protection of Consumer Rights and Interests) promulgated on 28 October 2002, in force 1 January 2003.

16 According to a nationwide survey carried out by the China Consumers' Association in 1997, nearly 80 per cent of consumers interviewed believed that they had been subjected to consumer fraud; see China Consumers' Association 'Writings on Theme for Publicity in the Past Six Years Good Faith and No Fraud – Annual Theme for 1997' available online (accessed 24 February 2006) at http://eng.cca.org.cn:801/page/browseinfo.asp?db = zthd&order = 2

17 See, for example, Article 13 of the fourth-draft national 'Regulations on Consumer Protection', 25 October 1985, which also contained a range of 'consumer obligations' such as acquiring knowledge of consumption and consumer goods, to be morally upstanding, to acknowledge unreasonable use of products, and to refrain from seeking reprisals or deliberately 'causing trouble' for industrial and commercial enterprises (King and Gao 1991: 115).

18 See also Articles 46, 47 and 48, which deal with problems or issues of mail order, advance payment and return of goods respectively.

19 'Beijing shi baohu xiaofeizhe hefa quanyi tiaoli' (Beijing Municipal Regulations on Protection of Consumer Legal Rights and Interests), in Zhongguo falü nianjian bianjibu, *Zhongguo falü nianjian 1987* (*Law Yearbook of China 1987*) (Beijing: Falü chubanshe, 1987), pp. 339–41.

20 See also the comments made by Liu in the news article 'Gongshang zongju gongyuan zhizhi "Xiaofeizhe Quanyi Baohu Fa" zhuduo biduan' (SAIC General Bureau Official directly points out many weaknesses in the 'Law Protecting

Consumer Rights and Interests'), originally published in *Zhongguo Qingnian Bao*, (China Youth Daily), 14 March 2005.

21 'Zhi'an Guanli Chufa Tiaoli' (Regulations on the Administrative Penalties for Public Security), 1994, Zhongguo falü nianjian bianjibu, *Zhongguo falü nianjian 1995* (*Law Yearbook of China 1995*) (Beijing: Zhongguo falü nianjian chubanshe, 1995), pp. 169–74.

22 'Xing Fa' (Criminal Law), 1997, Zhongguo falü nianjian bianjibu, *Zhongguo falü nianjian 1998* (*Law Yearbook of China 1995*) (Beijing: Zhongguo falü nianjian chubanshe, 1998), pp. 206–41. 'Zhi'an Guanli Chufa Tiaoli' (Regulations on the Administrative Penalties for Public Security), 1994, Zhongguo falü nianjian bianjibu, *Zhongguo falü nianjian 1995* (*Law Yearbook of China 1995*) (Beijing: Zhongguo falü nianjian chubanshe, 1995), pp. 169–74.

23 See 'Quanguo Renmin Daibiao Dahui Changwu Weiyuanhui Guanyu Chengzhi Shengchan Xiaoshou Wei Lie Shangpin Fanzui de Jueding' (Decision of the Standing Committee of the National People's Congress on the Punishment of the Crimes of Production and Sale of Fake and Substandard Commodities), 1993, Zhongguo falü nianjian bianjibu, *Zhongguo falü nianjian 1994* (*Law Yearbook of China 1994*) (Beijing: Zhongguo falü nianjian chubanshe, 1994), pp. 310–11.

24 Criminal detention (*juyi*) is a punishment imposed for relatively minor offences. The local public security organ confines the convicted person in a detention house and the prisoner may be permitted to go home several times each month as well as receive some payment for work.

25 See generally Lubman 1997 and Palmer 1998.

26 See also Palmer 1989.

27 'Xingzheng Chufa Fa' (Law on Administrative Penalties), 1996, Zhongguo falü nianjian bianjibu, *Zhongguo falü nianjian 1996* (*Law Yearbook of China 1996*) (Beijing: Zhongguo falü nianjian chubanshe, 1997), pp. 236–40. In addition, there have been continuing developments in the system of administrative punishments in consumer cases – for example, the provisions issued by the Sate Council under the title 'Shangpinliang jiliang weifa xingzheng chufa guiding' (Rules on the Administrative Penalties Concerning Product Quantity Measurement), 1999.

28 See, e.g., Note, *Harvard Law Review*, 1998, 1528–9.

29 See, e.g., Li 1996.

30 With its own website, at http://www.wanghai.net (accessed 24 February 2006).

31 A further criticism of Wang is that he has allowed himself in some of the litigation that he has initiated to become caught up in business rivalries, in effect bringing an action on behalf of one factory against another.

32 See, e.g., *Fazhi Ribao* (Legal Daily) 'She ge xiaofei fating ruhe' (How to Establish a Consumer Chamber), 13 December 13, 1998, p. 3; Wang Yang, 'Xiaofeizhe yan song pubian: sheli "xiaofeifating" ruhe' (Consumers show widespread dissatisfaction with litigation: how to establish a consumer chamber), *Ningbo Daxue Kexue Jishu Xueyuan, Keyuan Yuekan*, (*Monthly Journal of the Ningbo University College of Science and Technology*), 10 April 2003.

References

Chai, Joseph (1996) 'Consumption and Living Standards in China', in Robert F. Ash and Y. Y. Kueh, *The Chinese Economy Under Deng Xiaoping*, Oxford: Clarendon Press.

Chen Lijun, Xie Cheng'an and Wang Chongli (1996) *Shehui Jituan Xiaofei Guanli Yanjiu* (Research into the Management of Consumer Social Groups), Beijing: Zhongguo Shuiwu Chubanshe.

Epstein, Edward (1988) 'Tortious Liability for Defective Products in the People's Republic of China', *Journal of Chinese Law*. Fall 1988, vol.2, no.2, 285–21.

Howe, Christopher and Walker, Kenneth R. (1984) 'Introduction', *The China Quarterly*, no. 100 (December), ii–v.

King, Donald B. and Gao Tong (1991) *Consumer Protection in China: Translations, Developments and Recommendations*. Colorado: Littleton.

Lardy, Nicholas (1984) 'Consumption and Living Standards in China, 1978–1983', *The China Quarterly*, no. 100 (December), 849–65.

—— (1995) 'The role of Foreign Trade and Investment in China's Economic Transformation', *The China Quarterly*, no. 144 (December), 1065–82.

Li Na (1996) '"Wang Hai xianxiang" lüshi tan' (A lawyer discusses the 'Wang Hai phenomenon'), *Zhongguo Lüshi*, no. 3 for 1996, 22–3.

Liu Xiaoping (2004) 'Xiaofeizhe quanyi baohu fa – ba da wenti kepan jiejue' (The law protecting the rights and interests of the consumer – eight major problems that we hope to solve), *Fazhi Ribao* (Legal System Daily), 11 November, 8.

Lubman, Stanley B. (1994) 'Introduction', in Pitman B. Potter (ed.), *Domestic Law Reforms in Post-Mao China*, Armonk and London: M. E. Sharpe.

—— (1997) 'Dispute Resolution in China after Deng Xiaoping: "Mao and Mediation" Revisited', *Columbia Journal of Asian Law*, vol. 11, no. 2, 229–391.

Note (1998) 'Class Action Litigation in China', *Harvard Law Review*, Vol. 111, 1523–41.

O'Brien, Kevin J. and Li Lianjiang (1995) 'The Politics of Lodging Complaints in Rural China', *The China Quarterly*, no. 143, 756–83.

Palmer, Michael (1988) 'The Revival of Mediation in the People's Republic of China: (1) Extra-Judicial mediation', in W. E. Butter (ed.), *Yearbook on Socialist Legal Systems 1987*, New York: Transnational Publishers.

—— (1989) 'The Revival of Mediation in the People's Republic of China: (II) Judicial mediation', in W. E. Butter (ed.), *Yearbook on Socialist Legal Systems 1988*, New York: Transnational Publishers.

—— (1998) 'Environmental Regulation in the People's Republic of China: The Face of Domestic Law', *The China Quarterly*, no. 156, 788–808.

Ren Jianxin (1998) 'Zuigao Renmin Fayuan Gongzuo Baogao' (Work Report of the Supreme People's Court), Zhongguo falü nianjian bianjibu, *Zhongguo falü nianjian 1996* (*Law Yearbook of China 1996*) (Beijing: Zhongguo falü nianjian chubanshe, 1997), 29–34.

Saywell, Trish (1999) 'Demanding Action', *Far Eastern Economic Review*, May 13, 42–3.

Shi Fu, Gu Shi, Yang Hua and Xu Hao (1994) *Xiaofeizhe Quanyi Baohu Fa Shiyong Wenda* (Questions and Answers on the Applications of the Law for the Protection of Consumer Rights and Interests), Beijing: Xinhua Chubanshe.

Wang Yuncheng and Xiao Yuping (eds) (1991) *Difangxing Fa Gui Xuanbian* (Selection of Local Laws and Regulations), Beijing: Zhongguo Jingji Chubanshe.

Xiao Yang (2005) 'Zuigao Renmin Fayuan Gongzuo Baogao' (Work Report of the Supreme People's Court, March 9).

Zhongguo Xiaofei Zazhi Bianjibu (Editorial Department of the China Consumer Affairs Magazine) (1998) *Zhongguo Xiaofeizhe Shouce* (The China Consumers' Handbook), Beijing: Zhongguo Xiaofeizhe Zazhi.

Zhou Yong (1997) '"Da Yang", che dao shanqian lu zai he fang' ('Da Yang': the car has come to the mountain, but where is the road?), *Zhongguo Lüshi*, no. 11 for 1997, 29–31.

5 Powers of imagination

The role of the consumer in China's silent media revolution

Kevin Latham

Introduction

In the last two-and-a-half decades under reform, China's media have undergone major transformations and changes which have introduced the rhetorics and practices of market competition, commercialism and populism into industries none the less still strictly under government and Party control (Hemelryk Donald, Keane and Yin 2002; Latham 2000; Zhao 1998; Li Zhuren 1998; Barme 1999; Huang 1994; Hussain 1990). Consequently media production in China is marked by contradictions and tensions characterized by its situation always somewhere 'between markets and mandarins' (Latham 2001). Furthermore, these contradictions and tensions are vital for understanding the slow but sure transformation of China's propaganda hegemony, which has been dominated for so long by the Chinese Communist Party (CCP). Although the Party's domination of this hegemony is certainly not yet in question, it is none the less increasingly susceptible to scepticism and the exposure of its anachronisms (Latham 2000). In this chapter I shall investigate the fundamental role of the consumer in the transformations taking place in one central area of Chinese media production: newspapers.

Although 'the consumer' is an elusive entity whose actual existence must surely remain in doubt (Hartley 1992; Ang 1991), s/he is none the less a powerful conceptual category which advertisers, marketing professionals, media producers, sociologists, economists, historians and others have long since found indispensable for their understandings of contemporary societies around the globe (see, for example, Miller *et al.* 1995; Baudrillard 1988; Campbell 1987; Galbraith 1970, for general accounts; and Davis 2000; Li Conghua 1998; Chao and Myers 1998, on China). In the case of newspapers in contemporary China, the consumer, as reader, has a dual significance in the imaginations of editors and journalists. On the one hand the consumer is the end user of their product. S/he is the reader and purchaser of their newspapers, which must therefore be produced to meet such a reader's demands. On the other hand, s/he is also the end user of other people's products and services. As a result, in the minds of editors s/he has a strongly perceived interest in consumer information, advertising and marketing to which they therefore cater in the pages of their newspapers. For most Chinese newspapers, we should remember, advertisers constitute the primary source of revenue.

The force of the argument presented in this chapter can be applied to many if not all parts of China. However, I shall illustrate the argument with particular reference to Guangdong Province, neighbouring Hong Kong in southern China, which has been at the forefront of China's economic reforms over the last twenty-five years (Vogel 1989; Ikels 1996) and where I have conducted fieldwork.[1] I shall refer specifically to the founding and the early years of *New Express*, a city-level newspaper launched by a long-established newspaper group with the specific intention of tapping into an emerging consumer market. I shall argue that the imagined consumer, as newspaper reader, is playing a fundamental part in the understated transformations that together amount to China's silent media revolution. The voices of dissent in the world of China's media production are, on the whole, economically rather than politically motivated, and the revolutionaries of this revolution have their eyes firmly fixed on an economic rather than a political utopia of the future. However, the power of the changes that are taking place to dramatically alter China's social landscape should not be underestimated simply because such changes eschew the language of political confrontation. In important ways the new market-oriented understandings of editors, journalists and newspaper executives chip away daily at the bedrock of China's media hegemony: the Party's self-perceived need and ability to control the production and content of its media. This chapter looks at the crucial role that the consumer plays in this process of silent revolution.

China's changing media

Over the last quarter-century, China's media landscape has changed beyond all recognition. Mass communication had always had an important part to play in the CCP's strategy for maintaining its grip on power. From the 1950s wired radio and newspapers played their part alongside political meetings, mass rallies, wall posters and to some degree cinema. However, in the 1980s, the combination of economic reform and technological development brought about a sea change in China's practices of media production and consumption. When Deng Xiaoping came to power in 1978 television sets were a luxury beyond most families' dreams, and television broadcasting was accordingly limited. However, by the end of the next decade, television was commonplace in the main cities and rapidly penetrating the rural areas also, with the majority of the population having access to television broadcasts (Li 1991; Lull 1991). Ten years further on, China's television stations were preparing for broadband digital broadcasting and planning for convergence with telecommunications and internet service provision (Wang 1999: 11). By early 2005, this was already becoming a reality with the emergence of China's first internet protocol television (IPTV) channels (China Media Intelligence 2005).

Economic reform had dramatic effects on Chinese family economies (Davis and Harrell 1993). Between 1978 and 1985 rural per capita income and consumption had both doubled (Chao and Myers 1998: 353) with urban per capita income doubling in the first twelve years of reform and increasing by another 50 per cent between 1990 and 1994 (Davis 2000: 1–2; *Zhongguo tongji nianjian* 1995: 257). China's families found themselves spending proportionately less of their income on food and other essentials, leaving them more to spend on consumer durables such as televisions, radios, VCRs, washing machines and refrigerators (Chao and Myers 1998: 363; Lull 1991: 20–1; Davis and Harrel 1993: 3; Davis 1993: 75; Davis 2000: 2). At the same time there was a dramatic expansion of media production. Television stations, radio stations and newspapers all proliferated through the 1980s and 1990s. Between 1991 and 1995 alone, the number of television stations increased from 543 to 837 and the number of radio stations expanded from 724 to 1202 in the same period (Zhao 1998: 57). Newspaper growth in the 1980s was an impressive one new title every three days, a rate that had doubled by the early 1990s (Zhao 1998: 57). However, the greater availability and accessibility of mass media created heavy demands on media producers who, prior to reform, had been entirely dependent on state subsidy. Faced with stagnating state budgets and the pressures of consumer demand, the commercialization of media production became an economic necessity (Zhao 1998: 52–3).

Throughout the 1980s, prior to the brutal crackdown on Tiananmen demonstrators in 1989, this expansion of China's media had been accompanied by an increasingly liberal attitude to media production (Zhao 1998; Li 1991). There were proposals from various high-ranking Party officials, journalists and scholars to allow the establishment of independent newspapers, calls for increased freedom of speech and even some questioning of the fundamental principle of Chinese media production: that it is to serve above all else as the mouthpiece of the Party (Zhao 1998: 34–45). Post-1989, the Party tightened its grip on media organizations, and such calls for media democratization were effectively silenced, at least in public. In the 1990s, media reform was therefore dominated by economic rather than political changes. It is not possible entirely to separate commercialization from political issues. For instance, the arguments for greater and more efficient commercialization have also provided a useful springboard for arguing, on economic and commercial grounds, for the politically defined role of the media as the mouthpiece of the party to be abolished (for recent examples see, e.g., Yin and Li 2004; Yu 2004; Zhang 2005). None the less, from the 1990s on, the energies of journalists to transform China's media were channelled into its commercialization rather than its democratization.

The immediate marker of media commercialization was the growing importance of advertising in the 1980s. By the 1990s, however, advertisements had become thoroughly commonplace in newspapers, on television, on radio and as part of Chinese urban environments. Furthermore, the fierce competition between media organizations in contemporary China is now over advertising accounts. Increased sales of newspapers or increased audience ratings translate directly into increased advertising revenues. However, it is not simply the insertion of advertisements into the media that has changed their content. On the one hand, Chinese media have become increasingly populist as they have moved from 'revolutionary modernity to popular modernity' (Li Zhuren 1998). In journalism this has led to an abundant reporting of 'social news', such as reports of emerging social problems like unemployment or corruption. Social news also focuses on other social changes like educational and consumer trends or the emergence of new socio-economic groups. These are undoubtedly popular with readers who were accustomed for decades to the bland, one-dimensional reporting of the Mao era. Human-interest stories and crime reporting are similarly attractive. On the other hand, Chinese media have succumbed, in part, to the pressures of corporate finance. Such pressures manifest themselves in a variety of forms, from 'invitation journalism', where the news source pays the expenses of the journalist, to 'paid journalism' in which journalists or organizations receive payments or other benefits in return for promotional materials being written as news stories (Zhao 1998: 72–84).

What is characteristic about Chinese media commercialization, however, is that the CCP has never relinquished its perceived need to control media production. Indeed, since 1989 this need has in many ways been perceived all the more strongly. This has produced a range of contradictions and tensions within the systems of media production that 'simultaneously operate with two different logics – the Party's and the market's' (Zhao 1998: 84). Chinese audiences and media producers, for instance, find themselves juggling with contradictory 'regimes of truth' informed respectively by Party news theory, Western liberalism, media professionalism and economic practicalities (Latham 2000). At the same time media organizations may find themselves competing with their own immediate bosses for advertising revenue; bosses who are simultaneously in the position of monitoring and regulating the content of their output with regard to Party regulations.[2] The practical reality of these conflicting pressures on media professionals – to make profit by selling advertising, on the one hand, and meeting the expectations and demands of Party control on the other – is manifest on a daily basis in China's media output. Journalists now write articles not only with the expectations of Party propagandists in mind but increasingly with the expectations of readerships. Of course the former are still an important consideration but the game has become one of producing popular journalism that sells newspapers while not antagonizing local Party officials (see, e.g., Huang 2000; Zhao 2000). In fact, senior editors find themselves in the dual position of being simultaneously market-driven journalists and Party censors; an ambiguous position that inevitably introduces a degree of flexibility into the system.

Clearly one of the principle effects of this transformation of China's media over recent decades, has been to raise the profile of the media consumer. The consumer is the one who watches television programmes or reads newspapers and who, from media executives' points of view, must be persuaded to keep watching and keep reading. In this way media production has become increasingly driven by conceptualizations of what such consumers want. Of the different media in China, television stands at the top of the Party's propaganda hierarchy, which means, also, that its content, especially in terms of news production, is the most closely monitored and regulated for ideological content (Li 1991). Entertainment programming has certainly become more and more consumer driven, but news production on television is gripped more tightly by the hand of the Party than on other media. Hence, with regard to news, the trend towards consumer-driven production has been more clearly demonstrated in newspaper production than in television. Journalists working for newspapers, especially non-Party organs, which in the reform era had come to outnumber official Party organs (Zhao 1998: 17), could often find spaces for certain kinds of innovation or creativity, experimentation and boundary-pushing that their counterparts in television could only envisage in entertainment production.[3] The reform-era proliferation of newspaper titles has therefore also seen the massive expansion of non-Party organs catering to special interest groups like young people, farmers, women, police, students or soldiers (Zhao 1998: 17; Huang 2000). These newspapers always come under the auspices of government departments, business enterprises or other Party organizations, but because of their specialist nature and smaller circulation they are not perceived by the Party to pose such a major threat to social stability as their well-known daily counterparts might. As a result they have often enjoyed more relaxed political control and less direct interference in their editorial content than their Party organ counterparts. As we will see below, this has shaped the development of the newspaper market in recent years in important ways as large, recognized daily newspapers with high media profiles have also established subsidiary publications of this kind.

In the following sections I will offer a profile of one such newspaper, *New Express*, established in Guangzhou in March 1998. I will argue that the daily running of the newspaper is fundamentally premised not on Party propaganda but on commercial principles centred around the imagined figure of the consumer.

The launch of *New Express*

New Express, launched at the end of March 1998, was established as a subsidiary newspaper of the Yangcheng Evening News Group. The

Yangcheng Evening News is a nationally known and distributed, though regionally focused, evening newspaper of long-standing reputation in China. It was established in 1956, is widely recognized and appreciated for its high-quality analytical reporting, and in 1999 boasted distribution figures second only to the *People's Daily* in China, even if disputed by its local rival the *Guangzhou Daily*. It is the only evening newspaper in Guangzhou and hence, in that sense, it has no immediate competition. However, it is none the less in direct competition with the morning dailies, notably the *Guangzhou Daily* and the *Nanfang Daily*, and to understand the circumstances leading to the launch of *New Express* it is necessary first to consider the conditions of the local newspaper market in the 1990s.

From the end of the 1980s onwards, competition between newspapers in the region became intense with tangible effects on journalistic output from the region's newspapers. Throughout the 1990s, the *Guangzhou Daily*, the organ of the city Party Committee, more than doubled in size. In 1999, the paper routinely ran three broadsheet sections totalling thirty-six pages, making it by far the thickest of Guangzhou's daily newspapers. By 2005, the paper was nationally recognized as the largest newspaper in China by advertising revenue. The paper also included special sections on news from throughout Guangdong province and the Pearl River Delta aimed at its readership beyond the city of Guangzhou. In short, the *Guangzhou Daily*'s response to competition was to increase the number of pages of the paper to give the consumer better value for money, at least in terms of quantity.

The *Nanfang Daily*, the organ of the provincial Party Committee, adopted another highly successful strategy which over the years has raised the group's national profile (Wilson 1997). In the early 1990s, the *Nanfang Daily*, launched *Nanfang Weekend*, which soon established a national reputation for itself as a ground-breaking social news-oriented newspaper. The advantage of such a weekly edition was that it could minimize the political pressures to include dull Party news such as meetings reports and official pronouncements. Like the hundreds of other weekend editions which sprang up around the country, it wrote for its readers with the clear objective of selling popular journalism. It therefore ran human-interest stories, crime stories and social news stories as well as essays and commentaries by famous authors rather than the lack-lustre content normally associated with Party organs (Zhao 1998: 132–5). In 1995, following this success, *Nanfang Daily* launched a daily tabloid, *Nanfang Metropolitan Daily*, of sixteen pages in 1999, which continually pushed the limits of Party control to run more populist stories with more sensationalist presentation. Second only to the *Guangzhou Daily*, the paper rapidly became one of the most popular daily papers in Guangzhou.[4] The paper subsequently also blazed the trail for hundreds of other metropolitan daily newspapers up and down the country and, like the *Nanfang Weekend*, also established for itself a national reputation for innovative newspaper production.

Against this backdrop of mounting competition, the Yangcheng Evening News Group sought to expand its market share by launching a daily morning newspaper, *New Express*, to rival the *Guangzhou Daily* and the *Nanfang Metropolitan Daily* directly. This was, from the start, a purely commercial move by the publishing group. It drew upon its own substantial financial, human and material resources to set up the new title as a means of increasing the Group's market presence and enabling it to compete with the morning dailies in a way that it could never do while remaining solely an evening paper. Hence editors and journalists from the *Yangcheng Evening News* were transferred to *New Express* to take up new positions, particularly as senior editors. Successful young editors were also head-hunted for senior positions from other local publications. At the same time a recruitment drive was launched to attract young journalists to the new publication. The new paper was run from new offices in the already existing Yangcheng Evening News building, originally on a shoestring staff of around 60 people. This had nearly doubled to 113 by the summer of 1999. The paper was printed on the *Yangcheng Evening News* presses in the same buildings.

From the beginning, *New Express* adopted a highly visual strategy. It set out to be the most colourful paper on Guangzhou's newsstands with a large number of photographs, many in full colour, as well as extensive use of computer-generated graphics to accompany story text. An important feature of the paper's marketing strategy was readability and ease of absorption of information. As one of the senior editors told me, charts, maps and other graphic figures could convey information much more quickly and efficiently to the reader. If the reader could feel that s/he had received useful, up-to-date and accurate information without having spent ten minutes wading through descriptive text to get it, then s/he would feel satisfied.

The strategy of making the newspaper heavily visual was also adopted following influences from the North American *USA Today* and Hong Kong's highly successful *Apple Daily*. The former is renowned for its visual approach to news presentation, even going so far as to shape its streetside vending machines like television sets. The *Apple Daily*, meanwhile, was at the forefront of a newspaper transformation in Hong Kong in the intensely competitive environment of the 1990s. It was the first Hong Kong daily to adopt a highly colourful style with large eye-catching headlines and colour photographs, a style which was quickly copied and adopted by its main competitors, like the *Oriental Daily*, in Hong Kong's cut-throat newspaper market. *New Express* drew upon the personal experience of its own staff at *USA Today* and the expertise of Hong Kong computer graphics designers, some formerly from the *Apple Daily*, to build up their new striking image on Guangzhou's newsstands.

A standard edition of *New Express* in the early 2000s comprised three broadsheet sections. The first, eight pages long, included main news stories as well as national news, international news, Hong Kong, Macao and Taiwan news and a very colourful sports section with international soccer, basketball and other high profile sports featuring prominently alongside China's domestic sports news headed by the national soccer league. The second four-page section covered economic news, including share prices and market statistics, but also running feature stories on business and commerce in the region. The last 'lifestyle' section, also four pages long, ran a variety of entertainment, fashion and general consumer stories, including regular features on cooking and restaurant cuisine (see Chapter 6 in this volume, by Klein).

What is important to note about *New Express* is how the whole newspaper, from conception through launch and on to daily production, has been totally driven by a particular market niche centred around the notion of the reader and the reader as a particular kind of consumer. The colourful layout, high readability, the recruitment of young editorial and journalistic staff and the structure and layout of the paper, were all carefully and deliberately thought through with an eye to attracting an identified readership. Who constituted this conceptualized readership and how it figured on a daily basis in the production of *New Express* are the subjects of the next sections of this chapter.

The consumer at *New Express*

The consumer featured in the daily workings of *New Express* principally in two ways. On the one hand, editors and journalists at the paper constantly evoked the notion of their target reader as the person they hoped would buy their newspaper. In this sense the consumer, as imagined reader, was inextricably embroiled in the daily production of the newspaper. On the other hand, this imagined target reader was often conceived of *as a consumer* of other products. In this sense, the characterization of contemporary China as a consumer society, at least for a privileged, though sizeable minority of upwardly mobile urban professionals, had figured in the paper's understanding of itself from the planning stages through its launch and initial development. It also had a significant place in the plans of the paper's senior staff for the future development of the publication. In what follows, I deal in turn with these two ways in which the consumer featured in the paper's production: first the consumer as reader and then the reader as consumer.

The consumer as reader

The daily circulation of *New Express* in the summer of 1999 was over 100,000, rising to nearer 150,000 by the end of the year. However, this figure needed to rise to 300,000 for the paper to start to break even and, particularly in the early years of the newspaper, circulation figures were watched keenly. The newspaper therefore set itself a target to reach this level of distribution within the first three years of publication. The pressure on the paper's staff to achieve this goal was great in 1999, and various economies were also introduced in the summer of that year to reduce expenses. By 2001, the target was in sight but not yet met, although the paper's senior editors insisted that it was paying its way and even making a small profit. The result of this pressure in the early years, the focus of this chapter, however, was to concentrate editor's and journalist's minds more than ever on their target readers, the consumers of their product.

Editors at *New Express* had a very clear idea of their target reader. S/he was fairly well educated (higher middle school or above), probably a white-collar worker and in the age range of 30 to 50. S/he would be upwardly mobile with a relatively high disposable income, a mind for business and a penchant for consumption and leisure. This target reader was also more than likely male.[5] This target reader was in contrast to that of *New Express*'s two main daily rivals at that time, the *Guangzhou Daily* and the *Nanfang Metropolitan Daily*, who targeted more general, all-encompassing readerships. From its launch *New Express* had been aimed at this readership which senior editors at the paper recognized for its high spending power and therefore its attractiveness to advertisers. Compared to the *Yangcheng Evening News*, with around 40 per cent of its print space dedicated to fairly high-revenue advertising, *New Express* enjoyed a much lower advertising profile. Being a new title and therefore with an unproven readership record, this was inevitable, but its allotted advertising space had reached around 15 per cent by the summer of 1999 and senior editors seemed happy that advertisers were becoming more confident with the paper.

However, there was no room for complacency and the figure of the imagined reader loomed large in the offices of *New Express*. This was the case particularly after the results were received of a reader survey, commissioned by the paper on the occasion of its first anniversary. Senior staff on the newspaper were quite concerned that their actual readership, as deduced from the survey results, did not fit the profile of their target reader. The two principle findings of the survey which caused concern were that (i) only about 20 per cent of their readership was in the target age range with nearly 70 per cent below the age of thirty, and (ii) over 35 per cent of their readers, and the largest single occupational group, were students. In terms of building up loyal, long-term readers for the future, neither of these facts were particularly concerning, but in terms of appealing to advertisers, this was not the most favourable reader profile. Indeed, at one editorial meeting later that year the editor-in-chief was at some pains to stress that they did not want the paper to get the reputation for being a 'students' newspaper'.

After that meeting, editors worked keenly with two key aims in mind. First to develop and accentuate *New Express*'s specificity and unique characteristics, and second, related to the first, to re-align the paper with its target audience. Senior editors stressed the importance of the paper's business and economic section for achieving this task.[6] In the first place, the economic section was unique among Guangzhou's main newspapers, if not more widely. Second, the business section was seen to be of particular interest to the paper's target white-collar reader and of less interest to the dominant younger, student reader.

There were specialist economic newspapers available in Guangzhou, and other dailies also carried financial information such as market statistics. However, editors at *New Express* were keen to point out that the kind of news they carried in the economic section was of a different kind to either of these. The specialist business papers tended to be aimed at economists and those with a specialist knowledge of financial issues, and other dailies offered little in terms of financial commentary. *New Express*, on the other hand, offered economic and business news that was digestible for a non-specialist, though interested, reader. It aimed at a more magazine-like quality rather than technical analysis. There was, in fact, as much emphasis on business stories as on strictly economic ones. Rather than focusing on facts, figures and statistics, the economic section tended to run background stories on different aspects of the Guangdong economy, profiles or introductions to particular companies and businesses and general market information. For instance, the paper ran a regular column on company news at the back of the economic section. Following the reader survey report, editors worked hard to develop this section of the paper and devoted particular attention to it each day in editorial meetings. Increasing recognition of this section of the paper was clearly seen as one way of targeting the older, business-oriented reader.

Following the reader survey, senior editors also sought to re-align the paper with its target readership by aiming at greater 'depth'. One deputy editor explained to me that this required providing a higher level of analysis in their stories and fuller presentation of the background to news stories. The overall aim was to give the impression of deeper, more familiar and more knowledgeable news-reporting in order to build up confidence in the newspaper on the part of the target reader. At the same time, editors perceived a need to move away from what might have been an over-reliance on social news. This was still perceived to be important but was not the only thing that the target reader would be looking for in his or her daily paper.

In this way, the target reader, as the consumer of the newspaper, was a constant presence in the production process of *New Express*. Daily and weekly editorial meetings were often arbitrated by the notion of the target consumer. Particular stories were selected to give this reader what s/he was perceived to want. The framing and emphasis of stories would also be adjusted accordingly. There was also a general journalistic desire to run good or important news stories and important scoops or major news stories regularly ran as the front-page leaders to attract readerships of all kinds and to compete with other news coverage of the same stories. In this way the presence of the target reader was more clearly visible in relation to the inside pages and supplementary sections of the paper rather than the front-page headlines. Major stories would also be tailored to appeal to certain kinds of reader and often one thought of as a consumer, but the supplements and inner sections were more commonly thought of in relation to the more specific young professional target reader.

For example, editors stressed the importance of international news, pointing out that young, upwardly mobile business people often had their eyes partly directed overseas, whether as a source of potential markets or business competition or because of relatives living abroad or the attraction of an overseas holiday. Foreign news, of almost any kind, was seen as attractive. At the same time the paper sought to emphasize and develop its coverage of scientific and technological issues such as developments in communications, telecoms, computers and biological engineering. Indeed, articles on communications and information technologies regularly appeared in the economic section of the paper. These were seen as issues likely to be of direct interest to the target reader and also likely to shape the future development of the newspaper.

The reader as consumer

An important aspect of the target reader profile discussed in the previous section is how s/he was clearly perceived to have a strong interest in consumption. Earning more than the average worker, this reader was likely to have higher-than-average disposable income. It is not important here whether or not actual readers, either fitting this profile or not, in fact had such a disposable income. Nor is it important for this particular discussion whether or not China has been undergoing a 'consumer revolution' or not (see Chapter 1, the Introduction to this volume). What is important is that the editorial and journalistic staff at *New Express* perceived their readers *as* consumers. In fact, this was not restricted to the so-called target reader but included both the actual current readership, as revealed in the reader survey, and also their perceptions of the population at large. Even if readers did not actually engage in high levels of consumption, I was told by one senior editor, they none the less had an interest in consumer issues or aspired to consumption and for that reason should be thought of as consumers.

The section of the paper most clearly oriented to meeting this perceived demand for consumer-related stories was the daily lifestyle section. This section of the paper generally comprised articles on popular entertainment, leisure activities, fashion, consumer goods, food and eating, DIY and home furnishings, as well as regular articles giving advice on health issues (often related to eating). The lead stories of the section often discussed current cinema and television stars or popular films and serials. These articles and others on leisure activities such as music, travel, bowling, golf or keep-fit classes, centred on the reader as the consumer of leisure time. In the reform period urban Chinese have found themselves enjoying increased leisure time (Wang 1995) and these articles offered endless suggestions on how to make good use of it.

Fashion stories also featured regularly, often focusing the reader's gaze on expensive consumer items. For instance the 31 July 1999 issue ran a half-page collection of short articles and photographs on leather fashion accessories, principally hand and shoulder bags, from leading fashion houses

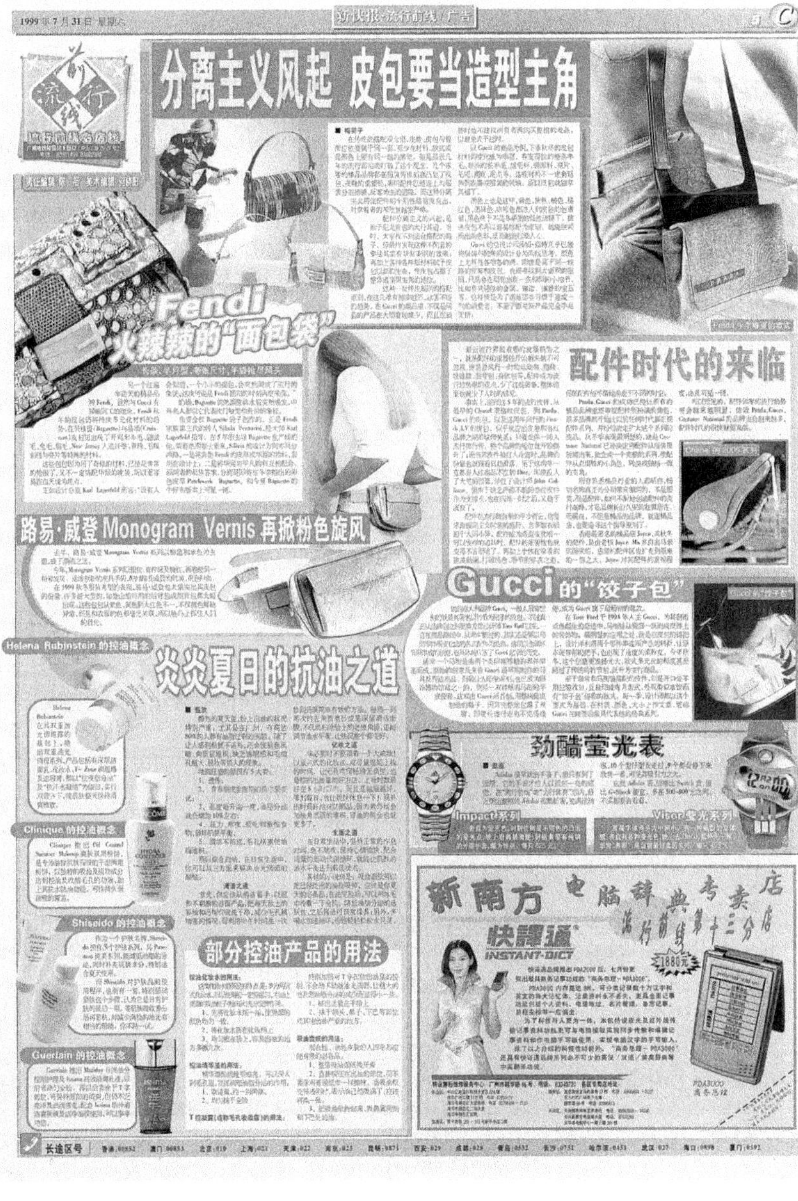
1999年7月31日 星期六

新快报·流行前线/广告

分离主义风起 皮包要当造型主角

Fendi 火辣辣的"面包袋"

路易·威登 Monogram Vernis 再掀粉色旋风

配件时代的来临

Gucci 的"饺子包"

Helena Rubinstein 的控油概念

炎炎夏日的抗油之道

Clinique 的控油概念

Shiseido 的控油概念

部分控油产品的用法

Guerlain 的控油概念

劲酷莹光表

Impact系列

Visor萤光系列

新南方电脑辞典专卖店

快译通 INSTANT-DICT

长途区号

Figure 5.1: Page C5 of *New Express* 31/7/99

like Prada, Chanel, Fendi and Gucci. The articles introduced the reader to the latest fashion trends and suggested where future ones would lead. The page was completed by accompanying articles introducing skin conditioning creams from Helena Rubenstein, Clinique, Lancôme, Shiseido and Guerlain, plus a short piece on Adidas designer sports watches (see Figure 5.1).

On 9 August 1999 the section led with an article questioning illegitimate late-night waiting charges levied by popular restaurants and discos on taxi-drivers. Although the article was an exposé of the treatment meted out to taxi-drivers by nightclubs, it was none the less clearly aimed at a readership accustomed to regular, and relatively expensive through-the-night socializing. This half-page spread was accompanied by one article discussing the pros and cons of the latest telephone technology and another discussing the respective merits of buying and hiring cars (see Figure 5.2). This page presents a clear picture of *New Express*'s imagined target reader as consumer. The article on telephones was headed by a picture of a man, probably in his late thirties, elegantly dressed in slacks and a roll-neck pullover, sitting on a designer bar stool with a micro-cellphone at his ear and gazing out knowingly into the eyes of the reader. The neighbouring article on car purchase and hire was headed by a photo of a sleek German luxury car. The article was also clearly aimed at a reader with much higher than average income. It was written as an informative and practical presentation of advice for those considering buying a car that could only be relevant to Guangzhou's high earners. In fact, the calculated cost of buying a car in the article comes to over 1.4 million renminbi. Meanwhile the opening article on taxi charges, accompanied by a large colour picture of a Guangzhou night-club and disco brightly lit up at night, gave a clear suggestion of the kind of lifestyle this reader is likely to relate to. Taken as a whole, this page offered a clear insight into the kind of reader the paper was trying to identify itself with. The inside pages of the section offered further clues as to the kind of leisure this reader may be likely to enjoy, including a prominent feature on white-water rafting and bathing holidays in natural spa resorts. Further on there was an indication of the reader's likely domestic consumption interests with a half-page introduction to dishwashers, headed by the question: 'Dishwashers: the latest craze in household consumption?' Dishwashers were luxury items rarely seen in the average home in Guangzhou at this time.

The lifestyle section related most blatantly to the values and interests of a projected consumer society. However, the conceptualization of the reader as consumer also came into editorial decision-making about other sections of the paper. The front page ran a daily mini-feature in which the results of a public opinion poll were presented with a small graphic and a few lines of explanation. The questions chosen for this feature were often consumer-oriented: 'Are prices high or low?' (31/7/99), 'Who is it best to present consumer complaints to?' (9/8/99), 'Above what price for goods would you consider making consumer complaints?' (10/8/99), to give but three examples.

1999年8月9日 星期一

新快报

生活副刊

何来深宵"等客费"?

保安私自收费?

这种收费没有法律依据

来电显示 几多方便几多烦扰

买车?租车? 哪个更合算

如果一年下来你用车的日子也不会超过100天,那就该考虑租车而非买车。

Figure 5.2: Page C1 of *New Express* 8/9/99

Editors often had the reader as consumer in mind while weighing up local news stories, and these too would often make their way onto the front page. For instance, on 26 July 1999 the front page was dominated by a large picture of a colourful northeastern-style restaurant, with two waitresses in traditional qipao dresses carrying plates of northeastern dishes to their customers (see Figure 5.3). The accompanying story, under the headline 'Regional Cuisines all the Rage in Guangzhou', explained how even in the city's competitive food market, in which supply outstripped demand, north-eastern style restaurants could currently attract customers in droves. A few days later, on 31 July, the front page carried another story explaining how long-distance phone cards could now be purchased from the comfort of one's home via the internet. Another story for several days in early August related to the ending of a government-enforced fishing ban in the South China Sea aimed at replenishing fish stocks. The stories around this event, however, were strongly focused on the subsequent changes and dramatic fluctuations in fish prices as the market was suddenly flooded with the newly landed catches. The significance of the story, from the editor's point of view, was how it impacted not so much upon fishermen but on the everyday life of the consumer in Guangzhou. In these various ways, stories dealing with everyday consumer issues relevant to the paper's readers, on housing, food prices or popular goods and services, were given high priority by the paper's editors. In fact, relevance to the reader featured as a prominent, if not the most prominent, principle in the daily production of the newspaper and this relevance was very often conceptualized in the various guises of the reader as consumer.

The role of the consumer in China's transforming media

The precise role of actual consumers in China in the transformation of China's media is very difficult to ascertain. Consumers and non-consumers are too numerous and differentiated to be able to deal with them comprehensively. What I have been dealing with in this chapter, however, is a conceptualized consumer, the imagined target reader or readers of *New Express*. What is clear from this discussion is that the conceptualization of this reader, as a consumer of the paper and of other products, was an important feature of how the newspaper was conceptualized and put together on a daily basis. In this sense it is possible to argue that the consumer, as an imagined stereotype or set of stereotypes, in fact has played a crucial role in the commercial transformation of China's media. To understand how this is the case, it is necessary to consider the role that the conception of the consumer-reader has played in leading editors and journalists to stretch the limits of permissible journalism in China.

Let us consider another example presented to me by a senior journalist at *Yangcheng Evening News*. He referred to a recent article that had appeared in *New Express* and subsequently in his own newspaper dealing with a mass killing in the township of Panyu, just south of Guangzhou. He explained that *New Express* had received some reprimand from the city's Party Propaganda Committee for running the article because it had done so without police clearance. For them, this kind of reporting fell into the category of 'sensationalism' (*chao zuo*). However, he pointed out that the

新快报

广州市区天气预报

新闻报料热线

电话:87776333

传真:87614349

A5 A8 B1 C1

解放军有把握以武力对付"台独"

《中国国防报》透露我军拥有"打、封、登"三种军事行动选择

中国驻南大使馆遇袭以来中美最高级别"面对面"接触

唐家璇会见奥尔布赖特

关于大使馆问题

关于台湾问题

坚持地方特色风味敢于推陈出新铺出成功路

外地菜馆火爆羊城

9904影响广州机会不大

未来两天天气仍不稳定

■广东青年喜迎八一

7·28可见月偏食

新快报视窗

操屠刀者焉能成"佛"

"法轮功"练习者李亭残杀父母

■害人害己

重要电话

Figure 5.3: Front page of *New Express* 26/7/99

Yangcheng Evening News did not get into any trouble over the article because *New Express* had already led with it. This kind of reporting of sensational crime stories was seen by journalists and editors at all the mainstream papers in Guangzhou as a sure way to sell newspapers. Here it was not the reader as consumer, but the consumer as reader that was important.

Newspaper editors had a clear understanding that sensational stories appealed to their readers and it was the figure of the consumer that often arbitrated editorial decisions about the content and presentation of the paper. Newspapers could not publish stories on violent crime, corruption, sex scandals or political scandals, except under the specific conditions permitted by the Party (see Li 1991). However, such stories were also often seen by senior editors as the forbidden fruit that would boost their sales enormously. In fact, editors often complained of the limitations placed on populist journalism. Hence, when chances arose to publish stories coming close to these categories, the opportunity was rarely missed.

For example, at the beginning of September 1999, a *Yangcheng Evening News* journalist was out shopping when he heard gunshots nearby. Having his camera with him, he rushed to the scene to find that armed police had just gunned down one of the most wanted gangs of criminals in the Province. It was too late to make the *Yangcheng Evening News* that day, but the front page of *New Express* the following morning carried large colour photos of a policeman, arms outstretched in front of him, still aiming his gun with the bodies of slain criminals on the ground. The story was not an exclusive for the paper but the photos certainly were, and the edge that the pictures gave to *New Express*'s coverage of the incident over its rivals was seen by the paper's editors as a minor but significant marketing coup.

One more example will help to demonstrate how these kinds of commercial pressures to sell newspapers through more seductive reporting simultaneously lead journalists to push the boundaries of state media control. Early in September 1999 there was an air crash in northern China with a sizeable number of casualties. One of the leading Guangzhou newspapers ran the story on its front page with a colour photo of the crash scene. However, after publication, the paper was reprimanded not just by the local Party Propaganda Committee but by the Central Committee. The complaint was that such a story lay beyond the local remit of the newspaper, which should have focused on local news of more immediate relevance to its readers. To give such prominence to a story like this one was unjustified sensationalism and likely to produce an unduly negative sense of China's social reality in the minds of its readers. The Party's concern in this case was that this was drifting too far in the direction of 'negative' reporting (see Li 1991). However, the point to be taken here is that the story was none the less run, despite the editors of the paper being fully aware of these concerns prior to publication and knowing that such a story carried considerable risk of criticism.

In the short term, as one journalist pointed out to me, in fact there was little that the propaganda committee could do. They could simply criticise articles or journalists after the event but, by that time, the story had already run. Indeed, as the example of the shooting article demonstrates, once a problematic story had run in one paper it seemed to be acceptable for others to follow. In the long term, of course, the dangers were rather greater. The

Party could, had, and continues on occasion to shut down newspapers without warning (cf. Zhao 1998: 7, 22, 159), and this was always the danger facing titles that tested the limits perhaps once too often. Clearly the Party organs (in Guangzhou that was the *Guangzhou Daily* and the *Nanfang Daily*) and large circulation papers like the *Yangcheng Evening News* had much less room for manoeuvre, in terms of daring journalism, as the Party tended to keep them under closer scrutiny. However, the new commercially oriented newspapers, especially the *Nanfang Metropolitan Daily* but also to some extent *New Express*, considered it part of their task to stretch the restrictions laid upon them whenever and as far as they could. Importantly, however, the motivation for this kind of challenge to authority was distinctly commercial rather than political, even if long-term political consequences could be envisaged. Hence this boundary testing, since 1989 at least, has on the whole been commercially and not politically driven:

> The critical capacities of journalists have for the most part been contained. Commercialized outlets survive and flourish not by directly challenging the Party principle and discarding political propaganda but by softening the tones of political propaganda, moving beyond narrow political propaganda, and broadening content to include social and personal issues. Their contents are supplementary rather than oppositional to the more conventional Party organs.
>
> (Zhao 1998: 159)

However, this should not be allowed to undermine the significance of these minor challenges to Party control of the media. In fact, the indications in late 1999 were that newspapers, in Guangzhou at least, were increasingly willing to move beyond simply 'social and personal issues' to experiment, in a circumspect manner, with more sensational aspects of reporting.

To understand how China's print media is undergoing this 'silent' transformation it is important to appreciate the ambiguous but crucial role that senior editors play in the system of State and Party control. Senior editors are, of course, more or less senior Party members. As such, they are responsible for monitoring the content of their publications and ensuring that they conform to the Party's strictures on media production. In the past, when the media were fully financed by the state, this was a straightforward responsibility. However, as the media have been commercialized, these very same editors are now also responsible for very different kinds of decisions, driven not by Party ideology but by their conceptions of the reading or viewing public; in the case of newspapers, of their readers as consumers. It is precisely because the mechanisms of censorship rely, in fact, on self-censorship and because the responsibilities for implementing and monitoring this self-censorship fall on precisely the same shoulders as the responsibilities to produce popular, market-sensitive journalism, that there is always a degree of flexibility wrought in this contradiction, which is intrinsic to the system of press journalism as it is now emerging. It is in the figure of the senior newspaper editor that the anachronisms of outdated ideas of Party control confront the forces of the competitive market visualized in the form of the target reader.

Conclusion

John Hartley, writing about Western television, has argued that audiences are 'the invisible fictions that are produced institutionally in order for various institutions to take charge of the mechanisms of their own survival' (1992: 105; cf. also Ang 1991). His point was that television audiences are too complex, diverse, individualized and unknowable for anyone to have a true idea of what they are or what they do. However, television broadcasters cannot manage without a notion of the audience. They have to imagine the audience in some way so that they can be entertained, educated and informed. In this way, Hartley argues,

> Audiences may be imagined empirically, theoretically or politically, but in all cases the product is a fiction that serves the need of the imagining institution. In no case is the audience 'real', or external to its discursive construction. There is no 'actual' audience that lies beyond its production as a category, which is to say that audiences are only ever encountered *per se* as *representations*.
>
> (Hartley 1992: 105)

The situation I have been discussing in this chapter is in some ways similar. The reader that we have been dealing with was similarly a 'discursive construction' imagined by journalists in order to 'take charge of the mechanisms of their survival' in a competitive media market. However, whereas Hartley focuses on the childlike qualities attributed to Western television audiences by broadcasters in what he describes as a 'paedocracy', far more important for Guangzhou's newspaper editors were the readers' qualities as consumers. This imagining was double-layered. On the one hand the reader was the purchaser of the newspaper and therefore needed to be informed, pleased, entertained and above all enticed to buy the paper again in the future. On the other hand, the reader was clearly imagined also to be firmly rooted in a new urban China characterized as a flourishing consumer society.

In this chapter I have drawn principally on how the editors and journalists at *New Express* imagined their target reader as a consumer in these two ways. To some degree this was particular to *New Express*, whose editors had a clear idea of their target reader quite distinctive from that of other papers like the *Yangcheng Evening News*, the *Guangzhou Daily*, the *Nanfang Daily* or the *Nanfang Metropolitan Daily*. These competitors were aiming at far more general readerships. For this reason *New Express*'s focus on the young, upwardly mobile professional and his/her associated consumer tastes was not strictly replicated on the pages of its rivals. However, these other papers were no less embroiled in the tough competition of Guangzhou's newspaper market and, as such, were equally obliged to think of their readers as their consumers. At the same time, general consumer stories relating to food, electrical goods, clothes, music and entertainment were equally present in these other papers. Of these rivals, the *Nanfang Daily* held most closely to its responsibilities as a Party organ, though its subsidiary the *Nanfang Metropolitan Daily*, was one of the most sensationalist of Guangzhou's newspaper titles. The *Guangzhou Daily,* by contrast, went for size over specificity, aimed at any and every potential reader that it could. Therefore, although there were definite and significant differences between the rival papers in Guangzhou, the general conclusions in this chapter regarding the imagined consumer-reader hold relevance across the city's newspaper spectrum. At the same time, the dual and conflicting pressures that characterize Guangzhou's media markets are similarly felt throughout China.

There are, indeed, valid and important questions to be asked of China's so-called 'consumer revolution' (see Chapter 1, the Introduction to this volume). There are also most certainly specific characteristics of China's emerging consumer markets that are not found in consumer societies elsewhere. With regard to media, for instance, the legacy of Party controlled and owned media alongside the commercial pressures of contemporary China have produced forms of media with distinctly Chinese characteristics. However, what this paper has shown is that the *image* of the consumer and the associated *assumption* on the part of newspaper journalists, that urban Chinese are, at the very least, aspirational consumers, have played a fundamental part in transforming China's media. The notion of the consumer-reader has provided one of the important mechanisms whereby journalists have found themselves drawn into challenging the Party's control of media content.

Notes

1 This paper is based on fieldwork conducted principally in Guangzhou and the Pearl River Delta, but also in Beijing, since the summer of 1996. I have made annual trips to Guangzhou and worked with journalists at several of Guangzhou's leading newspapers and television stations. I have had the good fortune to follow the development of *New Express* from before its launch in 1997 through to the present. Fieldwork has involved participant observation at the newspaper, especially in the summers of 1999 and 2001, when I was able to attend editorial meetings and wrote articles for the newspaper. I have also conducted extended interviews with editors and journalists at all levels in *New Express* and *Yangcheng Evening News*. This chapter is specifically focused on the early years of *New Express.* I am grateful to all the staff at the two newspapers and other media organizations who have been kind enough to welcome me and help me with my research. I am also indebted to all the members of the Journalism Department at Jinan University in Guangzhou, especially Professor Chen Weixing and former head of department Professor Wu Wenhu, who provided consistent support throughout this research. This research has been funded by awards from the Nuffield Foundation, SOAS research committee and the Sino–British Fellowship Trust. I must thank Silvia Ferrero and Stuart

Thompson for comments on an early draft of this chapter, although I am responsible for any errors or inaccuracies that remain.

2 For example, the Bureau of Television and Broadcasting, the administrative body overseeing all television stations in Guangzhou, was also itself responsible for re-selling advertising space on Hong Kong television relayed via cable networks in Guangzhou.

3 Some newspapers came directly under the control and management of city- or provincial-level Party propaganda committees. These newspapers are what I refer to as party organs. Although others were always owned by government organizations and ultimately responsible to local Party committees of some kind, they were not under the immediate control of such propaganda committees (see also Zhao 1998: 166–7; Huang 2000; Zhao 2000).

4 This is excluding *Yangcheng Evening News* as an evening rather than a morning paper and prior to the launch of *New Express*. By the summer of 1999, the editors of *New Express* claimed to occupy the number two position after *Guangzhou Daily* within the city of Guangzhou.

5 This was never explicitly stated but was often implicit in the newspaper's content (see example on p. 000, and Figure 5.2). It is important to note, however, that in addition to the principle target reader the paper clearly also aimed articles at women (see, for example, Figure 5.1).

6 In fact the economic section had been given some priority and importance in the conceptualization of *New Express* from before its launch. This was indicated by the fact that several senior and desk editors of the newspaper were head-hunted from one of Guangzhou's leading economic and business newspapers.

References

Ang, Ien (1991) *Desperately Seeking the Audience,* London: Routledge.

Barme, Geremie (1999) 'CCPTM & ADCULT PRC', *The China Journal*, 41, (January), 1–23.

Baudrillard, Jean (1988) 'Consumer Society', in M. Poster (ed.), *Jean Baudrillard: selected writings*, Oxford: Polity Press.

Campbell, Colin (1987) *The Romantic Ethic and the Spirit of Modern Consumerism*, Oxford: Blackwell.

Chao, Linda and Myers, Ramon H. (1998) 'China's consumer revolution: the 1990s and beyond', *Journal of Contemporary China*, 7 (18), 351–68.

China Media Intelligence (2005) 'IPTV in China: has the telecoms-television divide-been breached?'. Available online (and accessed 27.2.2006) at www.eight-and-eight.com/cmi

Davis, Deborah S. (1993) 'Urban households: supplicants to a socialist state', in D. S. Davis and S. Harrell (eds), *Chinese Families in the Post-Mao Era*, Berkeley: University of California Press.

—— (2000) 'Introduction: a revolution in consumption', in D. S. Davis (ed.), *The Consumer Revolution in Urban China*, Berkeley: University of California Press.

—— (ed.) (2000) *The Consumer Revolution in Urban China*, Berkeley: University of California Press.

Davis, Deborah S. and Harrell, Stevan (eds) (1993) *Chinese Families in the Post-Mao Era*, Berkeley: University of California Press.

Galbraith, John K. (1970) *The Affluent Society*, London: Pelican.

Hartley, John (1992) *Tele-ology: Studies in Television*, London: Routledge.

Hemelryk Donald, S. and Keane, M. (2002) 'Responses to Crisis: convergence, content industries and media governance', in Hemelryk Donald, S., Keane, M.

and Yin, H. (eds), *Media in China: consumption, content and crisis*. London: RoutledgeCurzon.

Hemelryk Donald, S., Keane, M. and Yin, H. (eds) (2002) *Media in China: consumption, content and crisis*. London: RoutledgeCurzon.

Huang, C. (2000) 'The Development of a Semi-Independent Press in Post-Mao China: An overview and a case study of Chengdu Business News', *Journalism Studies*, Vol. 1, Issue 4.

Huang, Yu (1994) 'Peaceful evolution: the case of television reform in post-Mao China', *Media Culture & Society*, 16, 217–41.

Hussain, Athar (1990) *The Chinese Television Industry: the interaction between government policy and market force*, London: London School of Economics and Political Science.

Ikels, C. (1996) *The Return of the God of Wealth: The Transition to a Market Economy in Urban China*, Stanford: Stanford University Press.

Latham, K. (2000) 'Nothing but the truth: media, power and hegemony in south China', *China Quarterly*, 163, September 2000.

—— (2001) 'Between Markets and Mandarins: Journalists and the Rhetorics of Transition in Southern China', in Brian Moeran (ed.), *Asian Media Worlds*. Richmond: Curzon Press.

Li Conghua (1998) *China: the Consumer Revolution*, Singapore: Wiley and Sons (Asia).

Li Xiaoping (1991) 'The Chinese television system and television news', *China Quarterly*, 126, 340–55.

Li Zhuren (1998) 'Popular journalism with Chinese characteristics: from revolutionary modernity to popular modernity', *International Journal of Cultural Studies*, 1 (3), 307–28.

Lull, James (1991) *China Turned On: television, reform, and resistance*, London: Routledge.

Miller, Daniel (ed.) (1995) *Acknowledging Consumption: a review of new studies*, London: Routledge.

Vogel, Ezra F. (1989) *One Step Ahead in China: Guangdong under Reform*, Cambridge, MA: Harvard University Press.

Wang, John (1999) 'Signs of opening in telecom', *China Business Review*, May–June 1999, 8–14.

Wang Shaoguang (1995) 'The politics of private time: changing leisure patterns in urban China', in D. S. Davis *et al.* (eds), *Urban Spaces in Contemporary China: The Potential for Autonomy and Community in Post-Mao China*, Woodrow Wilson Center Series, Cambridge: Cambridge University Press.

Wilson, T. (1997) 'Truth and Dare: Chinese weekend paper rakes scandal – and bucks', *Far Eastern Economic Review*, August 14.

Yin, H. and Li, D. G. (2004) '2003: zhongguo dianshi chanye beiwang' (2003: reflections on China's television industry), *South China Television Journal*, 2004: 1, 45, 32–7.

Yu, G. M. (2004) '2004: zhongguo chuanmeiye fazhan dashi tuixiang' (2004: thoughts on the general situation of development in China's broadcasting industries), *South China Television Journal*, 2004: 1, 45, 28–31.

Zhang, H. J. (2005) 'Shenhua tizhi gaige, dazao wenhua pinpai' (Deepen structural reform, forge a cultural brandname), *South China Television Journal*, 2005: 1, 51, 27–9.

Zhao, Yuezhi (1998) *Media, Market, and Democracy in China: Between the Party Line and the Bottom Line*. Urbana/Chicago: University of Illinois Press.

—— (2000) 'From commercialization to conglomeration: The transformation of the Chinese press', *Journal of Communication*, Spring 2000, 50, 2.

Zhongguo tongji nianjian (Chinese Statistical Yearbook) (1995) Beijing: Zhongguo tongji chubanshe.

6 Changing tastes in Guangzhou

Restaurant writings in the late 1990s

Jakob Klein

During the second half of the 1990s there was an upsurge of gastronomic writings in the Guangzhou (Canton) daily press. In December 1996 the *Yangcheng Evening News* (*Yangcheng Wanbao*) began to run a weekly food page entitled 'Cuisine today' (*Jinri meishi*). The *Guangzhou Daily* (*Guangzhou Ribao*) soon followed suit with an occasional section called 'Food and drink' (*Yinshi*). The *New Express* (*Xin kuaibao*), a subsidiary of the *Yangcheng*, was started up in March 1998 (see Latham, Chapter 6 in this volume). Soon after, it too began a weekly food section, which was entitled 'Look, smell, taste' (*Se xiang wei*). Each of these sections was one page long. The majority of the articles discussed here were drawn from these pages between late 1996 and early 1998.[1]

The proliferation of writings on food, and of lifestyle pages in general, was intimately bound up with the growing competition between newspapers and the increasing commercialization of the Chinese print media. While media institutions were still state-owned and supposed to be the mouthpieces of the Party, they also became increasingly dependent on advertising and sales (Latham 2001; Zhao 1998). 'Infotainment' was an important means of attracting readers and sponsors. With their colourful pictures, exciting layouts and titillating descriptions, food pages were not only guides to consumption but also highly entertaining in themselves, allowing those who lacked the financial capital to indulge in the latest trends vicariously to consume the city's culinary delights.

Although the food sections in the Guangzhou dailies also contained recipes, kitchen tips, shopping suggestions and dietetic advice, here I concentrate on articles on 'eating out', which included restaurant reports and advice on etiquette and ordering. I hesitate to refer to the restaurant writings as 'reviews', since I have not come across a single negative assessment of an establishment. A few articles included advertisements for the restaurants featured and thus were clearly sponsored by the restaurants. Furthermore, according to Zhao Yuezhi, a common form of advertising in Chinese newspapers was 'paid information services that [were] integrated into regular media content' (1998: 59), a sponsorship of which audiences usually were not informed. In other words, a good number of the reports discussed in this chapter may have been financed by the restaurants themselves.

According to Stephen Mennell, gastronomic writers in France and England in the nineteenth and twentieth centuries frequently attempted to educate diners and democratize food consumption by laying down the standards of 'correct' taste and disseminating these beyond the elite (1985: 266–90). He also maintains that, by the beginning of the twentieth century, 'the leading restaurant guides in France and England managed to establish a reputation for impartial and "objective" evaluations uninfluenced by backhanders from the evaluated' (1985: 268), and that, in Britain in the 1970s and 1980s, gastronomic guides became part of a general consumer movement in Western countries, often targeting powerful hotel and restaurant chains (1985: 281–90). By contrast, the very commercial restaurant writings in the Guangzhou press in the 1990s were not designed primarily to dispense impartial advice to the consumer. In this chapter I will argue that, none the less, Guangzhou's media gastronomes had an educational agenda for consumers. On my reading of their reports, these 'gastro-journalists' attempted to put order into an increasingly diverse culinary market, to guide the southern Chinese city's consumers through this diversity and even to 'civilize' readers' tastes. Moreover, I suggest, this 'civilizing mission' was quite compatible with journalists' dual responsibilities to the state and to the market.

Dealing with diversity

> It used to be the case that in Guangzhou one could get nothing to eat but Cantonese food. But now things have changed. Today's culinary market is no longer dominated by Cantonese cuisine. One after another, cuisines from other provinces and countries have come on stage.
>
> (Huang 1996)

Scholars of modern Chinese cuisine frequently stress its diversity. As in the case of the post-Independence Indian cookbooks discussed by Arjun Appadurai (1988), Chinese food scholars tend to emphasize a common framework underlying the variety. Oftentimes Chinese culinary diversity is represented in a spatial idiom of distinct regions, although, interestingly, the 'minority nationalities' (*shaoshu minzu*) tend not to be included in this culinary geography but are instead treated as a separate category. Some researchers (e.g., Lu 1992; Ren 1999: 397–583) attempt comprehensive accounts of the food and drink of China's provinces and cities. Others (e.g., Wang 1993: 146–61) define a small number (usually four or eight) regional 'culinary systems' (*caixi*) deemed to be of particular significance. The idea of 'culinary systems', which according to Wang Xuetai has only been developed 'in recent decades' (1993: 147), clearly builds on older classifications. E. N. Anderson writes that the 'classical' categorization was by city, which often stood metonymically for the cuisine of the surrounding regions (1988:

194). This may account for some of the confusion in terminology. I use the word 'Cantonese cuisine' to refer to '*Yuecai*' or '*Guangdong cai*'. Strictly speaking, the Chinese terms refer to the cooking of Guangdong Province, which most Chinese food scholars divide into the three sub-schools – Guangzhou cuisine, Chaozhou cuisine and East River (Hakka) cuisine (Han 1992). However, it is often clear from the context in the newspaper articles that what is meant by these terms is the culinary style of Guangzhou and the surrounding Pearl River Delta area. None the less, because '*Yuecai*' and '*Guangdong cai*' are ambiguous, I reserve the term 'Guangzhounese' for translations of phrases such as '*Guangzhou cai*' ('Guangzhounese cuisine'), '*Guangzhouren*' ('the Guangzhounese' or 'Guangzhou people') and '*Guangzhouren de kouwei*' ('Guangzhounese taste(s)').

Culinary specialization conceived of in terms of regional spatialization is prevalent in contemporary Chinese popular culture. People from different regions and localities are often described according to what they eat or are thought to eat. Many Guangzhounese I met during fieldwork explained what they called the 'light and mild' (*qingdan*) flavour of Cantonese food with reference to Guangdong's 'natural' characteristics, arguing that the hot and damp climate and the province's peculiar water and soil all carried 'heating vapours' (*reqi*) into the body, making it necessary for people in the region to avoid eating too many 'heating' foods such as chillies and deep-fried dishes, lest the body suffer from imbalance caused by excessive heating.[2] By contrast, the food eaten by 'Northerners' (*Beifangren*) – a term which often denoted any Chinese person from outside the province, including those from neighbouring provinces such as Hunan and Jiangxi – was described by Guangzhounese as being 'spicy' (*la*) and 'rich' (*nong*). In 1999, the ditty 'Hunanese fear food that isn't spicy, Jiangxi people are not afraid of spicy food, Sichuanese fear not spicy food' (*Hunanren pa bu la, Jiangxiren bu pa la, Sichuanren la bu pa*) was even printed on the jar of a leading brand of chilli sauce, which in fact was produced in Guangdong Province. This use of food to classify selves and others was not merely descriptive, but at times took on moral and competitive overtones. For example, some Guangzhounese described people from Hunan and Sichuan – provinces of origin of many of the migrant workers in and around the city – as being aggressive because of the amount of chillies they were thought to consume. By contrast, the Guangzhounese described themselves as being more 'civil' (*siwen*) because of their avoidance of 'heating' foods. Indeed, as Anderson points out, people in China take considerable pride in their local cuisines (1994: 42). Rivalry between regions and localities is often expressed in a culinary idiom. Such rivalry is evident in an article on the recent fate of Hong Kong chefs in Guangzhou (Shi 1997). While the anthropologist Siumi Maria Tam (1997: 298) claims that Hong Kong now sets the standards for southern Chinese cuisine, Guangzhou gastronomist Shi Peilin proudly describes the diminishing pull of Hong Kong cuisine on local appetites:

> 'Old gluttons' may remember that years ago in Guangzhou, Cantonese restaurants would take pride in having a Hong Kong master chef. For a time, the sign 'Hong Kong Chef in Charge' was a common sight. Yet nowadays, Hong Kong food has lost much of its former power to attract customers. The great majority of Guangzhou's first-rate Cantonese restaurants now have local masters as head chefs.
>
> (Shi 1997)

While Hong Kong perhaps now poses less of a threat to Guangzhou's culinary reputation,[3] the quote at the beginning of this section suggests that Cantonese cuisine in Guangzhou may instead be under pressure from foreign and non-Cantonese Chinese cuisine. This new diversity problematizes the culinary regionalizations of popular culture and scholarly works. According to Huang Zhihai (1996), the large-scale arrival of new styles was largely a development of the 1990s. It was closely related to the huge influx of migrants from all over China which Guangzhou began to experience around 1985 (Zhou 1992), and to the increasing openness of the Chinese market to foreign restaurants and food brands (Jing 2000; Watson 1997). As I will argue elsewhere (Klein in progress), Guangzhou's culinary boundaries had been strengthened between the mid-1950s and mid-1980s, during which time there was, in comparison with the late 1940s, relatively little movement of people, goods and capital between the city and the wider region and world (Chan 1995; Guldin 1992). Whereas teahouses and restaurants in Hong Kong and in the Cantonese-speaking diaspora continued, as had previously been the case in Guangzhou, to develop new varieties and styles through contact with foreign and other regional Chinese cuisines (Tam 1997; Cheung 2001, 2002), the Guangzhou catering trade, nationalized and centrally planned from the late 1950s, continued on the whole to reproduce – albeit in dwindling numbers – recipes laid down by Republican-era (1912–49) masters. The early, tentative years of urban reform in the 1980s, while bringing in a large number of individually and family-operated eateries and a small number of foreign and Hong Kong-style luxury hotel restaurants, also strengthened the position of the state-run catering trade, which was able to re-introduce a large number of delicacies and to re-open businesses that had been closed during the Cultural Revolution of the 1960s and early 1970s.[4] While people I spoke to in 1999 and 2000 were almost without exception positive about the greater general prosperity, abundance and choice of the reform years in comparison with the revolutionary period, many also spoke nostalgically about a sense of culinary order and respect for 'traditional' Guangzhou cooking techniques and recipes, which they argued had characterized the teahouses and restaurants of the 1970s and 1980s.

Unsurprisingly, then, the recent proliferation of eating places in the city and the growing variety of tastes and styles were *the* major themes in the food writings of the late 1990s. Significantly, Huang's article on the incursion of non-Cantonese foods took the lead in the very first edition of the

Yangcheng's 'Cuisine today'. That these new eating places were seen as somehow problematic is clear from the extent to which issues of 'taste' and 'place' were discussed in the reports. Foreign restaurants and Chinese restaurants from outside the province – the latter often collectively named 'restaurants from outside places' (*waidi caiguan/canguan*) and referred to in this chapter as 'regional restaurants' – were not simply described but commonly articulated with issues such as 'authenticity', 'nation', 'culture', 'Cantoneseness' and 'social status'. In their attempts to organize and manage the city's culinary diversity, gastronomic journalists attempted to shape consumers in accordance with particular ideals and to reaffirm – or perhaps reinvent – the idea of an essential Guangzhounese taste and cuisine.

Foreign fare

Quite a few of the articles are written in a strongly didactic style. Consumers are taught how to compose a proper meal when taking people out to dine (Zhang 1997), how to distinguish between 'hot-plated' fish and fish served on the 'original plate' (Gang 1997) and how to avoid wasting when ordering seafood (Xiao 1997). This explicit educational ambition is especially prominent in writings on foreign cuisine. For example, the author of a short comment entitled 'Eat Western food, know the proper etiquette' (Feng 1996) stresses that when eating in a Western restaurant one should eat quietly and, in particular, not slurp one's soup. The potential consumer is taught the 'correct methods' of eating Italian spaghetti, snails, crab, lobster and asparagus. Then come desserts, which one is supposed to eat 'with a fork in one's left hand and a spoon in one's right, using the spoon like a knife to cut off pieces of cake' (Feng 1996). The reader is urged not to drink tea or coffee with a spoon, but to sip directly from the cup, not to use a knife to shovel food into his mouth and not to speak with his mouth full. The final warning reads: 'The most vulgar behaviour possible would be to wave one's knife and fork around and use them to point at things' (Feng 1996).

In an article on steak-houses written by Shi Peilin and Hu Xianying (1997), the fear of embarrassing oneself because of ignorance of proper etiquette is given as one of the reasons why Guangzhounese shun Western haute cuisine. The authors lament that, despite the growing number of opportunities to try out Western food, Guangzhounese remain indifferent towards 'authentic' steak-houses. They are at great pains to teach consumers to distinguish between high and low. Citing the manager of the steak-house in the Garden Hotel, one of Guangzhou's fanciest hotels, the journalists point out that, with the rise of Western fast food, bars and buffets, people in Guangzhou have become used to 'that kind of carelessly made mix of Chinese and Western food served up as Western cuisine. By contrast, people find it difficult to accept the authentic Western culinary culture offered in steak-houses' (Shi and Hu 1997). They do admit that at around 400 yuan per person, the cost of going to a steak-house is somewhat prohibitive to the 'wage-earning stratum' (*gongxin jieceng*), but add that these prices are not uncommon in the city's first-rate Chinese restaurants, either. However, the main reason for people's lack of interest, they argue, is ignorance, and Shi and Hu set out to educate the public by explaining to them what a real steak-house is all about.

Like steak-houses, European-style coffeehouses were described as being refined and cultured. They were held up as cultivated alternatives to bars and discos:

> Now that the short-lived rage for bars has gradually died down, elegant coffeehouses have quietly been appearing on the Guangzhou streets. A cup of fragrant, mellow coffee in one's hand, one's mood as delicate and pure as fine porcelain – this is the kind of sentiment that Guangzhounese go to the coffeehouses to enjoy.
>
> (Shi and Li 1997)

In this article, 'Coffeehouses, more than just coffee', it is maintained that Guangzhou's coffeehouses use a refined and cultured environment to attract customers. Shi Peilin and Li Yunxian remark that: "In coffeehouses, alcohol, instant coffee and packaged teas are considered vulgar" (1997). The manager of one coffeehouse is cited as explaining that what they offer is more than the coffee itself, but 'coffee culture', which comprises 'the study of the properties, selection, roasting, grinding and blending of coffee beans, brewing, drinking methods and more' (Shi and Li 1997). Shi and Li go on to describe different kinds of beans and various methods of preparing and drinking coffee. To bring home the message of refinement and European exotica, the article is accompanied by two colour photographs, the larger of which depicts coffee beans laid out next to a porcelain cup full of coffee and an old-fashioned manual coffee grinder. The other photograph shows groups of fashionable young people sitting around tables in an immaculate coffeehouse.

Consumers are encouraged to be cosmopolitan in their tastes, to dine in 'authentic' Western restaurants and to behave 'properly' and order correctly when doing so. However, 'authenticity' is treated quite differently in writings on 'middle' and 'low range' Western food, including fast food. In a sense, 'authentic' Western food is equated with haute cuisine. Less prestigious food is treated with much less awe. Instead, adaptations to Cantonese tastes are actually applauded. One writer in the *New Express* argues that a popular restaurant chain called The Greenery owes its great success to its skill at adapting itself to different kinds of taste while remaining true to 'Guangzhounese taste'. 'Why is it', she asks, 'that this place is able to attract so many people of different ages, different tastes and different levels of education?' (Chen 1998). She explains that, in addition to serving a wide variety of foods at reasonable, middle-range prices, the answer lies in part in the fact that each of the nine branches has its own distinctive style, each attracting different kinds of customers. She continues:

> In the beginning, The Greenery was an ordinary café, now it has become a lifestyle . . . This is even apparent in the menu, which will satisfy those who like Western food and those who like Chinese food. Of course, there are also regional specialities. The most laudable thing is that Guangzhounese touches have been blended into the food here. This is particularly true of the Western food, which is adapted to the great majority of Guangzhounese tastes.
>
> (Chen 1998)

'Why,' Chen Yi concludes, 'do so many people like The Greenery? Simply because it has adapted to the vast majority of people's tastes, to Guangzhounese taste, this is why people like it' (Chen 1998). In other words, underlying the diversity of styles and tastes of the customers, there is a uniform, Guangzhounese taste.

The food served at The Greenery is precisely the kind scorned in the steak-house piece. In the *New Express* article, however, this food is lauded for not making demands on Guangzhounese taste-buds. The issue of adaptation to local demands lies at the heart of the numerous reports on fast food which appeared in 1997. The authors of *Golden Arches East: McDonald's in East Asia* (Watson 1997) argue that, far from being a simple agent of Western cultural imperialism, the American fast-food chain has in fact been 'localized' in various ways by Asian consumers and by the business itself. However, they neglect to look into the extent to which the 'localization' of fast food may itself be part of East Asian discourses (though see Yan 1995: 52).

On 13 July 1997, the *Yangcheng Evening News* devoted nearly its entire second page, the 'Assorted news' section of the paper, to several articles under the heading 'Do the Guangzhounese want to eat Cantonese-style fast food?' (Zhou and Gu 1997). In the leading article it is argued that, while Western fast food restaurants are closing down one after another, Chinese-style fast food is more popular than ever, with already more than 16,000 (!) establishments in the city. Yet the writers lament that most of these are small, individually run restaurants.

> Caught between, on the one hand, expensive Western fast food restaurants which do not suit local tastes and, on the other hand, rice boxes from individually run eating places, which cannot guarantee good hygiene, Guangzhounese demand reasonably priced, hygienic and reliable 'Cantonese'-flavoured fast food.
>
> (Zhou and Gu 1997)

The authors call for more government support and conclude that the time is ripe for the rapid development of Chinese-style fast food. They even imply that the substitution of fast food restaurants for small eateries is an inevitable consequence of modernization:

> In Hong Kong, there is one fast food restaurant for every ten thousand people, whereas there aren't even a hundred proper fast food establishments for the millions of people living in Guangzhou. If we also take the sizable floating population into account, then the market potential is enormous. Moreover, the trend is already that fast food restaurants are replacing the eateries (*dapaidang*). The food stalls selling rice boxes have no future.
>
> (Zhou and Gu 1997)

The page also includes an interview with Liu Shisheng, general manager of McDonald's in Guangzhou. Mr Liu is asked whether Guangzhou's fast food market will be 'carved up like a melon' (*guafen*, a term generally used to describe the post-Opium War imperialist encroachment on China) by Western fast food companies, and whether McDonald's will monopolize that market. He replies that there is enough market space to accommodate both foreign and Chinese fast food, and compares Guangzhou with Hong Kong in the 1970s, when people there were worried that local food would be corrupted by McDonald's. In Hong Kong, Liu argues, McDonald's actually had a positive effect on the development of 'Sino-Western' fast food and on the hygiene standards of local restaurants. He maintains that, similarly, Western fast food could be good for Guangzhou. The interview concludes on an even higher note:

> Mr. Liu says the culinary culture of the East is broad and deep, Cantonese cuisine is profound and has endless varieties. Western food cannot replace this. The task that Chinese-style fast food faces today is to learn from modern Western management without discarding its own traditions.
>
> (Zhou and Gu 1997)

Interestingly, when we turn from the news pages to the lifestyle pages, the issue of developing a Chinese fast food industry becomes less important. Instead, what is emphasized is the already ongoing indigenization of the existing fast food trade. In a leading article in 'Cuisine today' (Wu and Liang 1997) it is maintained (in contradiction to Zhou and Gu 1997) that, although people began to lose interest after the initial boom following the arrival of McDonald's in the early 1990s, after 1996 foreign fast food again began to flourish. Analysing the reasons behind this development, Wu Xiaopan and Liang Yanbing emphasize that 'Western restaurants offer primarily Western food, [yet] since arriving in Guangzhou many have worked hard to adapt to Guangzhounese tastes' (1997). An example is given by Wu Xiaopan (1997) in another article, where he writes that 'modern fast food establishments and Western restaurants' have begun to serve 'Chinese-style morning tea', in particular in order to attract customers outside of peak mealtimes. Wu describes a scene at *Dakuaihuo*, a Hong Kong fast food chain which had been serving morning tea for over a year:

> Every morning, in the bright and spacious *Dakuaihuo* fast food restaurant, aunties and uncles can be seen sitting around colourful tables in threes and fours, slowly sipping their tea and nibbling their snacks. Every now and then, the serving staff, wearing white uniforms with green caps, push their food trolleys past the customers.
>
> (Wu 1997)

Wu interviews three of the 'aunties' in a *Dakuaihuo*, who feel that the fast food restaurant, with its air-conditioning, is even more comfortable than an old-style teahouse. 'They often sit here exchanging mah-jong tips, not going home to eat until noon' (Wu 1997). Another customer they interview, 'Uncle Chen', 'frequently goes to fast food restaurants to enjoy his morning tea. He says that in the old part of town fast food restaurants serving tea are often terribly crowded, sometimes one even has to make reservations' (Wu 1997). Moreover, 'Uncle Chen' enjoys the fact that, in addition to the 'prawn dumplings commonly served in Cantonese-style teahouses, in the fast food restaurants they also have steaks, tuna-fish sandwiches and other Western-style snacks' (Wu 1997). According to the article, in June 1997, six Pizza Hut outlets had begun to serve afternoon and evening tea. In addition to Chinese teas, they also served tea with milk, lemon tea and other 'Western-style' teas, and five or six kinds of 'Western cakes'. Wu quotes one old gentleman, surnamed Huang: 'I've been drinking teas for many years, now I've come here to have a look at the Western scenery' (Wu 1997). What is striking about Wu's piece is that the same examples could easily have been used to argue that Cantonese tea-drinking practices were being changed – even 'Westernized' – by the fast food industry. Instead, he uses these examples to make the point that for foreign and Hong Kong fast food chains to succeed in Guangzhou, *they* must adapt to *local* customs and tastes.

Regional restaurants

In their accounts of Western food, gastro-journalists were very much concerned with distinguishing between 'high' and 'low', encouraging consumers to embrace the former as 'authentic' Western culinary culture, and at the same time commending what they saw as the ongoing indigenization of the latter. When it came to regional Chinese restaurants, there was much less of an interest in differentiating between 'high' and 'low' and a much more ambivalent approach to the question of authenticity. On the one hand, there was a great concern over whether Guangzhounese could accept the different 'local flavours' (*fengwei*), and adaptations to Guangzhounese tastes were frequently described as 'improvements' (*gaijin*). On the other hand, reporters also tried to teach local consumers about regional foods. They encouraged Guangzhounese to try out new cuisines and 'to seek authenticity' (*qiu zhengzong*).

In March 1998, the *Guangzhou Daily* devoted a whole page to regional cuisine in the city. The article begins:

> Cantonese cuisine is one of the eight great culinary systems. [The saying] 'For eating, it's Guangzhou' (*shi zai Guangzhou*) is definitely not a misnomer. In recent years, regional flavours from around the country have arrived in the South in rapid succession. Without leaving the city, Guangzhounese can enjoy every delicacy under heaven. However, it will take time before Guangzhounese can accept regional foods. It is no easy task for regional styles to take a spoonful of soup from Cantonese cuisine's market.
>
> (Hu *et al.* 1998)

The writers go on to describe the defining characteristics of cuisines from Sichuan, Hunan, Shandong, Shaanxi and Yunnan Provinces, from the Northeast and from Shanghai. They conclude with a discussion of *Qingzhen* (Muslim) cuisine, a residual category as it is not strictly regionally-based but here includes food prepared by Uyghurs from Xinjiang and Hui from Qinghai and Gansu Provinces. They list representative restaurants of each culinary group and discuss to what extent these restaurants have adapted to local tastes. For instance, Hunanese restaurants were found reluctant to adapt to local conditions. The journalists felt that the 'smoky, sour and spicy flavours would not easily interest the Guangzhounese, who are so afraid of "heating"' (Hu *et al.* 1998). By contrast, the Shandongese restaurant The Confucius had once served authentic Shandong cuisine, but received mostly customers hailing from Shandong and the Northeast. In order to attract more Guangzhounese, the restaurant added Cantonese dishes to the menu. In the case of a restaurant serving Shaanxi cuisine, it is argued that, although it does not plan to conform to Guangzhou tastes, it has made some small adjustments. Most noticeably, 'the huge pancakes of Shaanxi are much smaller here', yet 'Guangzhounese still stare at them in utter amazement' (Hu *et al.* 1998). The authors conclude that, on the whole,

> . . . while preserving their own characteristics [regional restaurants] also try to adapt as much as possible to Guangzhounese taste. From décor to the improvement of dishes, everything is steeped not only in exotic fragrances, but also in the fusion with Guangzhou's culinary culture. Here, outsiders come for a taste of their native places, while Guangzhounese try out novelties.
>
> (Hu *et al.* 1998)

A special edition of the *New Express*'s 'Look, smell, taste' feature concentrates on regional kitchens in Guangzhou (Shangguan 1998). The restaurant reports are preceded by a section in which Guangzhounese are interviewed about their views on regional cuisine. The seven interviewees are divided into two columns: those who like it and those who do not. The four who are positive about regional cuisine are either professionals or students in their twenties, whereas the three who dislike it are a housewife in her fifties and two female workers in their forties. All the respondents are women except for one 25-year-old section manager at a bank. Those in favour of regional cuisine are cited at some length. 'Miss Feng', a 21-year-old secretary, is quoted as saying:

> I eat it often, and frequently change styles. Usually I go to the Heavenly Abode, the Puli Mansion or the Red Sorghum for Sichuanese food, or to the Drunkard for Hunanese. I don't like Zhejiang food, it's too sweet.
> (quoted in Shangguan 1998)

By contrast, those who dislike regional cuisine are given much less space to express their views. 'Aunt Chen', the housewife, remarks: 'The taste is different, I'm not used to it', while 'Ms. Ying' curtly replies: 'I've never tried it and I don't want to' (quoted in Shangguan 1998). On my reading, it is suggested in the article that an open-minded, curious attitude towards taste is typical of the educated, the young and the successful, whereas conservatism is typical of the old and uneducated. The reader should want to emulate the former rather than the latter.[5] That readers are encouraged to embrace regional foods is more than clear from the reports, which include vivid descriptions of décor, dishes and atmospheres, and colour photographs of the restaurant interiors. The report on the Old Shanghai is full of pre-Liberation nostalgia and urban chic. By contrast, the *Qingzhen* food served in the Qinghai Restaurant is described as being served in hearty portions, 'keeping to Northwestern standards', with heavy, fragrant, sour and pungent flavours. The chef and his apprentice have made 'improvements on some of the rather coarse (*cuzao*) cooking methods. In addition to paying attention to the "smell" (*xiang*) and "taste" (*wei*) [of the dishes], they are now beginning to attach importance to their "look" (*se*)' (Shangguan 1998). A third restaurant, the Yunnan-style Spring City, seems both exotic and eclectic. It is said to specialize in healthy 'mountain treasures' such as different kinds of fungi. According to Spring City's manager, the cooking methods used are meant to preserve the nutrients and natural flavours of the ingredients. The journalist claims that the restaurant is the first in Guangzhou to serve authentic 'cross-the-bridge' noodles. He points out that the flour needed to prepare the noodles is made from a strain of rice grown only in a certain Zhuang Nationality village in Yunnan's Wenshan County, the owner's place of origin. Spring City is also said to specialize in something called 'minority nationality cuisine'. The décor is presented in 'minority nationality style' and the waiting staff wear a range of 'minority nationality costumes' and perform various songs and dances. The festivals of several of Yunnan's nationalities are celebrated with customers, 'creating a propitious and happy atmosphere' (Shangguan 1998). In addition to this, Spring City also serves 'the best of Cantonese cuisine' (Shangguan 1998), including morning, afternoon and evening tea with snacks.

Both the special issue in the *Guangzhou Daily* and that in the *New Express* encourage local consumers to try out new tastes. They also welcome adaptations to Guangzhounese taste made by regional restaurateurs. Other reports argue that regional cuisine has already induced changes in Guangzhounese tastes and that the city's consumers are becoming more sophisticated in their appreciation of regional cuisine. In a report on a recently-opened Sichuanese restaurant, one writer argues that the Guangzhounese have become used to regional foods. They have 'already satisfied their initial curiosity for novel tastes and have now matured to a point where they pursue authenticity' (Lin 1997). Another reporter for the *Yangcheng* goes even further, arguing that 'Cantonese cuisine, which has always been light and mild, has now begun to move towards spiciness' (Ju 1997). Ju maintains that Guangzhounese have recently begun to add chillies to quick-fried and clay pot-fried dishes, to mini-casseroles and to certain kinds of fish. He attributes this primarily to the flourishing of regional restaurants, in particular from the spicy provinces of Sichuan and Hunan, and also points to a growing interest in 'country flavour' and 'home cooking' more generally. Ju seems to be very much in favour of the change:

> According to gourmets, chillies not only whet the appetite, they also dispel the foul smells of fish and meat and make foods taste terrific. Even more interestingly, chillies are seductive . . . A customer who has eaten a spicy 'snail and chicken casserole', and reverts to eating it without chilli, will no longer . . . be able to taste the country flavour.
>
> (Ju 1997)

However, despite his assertions about changes in Guangzhounese tastes, in his conclusion Ju makes sure to clarify the boundaries between Cantonese and other regional flavours:

> None the less, the spiciness of the Cantonese is not the same as Sichuanese or Hunanese spiciness. It mustn't get too spicy and there is no interest in 'hot and numbing' (*mala*) flavours. Spiciness in Cantonese cuisine comes primarily from chilli, and sometimes a bit of ground pepper is used. Flower pepper, star anise and the like are rarely used.
>
> (Ju 1997)

Conclusion

The fact that Ju Guokun emphasizes the differences between Cantonese and 'outside' tastes is significant. While it was accepted in the food articles that regional styles may undergo change and influence each other, the assumption of a discrete spatialization of taste was underlined repeatedly. By frequently juxtaposing and comparing the tastes of different places, any boundaries which may have become blurred were reaffirmed. Moreover, the impact of Cantonese styles on foreign and regional cuisine was written about much more frequently than vice versa. Any signs of an indigenization of foreign fast food were warmly welcomed and influences on regional cuisines were explicitly described in terms of 'refinement' and 'improvement'. Often, regional restaurants seem to have been associated with the rural – with hearty portions and heavy flavours which had to be refined in order to be accepted by the more urban tastes of the Guangzhounese.

None the less, similar to the contemporary Bombay food media, where readers were encouraged 'to consume new cuisines and innovative restaurant styles' (Conlon 1995: 108), Guangzhou papers urged consumers to be cosmopolitan in their approach to regional and foreign cuisine. At the same time, however, the importance of Guangzhounese and Chinese tastes was constantly emphasized. If cosmopolitans depend on the existence of locals in order to define themselves as being cosmopolitan (Hannerz 1990), then gastro-journalists in Guangzhou envisioned an ideal consumer who was both cosmopolitan and local wrapped up in one. This ideal consumer was one who was open to and knowledgeable about culinary cultures from near and far. She was equally at home in an 'authentic' French steak-house, a Qinghai Muslim noodle shop, a stylish coffeehouse or a Sichuanese restaurant. Moreover, she ordered with deliberation and moderation, never wasting food or taking part in the eating and drinking competitions or other 'uncivilized practices' engaged in 'by the lower orders of the towns and villages' (Tang 1997). Food writings in 1990s Guangzhou were thus embedded in the overlapping discourses of regional identity and social hierarchy. They were involved in the redefinition of social boundaries in urban China, boundaries which were being defined not only by criteria such as occupation, wealth and access to state benefits, but increasingly also in terms of consumption, taste and lifestyle (Croll, Chapter 2 in this volume).

Furthermore, gastro-journalists' attempts to educate Cantonese eaters cannot be entirely separated from the interests of the reform-era Party-State. The promotion of an ideal eater who is patriotic, frugal and restrained accorded well with the state's emphasis on 'the construction of spiritual civilization', an ongoing pedagogical project aimed at improving the 'quality' of the population (Anagnost 1997; Murphy 2004). The assumption underlying this project, according to Ann Anagnost (1997), is that a 'civil' or 'civilized' (*wenming*) populace is a prerequisite for establishing a truly 'modern' China, a China able to stand on equal footing with Japan and the West. Significantly, the reform state's 'civilizing project' (Harrell 1995) has been promoted as a corrective to recent materialism, not as a critique of the market economy (Anagnost 1997; Bakken 2000). Similarly, while Guangzhou gastronomists did display a certain unease with indulgent consumerism, an unease which, following Judith Farquhar (2002), may have been rooted in the frugality and self-denial emphasized in the political morality of the Mao years, their 'civilizing mission' clearly did not amount to a critique of consumerism. On the contrary, diners were strongly encouraged to partake of the growing diversity of the city's restaurant scene, but to do so with knowledge, selectivity and self-restraint. As Latham (2001) and Zhao (1998) point out, journalists' dual responsibility to market and state quite often has not taken the form of a contradiction. After all, economic development through the growth of private industry and consumerism has been a cornerstone of recent Party rhetoric. In the gastronomic press in late 1990s Guangzhou, both the market and the Party seem to have been served quite well.

Notes

1 The first version of this chapter, presented at the London China Seminar in January 1999, was based on a close reading of Guangzhou dailies. Thanks to everyone who commented on my presentation at the seminar, and especially to Kevin Latham and Stuart Thompson for their helpful comments on several versions of the paper. I am particularly indebted to Kevin Latham for allowing me access to his private collection of Guangzhou newspapers. Thanks also to Stuart Thompson for suggesting the title, 'Changing tastes in Guangzhou'. While the focus of this chapter is still on newspaper reports, in updating the piece for publication I have also drawn on material collected during ten months of fieldwork on Guangzhou's teahouses carried out in 1999 and 2000 (Klein 2004).

2 On 'heating' and 'cooling' foods in Chinese folk dietetics, see Anderson (1988: 229–43) and Anderson and Anderson (1975).

3 I have argued elsewhere that, although Hong Kong in fact continued to exert a great influence on food trends in Guangzhou, by the turn of the twenty-first century restaurateurs, chefs and cookbook writers in the city had become quite deft at appropriating Hong Kong fashions as their own and blurring the distinctions – very apparent in the 1980s and early 1990s – between the commercial cooking styles of the two neighbouring cities (Klein 2004: 125–57).

4 The number of eating and drinking establishments in the city was greatly diminished during the revolutionary decades, from perhaps 12,000 in 1948 (Qiong'an 1948: 24) to 2,800 in 1958 and just 512 in 1972 (Gao and Gong 1999: 60–1). Numbers quickly recovered during the reform years, with nearly 8,000 registered eating and drinking places in 1987 (Guangzhou Nianjian 1988: 250) and over 16,000 in 1998 (Guangzhou Nianjian 1999: 273).

5 Stanley Rosen (2004) argues that, since the 1990s, young urban professionals have emerged as China's new, officially sanctioned role models, replacing the 'model workers' of previous decades.

References

Anagnost, A. (1997) *National Past-Times: Narrative, Representation and Power in Modern China*, Durham, NC: Duke University Press.

Anderson, E. N. (1988) *The Food of China*, New Haven: Yale University Press.

—— (1994) 'Food', in Wu Dingbo and P. D. Murphy (eds), *Handbook of Chinese Popular Culture*, Westport: Greenwood Press.

Anderson, E. N. and Anderson, M. L. (1975) 'Folk Dietetics in Two Chinese Communities, and Its Implications for the Study of Chinese Medicine', in A. Kleinman (ed.), *Medicine in Chinese Cultures*, Washington, DC: U.S. Government Printing Office.

Appadurai, A. (1988) 'How to Make a National Cuisine: Cookbooks in Contemporary India', *Comparative Studies in Society and History* 30: 3–24.

Bakken, B. (2000) *The Exemplary Society: Human Improvement, Social Control, and the Dangers of Modernity in China*, Oxford: Oxford University Press.

Chan, M. K. (1995) 'All in the Family: The Hong Kong – Guangdong Link in Historical Perspective', in R. Y.-W. Kwok and A. Y. So (eds), *The Hong Kong – Guangdong Link: Partnership in Flux*, Armonk, NY: M. E. Sharpe.

Chen Yi (1998) 'Lüyingge Zoubian Guangzhou Cheng' (The Greenery Is Spread All Over Guangzhou City), *Xin Kuaibao* (New Express), 4 April.

Cheung, S. C. H. (2001) 'Hakka Restaurants: A Study of the Consumption of Food in Post-War Hong Kong Society', in D. Y. H. Wu and Tan Chee-beng (eds), *Changing Chinese Foodways in Asia*, Hong Kong: The Chinese University Press.

—— (2002) 'Food and Cuisine in a Changing Society: Hong Kong', in D. Y. H. Wu and S. C. H. Cheung (eds) *The Globalization of Chinese Food*, Richmond, Surrey: Curzon.

Conlon, F. (1995) 'Dining Out in Bombay', in C. A. Breckenridge (ed.), *Consuming Modernity: Public Culture in a South Asian World*, Minneapolis: University of Minnesota Press.

Farquhar, J. (2002) *Appetites: Food and Sex in Postsocialist China*, Durham, NC: Duke University Press.

Feng Feng (1996) 'Chi Xican, Shi Liyi' (Eat Western Food, Know the Proper Etiquette), *Yangcheng Wanbao* (Yangcheng Evening News), 4 December.

Gang Yu (1997) '"Yuan" Die Yu "Guo Die"' ('Original Plate' and 'Hot-Plating'), *Yangcheng Wanbao* (Yangcheng Evening News), 8 July.

Gao Xuzheng and Gong Bohong (1999) *Guangzhou Meishi* (Guangzhou's Cuisine), Guangzhou: Guangdong Sheng Ditu Chubanshe.

Guangzhou Nianjian Bianzuan Weiyuanhui (ed.) (1988) *Guangzhou Nianjian* (Guangzhou Yearbook). Guangzhou: Guangzhou Nianjian Chubanshe.

{mmdash} (1999) *Guangzhou Nianjian* (Guangzhou Yearbook). Guangzhou: Guangzhou Nianjian Chubanshe.

Guldin, G. E. (1992) 'Urbanizing the Countryside: Guangzhou, Hong Kong, and the Pearl River Delta', in G. E. Guldin (ed.), *Urbanizing China*, Westport, CT: Greenwood Press.

Han Boquan (1992) 'Guangdong juan' (Guangdong), in Lu Kecai (ed.), *Zhonghua Minzu Yinshi Fengsu Daguan* (Survey of the Culinary Customs of the Chinese Nation), Beijing: Shijie Zhishi Chubanshe.

Hannerz, U. (1990) 'Cosmopolitans and Locals in World Culture', in M. Featherstone (ed.), *Global Culture: Nationalism, Globalization and Modernity*, London: Sage.

Harrell, S. (1995) 'Introduction: Civilizing Projects and the Reaction to Them', in S. Harrell (ed.), *Cultural Encounters on China's Ethnic Frontiers*, Seattle: University of Washington Press.

Huang Zhihai (1996) 'Guangzhouren Zhangkou "Shi Sifang"' (Guangzhounese Open Wide to Eat Food From Near and Far), *Yangcheng Wanbao* (Yangcheng Evening News), 4 December.

Hu Qiping *et al.* (1998) 'Dong Nan Xi Bei Zhongguo Cai, Suan Tian Ku La Ju Yangcheng' (Chinese Cuisine From the North, South, East and West; Sour, Sweet, Bitter and Spicy Flavours Converge on Guangzhou), *Guangzhou Ribao* (Guangzhou Daily), 7 March.

Jing Jun (ed.) (2000) *Feeding China's Little Emperors: Food, Children, and Social Change*, Stanford: Stanford University Press.

Ju Guokun (1997) 'Yuecai Zai Qiaoqiao "Geming" – Guangdonglao Ye Shuo "Pa Bu La"' (The Silent Revolution in Cantonese Cuisine – Guangdongnese Are Now Also Saying "I'm Worried the Food Isn't Spicy"), *Yangcheng Wanbao* (Yangcheng Evening News), 17 June.

Klein, J. A. (2004) 'Reinventing the Traditional Guangzhou Teahouse: Caterers, Customers and Cooks in Post-Socialist Urban South China', unpublished PhD thesis, University of London.

—— (in progress) '"For Eating, It's Guangzhou": Regional Culinary Traditions and Chinese Socialism', in H. West and P. Raman (eds), *Enduring Socialism*.

Latham, K. (2001) 'Between Markets and Mandarins: Journalists and the Rhetorics of Transition in Southern China', in B. Moeran (ed.), *Asian Media Productions*, Richmond, Surrey: Curzon Press.

Lin Lin (1997) 'Guangzhouren Shi Chuancai Qiu Zhengzong' (Guangzhounese Demand Authentic Sichuan Cuisine), *Yangcheng Wanbao* (Yangcheng Evening News), 14 August.

Lu Kecai (ed.) (1992) *Zhonghua Minzu Yinshi Fengsu Daguan* (Survey of the Culinary Customs of the Chinese Nation), Beijing: Shijie Zhishi Chubanshe.

Mennell, S. (1985) *All Manners of Food: Eating and Taste in England and France from the Middle Ages to the Present*, Oxford: Basil Blackwell.

Murphy, R. (2004) 'Turning Peasants into Modern Chinese Citizens: "Population Quality" Discourse, Demographic Transition and Primary Education', *The China Quarterly*, 177: 1–20.

Qiong'an (1948) 'Guangzhou Qingdiao' (The Feel of Guangzhou). *Lüxing Zazhi* (China Traveller), 22 (8): 24–5.

Ren Baizun (ed) (1999) *Zhongguo Shijing* (China's Classic of Eating), Shanghai: Shanghai Wenhua Chubanshe.

Rosen, S. (2004) 'The State of Youth/Youth and the State in Early 21st-century China: The Triumph of the Urban Rich?', in P. H. Gries and S. Rosen (eds), *State and Society in 21st-century China: Crisis, Contention, and Legitimation*, New York and London: RoutledgeCurzon.

Shangguan Qiuqing (1998) 'Guangzhou Waidicai Hui Wan Xin Yisi' (Enjoy New Experiences with Regional Cuisine in Guangzhou), *Xin Kuaibao* (New Express), 4 April.

Shi Peilin (1997) 'Guangzhou Shisi Gaobie Gangchu' (Guangzhou Restaurants Bid Farewell to Hong Kong Chefs), in *Yangcheng Wanbao* (Yangcheng Evening News), 29 July.

Shi Peilin and Hu Xianying (1997) 'Pafang: Yang Zai Shengui Ren Wei Shi' (Steak-Houses: Hidden Away Where People Cannot Learn About Them), *Yangcheng Wanbao* (Yangcheng Evening News), 15 July.

Shi Peilin and Li Yunxian (1997) 'Kafeiwu, Hezhi Yin Kafei' (Coffeehouses, More Than Just Coffee), *Yangcheng Wanbao* (Yangcheng Evening News), 22 July.

Tam, S. M. (1997) 'Eating Metropolitaneity: Hong Kong Identity in *Yumcha*', *The Australian Journal of Anthropology* 8 (3): 291–306.

Tang Zi (1997) 'Zhe Ban Jingyin You Ru Siwen' (Drinking Competitions Are a Disgrace to Gentility), *Guangzhou Ribao* (Guangzhou Daily), 13 June.

Wang Xuetai (1993) *Huaxia Yinshi Wenhua* (China's Culinary Culture), Beijing: Zhonghua Shuju.

Watson, J. L. (ed.) (1997) *Golden Arches East: McDonald's in East Asia*, Stanford: Stanford University Press.

Wu Xiaopan (1997) 'Kuaicandian Jingying Zhongshi Chashi' (Fast Food Restaurants Serve Chinese-style Tea), *Yangcheng Wanbao* (Yangcheng Evening News), 31 July.

Wu Xiaopan and Liang Yanbing (1997) 'Yang Kuaican Zuo Wang Guangzhou Cheng' (Western Fast Food Flourishes in Guangzhou City), *Yangcheng Wanbao* (Yangcheng Evening News), 24 June.

Wu Zhen and Zhi Liang (1997) 'Guangzhou De "Chaba"' (Guangzhou's "Tea Bars"), *Yangcheng Wanbao* (Yangcheng Evening News), 7 August.

Xiao Yu (1997) 'Zhenzhuo Dian Haixian' (Order Seafood Carefully and with Deliberation), *Yangcheng Wanbao* (Yangcheng Evening News), 8 July.

Yan Yunxiang (1995) 'Beijing De Kuaican Re Ji Qi Dui Chuantong Yinshi Wenhua De Yingxiang' (The Rise of Fast Food and Its Impact on Local Dietary Culture in Beijing), in Lin Qinghu (ed.) *Di Si Jie Zhongguo Yinshi Wenhua Xueshu Yantaohui* (The Fourth Symposium on Chinese Dietary Culture), Taipei: Foundation of Chinese Dietary Culture.

Zhang Hongsheng (1997) 'Hua Dian Xinsi Dian Jia Yao' (Put Some Effort into It and Order Exquisite Dishes), *Guangzhou Ribao* (Guangzhou Daily), 18 August.

Zhao Yuezhi (1998) *Media, Market, and Democracy in China: Between the Party Line and the Bottom Line*, Urbana and Chicago: University of Illinois Press.

Zhou Daming (1992) 'Zhujiang Sanjiaozhou Wailai Laodong Renkou Yanjiu' (A Study of the Labour Migrant Population in the Pearl River Delta), *Shehuixue Yanjiu* (Sociology Research) 5: 71–9.

Zhou Fangping and Gu Xiaofang (1997) 'Guangzhouren Xiang Chi Yueshi Kuaican?' (Do the Guangzhounese Want to Eat Cantonese-style Fast Food?), *Yangcheng Wanbao* (Yangcheng Evening News), 13 July.

7 On (not) eating the dead

A reader's digest of a 'Chinese' funerary taboo

Stuart Thompson

Re(con)sumption after last (w)rites

Consuming China – the title of this book – involves and invokes a deliberate ambivalence: is the gerund to be read in an active or in a passive sense? Ambivalence over consumption is a central motif of this chapter. 'Consumption' is itself a term which can be 'consumed' in a variety of ways that are neither necessarily consistent nor commensurable. The concept of the consumer has 'assumed centre-stage in academic debates' (Gabriel and Lang 1995: 1) in Western economics and social sciences. Daniel Miller 'contends that the study of consumption and commodities represents a major transformation in the discipline of anthropology' (1995: 141). It seems indisputable that the rate of acquisition of consumer goods in China has, in the last two decades, been increasing impressively as China has incorporated itself into the global economy. None the less, 'consumption and consumerism' are suspect heuristic devices if transplanted unreflectively into culturally Chinese contexts. There is a definite risk of trying *to nourish a bird with what would nourish you instead of what would nourish a bird,*[1] of imposing insufficiently critiqued Western folk models onto Chinese practices. The trick (and paradox) is to recognize differences without insinuating that 'Chinese' consuming practices constitute a creature that is radically and inexorably Other. Rather than reduce so-called Chinese consumption to its supposed inert and essential characteristics, the analyst needs to be alert to the complex and perhaps volatile congeries of similarities and differences, continuities and disjunctions, and the varied vantage points of differently-situated social categories, that are a concomitant of consuming practices across time and space (irrespective of whether our referent is 'Chinese' or not). My way of tackling (or is it obviating?) this fraught issue is to eschew 'one sweep of the knife' (*yi qie dao*) typologism (caricaturing?) in favour of a more detailed examination of a specific notion of consuming embroiled in the funerary ritual practices I witnessed in the west of Taiwan. Before undertaking that task, I will venture some sketched contextualization.

A comprehensive delineation and understanding of the place of consumption in contemporary Taiwan is well beyond the scope of this chapter.

Account should be taken of globalized and trans-national developments, but it would be analytically misconceived to presume that consuming has an essential, in-built, and universally convergent character to it, unfurling in a preordained fashion over time. Localized consuming practices in contemporary Taiwan (as anywhere else in the world) are best thought of as the moving resultant of historico-cultural factors in conjunction with the localizing strategies of people trying to get by in changing politico-economic situations. We can conceptualize that elements of an historico-cultural legacy, to some extent, inscribe or (w)rite the practices of everyday life in the present, but also expect that, to some extent, subjects are not fully subjected to the cultural logic, but can 'consume' history or culture tactically, in ways of their own choosing, and in accordance with their perceived needs (cf. de Certeau 1984).

I would venture that there has been a cultural imaginary propagated actively by China's literati-elite in the past as a sort of ideal-typification of a social order premised on a neo-Confucian notion of 'happy families'. Implicit in the Chinese language itself is an idea that each person is a consumer, in the sense of a 'mouth to be fed' (*kou* is the measure-word for a 'member' of a family, and *renkou* – literally 'people mouths' – is the word for 'population') rather than being portrayed metonymically as a producer, as, say, a 'work-*hand*'. In Imperial China, it was a function of the neo-Confucian orthodoxy that the literati-officials had, in theory, a moral responsibility to ensure that the population was adequately fed, and, in line with this cultural logic, commerce was viewed, again in theory rather than in practice, as parasitic consumption. There was varying awareness of a cultural imagination of the peasant family as a veritable symbiosis of 'man' and land, with family members sharing the labour of production and entitlement to consume the fruits of that labour. In the packaged co-identity of land and *jia* (family), production and consumption were seen as co-implicated: the family produced and consumed (the produce of) the land, whilst the land produced and consumed the family.[2] This imagination of a symbiotic harmony between family and land, and of a self-sufficient and mutually-striving family, propounded an ideal which influenced but misrepresented the life-situations of families. It served to license both patrilineality and patriarchy: men who joined the family through uxorilocal marriage were regarded as parasitical consumers (cuckoos in the nest), whilst women were only grudgingly entitled as consumers, since they were not conceived of as fulcrum family members.

In her combative book, *China's Motor*, Hill Gates has argued that 'Chinese people have lived for at least a thousand years within the reach of two different political-economic patterns that offered them different and partially contradictory possibilities and limitations' (1996: 7). One pattern, that of petty-commodity producers, was 'embedded in [the other,] a dominant tributary mode managed by state officials who put their own requirements for reliable revenues, stable class relations, and continued hegemony above any perceived need for economic expansion' (1996: 7).

These two modes of production in tension with each other generated contrary modes of, and attitudes towards, consumption, which (potentially) challenge much of the idealized, Confucian-elite imagination of the place and role of consuming in Imperial China. Consuming commodities – and the selling of one's labour to be consumed as a commodity – are not new-fangled Western imports or impositions, but have a centuries-long history in Chinese societies.

In the last fifty years, Taiwan's economic development has featured high growth rates in per capital income, and has been accompanied by remarkable levels of urbanization and purchasing of consumer goods and services. The most obvious sources of expenditure have been on housing and vehicles, but the uptake of electrical and electronic goods has been especially phenomenal. The consumption of leisure and tourist activities has increased apace, whilst the proportion of income spent on food has diminished, and the nature of what is eaten has also changed markedly away from reliance on rice. Contrary to the expectations of convergence theorists, increased consumption has not jeopardized savings rates which, in Taiwan, have remained comparatively high. Family life and relationships continue to be significant in contemporary Taiwan, though decreasingly so, in inverse proportion to the extent that individuals have been 'consumers' of education (Thornton and Lin). The boom in consumption did not, as I have suggested via Gates above, herald a turn to commodification – since commodification was already in evidence – but the move away from agricultural production has generated a significant change in household economies, strategies for their future, and the 'consumability' of family labour. Even with the preponderance of family firms in Taiwan, the reliance of the younger generation on parents for jobs and livelihood has been undermined, as the opportunities for the workforce to be 'free labourers' (free to sell their labour on the open market as opposed to being consumed domestically) have increased manifold. Family farmland is now seldom vital to a family's economy – with the partial exception of some agribusinesses – and often the family farm has become a 'failed consumer' of the family's labour-force.

If 'consumerism' differs from 'consumption' in terms of its discursivity, that is, the emergence of a systematic attitude toward, or discourse about, 'consumption', then 'consumerism' has become a feature of Taiwan's civil society. The Kuomintang (KMT) regime, at least until the 1980s, used to trumpet rates of material consumption in its 'standard of living' indexes. Consumerism in Taiwan was something to be celebrated and contrasted with the material austerity of an anti-consumerist PRC. As a means by which to win the 'hearts and minds' of its citizenry – and garnishing support for the legitimacy of the KMT's single-party governance – the consumption gambit was more successful than the double-edged effort to inveigh the KMT's version of 'Chinese culture' (see Chun 1994) and myth of an ROC nation that would 'recover the Mainland'. The latter effort was, in the end, roundly rejected by its targeted consumers, and rebounded on the KMT as the population became increasingly ready to 'consume' a proactively forged and popularized Taiwanese consciousness, and to espouse Taiwanese identity.

Attitudes towards Taiwan's consumerism have not all been positive. There seems increasingly to be a view among the chattering classes that over-consumption has resulted in resource depletion and serious environmental consequences. There have been various civil and governmental efforts to promote 'green consumption' for the betterment of the environment. Various Buddhist and 'new religious' groups try to proselytize the view that true happiness and wellbeing is to be derived from a substantial curtailing of unethical consumption, and a cessation of pandering to hedonistic desires. Others see Taiwan's inordinate consumption of 'things American' as damaging and invidious. June Yip combines these concerns when she lists the costs as: 'overcrowding, pollution, an increasingly pronounced gap between metropolitan cities and rural villages, a breakdown of traditional social relationships, and manic consumerism precipitated by a deluge of American, European, and Japanese products into the Taiwanese market' (2004: 10). Other commentators are concerned about the price of what they see as rampant consumerism on a younger, self-indulging generation for whom 'what is gratified through this perpetual consumption and search for self is the appetite for ego-worship . . . No longer are motorbikes symbols of the working-class's hard work, having instead now become the spaceships of idle youth on a voyage to self . . . no longer is work seen as an important vehicle for realization of individual self' (Chang 2002: 2).

Convergence theorists would predict that consumerism on the scale experienced and practised in Taiwan would be accompanied by a trend towards secularization. I would argue that participation in religious activities has remained ebullient, and that consumption on ritual accoutrements and ceremonies, and contributions to temples and shrines, have increased, certainly in absolute terms. There is still (spirit) money to burn for the gods, and replica consumer items – as parodied in Chi Yin's 2003 film *Hei Gou Laile* (*Comes the Black Dog*)[3] – to be conveyed to the recently deceased, as well as regular attention to their other *post mortem* quotidian needs. The feeling of the continued efficacy of death rituals and related consumption practices may be a manifestation of '[t]he enthusiastic rediscovery of Taiwan's historical past and indigenous culture – discouraged if not altogether forbidden in the days before reform' (Yip 2004: 7). There is no more crucial and poignant a time to set down markers of identity than when confronted by death. Perhaps ironically, Taiwanese villages have become sites of consumption as much as, or more than, places of agricultural production.

Zygmunt Bauman has argued that '[i]t is one thing to be poor in a society of producers and universal employment; it is quite a different thing to be poor in a society of consumers, in which life-projects are built around consumer choice' (1998: 1), and if we think of what he terms the 'plight of the flawed consumer' (1998: 1) in relation to the dead who are not fed, to the unsupported, non-consuming dead (pitiable as *gui*, ghosts), then the continued obligatory and identificatory appeal of ensuring the material well-being of one's ancestors makes a heightened sense. Baudrillard writes about 'the extradition of the dead' (1993: 125) in modern society, claiming that 'little by little, *the dead cease to exist*. They are thrown out of the group's symbolic circulation' (1993: 126). That symbolic exchange with the dead seems alive and well in Taiwan would seem to indicate that Taiwan does not fit Baudrillard's unduly reductionist simulation of what constitutes a 'modern society'.

My way of proceeding in this chapter involves what might be styled a re(con)sumption of a seminar paper initially presented more than two decades ago (Thompson 1982). Following Appadurai's lead, my text could be thought of as having (had) a biography, a 'social life' with changing signification, as it accrued and lost value till discarded as a dead letter, separated from the processes of social exchange (until now). I present a mostly verbatim version of the earlier text, though somewhat abbreviated, leaving in my theoretical posturing, 'warts and all'. Through this disinterment and anachronistic reinsertion back into a changed 'market in theory' (Fardon 1991: 2) – as the appetite of the interpretive community of anthropology has shifted – I am conscious (or hopeful) that 'there are no limits to the dialogic context . . . Nothing is absolutely dead: every meaning will have its homecoming festival' (Bakhtin 1986: 170).

In QingHan (Wild Clam) village, and the surrounding area of west-coast Taiwan, there is a consensus that when someone dies his or her descendants should refrain from consuming pork. Villagers assert that eating pork at such a time would be like eating the flesh of the dead person. Eating pig-flesh is construed as being equivalent to eating the flesh of the deceased.

Informants' interpretations

The assertion that it is wrong to eat pork when one's parent or other direct ascendant has died is not one which I have found referred to in any anthropological work on Taiwan or China, nor in any books written about Taiwan's customs and folklore published in Chinese. The notion is not, however, just specific to QingHan village, for the same abstinence was prevalent in several other villages where I observed funerals.

Informants' formulations of the notion that it is wrong to eat pork after the death of an ascendant sometimes varied in terms of detail. However, all informants whom I questioned on this matter at the very least emphasized that pig-meat should not be eaten. Most informants agreed on the duration of the pork abstinence, stating that the restriction applies from time of death until time of burial. The descendants can eat meat again on their return from the corpse's interment.

Informants are in agreement as to whom the abstinence should apply. When someone dies then all those in his/her family who are junior in generation to the deceased should refrain from eating pork. An unmarried daughter is subject to the prohibition, but a daughter who has married out is not, for she belongs to her husband's family, not her natal family. Wives of sons and grandsons are also encompassed by the restriction.

To my question "why should descendants not eat pigmeat?", villagers gave different answers. Some replies were unreflective. Other replies were more discursive. The fact that informants did offer me various interpretations of the need for pork abstinence testifies to at least a minimal interest in exegesis. But, for villagers, questions about the performing of ritual loom larger than those about its meaning. 'What is clear and explicit about ritual is how to do it – rather than its meaning . . . The ruling is explicit but its meaning may be implicit' (Lewis 1980: 19). The rules that prohibit the eating of pork, to use Gilbert Lewis's appraisal of food taboos, 'may touch the person to whom they apply so as to bind him to awareness of an aspect of his identity . . . What gives such rules their power is the knowledge that others may eat the food and do so, but not me because I am who I am now . . . Restriction derives its force from its contraries, permission and possibility' (1980: 146–7).

My informants do offer some interpretations for the pork prohibition, though many did not venture beyond attributing the taboo to 'custom' or 'tradition'. By and large, three different types of interpretation were offered.

1. One commonly cited interpretation linked the custom of pork abstinence to Buddhism, specifically the moral injunction against killing animals and the concomitant merit of vegetarianism. Since eating meat can be construed as morally wrong, to abstain, even if only temporarily, from meat-eating is an act of moral rectitude. The injunction could be seen as an attempt by descendants to build up merit for the deceased, though no informant explicitly posited a direct connection between abstaining from eating pork and the building up of merit for the deceased ascendant.
2. A second interpretation often given emphasized that the death of a relative is obviously a very sad time, and so it is only right and proper that one should curtail one's activities and deliberately refrain from enjoyments. Accordingly, for mourners, there are a number of 'forms of abstinence implying renunciation of comfort and ease' (de Groot 1969, vol. 2: 504). Thus mourners should refrain from certain life-renewing activities such as participating in festivities, drinking alcohol, dressing in bright or new clothes, shaving or cutting one's hair, and the like. This interpretation would see meat-eating as enjoyment, and, by extending the logic, to eat the meat of meats, pork, would be the height of enjoyment at what should be a sad time.
3. A third, and the most frequently expressed, interpretation given by informants suggested that it is filial not to eat meat on the death of an ascendant, or, stating it another way, eating pig-meat would be an unfilial act. The filio-parental relationship is the kernel of Chinese rela-

> tionships, and the concept of filial obedience (*hau-sun*) pervades Chinese society at all levels. Informants did feel that there was a strong connection with the idea of filial obedience, though they were unable to formulate the nature of the linkage. De Groot, in his own inimitable style, concurs with the importance of filial obedience in the mourning process. He notes that devout self-starvation is recommended in the ancient Book of Rites, and he states that 'the observance of (fasting) . . . was imperiously demanded by filial piety . . . which . . . claimed just as much sacrificial devotion for defunct as for living parents' (1969, vol. 2: 647). Further, de Groot notes, in Imperial China the zenith of filial behaviour was the cutting of flesh from one's own body to give to one's ailing parent in the hope of effecting a cure (see de Groot 1969, vol. 4: 386–7). Certainly, if eating pig-meat is construed as equivalent to eating the flesh of a deceased ascendant, then it would be the grossest act of unfilial behaviour imaginable, and could not be in more marked contrast to the epitome of filial behaviour just described.

Often the response to my question as to why descendants refrain from eating pork brought a reply such as *ciaq ti-baq si kap ciaq si-lang e baq kang-kuan* (or *siang-kuan*); that is, 'eating pork is like (or the same as) eating the dead person's flesh'. When I asked villagers directly if they could explain why these two acts of eating are said to be similar, my informants either admitted ignorance, or ascribed the likeness to time-honoured custom, or gave one of the three interpretations which I have reported as answers to my first question – that is, due to Buddhist influence, being a sad time, or filial piety. Only a very few informants even attempted to unpack the similitude any further. The most interesting informant-suggested interpretation relates the restriction on eating pork to a myth about a time when men had yellow tails and endonecrophagy was the norm.

The 'yellow tails' interpretation

This informant-suggested interpretation relates the similitude of eating pork and the deceased's flesh to the yellow tails myth. The accounts of this myth are similar to those Emily Ahern reports (1973: 205f) from Ch'inan in the north of Taiwan. Qing Han villagers have no contact with the Ch'inan area. Though I have searched extensively in published materials I have found no other references to this myth.

When I asked why descendants should refrain from eating pork at funerals, this first version of the myth was related to me by a 50-year-old widow, said to have an extensive knowledge of customs:

> This story that I heard is passed down from the old days. In the old days when people died they used to leave their flesh for their children to eat. So children would eat the flesh of their parents when they died. Then once there was a man who knew he was dying, but he didn't want to let

> his children eat his flesh, so he climbed to the rooftop and died there without his family knowing. . . . Because they didn't find him, he rotted up on the rooftop, and the worms ate his flesh. Eventually his family did find him, and they buried him. They didn't eat his flesh. They cried and they buried him. And so from that time onwards people wouldn't eat meat, because it would be like eating the dead person's flesh.

The second version was given by an elderly man who helps professionally at funerals:

> In the old days men used to have yellow tails. When they were about to die, the children used to kill them to eat their flesh. Once there was a man who didn't want his children to eat his flesh, so he hid in a store where there was a lot of wood and hay piled up. So the children couldn't find him. When, at last, they did find him, his flesh was already so rotted that they couldn't eat it, so they cried. So that's why people cry nowadays when their parents die.

My raconteur said that the story explains why people do not eat pork at funerals.

When I asked specifically if he knew the 'yellow tails' story, another of my more knowledgeable informants, a man in his sixties, gave this account:

> In earlier days men used to have tails, and when the tail went yellow it meant they were about to die. It used to be that the descendants would eat their flesh once they died. But one time a man hid and his flesh rotted and the descendants couldn't eat it, so they buried him.
>
> Tudi Gong [the local earth god] tricked them, saying that after seven days they could dig him up again to eat him, but when they did, the flesh had rotted and gone smelly. And from then onwards it's always been that they've always buried parents, and cried, and not eaten them. Nowadays we don't eat meat till a dead parent has been buried, to show filial piety. For to eat meat would be like eating the dead person's flesh. And because children no longer eat the flesh of their dead parents, they now don't eat meat [when mourning] to show their filial piety.

Another informant, a widow in her forties, gave me a truncated version of the myths related above, but then, without prompting, told this version in which there is an inversion of the generations:

> There were two men who were very good friends. One went to visit the other who was very poor. So the host had nothing with which to treat his friend. So he wanted to kill one of his children to treat his friend. The child heard about it and went to hide. He died and his flesh rotted. And so, when the father eventually did find him because of the smell, he could not eat the son. So the father cried, because he couldn't bear the remorse. And so, from then onwards people said that one shouldn't eat

> people's flesh. From then on people were buried after they died, and they [descendants] cried. The meaning is that now you bury everybody.

What are we to make of these myths? As I see it, if we discount any suggestion that the myth refers to an actual historical past, there are three ways in which we might interpret the stories. Myth is a form of speculation, and, in a sense, we can only speculate as to how to interpret it.

One plausible interpretation is the view that such a story represents a horribilized, barbaric past, an extreme and repugnant Other, against which we, in the here and now, can compare ourselves. This is the sort of interpretation that Arens favours in his book *The Man-eating Myth.* He would see such myths as 'an aspect of cultural-boundary construction and maintenance' (1979: 145). Groups 'often cherish a myth about an obscure "once-upon-a-time" past, which includes an account of eating human flesh. These stories pinpoint the emergence of their culture from a pre-civilized stage by recounting the deletion of human flesh from the food category' (1979: 146). There does indeed seem to be an aspect of seeing oneself more clearly by reference to what one is not in the yellow tails story, and one villager did, in fact, give an interpretation somewhat along these lines. The myths, in this view, portray an earlier age when children treated parents with the absolute opposite of filial piety – remembering that a child's cutting off his own flesh is seen as the pinnacle of filial piety.

It is a measure of the speculative openness of myth – is it? – that we can posit other interpretations as plausible. Instead of the myth representing a horribilized version of the past, it can be looked upon as representing the ideal order of society, ideal but unattainable. In the myth the children eat the flesh of their father and thus incorporate into themselves and their generation the vital substance of their father. The sons' eating of their dead father can be construed as a mythical representation of the ideal: patrilineal descent in its pure, ideal, ideological form.

A third way of looking at the yellow tails myths is to see them as expressing the deeply-felt ambivalence and tension that exists in the filio–parental relationship. In Chinese society, mutual dependence and support between father and son is constantly affirmed as the desired state of affairs. As Eberhard has written, 'the love between father and son is a predominant ethical precept, so much so that even a hint of difficulties in the relation between father and son would be regarded as improper' (1967: 77). But in reality there are difficulties, strains and potential proclivities in the relationship. The yellow tails story can be seen as illustrative and evocative of the ambivalence in the relationship. The sons want to eat the father's flesh – and, in one account, the father wants to eat his son – but, at the same time, the sons cry when they bury the father.

We ought, perhaps, to examine the bundle of meanings carried by the Hokkien work *ciaq*, which I have translated as 'eat'. In some usages the sense conveyed by *ciaq* is one of aggression. Thus *ciaq* can mean to annihilate, as in the sense of one army 'eating' another, a sense carried over into the game of chess, where one piece 'eats' another. To 'eat' a prostitute connotes using her for sex. To 'eat' people can mean to cheat them – as in the term of abuse '(you) eat people, cannot eat enough', recorded by Eberhard (1971: 322). But *ciaq* does not always carry with it this aspect of aggressive consumption. The term *ciaq thau-ke*, which literally seems to mean 'to eat the boss', actually connotes 'eating on the boss' (i.e. the boss includes food with the wages) (Bodman 1955: 126). Similarly, '*ciaq* the god X' means to 'eat food through the grace of the god X', as in *ciaq Sien Kong,* which means 'eating (by courtesy of) Sien Kong' (Feuchtwang 1974: 174). So *ciaq* has various non-aggressive meanings such as 'live off', or 'eat on', or 'eat by courtesy of'. *Ciaq* is also used in the sense of absorbing or assimilating – blotting paper, for instance, 'eats' ink. The point I want to make is that the term *ciaq* has no single specifiable meaning which holds constant in all contexts. Its meaning wavers according to context, and it is not always easy to determine which sense is implied.

If a baby is born with teeth, or an old man should grow teeth, it is thought inauspicious, and villagers say that the child will 'eat' his parents, or the old man will 'eat' his children. Apparently here *ciaq* is used in the sense of 'eating up the wealth and resources of', or, at least, that is what my informants seemed to surmise. But if we take the statement in its own right we would be perplexed as to which sense of 'eat' should be applicable. In the yellow tails myth there is an indeterminacy as to which sense or senses the word *ciaq* signifies. I intend to examine the latter two interpretations of the yellow tails story at some length. The two differing interpretations hinge, partly, on different interpretations of the meaning of the word *ciaq* as used in the myth. One interpretation supposes *ciaq* to have aggressive connotations; the other presumes more a sense of absorption or assimilation.

Jonathan Culler, in his discussion of Jacques Derrida's two interpretations of interpretation, writes cogently that 'one cannot simply or effectively choose to make meaning either the original meaning of an author or the creative experience of the reader . . . whatever the theorist's choice, the theory seems to present a divided meaning or interpretation – divided, for example, between meaning as a property of a text and meaning as the experience of the reader'(1983: 132). So far, I have tried to interpret on the basis of the text, by which I mean the statements given me by my informants. Not that these statements were somehow spontaneously given, for the particular types of questions that I asked obviously influenced the answers given, so that the text was grafted, as it were, jointly by my questions and their answers, and the dialectic between the two. In a sense I am both co-author and reader of the text. As a reader I am influenced by my experience of what other anthropologists write about. And, as a reader so influenced, I may 'read meaning into what . . . (I) see (where it does not belong)' (Lewis 1980: 18). But, having pushed the logic of my informants' interpretations as far as I feel I can – indeed, perhaps further than the 'text' justifies – and still feeling that there is more to the situation than my informants (explicitly) realize, a 'reading' of the text for further interpreting is ventured.

The 'filio–parental ambivalence' interpretation

Many villagers, as I have said, posited a connection between pork abstinence and filial behaviour: a case, perhaps, of abstinence makes the heart grow fonder. Meyer Fortes views West African ancestor worship as 'in essence the ritualisation of filial piety' (1959: 18), sanctioning the transfer of authority in a patrilineal system from dead father to living son. The ritualization is, however, ambivalent and latent with disrupting potential, for '[i]n their ancestor worship Tallensi make clear to themselves the fact that, though parents depart, the authority and jurisdiction they wielded . . . still goes on' (1965: 139). His interpretation stems from a Freudian perspective. Sons, since they replace their father when the latter dies, feel self-guilt, albeit subconsciously, for they seem to gain from the father's death, and, in a way, live off the death of their parents. The rites of ancestor worship, which involve the feeding and tending of the dead antecedent, serve to assuage the conscience of the living. Just as the parent was responsible for feeding his son as an infant, so, now, the son in turn is responsible for feeding his defunct parent, an *infant* in a different sense.

Ahern, in an ingeniously constructed interpretation, also focuses on the filio–parental relationship, though she posits an emphasis somewhat different from that of Fortes's formulation. In Ch'inan village most sons gain through acquiring property or jural authority when their fathers die, though parts of either or both may have been transferred prior to the father's death. Ahern makes the bold suggestion that the flesh of the deceased may stand for those aspects of the father's authority which transfer to his sons on death. In the Taiwanese system of burial the flesh of the deceased is allowed to rot, whereupon the bones must by exhumed for secondary burial. In Ahern's view 'the relinquishment of flesh may correspond to the deceased's abdication of some of his earthly powers'(1973: 205). The flesh must be allowed to decay naturally, without the active intervention of descendants. 'In no case can the descendants scrape off the remaining flesh . . . because "cutting off the flesh would be just like killing the ancestor"' (1973: 205). The deceased must yield his flesh – his earthly power – voluntarily. The descendants must not seem to wish to wrest authority from their father. I would suggest that pork abstinence practised by the heirs of the deceased (a practice that Ahern does not record) can be given a meaning which fits into this complex. By the symbolic act of deliberately refraining from eating pork flesh – which in Qing Han is explicitly associated with the deceased's flesh – the descendants indicate that it is not their wish to wrest authority from their father, and by this formal act they deny the implication, or even the self-guilt, that they desired the hastening of their father's death so as to acquire his earthly power. By not eating pig-meat they express, formally, their filial piety. All of this also seems to fit well with Fortes's formulation that self-guilt felt as a result of gains made at a father's death is culturally assuaged in the processes of ancestor worship.

However, there is a twist in the yellow tail. Flesh is allowed to putrefy, but bones are exhumed, placed in a ceramic pot, and preserved. In Ahern's view, bones represent the perduring authority of the ancestors that the living cannot escape, exemplified by the necessity incumbent on the living to assume the burden of caring for and feeding the ancestors. The myth represents, Ahern suggests, the deeply-rooted, indigenous view of ancestor worship. In her versions of the story, descendants want to kill and eat their ascendants, but in all but one version they are thwarted from so doing. The descendants want to consume aggressively, to annihilate their elders and the control that their elders have over them even in death. The descendants want to eat the flesh of the ascendant, which is directly contrary to the culturally-projected image of caring for and sustaining the ancestors. But the descendants fail, they are unable to eat the elder, and so cannot escape the permanent authority of the ancestors. It is Ahern's view that, contrary to Fortes's formulation, 'the story reveals not people's guilt, but people's regret at their inability to wrest all control from the dead'(1973: 213). She concludes her monograph with the assertion that the yellow tails myth 'is in many ways the most important part of this study' (1973: 266).

Ahern sees the symbolism of eating the elders in the myth as reflective of the desire of the living to seize, consume, and escape the authority of their dead antecedents, an authority rooted in 'the cumulative weight of that authority (exercised in childhood) extended over a lifetime'(1973: 219). There is, I believe, an alternative interpretation, linking the myth to patrilineal ideology, an ideology prevalent throughout Chinese society.

The 'retention of kinship substance' interpretation

While Ahern interprets 'eating' in the myth as an aggressive act, a metaphor for the annihilation of ancestors, I think that we can, alternatively, interpret 'eating' in the sense of assimilation, of absorption, as a metaphor expressing the retention of kinship substance. I will argue that we can view bones and rice as agnatic substances, whereas flesh and pork are construable as anti-descent substances. To start with, I want to establish that rice and pork are the key Chinese foods, and that the symbolism of eating rice is radically counterposed to the symbolic implications of eating pork.

A fundamental dichotomy characterizes Chinese ethnohoptology. There is rice (or other substitute staple); and there is *chhai* (the vegetable and/or meat dishes). Of the two, rice is very much the primary, the key, element. *Rice is the core, the marked element of a meal. A family is the unit attached to a rice pot (Jordan 1972: 118). The daily reiterated act of sharing rice sustains and nourishes the family both literally and metaphorically.*[4]

Pork is very much the favourite *chhai* of the southern Chinese. It seems very much to be 'substance given'. It is the most significant food exchanged with other families. It is the ultimate prestation conferred on wife-givers in marriage exchanges. At a parent's funeral, daughters who have married out must each offer a pig's head and tail to the deceased. Pork is also *the* Chinese festive food. Feasts are times when interaction between families is paramount. At a meal (*ciaq png*), rice is the core element; at a feast (*ciaq douq*), *chhai*, and particularly pork, becomes the core element – rice may not even be provided. The usual rice–*chhai* dichotomy is reversed. Pork, prototypically the food for exchange, comes to the fore.

There is a clear tendency for rice to be retained within the family for, *like males in the patriline, it is not a substance for exchange. In the sense that rice is a product of the land worked by and inherited from ancestors, land which, ideally, should be inalienable to non-agnates, rice can be identified as stuff of the ancestors. And, as ancestral stuff, its retention within the family and descent line makes sense. Bones, as agnatic matter, are similarly retained, for they are exhumed and repotted for preservation. Bones are also explicitly associated by villagers with semen.* As agnatic stuff, then, rice, like ancestral land, like semen, like ancestors' bones, and like living male agnates, should be retained, should be hoarded within the family, and should be transmitted only along the descent line.

*At a funeral the transmission from deceased to his/her descendants is symbolized in terms of apportioning rice. If the deceased dies after the third meal on the day of death, then a special rite called 'begging rice' (*to png*) is performed. A* tau *measure of rice is divided, two parts (two meals) for the living, and one part (one meal) for the deceased.* One might infer that the deceased was hoarding his agnatic substance, and not allowing it to be transmitted along the patriline to the descendants. Also at funerals, a *tau* measure of rice, wrapped in a cloth bag, is set on top of the coffin. This rice is to be eaten by the sons of the deceased, and the sons' wives and families – the very people prohibited from eating pork. Eating this rice is said to ensure that the family will always have plenty to eat, and will be blessed with peace and prosperity.

The tau *plays a very central role in funerary ritual. We can learn a great deal about what mortuary rituals express by unpacking the symbolism associated with it. The* tau *refers both to the traditional standard measure for rice (approx. one decalitre), and to a circular wooden tub which can hold a* tau *of rice. A* tau *containing a temporary ancestral tablet for the deceased is carried by a son, or preferably a senior grandson, of the deceased at the head of the funeral procession to the grave site. If the deceased died without heirs, then whoever is charged with carrying the* tau *to the grave becomes his posthumous heir.*

If we look at what the *tau* tub contains in the course of mortuary ritual then some intriguing juxtapositions become exposed. The *tau* tub is a container very much associated with rice. In the mortuary rites, a *tau* measure of rice is placed in a cloth wrap on top of the coffin, and, in its place in the *tau* tub are put articles representing the deceased, most importantly the temporary ancestral tablet. Also put in the *tau* tub for carriage to the grave are grain seeds (the 'five grains'), coins and nails. The seeds signify fertility of crops, the coins wealth, and the nails (by means of a pun) male offspring. These items are distributed to the mourners at the grave. At the funeral of my landlord's brother, which took place in Chia-yi city, I saw the son of the deceased pull a nail from the coffin with his teeth and then deposit it into the *tau* tub. The nail was said to represent future male descendants.

My reading of this series of items contained in the *tau* is that rice and the deceased-as-ancestor-tablet are interchangeable, both being aspects of agnatic substance. Further, the death has been transformed into regeneration, releasing a potentiality for fertility from which the descendants gain. The individual degeneration of death is compensated for by the fertility of crops (symbolized by the five grains) and the fertility of the descent line (symbolized by the nails). Pulling a nail (representative of male descendants) out of a coffin of a deceased ascendant is a remarkable ritual expression of death being transformed into a source of fertility. The death of the ascendant is represented as promoting the fertility of those who survive.

We can push such an interpretation still further. Given that the bag of rice on the coffin, and an aspect of the deceased, are equatable, then it follows that the descendants by consuming the rice, an agnatic substance, are metaphorically indulging in endonecrophagy. *The resonances become still more 'sinister' if we further consider that the word* tau *'is used by some people in the binome* kim-tao *(golden* tao*) both for the urn into which the bones of a dead person are put for reburial and for the red bag into which traditionally women gave birth or, in slang, for female genitals themselves' (Feuchtwang 1974. 314). A* tau *in this broadened terminology can then be a container for semen, for rice, for an ancestral tablet, for reburied ancestral bones, and for a new-born baby – each of which can be construed as aspects of agnatic substance. Semen, rice, bones, offspring can again be seen as co-associated, and, also, as elements in the cycles of agnation spiralling through time. Semen, agnatic substance, creates offspring, agnates, who are sustained through life by consuming rice, another agnatic substance. At death an agnate becomes ancestor, preserved as bones and ancestral tablet, but for descendants the death of an ascendant releases life-forces, fertility, of which semen is a facet, thereby closing one cycle and generating another. Agnatic substance is retained, at least metaphorically, within the descent line.* The eating of the *tau* of rice, then, represents not only the retention of kinship substance, but also the retention of fertility derived from the deceased. The ritual expresses the ideal of reproduction by descent alone (see Bloch 1985). The transfer of rice does not just narrowly symbolize the transfer of property, but, more than that, the transfer of agnatic substance and the potentiality for growth and fertility.

Reproductive capacity is not squandered, for, by symbolically eating the deceased-as-rice, it is retained within the descent line.

In their volume *Death and the Regeneration of Life* (1982), Bloch and Parry develop an argument about how particular, idealized assertions of social structure are created through the communications of mortuary ritual. 'Mortuary rituals (are) one of the most important occasions for asserting (an) eternal order' (1982: 15), there being a 'fabrication of an ideal order out of the transformed remains of the dead' (1982: 36). This ideal social order is, in large measure, created by refuting those aspects of the empirical, practical world which are antithetical to the transcendent, eternal, ideal version of social order being asserted. By this 'socio-logic', descendants, by eating the deceased-as-rice, absorb the agnatic stuff of the deceased, thereby conforming to the ritual conception of the ideal social order as reproduction entirely contained within the eternal line of descent.

By contrast, the deceased-as-pig-meat is prohibited food. Those descendants of the deceased who are supposed to eat the *tau* of rice are the very people also subject to the pork abstinence. For them to eat pigmeat rather than rice would be to emphasize aspects of the dialectic of life in the empirical world of interaction which, from the viewpoint of the patrilineal ideology promoted in the ritual, are unsavoury, contradictory, and, indeed, threatening.

The mortuary ritual in trying to create an ideal, eternal social order, premised on reproduction by descent alone, must deny this world of pork, affinity, women and exchange. The sexuality and fertility of women is anathema to the fertility generated within the descent line itself. In the mortuary ritual, reproduction through women is denied, and reproduction by descent alone is given emphatic expression. Women are outsiders who come as virtual intruders into the line of descent, and as boundary crossers their position is paradoxical. They have the capacity to provide sons for the family, but they are depicted as "pillow ghosts" responsible for turning brother against brother, thus splintering the family group so that it cannot be perpetuated through time. Women's reproductive capacity is shrouded by notions of pollution. In mortuary ritual women's reproductive capacity is displayed in a negative light, is refuted, while self-regeneration within the agnatic line, the fertility transmitted from deceased agnates, is stressed.

Bones endure, and through secondary burial are deliberately preserved. They are representations of the family's continuation through time, of the descent line perpetuated. Bones are agnatic substance. Flesh, on the other hand, is ephemeral. It decays and decomposes on death, and is deliberately – though not actively – discarded. Flesh is said to be inherited from one's mother, and thereby derives from outside the agnatic line. Flesh is closely associated with women, and with affinity. It is not of enduring importance, just as affinal relationships, which start to wither after the death of the woman exchanged. Flesh, like affinal relationships, is allowed to decay after death. Bones and agnates are the core, the permanent units of society as ideally construed; flesh and affines are of only ephemeral significance, are not everlasting.

Bloch and Parry reckon that 'the dominant ideological representation is created out of its contrary' (1982: 18), and, in the Taiwanese case, we can see pork bearing, with a broad back, the burden of several key antithetical elements, aspects of the dialectic of life which have to be refuted for the ideology to be upheld. Eating pork at a funeral seems to be anti-descent, for the descendant would be stressing exchange instead of retention, affinity rather than agnation, flesh and decomposition rather than bones and the continuity of the descent group, transformation rather than unchangeability, and so on. The symbolic implications of eating pork at a funeral, then, are diametrically opposite to the symbolism implied by eating the *tau* of rice.

The symbolic representation of pure patrilineal descent given phenomenological expression in funerary ritual is also mooted in the yellow tails myth. The myth has essentially a binary structure. In the first part a distant past is depicted in which children, as a matter of course, eat their ascendants. By contrast, in the second part of the myth, descendants bury the dead – as is the case nowadays. I interpret the first part of the myth as positing a time of pure, idealized descent, while the second part depicts the present-day situation, a compromise that has had to be effected for the ideal has to confront pragmatic reality, the everyday processes of life.

The endonecrophagy described in the myth seems to echo the symbolic endonecrophagy given expression in the funerary rites. Children's cannibalism of their elders is not depicted as a heinous act, nor even in a negative light in the myth. Nor is murder necessarily a prelude to eating the elder, for in two of the Qing Han versions no mention is made of killing the elder, and in the first version I was told that 'when people died they used to leave their flesh for their children to eat'. My reading of the first part of the myth sees eating more as ingestion or absorption than as aggression. Endonecrophagy can be viewed as a supreme representation of pure patrilineal descent, self-encapsulated and self-reproducing from one generation to the next without the absorption of alien, non-patrilineal substances, or the dissipation of agnatic substance/fertility. Children by the act of eating their dead parent do two things: they prevent the corpse from putrefying; and they incorporate, they ingest, good kinship substances which are thereby transmitted from one generation to the next. Reproduction is by descent alone, without need of women, affines or exchange. Individual death is merged into cyclical time as death, through endonecrophagy, immediately becomes regenerated as new life. In this mythologized enactment of patrilineal descent in idealized form, unshackled by empirical reality, the living act merely as trustees or caretakers of the position till the next generation takes over. They 'should be nothing else but continuators of the ancestors, the present incarnation of the continuing entity' (Bloch 1982: 211).

Resonances and consuming (on) good authority

From today's perspective (2005) I feel that a number of features of my presentation no longer stimulate a contemporary disciplinary appetite in quite the same way as they did when first written. Though informants' views were solicited and briefly reiterated early in the piece, those voices have been superseded by a markedly structuralist analysis which aims to 'go beyond' informant testimony. There is an ambivalence as to which 'interpretation' of the pork taboo is the more persuasive, but the way ritual is 'read' (as an ideological instrument of social control) is too uni-dimensional. There are further problems in my ethnographic consumption of the material which I will address in this chapter's final section. But there is one particular paradox, and one blatant omission, which I will mention first. The paradox is that old (and perhaps weary) chestnut of the extent to which a cultural analysis can legitimately manufacture an interpretive model which bypasses the imaginary of interlocutors. The blatant omission is my failure to contemplate counter-perspectives for how women (or others lacking recognized power and authority) might experience or understand the death rites. The Bloch and Parry approach on which I drew assumes that actors are 'consumed' and dominated by the ideological moment of the rites, and denies space for alternative modes of consumption or for what de Certeau (1984: xii) refers to as 'poaching' meaning.[5] I would claim that this absence has, in some respects, been made good in Thompson 1988.

The contemporary me is more hesitant about structuralist analysis. Yet a number of works published since 1982 seem to suggest, on good authority, that I was broaching issues and tensions fundamental to what I'll risk calling the Chinese 'cultural unconscious'. Corroborative support can be found in (and beyond) an interpretive community of cultural analysts.

I find my first support in the work of Goran Aijmer who, for some four decades, has provided intriguing interpretations of the symbolic significance of the Chinese ceremonial calendar, and – in particular – the analogical parallels that can be drawn with the rice-growing cycle, the waxing and waning of *yin* and *yang*, and yearly series of symbolic exchanges between the living and the(ir) dead. Most of Aijmer's 'symbological exegeses' (2003: 11) have been based on information from local gazetteers from the Dongling Lake area of central China. In one foray away from the central China gazetteer material, Aijmer (1985) deployed the same technique to conjure up an insightful structuralist interpretation – modestly subtitled 'musings on a Taiwan corpus' – of the rather fragmented ethnographic references to rites of passage written on the basis of fieldwork on the island. The strategic procedure which Aijmer employs for *reading* his corpus of textual data is to adopt 'a notion of "cultural system" . . . as a "hidden" device to bring some order to the textual fragments which provide the evidence for our present endeavour' (2003: 10). 'This procedure of interpretative investigation . . . should never be regarded as finally conclusive . . . yet, as long as there are no other, better explanations at hand – for instance, those which are more conclusive with regard to data – we should feel at least temporarily satisfied with accounts that seem to make sense of the few and scattered items of information we have . . . The anthropological sense opens up motifs and meanings which go beyond what the data *qua* data say' (2003: 11).

This is a sturdy justification for his methodology, and, with hindsight, the mode of investigation and interpretation which I used to 'consume' the diverse fragments of the information I amassed on death rites in and around Qing Han village could have been articulated in the words I have quoted above from Aijmer. Perhaps it is the similarity of our *will to structure* – our theoretical appetites – as much as what was (actually/somehow) in the minds of local ritual participants – that fed itself – albeit from different points of origination – into some key interpretations that are either congruent or intriguingly resonant. With reference to what I was arguing in Thompson 1982, two aspects of Aijmer's work especially stand out.

First, there is Aijmer's equation that 'rice is agnatic stuff which mediates between living and dead and sustains both (1991: 184). 'I have asked the reader to accept that rice is ancestral stuff – it is a gift from the dead ancestors to the living . . . rice is agnatic matter, matter which creates agnation by way of consumption (1985: 26) 'Married-in . . . women are converted into agnates by the consumption of agnatic rice' (1991: 184) 'Ancestors somehow "are" the land which produces rice – and rice is an ancestral manifestation' (1991: 194). This symbolic valorization reinforces my argument on the cultural semantics of a taboo on consuming pork (an affinal food, the epitome of 'not-rice') tallied with an insistence on eating (the *tau* measure of) rice, the food that confers patrilineality by dint of its consumption.

Second – and interrelated – the (ana-)logic of Aijmer's interpretive practice leads him to make a brilliant observation on Ahern's analysis of the yellow tails myth. He notes that Ahern's four versions of the myth all start like this:

> In early times men had tails. When they got old, their tails turned yellow. As soon as this happened their descendants killed them and ate their flesh.
>
> (Ahern 1973: 206)

Aijmer's epiphany of a suggestion is that 'The tail that turns yellow could be seen as ripening rice. The killing is the harvest. The killing provides food (rice) which is the flesh of the dead forefathers' (1985: 27). Aijmer's interpretations on the centrality of consuming rice boosts the view that the taboo on eating pork, the insistence on eating rice, and the ambivalences inherent in the yellow tails myth might be taken as symptomatic of a crucial Chinese 'cultural unconscious'.

Enter, stage left, Steven Sangren, whose most recent and ambitious book, *Chinese Sociologics* (2000) can be viewed as the culmination of almost two decades of involvement in the ethnography of Taiwan. *Chinese Sociologics* strives to be an anthropological account of – but also accounting for – the role of alienation in social reproduction. In examining the production of Chinese cultural subjects with reference to a co-implicated dialectics of alienation, Sangren argues that 'analysis of a genre of Chinese mythical narratives can reveal aspects of what might be termed a patrilineal mode of production of desire' (2000: 189). His primary focus is upon the story of Nezha. 'Like the story of Oedipus, the Nezha story revolves around tensions between a son and his father. In this respect, the story provides insights into Chinese culture repressed by normative convention valorizing filial piety in the more familiar self-representations of Chinese philosophy and elite literature' (2000: 190). Thus he reckons the Nezha story to be symptomatic of a crucial – if normally unmentionable – cultural unconscious.

Remarkably, Sangren has not spotted the parallels that would seem to exist – not least in the 'sociologic' he seeks to infer – between the Nezha stories and the 'yellow tails' myths (as recounted by Ahern 1973). The Nezha stories dwell on 'the son's patricidal hatred, the father's murderous intentions towards his son' (Sangren 2000: 198), and Sangren recounts how 'to escape divine punishment for his insubordination, [Nezha] returns his flesh and bones to his father, a suicidal act explicitly intended to abolish his filial obligations' (2000: 198). Sangren claims that 'Chinese readers clearly identify most with Nezha [whose] bloodlust [*shaqi*] and exuberant rebelliousness . . . must be controlled by the "banal" Confucian father figure' (2000: 204).[6] In a complex and sophisticated train of argument too difficult to condense satisfactorily, Sangren has a further speculation that 'the fantasy or desire figured in the Nezha narrative is closely linked to what appear to be similar desires implicit in the rhetoric and structure of Chinese rituals' (2000: 210). 'Chinese cosmology and ritual make implicit claims to the effect that female productive powers derive from transcendent patrilineal ancestors and that patrilineal ancestors are egocentrically assimilable to male subjectivities [so] patriliny itself can be viewed as institutionalized, male-subject-focused, egocentricism' (2000: 208). The former claim about transcendent patrilineal reproduction by-passing female fertility resonates closely with my (by way of Bloch and Parry 1982) insinuations about the retention (through consumption) of rice as kinship substance, whilst the (at times) murderous ambivalence between father and son portrayed in the Nezha stories echoes the strikingly similar ambivalence in the versions of the yellow tail myth which I collected. 'For men the issue focuses on whether one is to be the agent/subject of one's own desires or the instrument/object of the desire of some "other" – specifically one's son or one's father. Stories like that of Nezha focus on this struggle for the empowered (male) subject position' (Sangren 2000: 221). Likewise in the yellow tails myth, the crucial tension of the 'cultural unconscious' manifests itself in the form: 'eat or be eaten'.

Further support for the thesis that there is a Chinese cultural unconscious hinged on an 'eat or be eaten' tension crucial to the cultural production of subjects in a patrilineal and patriarchal society comes from two quarters: analyses of modern Chinese literature, and efforts to make sense of the gruesome events reported by Zheng Yi in his *Scarlet Memorial* account of mass cannibalism in Guangxi Province in 1968.

For many, the signature birth pangs of modern Chinese literature were the New Culture Movement's onslaught on Confucian morality and the oppressiveness of China's traditional culture. Lu Xun's 'Diary of a Madman', published in May 1918, was pivotal to the movement. In the story, the 'hero . . . a fairly young man . . . imagines that people are planning to eat him' (Chinnery 1960: 311). By the third entry in his diary, 'the madman discovers that not only does cannibalism exist today, but it has existed throughout Chinese history' (Chinnery 1960: 313). Chinnery concludes that 'the central idea of the story is that society is cannibalistic and that the orthodox Confucian morality was merely a cover for cannibalism' (1960: 314). It is no coincidence that the work most associated with denigrating China's moribund Confucian values and patriarchal family system should have portrayed the old regime as cannibalistic.

Sun Lung-Kee's (1986) exposition of Lu Xun's Dilemma of Political Engagement is strikingly titled 'To Be or Not to Be "Eaten"', and seems to provide further authoritative corroboration of the view that 'at the core of the entire edifice of Chinese patriarchy lies a profound tension' (Sangren 2000: 213), locked in the 'cultural unconscious' as a cannibalistic dilemma. In terms which seem to accord well with Sangren's very differently situated deciphering of the Nezha myth, Sun outlines how, 'in the eyes of the May Fourth iconoclasts, one of the accursed aspects of Chinese culture was its blighting effect on individuality (*gexing*) [leading them to] call for the "emancipation of self" [*gexing jiefang*] (1986: 459). Yet Lu Xun's desire for a China strengthened by socialism meant that he 'was an individual trapped in the dilemma of deciding whether he should let himself be "eaten" for the sake of others' (1986: 481).

Yue's (1999) examination of the literary culture of modern China, covering writers from 1918 till 1996, builds on Lu Xun's metaphorical characterization of social relations in China as cannibalistic to suggest that cannibalism has been the central trope for key writings since Lu Xun. The cultural valency of cannibalism has also been noted independently in a critically incisive article by Carlos Rojas (2002) entitled 'Cannibalism and the Chinese Body Politic'. Rojas goes beyond 'Lu Xun's identification of cannibalism as the metaphorical condition for which society must attempt to extricate itself', to offer interpretations of the figure of cannibalism in other contexts. Taking rumours that circulated on the internet in 2001 of the eating of human flesh in Taiwan restaurants as his starting point, Rojas 'elaborates a selective discursive genealogy of cannibalism in twentieth-century Chinese', and strives to show how 'the figure of cannibalism itself involves a paradoxical combination of identification and alterity, of violence and desire'. It is a headily seductive itinerary, but not one that can be pursued further in this chapter, other than to recognize through Rojas the vibrant resonances of the figure of cannibalism across a range of different discursive contexts.

Which brings us back to cultural anthropology, and Donald Sutton's efforts to make cultural sense of the macabre episodes of cannibalism reported by Zheng Yi – and apparently amply substantiated by others – in Guangxi province. In his 'Consuming Counterrevolution' article, Sutton (1995) argues that 'beliefs about the dead . . . play a key role in cannibalism [and, despite the horror of the practices of eating human flesh] . . . there is little that is random and arbitrary in the practices of consumption and disposal extemporized in the spring of 1968' (1995: 147). He attempts to delineate 'various cultural resonances of cannibalism, most noticeable [of which] is the availability of moral underpinnings for the practice' (1995: 154). He concludes that 'if Chinese culture is seen . . . as a repertoire of ingrained but not unchanging habits and preferences, linguistic and symbolic associations, folk and elite images . . . then . . . even cannibalizations were grounded in familiar cultural symbols and associations' (1995: 169). Once more, there seems justification for viewing the Qing Han complex of 'eating and not eating the dead' as aligned with a key and familiar tension in the Chinese cultural unconscious.

Philippe Aries has made the case for the comparative atypicality of contemporary Western attitudes to death. Death has been hushed up, and is a taboo subject. 'Death in the hospital is no longer the occasion of a ritual ceremony, over which the dying person presides amidst his assembled relatives and friends' (Aries 1976: 88). Baudrillard takes up this theme in his *Symbolic Exchange and Death*: 'Strictly speaking, we no longer know what to do with them, since, today *it is not normal to be dead*, and this is new. To be dead is an unthinkable anomaly; nothing else is as offensive as this' (1993: 126). For Baudrillard, in modern society, symbolic exchange with the dead has, itself, died a death. The predominant Western attitude towards 'cannibalism' is still Dickensian.[7] Maggie Kilgour, on the other hand, examines cannibalism in terms of metaphors of incorporation, and the most basic binary opposition of inside–outside. She writes that, '[a]s Bakhtin . . . notes, one of the most important characteristics of eating is its ambivalence . . . an act that involves both desire and aggression, as it creates a total identity between eater and eaten while insisting on the total control – the literal consumption – of the latter by the former. Like all acts of incorporation, it assumes an absolute distinction between inside and outside, eater and eaten, which, however, breaks down, as the law "you are what you eat" obscures identity and makes it impossible to say for certain who's who' (Kilgour 1990: 7). This ambiguity over consumption, incorporation and identity resonates with the yellow tails myth as well as with Lu Xun's dilemma of political engagement.

Baudrillard's reductionist nostalgia for a primitive order where symbolic exchange with a society's dead is alive and well, seduces him toward some none the less interesting claims about the cultural unconscious of cannibalism. 'This devouring is a social act, a *symbolic* act, that aims to maintain a tissue of bonds with the dead man . . . We think of anthropophagia as despicable in view of the fact that we despise what we eat, the act of eating and ultimately even our own bodies. Primitive devouring is ignorant of the abstract separation of the eater and the eaten into the active and the passive . . . Devouring . . . is a *social* act, a sacrificial process where the metabolism of the whole group is at stake . . . an act of expenditure, consumption or consummation, and of the transmutation of the flesh into a symbolic relation, the transformation of the body in social exchange' (Baudrillard 1993: 138). If we are only prepared to view cannibalism from the Freudian vantage point of unleashed aggression expressed toward the father, then we are not receptive to a Chinese cultural unconscious in which (to reiterate Rojas's phrasing) 'the figure of cannibalism itself involves a paradoxical combination of identification and alterity, of violence and desire' (Rojas 2002).

In this section I have exhumed my earlier presentation, and inserted it into the context of ongoing dialogues in an endeavour to suggest that the ideas I was grappling with in 1982 can be read in such a way as to resonate with a range of theoretical stances adopted since then by authoritative writers including Aijmer, Sangren, Gang Yue, Rojas, Sutton, and even – ill-digestedly – Baudrillard. I have been touting the idea that 'eating and not eating the dead' fits intriguingly and aesthetically with the notion of a Chinese cultural unconscious in which cannibalism is a crucial trope. The reader might, though, wish to consider whether I have been like the fox (in the four-character idiom *hujia huwei*) who foils the tiger's desire to consume him by parading in front of the tiger, thereby appropriating the tiger's authority, so that the latter is persuaded that it is the fox that the other animals hold in awe.

Post-mortem re(con)sumption, post-modern palatability: a cultural autopsy

In what may be viewed as an effort to devour my own tale, in this section I suggest some problems with this conception of a Chinese cultural unconscious, problems that have become evident as what is theoretically palatable has been subject to the dismantling effects of post-modernism. The first point of wariness in re-consuming my earlier presentation has to do with the extent to which I have, unintentionally, been prone to what would now be called Orientalist suppositions. Hsieh (1988) records how Victor Segalen, champion of 'the exotic', symbolized pre-1911 China as a 'juicy, incomparably savorous fruit' (1988: 201) 'ripe for literary exploitation' (1988: 246). To what extent was my original writing a consuming of the 'other', a sort of 'foreign-sic' exploitation dressed up as ethnography? Was my focus on death rites really a product of what was crucially important in the mindset of those in my fieldwork village, or was it part of an exoticization of the other, a pandering to what might be of most interest to a Western readership? In my bid to make sense of what I came across in fieldwork I worked too cosily with the assumption that the diversity of unfamiliar, at times quirky, happenings and conversational snippets could be susceptible to some sort of 'generative' interpretation. Gregory Blue has demonstrated that 'one of the major problems with Western analyses of Chinese society over the last three hundred years has been that principles and categories stemming from the Western tradition of social theory have often distorted that which they were meant to clarify' (1999: 109). My 'will to pattern' probably nourished my analytical model by being selectively economical with the diversity of local discourses.

One device for Orientalist probing that is difficult to disentangle in ethnographic consumption is Freud's influence, not least his 'belief that ritual practice must be deciphered as a *symptom* of hidden psychic realities' (Seeman 2005: 359), thereby endorsing distinctions between so-called manifest and latent meanings. Freud's account of the cultural production of the individual subject is still fiercely contended, as is the ubiquity of the Oedipus complex, and may privilege a particular Western take on individuality and sexuality. Psychoanalytical theorizing is a heuristically suspect device, not least when it foists complexes (whether oedipal or edible) as universal. Clough outlines the 'pressure in terms of which identity form arises as the writer's oedipal struggle with a precursor writer or writing – the struggle, that is, to appropriate the phallic function of writing itself' (1992: 19), which generates the suspicion that the deployment of Freudian styles of analysis may be persuasive for reasons internal to the ethnographer's struggle with the self-production of his own unified subject identity.

Re-digesting my earlier text, it is now evident to me that it was written in the 'ethnographic present' (see Fabian 1993), in which my interlocutors have been frozen in a timeless present, along with an apparently unchanging Chinese culture. History, if not overtly denied, was certainly ignored, in the way that I sought to derive something essential about the other. It is not an exoneration that others, including Aijmer and Sangren, have similarly posited a sort of strategic synchronicity in order to capture their object of study – ethnography, perhaps, as a form of cryogenics.

The denial of co-evalness is one of the problems inherent in a structuralist approach to ethnographic quandaries. As a methodology, structuralism is prone to the Procrustean style of consumption, a sort of intellectual Taylorism, where the essential parameters are laid out by 'the ethnographer as the heroic subject of knowledge' (Clough 1992: 19) able to read between and beyond the lines of the conscripted other. There seems to be an inverse correlation between the 'heroism' of the anthropologist and the passivity of 'the voices of local interlocutors [who] were usually silenced altogether' (Fardon 1991: 8). The dialogic nature of language is thereby ignored as data is corralled into the prison-house of language (from which there is no parole) for structuralist decoding. The approach becomes cryptological in character, but cryptology invokes the logic of the crypt, an 'abstract objectivism' (Volosinov 1986: 81) which works most efficiently (on its own terms) on language (or cultural data) as cadaver, stripped from its living context. The first meaning of 'autopsy'[8] is 'seeing with one's own eyes': personal observation. The more prevalent meaning of 'dissection of a dead body', post-mortem examination, is of more recent vintage. Though I paid some attention to my informants' interpretations at the outset of my earlier text, they receded as my structuralist quarrying proceeded. Were the Malinowskian claims of having seen with my own eyes a standard rhetorical trope to deflect from my conducting an 'autopsy' in the now more conventional sense? In this structuralist consumption of the other, individuals are liable to be reduced to objects of observation, mere signifiers – sinology as signology. Sangren endeavours to obviate this problem by stipulating that 'in all of the preceding discussion one should not confuse "subjectivity" and "subject position" with real people' (2000: 221) – as the film postscript has it, any resemblance to actual persons is purely fortuitous!

Another difficulty with the structuralist approach taken by Thompson 1982 is that of what constitutes the unit of cultural account. To what extent is it viable to extrapolate from a structural analysis of local culture to some holistic notion of Chinese culture or essential characterizing of a Chinese cultural unconscious? Is it anything other than naive to expect that findings from Qing Han village, or eighteenth-century gazetteers from central China, or versions of the Nezha myth, or analysis of Lu Xun's texts, can furnish some universal propositions about 'China' – irrespective of time or space? Whatever 'unit' is posited for cultural analysis, it is always already hybridized, differentiated and unstable. Yet, as Mark Hobart (2000) suggests, 'To be possible professional ethnography required an extraordinarily closed and holistic notion of culture, as without it the ethnographer had no idea how what she recorded related to anything else, or what had happened before. It was a brilliant way of articulating a problem, even if it effectively disarticulated those whose lives it depicted.' (2000: 25) The term *culture*, then, is one that is deeply problematic, and perhaps best consumed critically and reluctantly, *sous rature.* Murray and Hong (1994) vehemently accused the anthropological establishment working on Taiwan of 'seeing through Taiwan' to the more prestigious and privileged 'Chinese culture' as their object of study, in the process 'obliterat[ing] Taiwanese culture' (1994: 4). Taking the contingent identity[9] of 'Taiwanese culture' as a unit of cultural account is in its turn also stacked with difficulties. At best, the adjective 'Chinese' – even if somehow absolved of its political connotations – can itself only be applied *sous rature*, and, once broken of assumptions about inherent cultural unity, cannot easily be put together again.

Carrier and Heyman (1997) express an 'intellectual and political dissatisfaction with the anthropology of consumption' (1997: 356), accusing many of its practitioners of ignoring 'issues that come under the general heading of political economy' (1997: 355). Just as the political transformation of Taiwan since the late 1980s should be taken into account, so, too, should the radical changes in Taiwan's economy (in modes both of production and of consumption) feature in a more nuanced examination of the 'eating and not eating of the dead'. There are many changes, but I will content myself with sketching some changes that may have a substantial bearing on the ritualized co-identification of land and families, of rice-farming and the ceremonial calendar, and implications for the symbolic exchanges and cannibalistic tensions between the living and the dead. Taiwan's population has, in the last fifty years, moved comparatively from 'rags to riches', leading to a surge in mass (and conspicuous) consumption. A previously rural society based on agricultural production has become a highly urbanized and capital-intensive economy geared to manufacturing consumer goods for export to the global market. The agricultural sector, not least the cultivation of rice, has slumped considerably in its economic importance; land has long since become a secular and alienable commodity. Family farms have, at best, become family firms, as family members, often dispersed around the island and beyond, maintain looser, less anchored, voluntaristic ties with each other, and with 'the land'. There has, in the process, been a relative unhinging of formerly stable relationships and identities. As the social relationships of everyday life – of production and of consumption – alter, so, too, the practice of everyday death (*pace* de Certeau 1984), what Baudrillard calls 'symbolic exchanges' with the dead, whilst bearing recognizable traces of the past, will gradually take on an altered significance. Ultimately, the cultural unconscious is not impervious to radical changes in the political economy. Where the production and consumption of rice could be conceptualized as a crucial qualification of key social relationships among the living, and between the living and their dead, consumption through the vehicle of money seems likely to give rise to a relativization of social relationships, and a further disaggregation of 'communities'.

A sceptical re-reading of my earlier text might suggest that, though ideas of 'eating and not eating the dead' (as practised in terms of the pork taboo, and the insistence on eating rice) are still extant, the sense of what this means (and knowledge of the yellow tails myth) is fading into relative insignificance. Given the epiphenomenalization of agriculture and family farms, the myth has slipped out of the cultural unconscious. Rather than being unmentionable because it touches a raw nerve at the heart of the tension in father–son relationships, it may be that it is not mentioned because it is thought of as too trivial to pass on through oral tradition. Sometimes a cigar is just a cigar. There is a 'can't lose' aspect to the notion of a cultural unconscious, though, for, by definition, it escapes people's conscious awareness. As Aijmer says, 'we cannot expect to find overt expression of a system which we postulate here as part of a fundamental deep structure' (1985: 26).

As I have indicated, there are plenty of swipes that can be aimed at the postulate that the 'eating and not eating of the dead' can make sense as a crucial feature of a 'Chinese cultural unconscious', in some ways analogous to (but significantly different from) the fundamental deep structure of the Oedipus complex proposed by Freud. The ethnographic digestive process – consuming the other – can be a matter of perspective and a matter of 'level of ambition'. There is a case for deflecting the iconoclasms of post-modernistic criticism, or at least to hold them in abeyance, to invoke what Spivak (1993) (in different circumstances) calls a 'strategic essentialism' to license some imaginative and suggestive ordering of the material. It is a ploy to make *a* sense of the material, but not *the only sense* that might be ventured. I have not sought to consummate a marriage between my structuralist approach and my post-modernist criticism of such an approach. I don't see the need to disambiguate. You decide, if the ambivalence offends. As reader-consumer of this chapter, 'you pays your money and you takes your choice'.

Notes

1 The reference is to a story in Zhuang Zi – see Watson 1968: 194.
2 I have drawn here on Marx's comment in *A Contribution to the Critique of Political Economy* (cited by Bourdieu 1976: 117) that 'The beneficiary of the entail, the eldest son, belongs to the land. The land inherits him.'
3 '*Brother Teh's funeral is too simple. Chin-Shan, give them 30 grand . . . Your father never enjoyed it when he was around. Make sure to burn a Benz, a mansion, and a TV for him, so he won't get bored, OK?*' [the eponymous 'Black Dog' in the film *Hei Gou Laile* (*Comes the Black Dog*), Yin 2003].
4 Some sentences on this page and the next were 'consumed' verbatim in Thompson 1988. I have indicated the five instances of this 'post-quotation' by employing a contrasting typeface.
5 For de Certeau, culture is not simply consumed for, in everyday life, it is invented 'by poaching in countless ways on the property of others' (1984: xii). In its contemporary guise, the discipline of anthropology might be depicted as cultural gamekeeper turned self-acknowledged poacher.
6 If so, then it is tempting to think of the repressed tension as not necessarily being confined to the level of personal relations, but as reverberating with the tension that Hill Gates argues to have long existed between aspirant petit-bourgeois-type entrepreneurs and a commercially-conservative state.
7 'Cannibalism for Dickens was always a paradigm of supreme degradation and inhumanity' (Stone 1994: 255–6).
8 According to the Shorter Oxford English Dictionary.
9 'A contingent identity only constitutes itself *in relation to that which it is not . . .*' (Paul du Gay 1996: 2).

References

Ahern, E. M. (1973) *The Cult of the Dead in a Chinese Village*, Stanford: Stanford University Press.
Aijmer, G. (1985) 'Birth and Death in China: Musings on a Taiwan Corpus', *Ethnos* 49: 5–42.
—— (1991) 'Chongyang and the Ceremonial Calendar in Central China', in H. R. Baker and S. Feuchtwang (eds), *An Old State in New Settings: Studies in the Social Anthropology of China in Memory of Maurice Freedman*, Oxford: JASO.

—— (2003) *New Year Celebrations in Central China in Late Imperial Times*, Hong Kong: Chinese University Press.
Appadurai, A. (ed.) (1986) *The Social Life of Things: Commodities in Cultural Perspective*, Cambridge: Cambridge University Press.
Arens, W. (1979) *The Man-Eating Myth: Anthropology and Anthropophagy*, Oxford: Oxford University Press.
Aries, P. (1976) *Western Attitudes Toward Death from the Middle Ages to the Present*, London: Marion Boyars.
Bakhtin, M. M. (1986) *Speech Genres and Other Late Essays*, C. Emerson and M. Holquist (eds), V. W. McGee (trans.), Austin: University of Texas Press.
Bauman, Z. (1998) *Work, Consumerism and the New Poor*, Milton Keynes: Open University Press.
Baudrillard, J. (1993) *Symbolic Exchange and Death*, London: Sage.
Bloch, M. (1982) 'Death, Women and Power', in M. Bloch and J. Parry (eds), *Death and the Regeneration of Life*, Cambridge: Cambridge University Press.
—— (1985) 'Almost Eating the Ancestors', in *Man (ns)*, vol. 20, 631–46.
Bloch, M. and Parry, J. (1982) 'Introduction: Death and the Regeneration of Life', in M. Bloch and J. Parry (eds), *Death and the Regeneration of Life*, Cambridge: Cambridge University Press.
Blue, G. (1999) 'China and Western Social Thought in the Modern Period', in T. Brook and G. Blue (eds), *China and Historical Capitalism. Genealogies of Sinological Knowledge*, Cambridge: Cambridge University Press.
Bodman, N. C. (1955) *Spoken Amoy Hokkien*, Kuala Lumpur: Charles Grenier.
Bourdieu, P. (1976) 'Marriage Strategies as Strategies of Social Reproduction', in R. Forster and O. Ranum (eds), *Family and Society*, Baltimore: Johns Hopkins University Press.
Carrier, J. G. and Heyman, J. M. (1997) 'Consumption and Political Economy', *Journal of the Royal Anthropological Society (n.s.)*, vol. 3, no. 2, June, 355–73.
Chang Shr-syung C. (2002) 'Personalized "consumer ego" and the vanishing of social inequity consciousness', *Taiwan News*, 11 February.
Chinnery, J. D. (1960) 'The Influence of Western Literature on Lu Xun's *Diary of a Madman*', *Bulletin of the School of Oriental and African Studies*, vol. 23, no. 2, 309–22.
Chun, A. (1994) 'From Nationalism to Nationalizing: Cultural Imagination and State Formation in Postwar Taiwan', *The Australian Journal of Chinese Affairs*, no. 31, January, 49–69.
Clough, P. (1992) *The End(s) of Ethnography: From Realism to Social Criticism*, London: Sage.
Culler, J. (1983) *On Deconstruction: Theory and Criticism After Structuralism*, London: Routledge and Kegan Paul.
de Certeau, M. (1984) *The Practice of Everyday Life*, Berkeley: University of California Press.
du Gay, P. (1996) *Consumption and Identity at Work*, London: Sage.
de Groot, J. J. M. (1969) *The Religious System of China* (6 volumes), Leyden: Brill.
Eberhard, W. (1967) *Guilt and Sin in Traditional China*, Berkeley: University of California Press.
—— (1971) *Moral and Social Values of the Chinese: Collected Essays*, Taipei: Chinese Materials and Research Aid Service Center.
Fabian, J. (1983) *Time and the Other: How Anthropology Makes Its Object*, New York: Columbia University Press.
Fardon, R. (1991) 'Introduction' to R. Fardon (ed.), *Localising Strategies*, Edinburgh: Scottish Universities Press.
Feuchtwang, S. (1974) '*Religion and Society in Northern Taiwan*', PhD dissertation, University of London.

Fortes, M. (1959) 'Oedipus and Job in West African Religion', in C. Leslie (ed.), *Anthropology of Folk Religion*, New York: Doubleday.
—— (1965) 'Some Reflections on Ancestor Worship in Africa', in M. Fortes and G. Dieterlen (eds), *African Systems of Thought*, London: Oxford University Press.
—— (1976) 'An Introductory Commentary', in W. H. Newell (ed.), *Ancestors*, The Hague: Mouton.
Gabriel, Y. and Lang, T. (1995) *The Unmanageable Consumer: Contemporary Consumption and its Fragmentation*, London: Sage.
Gates, H. (1996) *China's Motor: A Thousand Years of Petty Capitalism*, Ithaca, NY: Cornell University Press.
Hobart, M. (2000) *After Culture. Anthropology as Radical Metaphysical Critique*, Yogyakarta, Indonesia: Duta Wacana University Press.
Hsieh, Y. Y. (1988) *Victor Segalen's Literary Encounter with China: Chinese Moulds, Western Thoughts*, Toronto: University of Toronto Press.
Jordan, D. K. (1972) *Gods, Ghosts, and Ancestors: The Folk Religion of a Taiwanese Village*, Berkeley: University of California Press.
Kilgour, M. (1990) *From Communion to Cannibalism. An Anatomy of Metaphors of Incorporation*, Princeton: Princeton University Press.
Lewis, G. (1980) *Day of Shining Red. An Essay on Understanding Ritual*, Cambridge: Cambridge University Press.
Lu Xun (1977) 'Diary of a Madman', in Lu Hsun: Selected Stories. Yang Hsien-yi and Gladys Yang (trans), New York: Norton.
Miller, D. (1995) 'Consumption and Commodities', *Annual Review of Anthropology*, vol. 24, 141–61.
Murray, S. O. and Hong Keelung (1994) *Taiwanese Culture, Taiwanese Society: A Critical Review of Social Science Research Done on Taiwan*, New York: University Press of America.
Rojas, C. (2002) 'Cannibalism and the Chinese Body Politic: Hermeneutics and Violence in Cross-Cultural Perception', *Postmodern Culture (An Electronic Journal of Interdisciplinary Criticism)*, vol. 12, no. 3, May.
Sangren, P. S. (2000) *Chinese Sociologics. An Anthropological Account of the Role of Alienation in Social Reproduction*, London: Athlone Press.
Seeman, D. (2005) 'Ritual Practice and Its Discontents', in C. Casey and R. B. Edgerton (eds), *A Companion to Psychological Anthropology. Modernity and Psychocultural Change*, Oxford: Blackwell.
Spivak, G. (1993) *Outside the Teaching Machine*, London: Routledge.
Stone, H. (1994) *The Night Side of Dickens. Cannibalism, Passion, Necessity*, Columbus: Ohio State University Press.
Sun Lung-Kee (1986) 'To Be or Not to Be "Eaten": Lu Xun's Dilemma of Political Engagement', *Modern China*, vol. 12, no. 4, October, 459–85.
Sutton, D. S. (1995) 'Consuming Counterrevolution: the Ritual and Culture of Cannibalism in Wu Xuan, Guangxi, China, May to July 1968', *Comparative Studies in Society and History*, vol. 37, no. 1, Jan., 136–72.
Thompson, S. E. (1982) 'Eating and Not Eating the Dead: A Taiwanese Case', paper presented at the London Intercollegiate Seminar Series, December.
—— (1988) 'Death, Food and Fertility', in J. L. Watson and E. S. Rawski (eds), *Death Ritual in Late Imperial and Modern China*, Berkeley: University of California Press.
Thornton, A. and Lin Hui-sheng (1994) *Social Change and the Family in Taiwan*, Chicago: University of Chicago Press.
Volosinov, V. N. (1986) *Marxism and the Philosophy of Language*, Cambridge, MA: Harvard University Press.
Watson, B. (trans.) (1968) *The Complete Works of Chuang Tzu*, New York: Columbia University Press.

Yin Chi (dir.) (2003) *Hei Gou Laile* (*Comes the Black Dog*), Taiwan.
Yip J. Chun (2004) *Envisioning Taiwan: Fiction, Cinema, and the Nation in the Cultural Imaginary*, Durham, NC: Duke University Press.
Yue Gang (1999) *The Mouth That Begs. Hunger, Cannibalism, and the Politics of Eating in Modern China*, Durham, NC: Duke University Press.
Zheng Yi (1996) *Scarlet Memorial. Tales of Cannibalism in Modern China* (ed. and trans. T. P. Sym), Boulder: Westview Press.

8 Images of the Chinese

Photography and consumerism in 1990s Hangzhou

John Bayne

Initial observations of photographic practices

Throughout my sixteen months of anthropological fieldwork in Hangzhou, I always derived enormous pleasure from riding my bicycle along the roads which bordered the edges of the city's iconic feature, West Lake (*Xihu*).[1] While the considerable beauty of the lakeside scenery was one reason for choosing to cycle there, so too was the opportunity to glimpse the many activities which took place along the lake. One of these activities was the taking of photographs.

I soon began to notice that there appeared to be a conformity in photographic practices, whether undertaken by visitors, residents, or professional souvenir photographers. Almost without fail, those being photographed would be wearing their best clothes, and would stand or sit facing the camera, with their backs bolt upright and feet together. Rarely were there more languorous poses with people leaning against walls or trees; if there were, then this tended to be the work of the professional souvenir photographer. Seated people would place their hands on their knees, while those standing would have their arms hanging straight down, or – more dashingly – place a hand on a hip. Otherwise, if the people being photographed were standing next to something, such as a tree or an architectural feature, then in most instances they would extend an arm to this 'prop' and place their hand on it or grasp hold of it, even if it meant having to raise their hand above their head to reach the overhanging branch of a tree. Certainly no motion shots were ever entertained. As for facial expressions, these varied from the sombre to a smile, but I never saw anybody being photographed indulging in any voluble laughter. Neither did I ever see photographs being taken without somebody posed in the foreground. Away from Hangzhou's tourist sites and parks, the same photographic 'conventions' appeared to persist. While the objects and/or locations privileged by those being photographed were foreign vehicles, the lobbies of expensive hotels, or modern buildings, the poses and facial expressions remained the same. That I should begin to notice similar 'conventions' in the photographic illustrations of modern Chinese wall calendars – the 'object' of my doctoral research – seemed to suggest then that such 'tendencies' went beyond the 'genre' of souvenir photography alone.

For many outside of China, the era of the photographic snapshot, heralded as long ago as the 1930s with the Kodak slogan 'You press the button and we do the rest', has resulted in photography becoming an ephemeral – even a throw-away – medium. While photographic equipment in the 1990s may have been no different in Hangzhou than it was in, say, Europe or America, in this chapter I suggest why it is that new forms of technology do not inexorably precipitate any trend towards a standard practice or 'reading' – at least not in the short term. Although this immediately refutes the idea that media technology and/or foreign-born products or activities are resulting in cultural interconnectedness and global homogenization – an idea also resisted by Parkin (1993), Appadurai and Breckenridge (1995), and Miller (1995), among others – my study of photographic practices also addresses a number of other considerations in the Western social science literature on consumerism, most particularly whether localizing characteristics of consumer practices should be considered inherently 'Chinese' or merely 'characteristics in China'. By way of addressing these issues I shall investigate a range of discourses which, although not exhaustive, did, I suggest, variably determine 'photographies' – to use the term preferred by Tagg (1988) – in mid-to-late 1990s Hangzhou.

I begin my investigation by describing the practices of professional photographers, the reason being that for the great majority of the Hangzhounese I encountered there was little doubt as to who was most influential in determining photography. It was '*sheyingzhe*' (photographers). Through this investigation, the significant part that technological development and politics have had to play in the 'history' of photographic practices in urban China will also become evident.

The professional photographer in Communist urban China

The influential role of photographic studios has been well documented, especially in analyses examining the early decades of photography in Europe and America (such as Reiakvam (1993) or Freund (1974)). In urban Hangzhou, and China more generally, there is a strong case to be made claiming the influence of the professional photographer on photographic practices, especially given the conditions which until recently prevailed on photographic practices. First, economic and political conditions in China limited the practice of photography to those working in the photographic business (and a small number of amateur enthusiasts). Aspiring photographers could not hope to find training, gain access to good photographic equipment or use their photographic skills outside of the work unit (*danwei*). Second, these constraints meant that photographic studios were almost the sole arena of photographic portraiture. Although camera ownership was increasing in Hangzhou in the 1990s (a consequence of increased personal incomes and wider availability of photographic equipment), none the less for most people this remained the case. Even those Hangzhounese lacking the financial resources to go to photographic studios for fun would still have experienced studio photography at first hand. Efforts at control by state regulatory bodies over the daily lives and activities of the population in post-1949 China meant a majority of urban Chinese having to have their portraits taken for identity cards and report files at least once in their lives. Third, even with the explosion of media production beginning in the 1980s, the influence of the professional photographer in urban China appears to have persisted in the 1990s. The vast majority of professional photographers were still taught at their place of work, because photography has been such a comparatively recent phenomenon in China,[2] and it was also rare for photographers to specialize – be it in fashion, press or creative photography. They had to be able to turn their hand or their lens to anything.[3] The need for such professional diversification became all the more necessary with many photographic studios diversifying into ever-new commercial activities, in particular undertaking photographic work for Hangzhou's burgeoning number of advertising agencies and publishing houses. For these reasons, photographic professionals were in a considerably advantageous position to determine photographic genres and styles.

I was consistently told by photo-portraitists that the aim in portrait photography was to produce as flattering a picture as possible of the people being photographed. They had little or no concern for issues of documentation or characterization, revealing the subject's *neixin* or 'innermost being', although being rendered totally unrecognizable was not something clients found desirable. To achieve this objective, portrait photography often entailed the following (in some instances the services being supplied by the studio): make-up (especially for women but occasionally also for men); hair styling; wearing fashionable or glamorous clothes (often connotative of 'the foreign', such as Western suits for men or white wedding dresses for women; and the glittery costumes beloved by Chinese television quiz show hosts were also popular); props (such as mock seventeenth-century-European fireplaces, plaster reproductions of classical Greek statues or architectural columns, artificial flowers, or soft toy animals); and backgrounds (usually plain but on occasion photographic reproductions of scenery or of Chinese or foreign cityscapes).

Lighting and body articulation too were important factors in photographic portraiture. Of paramount importance, photographers told me, was the need to soften the shadows – especially in the face – and to ensure that there was a glint of light in each eye (*yanshenguang*),without which the face would be 'lifeless'. Photographers would also suggest poses for clients to adopt; rarely did I witness clients overtly dictating the photographic agenda. However, professional photographers most favoured poses which avoided any stiffness (*jiangying*) and perpendicularity. As a consequence, for women a gentle S-shaped curvature in the body was the norm. And just as important as the articulation of the body in the photographic portraiture of women were the position of the hands. Two very characteristic hand poses (*shoushi*) women were asked to adopt were to place the tip of the vertical first digit of one hand against the jaw bone or chin, or to rest the side of the face against an open hand or vertically pointing first digit.[4] Men, on the other hand, were encouraged to be casual (*suibian*), natural and unrestrained (*xiaosa*).[5]

Although clients were constantly urged to relax and to smile a little, never were they encouraged to laugh openly, since this 'creased the face'. Rarely were there any motion shots either, because the success of such photography was much more difficult to predict and required much more film, for which most clients were unwilling to pay. Most top-market portrait studios used imported photographic film. The Chinese equivalent, although a fraction of the cost, was generally considered as being substandard for high-quality photographic work. The same budget constraints meant that most photographic studios tended to preclude location or outdoor photography (*waipaizhao*) where they lacked the controlled environment of the studio, although some advertising agencies, publishing houses and wealthy individuals were beginning to commission such photographs. The composition (*goutu*) of most photographs taken at photographic studios tended to conform to certain norms. A respectful distance from the person being photographed was maintained, with close-up shots being rare and the head clearly visible. While not necessarily looking straight at the camera, portraits were also never more oblique than three-quarter profile.

Looking at the work of many photographic studios, one could also be forgiven for attributing professionals working in such establishments with the recent bias in much of the media towards images of young women, children and babies. I was told that photography privileged considerations of beauty (*mei*) above all others.[6] As a consequence, certain subjects lent themselves better to photography than others. Among these were animals and children, but most importantly these were women, particularly young women. Because women are charming and beautiful (*meili*), they were felt to be the natural subject of photography. But just as perceptions of the medium predisposed it to the photography of young women, its associations with beauty therefore tended to preclude the portraiture of young men (photographs of wedding couples excepted).

That photographic portraiture appears to have privileged certain occasions – in particular weddings, work outings or leisure trips to tourist sites – also suggests the determining role of the professional photographer. In many large towns and cities in China, one did not have to walk the streets for very long before becoming aware of the plethora of photographic studios and wedding parlours which existed, with their window displays of framed photographic portraits and elaborate white or pastel coloured wedding dresses. (Many photographic studios were actually part of wedding parlours, which offered photographic portraiture as one of many services.)

However, it was also clear that professional photographers did not *necessarily* set the entire photographic agenda and, in particular, the way that photographs were read. For example, while the employees of one of Hangzhou's leading studios were very familiar with photographic works from outside China and were keen to incorporate new ideas into their portraiture or advertising, they were nevertheless constrained by the requirements of their clients. I was told on a number of occasions that the vast majority of their clients did not want something too abstract (*chouxiang*). By way of an example they showed me a portrait of a male whose face (photographed from the side) was largely indistinct through darkness – the profile being contrasted to the lighter background. The director said that such a portrait would be unacceptable to most of his clients because most of the face was hidden. Similarly, photographs they had taken for a fashion advertisement were rejected because they had cropped off the top of the models' heads. That the studio had done this to draw attention to the clothes and not the faces apparently cut no ice with the client.

Such examples of visual conservatism notwithstanding, to attribute such considerations as the privileging of certain kinds of clothing, body articulation, the absence of laughing, photograph composition, and even occasions for photography *entirely* to the influence and practices of portrait photographers would be to ignore – as I shall endeavour to demonstrate – a range of potential alternative determinants. Neither should the same professionals be considered the originators of the preponderance of images of young women in photography and the media. As analyses of photographic practices by Pinney (1995), Bourdieu (1984) and Appadurai (1997) suggest, other factors should be taken into consideration.

Photographs, people and society: the contemporary, the foreign and the expensive

Despite the alleged indexical superiority of a photo-chemical, as opposed to a manually wrought medium of visual representation, a number of analysts have argued that the medium of photography should not necessarily result in the kind of altered 'ethics of seeing' suggested by Sontag (1987: 2).[7] One such analyst – Tagg – posits that:

> [t]he photograph is not a magical 'emanation' but a product of a material apparatus set to work in specific contexts, by specific forces, for more or less defined purposes. It requires, therefore, not an alchemy but a history, outside which the existential essence of photography is empty.
>
> (Tagg 1988: 3)

Drawing on the work of Gombrich (1972) and Goodman (1976), Pinney (1995), in his study of photographic practices in present-day portrait studios in Nagda, India, also maintains that seeing is not a neutral activity but one conditioned and constrained by systems of representation standard for a given culture or person at a given time. Thus the 'correctness' of an image in any system 'depends upon how accurate is the information about the object that is obtained by reading the picture according to that system' (Goodman 1976: 38). Bourdieu is another analyst who suggests that 'photography should be the subject of a reading that may be called sociological, and that it should never be considered in or for itself, in terms of its technical or aesthetic qualities' (Bourdieu *et al.* 1990: 22). For Bourdieu, 'sociological' factors 'objectively determine the meaning which a group confers upon the photographic act as the ontological choice of an object which is perceived as worthy of being photographed, which is captured, stored, communicated, shown and admired' (1990: 6).

In a study of photographic 'picture-taking' practices in 1950s France (Bourdieu *et al.* 1990), Bourdieu notes the particular characteristics of portrait photography. He contrasts, for example, the photographic practices of rural dwellers in Bearn with those of white-collar workers, managers and members of photography clubs. The photographic predilection of the latter was for studied compositions of landscapes or still lives, or for more 'natural' spontaneous snapshots of holidays or their own babies and children. Among rural dwellers in Bearn, on the other hand, photographic conventions seemed to demand that people stand in 'dignified attitudes', motionless and face-on to the camera, and that only certain special occasions should warrant photography (weddings and christenings in particular). Similarities here with the photographic practices noted in Hangzhou continue: the Bearnais person being photographed had to be erect (whether seated or standing), they could not laugh, they had to be dressed as smartly as possible, and their face had to be clearly visible and identifiable. Further similarities in picture composition appear to exist when Bourdieu describes photographic portraiture in Bearn as favouring a 'respectful distance' from the person being photographed, while situating them in the centre of each photograph (1990: 82–3).

By way of an explanation for such 'sociological' photographic 'conventions', Bourdieu, in the main, falls back on his notion of class-based dispositions (1984).[8] As I shall demonstrate, there is much that is useful in such a status-based theory – in particular Bourdieu's notion of 'cultural capital' – but nevertheless caution has to be exercised. In particular, one has to question whether social distinctions in 1990s Hangzhou really demonstrated a division between, on one hand, the kind of Kantian aesthetics Bourdieu suggests pertains to those individuals and groups said to belong to the upper class, and, on the other, a non-Kantian aesthetic of overt sensualism for the mass-produced popular culture of the working class.

That said, taste-based social distinctions do appear to be particularly manifest in certain comments of professional photographers in Hangzhou, especially distinctions made between photographic portraiture considered to be 'art' (*yishuzhao*) and that which was not. Moreover, the exasperation of many professional photographers with the somewhat conservative tastes of their clients also reflects Bourdieu's taste-based distinctions. The popular appreciation, certainly after 1993, for black-and-white photography is another case in point. That black-and-white photographs were acknowledged by many Hangzhounese to be more 'artistic' than colour photography was largely premised on the fact that colour photography tended to be the preference of less 'cultured' (*wenming*) people.

However, Bourdieu's class-based dispositions of taste would appear to be less apposite in explaining other photographic conventions in mid-to-late 1990s Hangzhou, notably preferences for certain kinds of clothing (such as Western-style suits or white wedding dresses), and contemporary, expensive, or foreign props and backgrounds. Hangzhounese, if asked while being photographed or looking at photographs of themselves or of others, often commented that clothing, backgrounds and props played an important part in enhancing certain qualities of the sitter. I would be told that a brand label on an article of clothing, objects such as television sets or motorcycles and a background scene of a modern building or the lobby of a luxury hotel could denote the 'contemporaneity' (*xiandai*) or 'wealth' (*fuyu*) of those being photographed. It was for this reason that the prop or the background scene should be sufficiently prominent and visible for this symbiosis to be readily apprehended. That such preferences appeared to be nearly universal among urban Chinese – regardless of gender, age or socio-economic background – suggests that factors other than Bourdieu's class or status-based dispositions of taste prevail. As Appadurai notes on the use of backdrops in 'colonial' and 'post-colonial' studio photographic portraiture:

> If photo backdrops are seen as part of the pose into which the photographic object is positioned (whether by his or her choice or not), then they can no longer be regarded merely as backdrops, but rather must be considered as deliberately defined elements of the overall context of the photographed object.
>
> (Appadurai 1997: 4)

Thus, '[t]he significance of the visible backdrop (actually represented in the photograph) cannot be assessed without reference to the invisible backdrop (the discourses and images that inform the eye of the photographer)' (1997: 5). Appadurai concludes that, '[o]ne way or another, many photographic backdrops place the photograph in a potential space of debate about visual modernity as it is expressed in clothes and machines, as well as in bodily comportment and bodily accessories' (1997: 6). In order to understand why contemporaneity or wealth should have been so privileged for those I saw being photographed in Hangzhou, one has first to look at recent Chinese history.

Gamble's (1996) study of Shanghai residents, and Gold's (1993) analysis of *Gang-Tai* (i.e., Hong Kong and Taiwanese) culture, draw attention to the fact that the onus on contemporaneity and wealth owed much to the shock experienced by many Chinese at China's economic backwardness and cultural sterility when the PRC was opened up to the world of foreign goods and ideas following the post-1978 reforms. Until then, the Chinese had been led to believe that socialism had delivered for the population of the PRC an existence which was in every way more advanced and ideologically sound than anything enjoyed in the capitalist West. Exposure to *Gang-Tai* and Western-made products and media – which enabled most urban Chinese to achieve some measure of familiarity, however vicariously, with foreign products and lifestyles – demonstrated just how much at variance conditions in China were with those elsewhere. Far from living in some kind of utopia, what became immediately apparent was the extent to which the vast majority of Chinese existed in an environment characterized by tired ideologies and things which were old, dirty, in very short supply, and frequently in a sad state of repair.

It was little wonder, then, that 'foreign' products and ideas were accorded considerable cachet, as the yardstick by which to measure this rupture from pre-market reform existence.[9] Even when the effects of the reform process had come to be widely experienced by most urban Chinese, the allure of the foreign was to endure. One explanation for this was the considerable aura of exclusivity and one-upmanship that the far greater expense (or frisson) of foreign-born products and media productions gave to many individuals. More significant for many Hangzhounese, however, was that most foreign things or ideas were perceived to be superior in quality and were better looking (*haokan*) or more interesting (*you yisi*) than their Chinese equivalents. Above all, foreign-made products and ideas were demonstrably new and best fulfilled the desire of many Hangzhounese in the first half of the 1990s to be contemporary (*xiandai*).[10] The high esteem accorded to foreign-made goods meant that they remained the preferred consumer choice for many Hangzhounese, and the Veblenesque ostentatious flaunting of such products in public places attests to the allure in the 1990s of the foreign (for which, read expensive) product.

For those with restricted economic means, clothes were perhaps the most easily accessible signifiers of contemporaneity and wealth, whether in photographic portraiture or in public space. Schell (1988) and Finnane (1996) note that the emergence of Euro-American forms of dress after 1978 quickly eclipsed 'indigenous fashions . . . under the imperative of modernization' (Finnane 1996: 102). Apart from the folk costumes of so-called ethnic minorities, indigenous forms of dress quickly lost all status. This perception endured in the 1990s, as attested to by adverse comments about the cloth shoes (*buxie*) I regularly wore. The desire to be demonstrably modern meant that, for many Hangzhounese (in particular the young and the wealthy), the clothes and accessories they bought and wore not only had to be seen to be modern, they had to be clearly identifiable as such. As a consequence, brand names often assumed almost unparalleled importance. No product – foreign or otherwise – was complete without the *mingpai* (brand name) to describe it, and wherever possible that brand name was prominently displayed on the product. Thus the American practice of selling men's suits with the designer's label sewn on the outside of the left sleeve (to be removed upon purchase) became subtly altered so that a similarly adorned suit in Hangzhou (and in many other parts of China, too) would often retain the label after purchase. Other consumer products – such as household electrical goods, furniture or furnishings – underwent similar processes of distinction with the common sight of plastic labels deliberately retained on microwave ovens, washing machines, sunglasses and other consumer goods. That such markers of wealth and contemporaneity should be so significant for many urban Chinese explains their significance – and prevalence – in mid-to-late 1990s Chinese photography.

Professional photographers may have contributed to such a discourse in their photographic work, but to suggest that they alone generated such preferences ignores the greater socio-economic and political picture. The same refutation can also be made for the influence of professional photographers in determining the kind of props and backgrounds favoured in much photography. But just as the form and content of many photographs can be said to have been informed by a discourse of contemporaneity, so too can the practice of photography itself. Take, for instance, the growing number of amateurs pursuing photography. Contemporaneity and foreignness could be expressed just as much in the leisure pursuits of the 1980s and 1990s as it could in the consumer goods one bought.[11]

Photographs, people and society: leisure pursuits and the urban

As Wang (1995) notes in his analysis of leisure patterns in post-1978 urban China, leisure was considerably de-politicized (but still only where activities were deemed not to threaten the existing social order), diversified and domesticated, meaning that the home was fast becoming the main arena of leisure. Over and above the Westernizing influence of *gangtai* culture noted by Gold (1993), Wang further cites the important part that accommodating the leisure needs of foreigners in China had for the Chinese themselves. The bars, restaurants, photography kiosks, discotheques and health and sporting facilities that were initially built for the exclusive use of foreign guests in specially segregated hotels soon became popular among ordinary mainland Chinese, as access to such facilities was gradually opened to the wealthy and, following that, similar facilities were established elsewhere. The widespread popularity and photographic merit-worthiness of activities such as dancing, karaoke, ten-pin bowling and eating at fast-food restaurants, could all be attributed to such foreign-inspired influences.

That many such leisure activities took place in buildings that were recently constructed – and in many instances, lavishly adorned – meant that the buildings themselves and their decor were similarly connotative of modernity. As Goodman notes:

> In Hangzhou during 1992 a hint of foreign decor, be it Japan, Thailand or Southeast Asia, was regarded as necessary for the best of the new private restaurants (although all served basically the same kinds of local dishes). In 1993 the fashion was for the new private restaurants to emphasise exclusivity in small dining rooms modelled on English country houses of the eighteenth century with Palladian arches, statues of Greco-Roman gods, oil paintings of the master and mistress of the house, and appropriate table settings. In the process, of course, the new-style restaurateurs themselves became relatively wealthy trend-setters.
>
> (Goodman 1996: 239)

It is no coincidence, then, that many of the architectural features mentioned by Goodman – in particular the Greco-Roman and Palladian – also appeared as props and as backgrounds in many photographs.[12] Once again, this would seem to diminish the claim of professional photographers for setting the photographic agenda.

The popularity of photography as a leisure activity was clear from the number of photography manuals on sale in Chinese bookshops and the common sight of people taking photographs in the city's numerous parks or tourist sites. Indeed, as I was to discover, among those Hangzhounese who owned or had access to a camera, an increasingly common leisure pursuit was to go out for the day with a group of friends or family with the express intention of taking photographs of one another. Such photo-outings, along with travel as a leisure activity, served to popularize photography considerably. Although travelling around China remained difficult, looser residency regulations, better transport facilities and a reduced official working week (from six to five days) all facilitated opportunities for travel. Whatever the trip – be it to the local park or a conference organized by the work unit – an essential ingredient of any such venture was that of the souvenir photograph.[13]

As well as in parks, it was common to take photos in front of modern buildings and luxury cars. This indicates the significance of the urban as a further manifestation of the discourse of Sinicized contemporaneity. Living in Hangzhou – as in most cities in eastern China – it was impossible to ignore the extraordinary building spree that was taking place. This, together with the move towards greater differentiation and specialization in urban redevelopment, the growth of real estate and private home ownership for many urban dwellers, served to focus attention on the 'modern' urban landscape as perhaps never before. Moreover, large urban centres became the loci for the most desired employment, residence, education, medical facilities and recreation – the huge influx of rural dwellers to the cities since the mid-to-late 1980s being ample testimony of this.

However, this privileging of the urban also had other origins. A bureaucratic and social divide has long existed between urban and rural Chinese, a divide so fundamental that Whyte is moved to describe it thus:

> In explaining the contemporary patterns of social and cultural life in the PRC, such as fertility, religious activity, and family structure, rural versus urban appears to be the primary cleavage in China's contemporary social landscape, a factor more important than income, class, educational level, or other influences.
>
> (Whyte 1993: 358)

For these reasons, cities were considered to be 'developed and flourishing' (*fada*). The countryside, by contrast, was just seen as being poor and 'hick' (*tuli-tuqi*). Certainly for many urban dwellers who had been sent to work in agricultural production before the reform era began in 1978, the countryside was sometimes a place of unimaginable hardship. Similar commentaries comparing cities and the countryside were made about photographs I had taken of Hangzhou and of a mountain village in south Zhejiang province to which I made frequent visits. To the rural inhabitants, my photographs of Hangzhou were a visual representation of a 'paradise' few people would ever hope to visit (due to the oft-quoted phrase, 'In heaven there is paradise, on earth there is Suzhou and Hangzhou'). By contrast, any Hangzhounese looking at photographs of the mountain village would – without exception – comment on its poverty and lack of (the possibility for) development.[14]

The privileging of the urban can also be attributed to the ideological swing which took place after the implementation of the 1978 reform process – from the social ideal of the peasant to that of the (urban) intellectual and then entrepreneur. Once again such 'sociological' considerations (to use Bourdieu's terminology) appear to diminish the claim for the pre-eminent position of professional photographers to wholly determine conventions of photography.

That said, however, to consider 'sociological' discourses of contemporaneity, foreignness or wealth as the only discourses which informed photographic practices would be to ignore the significance of gender, the subject of the next section.

Photographs, people and society: gendered discourses in photographic production and considerations of the 'photographic occasion'

The symbiotic relationship between the person in the photograph and the backdrop or props used was often premised on criteria of gender. While men would more often be photographed with cars or modern buildings, objects and environments deemed most suitable for photographing women were those perceived to be 'natural', 'traditional' or 'beautiful'. I was consistently told, by both men *and* women, that flowers, trees or landscape settings (and cuddly toys) emphasized the beauty or charm of a female subject.[15] That many of my photo-respondents should have considered women (and to a lesser extent, children and babies) as the 'natural subject of photography' also suggests that a discourse of gender was of some significance. Indeed, this process of 'naturalization' was such that the preponderance of female images in media productions seemed to be a subject of little concern to most women. As a considerable number of middle-aged Hangzhou women told me, being able to wear feminine clothes, put on make-up, and have one's hair done was a marked – and desired – contrast to the strictures of the Cultural Revolution years. Only once did I hear dissent, when a 21-year-old female university student expressed exasperation at the long, lingering camera shots of swimsuit-clad Chinese women in karaoke laser disc video films.

It is also significant that most professionals involved in photographic production were men. Explanations of this near-absence of female photographers invariably cited the rigours of carrying the heavy equipment, and women's lack of the 'depth of thought' required for good photography.[16] Even among non-professionals – such as tourists or amateurs – photographic practices carried a strong gender bias. Most commonly, those being photographed would be women while those taking the photographs would be men.

While such a gender bias should not be discounted, more sociological considerations have also to be taken into account. In his study of twentieth-century (Euro-)American cinema, Denzin (1995) draws attention to similar processes of naturalization brought about by what he calls 'the voyeur's gaze'. Drawing on Baudrillard's theories of the hyperreality of signs, Denzin suggests that this male-produced voyeuristic gaze is one which has resulted from a diverse number of visualities, with the consequence that 'each individual has interiorized the hearing and visual gaze of an "objectified" external, generalized, nameless, often faceless, other' (Denzin 1995: 191).[17] Although care has to be taken in applying Denzin's more Hollywood-wrought theory of visualities to the context of China, Evans's (1997) study of discourses of female sexuality and gender suggests just how engendered state and media gazes have been since 1949. According to theorists such as Evans (1997) and Gilmartin *et al.* (1994), such processes of 'feminizing' and representing women are a product of changing 'dominant discourses' (Evans 1997: 15) on women in post-1978 China – a process identifiable in perceptible gender biases in media productions such as popular magazines, posters, karaoke videos and calendars and studio photography. Taking Woo's (1994) thesis of a discursive shift from the more 'societal' attitudes towards women during the time of the Cultural Revolution to the 'biologized' ones which emerged after the 1978 reforms (Woo 1994: 284), Evans notes:

> Inscribed in law, assumptions of an originating, essentialist biological difference between women and men effectively serve to underpin women's inferior status in employment and wage structures through legitimizing employers' decisions to exclude women from the work-force. Popular discourses, as represented in women's magazines or TV soaps, widely invoke a similar essentialism to suggest that women's natural interests may be best served by withdrawing from the labour market and returning home.
>
> (Evans 1997: 27–8)

Thus, while pre-reform media images depicted women as workers, whether in the fields or in the factory, the vast majority of pictorial images of women in media productions after the mid-1980s located women either in a domestic environment or against a backdrop commonly perceived to be 'beautiful'. There was rarely any suggestion that any of these women could be in full-time employment, let alone hold positions of authority – as was in fact the case with many urban Chinese women in the 1990s. Instead, where such media products were illustrated with images of Chinese women, the emphasis became one of femininity – a further consequence, Evans suggests, of the 'biologization' of dominant discourses on women:

> While the reassertion of a natural femininity may, in part, be a response to the absence of erotic interest in previous decades, naturalized assumptions about gender and sexuality have fed into the perpetuation – and in many instances the augmentation – of gender hierarchy and conflict.
>
> (Evans 1997: 31)

A discourse of gender can also be said to play a similar determining role in other conventions of photographic portraiture noted in this chapter. For example, the absence of open-mouthed laughter in photographs – explanations for which normally amounted to no more than the occasional comment that laughing was *bu haokan* (literally 'not nice to look at') – could be attributed to the socio-cultural aversion to open mouths and exposed teeth, most vividly exemplified in the enduring habit – inculcated at an early age in young girls in particular – of covering the mouth with an open hand when laughing. Preferences too for pale skin and large eyes – especially for women – have long predated photography, dark skin being equated with having to do manual work out of doors, usually in the fields (once again reinforcing the rural–urban divide). As for the gentle, 'S'-shaped body pose, this too has long existed in Chinese painting and sculpture, as have the various hand poses. In this way, to accord professional photographers with too much of a determining role in photography would be to ignore the significance of such socio-cultural considerations.

Similarly, to overly credit professional photographers for choosing which specific occasions were considered worthy of record in photography would be to ignore the socio-cultural aspects of much Hangzhou photography. By my observations, most photography appeared to be limited to the following specific occasions: *manyue* (the completion of a child's first month of life), *bairi* (the hundredth day of a child's life), *yi zhousui* (first birthday), *shengri* (birthdays during early childhood), *miaonian zhaopian* (attaining adulthood, usually the eighteenth birthday), *hunshazhao* (weddings), and *laoren jinian zhaopian* (commemorative photography for old people), along with *quanjiafu* (family gatherings) and *kaihui* (attending conferences).[18] That most such occasions are life-stage ceremonies which had long predated photography suggests that socio-cultural factors can indeed be considered as significant considerations influencing photographic practices.

Other considerations of suitability need also to be taken into account. While beauty-based considerations of aesthetics may indeed have been a significant determinant in those instances where my attempts at photography were deemed 'unsuitable' (such as photographs I took of rural dwellers, of buildings in the Hangzhou old town, or of people shopping), the knowledge that I was likely to be showing these photographs to a non-Chinese audience so that 'China' was not going to be represented in its best possible light was, as a number of respondents exhorted, a question of 'face' (*mianzi*). Similar considerations of face – defined by Yang (1994: 133 and 140) as a situational measure of self-respect (*zizunxin*) which is gained and lost *vis-à-vis* others[19] – can be said to have been manifest in reactions to the documentary film 'Chung Kuo' shot by the Italian director Antonioni in 1972. Sontag relates how he met considerable official displeasure when he filmed scenes perceived to be:

> . . . old, or old fashioned – 'he sought out and took dilapidated walls and blackboard newspapers discarded long ago'; 'paying no attention to big and small tractors working in the fields, [he] chose only a donkey pulling a stone roller' – and for showing indecorous moments – 'he disgustingly filmed people blowing their noses and going to the latrine' – and undisciplined movement – 'instead of taking shots of pupils in the classroom in our factory-run primary school, he filmed the children running out of the classroom after a class'. And he was accused of denigrating the right subjects by his way of photographing them: by using 'dim and dreary colors' and hiding people in 'dark shadows'.
>
> (Sontag 1987: 170)

In short, Sontag remarks, Antonioni 'was depriving people and things [of the photo-opportunity] . . . to look their best' (1987: 172). This notion of face, as I shall demonstrate below, also plays a central role in another key consideration in photographic practices and the 'reading' of photographs in China – its commemorative role.

The photographic portrait as immortalizing 'souvenir' and personal property

Explaining the photographic practices of the rural residents of Bearn in France, Bourdieu makes the important point that, far from being a documentary record of the random or inconsequential, photographs strove 'to solemnize and to immortalize' (Bourdieu *et al.* 1990: 7). For the majority of photographic portraiture in Hangzhou, too, this 'immortalization' was one of the most important aspects of the medium. Certainly for those without the economic means to have their photographs taken frequently, a photograph often served as one of the sole reminders to a future generation of that person's presence or likeness – although many wealthy Hangzhounese also accorded considerable significance to the immortalizing nature of a photo portrait.[20] Photographs were a way of overcoming separation which required something perfect with which to 'detain' (*liu*) somebody – in particular to detain the memory of them (*liu ge jinian*). For this reason, being portrayed in as dignified or awe-inspiring a manner as possible was often a great consideration for this commemorative function of the photographic portrait. Here the emphasis was on external likenesses rather than any metaphysics of being.

Vinograd has noted how this commemorative function of portraiture was also important in traditional Chinese painting (*guohua*), where portraits assumed considerable importance as ancestral or funerary images: 'Portraiture is grounded in social practices having to do with rituals of commemoration and claims of status and identity that are largely public' (1992: 1). As a consequence, '[m]ost Chinese portraits were very much formal sittings with posture and gesture restrained and facial expressions limited to a narrow range between dignified seriousness and mild good humor' (1992: 9). And just as with photographic portraiture, Vinograd notes that, while paintings did attempt to depict the sitter in their social and cultural milieu, characterization was minimal.[21]

Compounding this immortalizing characteristic of portraiture, however, was a widely-accepted notion of photographic practice which I can only best describe as 'proprietorial'. A number of diverse circumstances led me to consider such a thing. The first of these was the frequent situation in which I was given a photograph as one of the subjects of the picture and where there was never any thought of financial recompense demanded by the giver. That some of these gift-givers should have been close friends meant that initially I had little cause to question this gesture. However, that many more such donors were not close friends and some of them even near-strangers – meant that I began to take account of who was giving me photographs in this way, and why. I soon noticed that the gift-giver was invariably either mainland Chinese or Hong Kong, Singapore, Malaysian or Indonesian Chinese. Then when I eventually plucked up the courage to ask why I should be the recipient of their largesse, the matter-of-fact response was usually along the lines that 'the photograph belongs to you'. The reasoning behind this reply only became apparent once I started looking at my Chinese friends' photograph collections and albums. In addition to the usual composition of bodies in the photographs, what struck me about these collections was their anthropocentric and autophotographic nature. Not only was there the dominant presence of people in every photograph (I rarely saw any simple landscape photographs), but I also noticed that people rarely possessed photographs in which they did not appear. As a consequence, looking at a photograph album usually meant looking at a whole series of photographs, most of which were of the same person in a number of different circumstances and locations – in contrast to the albums I am familiar with in England where one is confronted by photographs peopled by individuals one does not know because the person whose album it is has, in most instances, been the photographer. It seemed, therefore, that one did not keep photographs where the self was not included.

I began to reconsider this theory once I began participating in photographic outings with my Chinese friends to Hangzhou's parks and tourist sites, after which I witnessed the distribution of the photographs once the films had been developed. Even before economic hardship began to bite in the late 1990s, photography for most Hangzhounese remained an expensive pastime (in 1996 the price of a film and the cost of developing amounted to about 40 *yuan*). For this reason, photography tended to be a group pursuit, with one person supplying the camera and – in many instances – everybody sharing the cost of the film and developing. It was the expense of photography, many people told me, which explained why poses tended to be 'stiff' – people could not afford to waste a shot. This is also why there were so very few photographs without somebody standing in the foreground. Economic considerations also explained – in part – how the shared developed film was invariably distributed: a photograph was automatically given to whoever was in that photograph (the only exception to this being group portraits when the common practice was to make copies of the same photograph so that everybody in the shot might receive a copy).[22]

However, I also observed similar distribution processes among my more affluent Hangzhou friends for whom the cost of photography was unimportant. Asked why nobody seemed interested in photographs of each other, they gave the same reply as that of my photo-gift-givers: 'They are not ours.' And as if to emphasize the fact that a photograph could only belong to the person in that photograph, it was not uncommon for the negative to be included with the photograph.[23] While I was to encounter such apparent photo-portrait 'proprietorship' on a number of separate occasions involving a range of people and circumstances, perhaps its most graphic exemplification took place when, on three separate occasions and with three different newly-married Hangzhou couples, I sat with them while they looked at photographs of their wedding banquet. In all three cases, once the couple had picked out all the photographs of themselves, they then proceeded to sort out all the remaining photographs (and negatives) according to who was in them in order that those friends or relatives might have a 'souvenir' of the wedding. Asked if they had not wanted to have a record of the people who had been with them on that important occasion, all three couples replied that the photographs of their friends and relatives 'were not theirs to do as they wished with'.

That such portrait proprietorship was often premised on considerations of expense cannot to be denied – as I have already suggested. However, the fact that I encountered this practice among Hangzhounese of all economic circumstances suggests that the photographic image of a person did indeed possess a considerable commemorative content. Such perceptions also go a considerable way to explain why so many times I should have been asked 'why take photographs of people you do not know?' when taking pictures of people in the street.[24]

Chinese photography or photography in China?

To return then to this article's problematic – namely whether there was something intrinsically 'Chinese' about photographic practices in 1990s Hangzhou (and by extension, consumerism in general) – much in this chapter would indeed seem to indicate that there was. From the near-monopolistic position enjoyed by professional photographers to the way that photographs were 'read', the case for a 'Chinese photography' would appear to be a strong one. Likewise, the privileging of the 'foreign' and 'the contemporary' as a direct consequence of China's political isolation, or the Veblenesque ostentatious flaunting of consumer goods noted by a number of authors in this book, similarly suggest some notion of 'Chinese consumerism'. However, closer analysis of many of the particular considerations mentioned in this chapter suggest otherwise. While it cannot be denied that there were a number of factors specific to China, such as its political isolation, its cultural history, or the system of household registration which led to disparities between China's urban and rural populations (to name but three factors), that many of the considerations mentioned in this chapter should find parallels in other societies and cultures militates against positing a specifically 'Chinese' form of photography and/or consumerism.

Let me take a number of examples pertaining to photography before considering consumerism more generally. While the determining role of the professional photographer in urban China can rightly be said to have been a consequence of particular economic and political conditions unique to China, professional photographers in other countries and at other times similarly determined photographic practices.[25] Likewise, that photographic composition and the positioning of bodies in much Chinese photo-portraiture should find similarities elsewhere, such as in the photographs of the Bearn inhabitants of 1950s France, suggests that many such photographic 'conventions' could be said to be more a question of cultural competence, or, as Bourdieu (Bordieu *et al.* 1990) would have it, social/status group distinctions of taste. They would not be anything uniquely 'Chinese'. And while the hand poses noted in this chapter may be specific to China, there is nothing unique to characteristic hand poses in general, as a cursory look at fashion or 'glamour' photographs, for example, would indicate. Likewise, the aversion felt by many women to exposing their teeth or opening their mouths is also shared by many Japanese and Koreans. Nor is there anything special about the privileging of 'the foreign' or 'the contemporary' in Hangzhounese photography, even though this was a consequence of China's economic and political circumstances. The same privileging is to be found in photographs elsewhere (see, e.g., Appadurai's (1997) study of 'colonial' photography). Moreover, the (young) female as the prevalent subject of the (ostensibly male) photographic gaze – together with the gendering of objects and background elements – is, as Denzin (1995) notes, rife in America. Neither should the privileging of the urban be considered something quintessentially Chinese – for all the uniqueness of the *hukou* system of population registration. Both Williams (1973) and Thomas (1983) note how attitudes towards cities and the countryside in England have shifted through history, for instance. Lastly, there is nothing uniquely Chinese about wanting to be photographed in as dignified or modern a manner as possible – whatever the 'Chineseness' of 'face'.

References made in this chapter to the clothing, props and backgrounds of preference in most photographic portraiture suggest that in Hangzhou there was some privileging of the foreign or the contemporary and of brand names, and even a tendency for an 'if-you-have-it, flaunt-it' ethos. Most Hangzhounese did indeed variously aspire to such things – my analysis of photographic portraiture demonstrates the extent to which such consumerist goals *were* aspired to and (oftentimes vicariously) achieved. Yet my study also demonstrates that there was often a considerable gulf between aspired-to and achieved consumption, and that these consumer aspirations were not necessarily shared by all Hangzhounese to the same degree or intensity. Photographic portraiture, for instance, was a pursuit indulged in by a certain minority only (principally the wealthy or the young), or was reserved for special occasions (such as special life-cycle occasions or when travelling). This suggests that, at best, we have no more than consumerism with certain 'characteristics in China' rather than any particularly Chinese consumerism.

There is one final caveat, however. Given my standpoint that notions about photographs are not premised on the 'pure mimesis' of visuality alone but are, in fact, socially (and sometimes culturally) constructed concepts, my final observation about the 'proprietorial-commemorative' element of much of photographic portraiture in Hangzhou indicates that in the particular medium of photography, and in the way that photo-portraits were 'read' and distributed, there may indeed be a case for considering 'Chinese characteristics'.

Notes

1 An edited version of this chapter – given in conjunction with the documentary photographer, Sandrine Rousseau – was presented on 3 December 1998 in the form of an illustrated talk to the 1998–99 London China Seminar series on 'Consumption with Chinese Characteristics'. This chapter is based on anthropological fieldwork undertaken in the city of Hangzhou between September 1994 and December 1995, and in October/November 1996. This was only made possible thanks to the financial assistance of the Economic and Social Research Council (ESRC), the University of London Central Research Fund, The Sino–British Fellowship Trust Fund, and the Radcliffe-Brown Trust Fund/Satusoma Award. I also wish to thank Stuart Thompson and Kevin Latham for their useful comments

on earlier draft versions of this chapter. My special thanks also to Andy Bilewycz for providing a replacement computer when mine ceased to function.

2 According to Minick and Jiao, photography came late to mainland China – 'in the thirties' – where it was limited to 'the urban Chinese in foreign districts' while being 'widely reviled as a form of black magic in the neighbouring countryside' (1990: 59). Zhou and He (1995) also cite the 1930s as being the time when portrait photography first became popular in Hangzhou.

3 Such adaptability became all the more apparent with changes in work practices. Whereas most photographers tended to work full-time for the one work unit before the 1990s, like many other urban Chinese who have opted entirely or in part to 'put out to sea' (*xia hai*) and go into business, a number of professional photographers have now established their own photographic facilities and undertake self-employed commissions. Many photographers working for, say, publishing houses or advertising agencies now also do photographic portraiture in their own studios and vice versa.

4 Asked about the origins of hand poses, some photographers suggested the Beijing opera or the eighteenth-century literary classic 'The Dream of the Red Chamber' written by Cao Xueqin and Gao E. I have not been able to substantiate either of these claims.

5 Gamble (1996: 294) notes how *xiaosa* also took on the meaning of 'stylish' and 'trendy' after a Taiwanese pop song of the early 1990s.

6 One or two professional photographers in Hangzhou suggested that pursuing beauty in photography might also have been a political expedient, as this was less likely to incur official displeasure given the strict censorship many photographs had to undergo prior to public display.

7 For Sontag (1987: 154), photographic images . . . are indeed able to usurp reality because first of all a photograph is not an image (as a painting is an image), an interpretation of the real; it is also a trace, something directly stencilled off the real, like a footprint or a death mask. While a painting, even one that meets photographic standards of resemblance, is never more than the stating of an interpretation, a photograph is never less than the registering of an emanation (light works reflected by objects) – a mental vestige of its subject in a way that no painting can be.

8 According to Bourdieu the pinnacle of the hierarchy of taste is the 'pure' aesthetic gaze possessed by only the very few with social cultivation and education. At the other end of his aesthetic spectrum lies the overt sensualism of the mass-produced popular culture of the working class (1984: 32).

9 However, for all the privileged position of 'the foreign' in this discourse of 'the contemporary', its appraisal was not entirely without discrimination. For almost all Hangzhounese, the vast majority of these products and ideas only came from a limited range of countries – most notably Hong Kong, Singapore, Taiwan, America, (Western) Europe, Australia and Japan. Hence, familiarity with the goods and ideas of these countries helped to enhance certain (mostly positive) 'Occidentalist' (Carrier 1996) perceptions of the lifestyles, consumer goods, and the lived environment of people from these places. On the other hand, perceptions of other countries (together with their inhabitants, technology and ideas) might, at best, be completely absent, or as was often the case with Africa or South America, almost universally negative. Often mediating these perceptions yet further were more racial discourses (see Dikötter 1992; Gladney 1994). For these reasons, Caucasians were often to be seen in advertisements for clothes, perfume or cars. Less foreign than 'Westerners' (where 'Western' was often synonymous with 'American'), but embodying modernity just as much, were Hong Kong, Taiwanese and Singaporean Chinese. Thereafter, other nationalities and races were accorded varying degrees of esteem. Japanese, notably, were

perceived to share the same culture as the Chinese and their technology was widely admired even though they were otherwise generally reviled for historical reasons.

10 In this chapter, *xiandai* is translated as 'contemporaneity' rather than 'modernity'. For informants in Hangzhou, *xiandai* implied above all a sense of being 'in vogue'. The term did not necessarily come with the same conceptual baggage as 'modernity' does in social science discourses. This is not to say that everything *xiandai* was necessarily brand new or foreign-derived. The fashion in early-to-mid-1990s Hangzhou for nostalgia (*huaijiu*) – manifested in such activities as wearing 1930s clothing, collecting Mao Zedong memorabilia, or photographing old Chinese buildings – was also deemed to be *xiandai*.

11 Not all foreign influenced leisure activities hailed from the post-1978 reform period. The common sight in urban public spaces of middle-aged and elderly couples ball-room dancing out-of-doors in the early mornings as a form of exercise was a Soviet influence from the 1950s, revived, post-Cultural Revolution, in the early 1980s.

12 In mid-1990s Hangzhou, it was the 'ancient Rome style' (*Gu Luomashi*) of architecture and interior decorative features which was most in vogue.

13 Interestingly, photographic picture-postcards of Hangzhou were very rarely found outside the foreigners' bookshop or hotels. Moreover, the greatly inflated prices of most postcards clearly indicated that postcard-buying was not a significant part of the 'Chinese' travelling experience.

14 This discourse may take a slightly different form in Taiwan. Alessandro dell'Orto related (in personal communication) how urban dwellers talk about images of the countryside as being *danchun* (meaning 'clear' – with overtones of Rousseauesque back-to-nature simplicity), whereas the popular perception of the Taiwanese city is *fuza* (meaning 'complicated' – with overtones of untidiness).

15 Even where women were photographed with objects or against backgrounds which were perceived to be more male – such as a motorcycle or a cityscape – this too can be said to have been informed by a discourse of gender. Analysing Indian calendar images, Uberoi notes that this is 'the consociation of women with material products' whereby '[t]he woman is assimilated to [a] range of status symbol consumer products and in the process she is commoditized herself. Neither the bicycle or the motorcycle is a 'feminine' product per se. They provide the occasion or excuse for the display of the female form' (1990: 45).

16 Wolf (1985) notes similar excuses as to why women did not drive tractors, and also relates views concerning the relative 'mental incapacity' of women.

17 Such visualities Denzin lists as 'the medical, investigative, technological, informational, erotic, accidental, inquisitive, comic, paranoid, obsessive, masculine, feminine, passive, active, direct, indirect, supplemental, legal, illegal, secret, illicit, loving, hostile, aggressive, official, regulated, unregulated and the indifferent' (1995: 191).

18 Bourdieu's privileging of 'the family' as the group which, more than any other, calls upon photographic practice as an instrument of integration is, in the context of modern-day China, to ignore the importance of the workplace. Although the greater part of photography in 1990s Hangzhou was family-oriented, a considerable amount of photographic work undertaken by professional photographers involved the workplace as well, an arena of collective social groupings which, as Gonzalez (1992: 128) indicates, may have determined photographic practices as much as the family.

19 Yang identifies two aspects of face. One – *lian* – she defines as 'the public recognition of ego's moral integrity in deep internalization of society's code of ethics' (1994: 140) while the other – *mianzi* – is linked to the context of *guanxi* prestige relations.

20 That a photographic portrait of the deceased would be displayed in funerals, and was frequently inserted on tombstones, suggests some similarity to the use of ancestral tablets. Considerations of the part played by a photographic portrait after death may – more contentiously – explain other photographic conventions, in particular the preference for full-length portraiture. The emphasis placed in 'Confucian' socio-cultural beliefs of being in possession of one's entire body at the time of death (de Groot 1892; Cohen 1988; Watson and Rawski 1988) might explain this.

21 One should be careful, however, about assuming that the art philosophies of the Chinese imperial elite were necessarily those of the Chinese population as a whole.

22 Because of the expense (especially among my student friends), group photographs tended to be rarely undertaken – especially of large groups. The exception to this was group photos of family members (when they shared access to the photographs) or work-outing group photographs (when the work unit usually footed the bill).

23 The only exception to this was in the case of group portraits when the camera owner or whoever paid for the developing kept the negatives.

24 I wish to point out, however, that my analysis of this intriguing element of photography in China has to remain unproblematized since I have not had the opportunity to compare photographic practices and 'philosophies' among a large number of diasporic Chinese, nor in other Far Eastern countries such as Japan or Korea.

25 Reiakvam, for example, suggests that 'studio pictures and the established visual schemas of postcards' were principal influences on the 'pictorial language' of a turn-of-the-century photograph album belonging to a 'bourgeois family from Bergen in Norway' (Reiakvam 1993: 42). Freund, too, argues for the influential role of photographic studios, this time in establishing certain conventions in the portraiture of Second Empire France (around 1865). Citing the routine use by photographic studios of a narrow range of props such as 'the column, the curtain and the pedestal table' (1974: 65; my translation) – together with other items such as pens, rolls of parchment deeds, and easels – these, Freund posits, helped establish a certain visual lexicon suggesting differing professional occupations and social aspirations (1974: 57–69).

References

Appadurai, A. (1997) 'The Colonial Backdrop', *Afterimage*, 24 (5): 3–7.

—— and Breckenridge, C. A. (1995) 'Public Modernity in India', in C. A. Breckenridge (ed.), *Consuming Modernity: Public Culture in a South Asian World*, Minneapolis: University of Minnesota Press.

Bourdieu, P. (1984) *Distinction: A Social Critique of the Judgement of Taste*, trans. R. Nice, London: Routledge and Kegan Paul.

—— with L. Boltanski, R. Castel, J.-C. Chamboredon and D. Schnapper (1990) *Photography: A Middle-Brow Art*, trans. S. Whiteside, Cambridge: Polity Press.

Carrier, J. G. (1996) *Occidentalism: Images of the West*, Oxford: Clarendon Press.

Cao Xueqin (1979) *The Story of the Stone*, trans. D. Hawkes and J. Minford, Bloomington: Indiana University Press.

Cohen, M. (1988) *Souls and Salvation: Conflicting Themes in Chinese Popular Religion*, Berkeley: University of California Press.

de Groot, J. J. M. (1892–1910) *The Religious System of China*, six volumes, Leiden: E. J. Brill.

Denzin, N. K. (1995) *The Cinematic Society: The Voyeur's Gaze*, London: Sage.

Dikötter, F. (1992) *The Discourse of Race in Modern China*, London: Hurst and Co.
Evans, H. (1997) *Women and Sexuality in China: Dominant Discourses of Female Sexuality and Gender since 1949*, London: Polity Press.
Finnane, A. (1996) 'What Should Chinese Women Wear? A National Problem', *Modern China*, 22 (2): 99–131.
Freund, G. (1974) *Photographie et société*, Paris: Éditions du Seuil.
Gamble, J. E. (1996) 'Opening the Door, Crossing the Stream: Changing Perspectives and Social Contours of 1990s Shanghai', unpublished PhD thesis, University of London.
Gilmartin, C. K., Hershatter, G., Rofel, L. and White, T. (eds) (1994) *Engendering China: Women, Culture, and the State*, Cambridge, MA: Harvard University Press.
Gladney, D. C. (1994) 'Representing Nationality in China: Refiguring Majority/Minority Identities', *Journal of Asian Studies*, 53 (1): 92–123.
Gold, T. B. (1993) 'Go With Your Feelings: Hong Kong and Taiwan Popular Culture in Greater China', *China Quarterly*, 136: 907–25.
Gombrich, E. H. (1972) *Art and Illusion*, London: Phaidon.
Gonzalez, J. A. (1992) 'A Contemporary Look at Pierre Bourdieu's "Photography: A Middle-brow Art"', *Visual Anthropology Review*, 8 (1): 126–32.
Goodman, D. (1996) 'The People's Republic of China: The Party-State, Capitalist Revolution and New Entrepreneurs', in R. Robinson and D. Goodman (eds), *The New Rich in Asia: Mobile Phones, McDonalds and Middle-Class Revolution*, London: Routledge.
Goodman, N. (1976) *Languages of Art: An Approach to a Theory of Symbols*, Indianapolis: Hackett.
—— (1978) *Ways of Worldmaking*, Hassocks: Harvester Press.
Holm, D. (1991) *Art and Ideology in Prerevolutionary China*, Oxford: Clarendon Press.
Jiangsu (1993–1996) *Lao Fangzi* (Old Houses), Jiangsu Fine Arts Publishing House.
Miller, D. (ed.) (1995) *Worlds Apart: Modernity through the Prism of the Local*, London: Routledge.
Minick, S. and Jiao Ping (1990) *Chinese Graphic Design in the Twentieth Century*, London: Thames and Hudson.
Parkin, D. (1993) 'Nemi in the Modern World: Return of the Exotic?', *Man (N.S.)*, 28 (1): 79–100.
Pinney, C. (1995) '"An Authentic Indian 'Kitsch'": The Aesthetics, Discriminations and Hybridity of Popular Hindu Art', *Social Analysis*, 38: 88–105.
Reiakvam, O. (1993) 'Reframing the Family Photograph', *Journal of Popular Culture* 26 (4): 36–67.
Schell, O. (1988) *Discos and Democracy: China in the Throes of Reform*, New York: Pantheon.
Sontag, S. (1987) *On Photography*, London: Penguin.
Tagg, J. (1988) *The Burden of Representation: Essays on Photographies and Histories*, London: Macmillan.
Thomas, K. (1983) *Man and the Natural World: Changing Attitudes in England, 1500–1800*, Harmondsworth: Penguin.
Uberoi, P. (1990) 'Feminine Identity and National Ethos in Indian Calendar Art', *Economic and Political Weekly*, 28 April, 41–8.
Vinograd, R. (1992) *Boundaries of the Self: Chinese Portraits, 1600–1900*, Cambridge: Cambridge University Press.
Wang Shaoguang (1995) 'The Politics of Private Time: Changing Leisure Patterns in Urban China', in D. Davis *et al.* (eds), *Urban Spaces in Contemporary China: The Potential for Autonomy and Community in Post-Mao China*, Cambridge:

Cambridge University Press, and Washington, D.C.: Woodrow Wilson Centre Press.
Watson, J. L. and Rawski, E. S. (eds) (1988) *Death and Ritual in Late Imperial and Modern China*, Berkeley: University of California Press.
Whyte, M. K. (1993) 'Adaptation of Rural Family Patterns to Urban Life in Chengdu', in G. Guldin and A. Southall (eds), *Urban Anthropology in China*, Leiden: E. J. Brill.
Williams, R. (1973) *The Country and the City*, St Albans: Palladin/Chatto and Windus.
Wolf, M. (1985) *Revolution Postponed: Women in Contemporary China*, Stanford: Stanford University Press.
Woo, M. Y. K. (1994) 'Chinese Women Workers: The Delicate Balance between Protection and Equality', in C. K. Gilmartin *et al.* (eds), *Engendering China: Women, Culture, and the State*, Cambridge, MA: Harvard University Press.
Yang, M. M.-H. (1994) *Gifts, Favors and Banquets: The Art of Social Relationships in China*, London: Cornell University Press.
Zhou Kanbu and Li He (1995) 'Hunsha Sheying' (Wedding Photography), *Qianjiang Zhoukan* (Qianjiang Weekly), Thursday, 5 May, 8–9.

9 Fashions and feminine consumption

Harriet Evans

The fashionable figure of the modern beauty is an emblem of China's consumer culture.[1] She features in diverse situations, walking along the pavements of down-town Shanghai, attending to eager customers in Beijing's elite fashion stores, or advertising the products of cutting-edge interior design companies. As a marker of cultural, social and national meaning, she has been the subject of extensive academic interest, across a number of disciplines. In the early stages of China's 'consumer revolution', the exaggeratedly sweet femininity of women's appearance in print culture and media advertising was widely interpreted as a response to the constraints on bodily and sexual expression of the Mao years. Many commentators saw her new form as an expression of women's desires to free themselves of the 'gender neutral' requirements of Maoist morality to explore diverse possibilities of self-identification. Linked to this was an interest in the symbolic use of her body to underline the emergence of a new 'public sphere' removed from direct intervention by the communist state, transcending the geo-political boundaries between different Chinese societies and cultures. In turn, the integration of China's market with global capital has inspired discussion about the influences of globalization and 'the West' in shaping public discourses of gender identities and relations in the People's Republic of China, including the cultural production of contemporary femininities.

The images of body and face informing these explorations mostly correspond with the mainstream representations of femininity prevalent in contemporary print culture. Whether locally produced under the auspices of state institutions, such as the Ministry of Sport, or the Ministry of Light Industry, or by local editions of international magazines such as *Elle* or *Vogue*, these representations collapse the multiple possibilities of femininity and femaleness into a composite image that is urban, educated, content, materially successful and beautiful.[2] It goes without saying that many other constructions of femininity are available in China, though these tend to be excluded from print culture by the commercial interests of magazine editors. Political constraints also limit the range of gender and sexual identities that magazine editors can publicize.[3] My purpose here is not to explore the different subject positions these represent. Rather, I want to survey some of the dominant arguments available in current scholarship about how to 'read' the images of fashionable femininity that are so prominent in China's consumer culture, and to suggest new ways of approaching these images which challenge the familiar dichotomies used in analysing them. I want to reflect on the nature of the contestations within and between local and global discourses of gender that are inscribed in these images. Is there a hegemonic politics of gender that emerges from the diverse readings of the fashionable feminine body? What are the effects of the globalization of these images on gender's operation as a fundamental principle of local social and cultural organization?

But first, some generalities. Fashion offers a rich terrain for exploring meanings of gender, social and political identity. As a prominent part of consumer culture, associated with designer labels, luxury cosmetics, changing hair styles and so on, it is, by nature, changeable and fleeting in its immediate effects. At any given moment fashions in clothing and make-up, for example, 'fashion' the body and face in multiple and influential ways, shaping, forming and moulding gender identities. They 'perform' gendered identities in literal ways, casting aside old items as new ones are needed, re-clothing bodies in an endless production of meanings differentiating the 'in fashion' from the 'out of fashion', the included from the excluded. Fashion transforms the possibilities of the body, and, following Baudrillard, summons women to treat their bodies as 'an investment through clothing and style' (Baudrillard, quoted in Gane 1991: 106). The notion of 'fashion' also contains a common conflation between the idea of a material object to be consumed, the desire to be beautiful, and the eroticization of female bodies for their own and others' consumption. Such a conflation was clearly at play in the rhetoric surround China's first Supermodel Contest, held in 1991, about which Susan Brownell (1998–1999) has recently written. In a context in which the All China Women's Federation had unequivocally announced its opposition to beauty contests on the grounds that they degrade women, public commentators took pains to emphasize that the Supermodel Contest was not a beauty contest, but rather an arena where contestants displayed fashions. However, as Brownell commented, contestants were judged on the basis of a range of criteria including their walk, movements, agility, coordination, level of ease, aesthetic appeal, and harmony of appearance. While the colour and shape of their swimsuits and evening gowns might, of course, have contributed to the panel's assessment of these categories, the fashions – in a sartorial sense – were not the object of the judges' gaze.

There is currently in China ample evidence of an unprecedented expansion of spaces and positions for individual and group experimentation with new gender and sexual identities. At the level of public debate and organization as well as the individual subject, marketization of the economy has permitted Chinese women to explore notions of self-identity that potentially signify fundamental shifts in social understandings of gender. At the same time, many practices and policies, including those designed to protect 'women's rights', seem to consolidate divisions between differently positioned women. While the differentiation and diversification of the reform era has given to women many unprecedented opportunities, it has, as Wang Zheng (2001) has argued, also brought accelerated gender discrimination and gender conflicts. From the most basic issues of son preference and missing daughters, to the feminization of agriculture and exploitation of unskilled female migrant labour, women continue to be marked on a large scale as unequal citizens, denied material remuneration and cultural recognition in a way that could classify them as 'equal' to men. Between these poles of empowerment and exclusion, however, multiple meanings of gender are produced and negotiated, within both local contexts and dominant media discourses. Given the possible, maybe limitless, range of readings, is it possible to ascribe transcendent meanings to any particular set of images?

This question was brought home to me in the late 1990s by a media studies scholar when I presented a paper on posters of the Cultural Revolution in Indiana University. In response to the semiotically-based arguments I put forward in this paper, he challenged my conclusions, not on the basis of any opposing argument, but to ask why I looked at the posters as visual closures on the gender positions they represented rather than visual invitations to exploration and empowerment?[4] With reference to the topic of this chapter, can we sustain the argument that contemporary images of consumer femininity, circulating within China as well as transnationally, are susceptible to any dominant or hegemonic interpretations? How might we challenge current widespread assumptions about the meanings of contemporary fashionable femininity to identify alternative readings, removed from the familiar binaries of dominant approaches?

In attempting to answer these questions, I first want to turn to some of the assumptions made about how to interpret fashionable femininity in China's globalized consumer culture. I then want to outline some of the major contributions scholars have made in recent years to thinking about how to analyse the standard images of femininity produced in popular culture. Young women's explorations through their own fashions, and through the discursive representations of contemporary femininity in the fashion magazines they read, offer diverse understandings of gender. Finally, therefore, I want to suggest that examining the ways young Chinese women look at images of fashionable femininity disturbs many of the assumptions about their meanings that continue to characterize mainstream narratives on women and gender in Chinese society.[5]

Questioning dominant narratives: Maoist and market eras

Recent Western research on women and gender in China has raised critical questions about many of the familiar narratives about Chinese history, society and culture. This research has produced perspectives on gender identities that are more nuanced, fluid, and historically plausible than the standard texts on family and society in China would suggest.[6] In insisting on the mediations of historical moment, region, ethnicity, economics and politics in shaping women's lives and the ways in which we analyse them, these writers have been able to critically re-examine a series of normative approaches to gender relations in China which have been, as it were, taken for granted – the conceptualization of 'inner' and 'outer' realms, the 'victim' status of women with bound feet, the assumption that Confucian patriarchy denied women access to education and learning, and so on.

In contrast, discussions about gender identities in the PRC still often rehearse familiar assumptions which add little to our understanding of Chinese society and culture. Two such assumptions need to be mentioned here, for they have significant repercussions for our understanding of the changes in gender representations and practice that have reshaped Chinese women's lives in the past three decades or so. The first is that the radical changes in public representations of women and femininity since the 1980s signify a total break with the Maoist era. Embedded in this is the second, that there is an essential difference between the dominant discourses of gender characterizing the Maoist and the reform periods. The immense diversity in women's identifications and their representations across these different periods is somehow reduced to a stark contrast between two generic types, roughly corresponding with the differential positioning of women indicated by the terms *funü* and *nüxing* (Barlow 1991: 132–60). On the one hand, there is the robust steelworker or young farmer, the woman (*funü*) of Maoist ideology, eyes shining with political zeal, dressed in the same greys, greens and blues as her male counterpart. On the other there is the fashionable, beautiful, consumer-oriented and Westernized urbanite, the emblem of the success of China's market reform. This 'rupture' in representation and meaning is predictably presented as a consequence of the marketization of the economy and consumer culture, the ideological shifts of the Party-State, Westernization and globalization. It is echoed in diverse ways, including in popular discussion about fashion, beauty and consumption. As a Chinese commentator put it in an article on feminine beauty, 'no beauties were allowed twenty years ago. . . . Today's beautiful women should thank the times, not themselves, for their beauty' (Anonymous 1998). The 'times' of the Mao era become a signifier of bodily constraint and puritan morality, when women's outward appearance was masculinized and stripped of any aesthetic and erotic appeal. In contrast, 'modernity' and the 'West', in the form of market reform and consumer culture, appear as the motors driving release from those constraints, facilitating 'choice for modern women' (*xiandai nüxing de xuanze*). Many young women I have interviewed who grew up in the 1980s upheld the same dichotomized understanding. That the 'socialist androgyny' (Young 1989) of the Mao decades precluded all overt expressions of femininity and bodily beauty has become one of the most familiar tropes of post-Mao memories.[7]

In contrast with such a view, all the more powerful for its prevalence in today's popular culture, narratives and images of the Mao years commonly made a gendered association with interests in appearance and beauty, albeit a negative one. For example, as I have argued elsewhere, women's and young people's magazines during the 1950s and early 1960s – such magazines ceased publication during the Cultural Revolution – made routine reference to feminine interest in appearance in framing descriptions of immoral and ideologically unsound young women. Indeed, expressions of female eroticism and feminine beauty were widely used as metaphors for ideological turpitude. Women who 'wasted their time' on their dress, or who spent money on fashionable clothes, were represented as self-seeking temptresses. The female 'third party' in divorce cases, or the hapless innocents seduced and abandoned by ruthless men, frequently appeared in narrative contexts that drew attention to their fondness for high-heeled shoes, tight skirts and sleek hair. Physical beauty and fashionable clothes, such narratives intoned, could disguise 'evil intentions' and even criminal behaviour (Evans 1997: 156).

State intervention in sartorial politics in the mid-1950s revealed the depth of the assumption of women's natural desire to acquire things beautiful, when a 'clothes reform campaign' was launched to boost the self-confidence of the urban housewife. Symbolic suggestions of femininity, such as dress patterns and instructions about how to refashion old clothes, started appearing in the print media alongside articles urging women to discard the view that being interested in appearance was bourgeois. Coinciding with rising pressure on the urban economy under the effects of large-scale migration to the cities, the slogan 'let's be pretty' encouraged women to make the best of 'returning home'. The new legitimacy given to permed hair styles and floral printed skirts appeared as a reward for withdrawing from the urban labour market. Alongside frequent assertions about women's natural identification with the domestic sphere, this 'refeminization' of female appearance was premised on a naturalized view of gender attributes which contrasts with reform-era images in degree and form, but not essentially in kind. The idea that gender differences were erased by neutralization of appearance thus has little more than a superficial applicability. The amnesia characterizing public accounts of the Cultural Revolution in the past two decades has to a great extent been ideologically driven by the interests of post-Mao leaders. The exclusions at work in current memories of the gender associations of the Cultural Revolution can similarly be seen as a kind of amnesia, but driven by the interests generated by the consumer market.

There is, however, evidence of a somewhat different approach in visual and autobiographical accounts. For example, posters of the Cultural Revolution indicate a range of visual clues suggestive of the 'legitimacy' of feminine interest in clothes and appearance. Many posters of the early 1970s depict young women dressed in bright clothes, with pretty red bows in their hair, or colourful and patterned blouses peeping out from under their sober

Mao jackets. It could further be argued that the imaging of women as young mothers of bouncy babies clad in patterned and colourful garments reinforced the naturalized association between femininity and colourful prettiness. Visual images of femininity occasionally went even further in the appeal they inscribed in the female body, and acquired a potentially erotic allure in the famous painting of Wu Qinghua, the strong and shapely heroine of the revolutionary model ballet *The Red Detachment of Women*. Entitled 'Full of hatred' (*Manqiang chouhen*), this oil painting was a copy of the stage photograph of the same image from the ballet performance. Writing about her own youthful fascination with the image of her 'handcuffed hands, whipped body, long and braided hair and torn red silk dress', Chen Xiaomei suggested that, looking back, Wu Qinghua's figure had a 'voluptuous appeal and bodily beauty' which, though 'securely disguised by the focus on an ideologically correct story and by equipping the womanly body with a "manly spirit", as it was traditionally defined', explained the power her image held (Chen 1999: 111–12).

Chen Xiaomei also describes her sense of freedom and delight in experimenting with guises of gendered and sexual identities represented by the fashions of the time. Between her delight in her dancer mother's feminine body and appeal and her excitement at 'disguising' herself through wearing the 'gender-neutral' clothes of the time, she enjoyed the possibility of moving between different kinds of identities. Associating this with her privileged background of being born into a family associated with a national theatre and her simultaneous attachment to the 'subalterns that [her] parents both devotedly represent[ed] on stage and used as models of social behaviour offstage', Chen Xiaomei addressed an 'ambiguous space' relating to gender identities, in which, 'by virtue of the androgynous play between the manly woman and the womanly man', she gained a sense of balance and freedom (1999: 110).

Another work, also by a woman of the Red Guard generation, is important to mention at this point, as an example of the ways in which the sartorial distinctions drawn between the constraints of the Mao era and the individual freedoms of the post-Mao period might be thought. *Spider Eaters*, by Rae Yang (1997), is an autobiographical account of growing up in China, one of the most memorable and moving parts of which narrates her experience, and her agency, as a Red Guard. She describes how her simple Red Guard 'uniform' did not obscure a feminine sense of longing to find expression, but gave her a sense of self in which her personhood as a political agent relegated concerns with gendered appearance to the status of something she never considered. Dress, far from being a constraint, was the symbol of her practice as an equal actor alongside other women and men of her age and outlook. That many women of the same generation experienced Cultural Revolution clothing in similar ways is apparent in some of the autobiographical accounts of *Some of Us* (Zhong *et al.* 2001), a recently-published collection of memoirs of Chinese women growing up in the Mao era.

These two examples show that the previous discourse, visual as well as textual, was far from holding out a closed set of positions for women's self-identification. They demonstrate that the apparel and bodily forms of the Mao period were not simply a closed book in terms of the possibilities of gender identifications. Even though the visual parameters of Maoist images were clearly limited, these limits did not simply determine the ways in which they were interpreted. The images of the time had nothing to do with the commercial interests of consumer culture, but they were far from representing centrally dictated modes of response from their audience.

However, the boundaries of exclusion and inclusion that these images represented were defined by very different interests to those informing the more recent commercially driven images. Social differentiation in consumer culture, as Baudrillard argued, is mediated by the object, and not by the subject. He also argued that consumer society 'generalises the feminine model across the whole field of consumption' (quoted in Gane 1991: 60). The possibilities of individual self-identification made available by the commercial 'object' were not available under Mao's rule. Hence, the lines of differentiation in the Mao images were determined by the ideological and political tendencies of the time, and not by the social hierarchies of consumption. In the class terms of the time, they included the rural, the elderly, the uneducated and the poor, leaving many potential spaces for a gendered and even sexual appeal across the boundaries of difference that operate in today's consumer culture. The accoutrements of fashion now displayed to appeal to women's consumer passions exclude everyday gendered identities that are not commercially valued by consumer culture. The rural, the older, the poor and the disadvantaged are virtually absent from the images that dominate the front covers of women's magazines. The limited exceptions are found on a few inner pages of women's magazines, where articles might focus on, for example, a grandmother's growing frustration at being expected to care for her grandchildren, or a migrant worker's success in setting up her own business. Contemporary femininity is fashioned through images of the urban-located female who has access to the clothes and accoutrements that urban consumption offers. The consuming urbanite thus functions to affirm hierarchical lines of distinction defined by consumer capacity and success. Those who cannot or do not participate in this project are relegated, silenced, and absented to the outer borders of the reform project.

One effect of this is the marginalization of alternative and potentially subversive gender identities, apparent in Chen Xiaomei's and Rae Yang's accounts, which cast the pre-reform years of the Cultural Revolution as liberating. The erotic appeal of many contemporary images of women undoubtedly reinscribes the feminine body with possibilities of exploration and desire that were, for many, denied by the discourse of the Cultural Revolution (Larson 1997: 204–5). But, corresponding with the dichotomized division between the Mao and post-Mao woman which I have critiqued above, the self-legitimization of the consumer project rests on the assumption that multiple readings of womanhood and femininity were denied by the discursive constraints on gender in the previous period. Put in other words, the erotic consumer of recent years is seen as the image of personal freedoms because she has been released – by the market – from the controls of the Mao era and a suppression of its effects. The 'forgetting' of experiences such as Chen's and Yang's thus emerges as a necessary component of the current 'socialist' market/Party-State's claims to facilitate individual opportunity.

In challenging the idea of a simple rupture between the Mao and post-Mao periods, and in pointing out the amnesia which seems to characterize contemporary reflections on the 'fashions' of the Mao era, I am not ignoring the specificities of history. It goes without saying that the affirmative construction of the feminine consumer of recent years has given to fashion and bodily appearance a privileged place in contemporary culture which did not apply to the Maoist era. The reform period's departure from the Maoist period has been articulated through inscribing positive values in the link between femininity and consumption, and, as a result, through legitimizing the effects of the latter in sexualizing public culture (Baudrillard 1976: 132–51). The emblematic use of the fashioned, feminine body has since the 1980s been used to demonstrate the rewards for participating in the market economy. The gender subjectivity of the 'modern woman' displayed in women's magazines condones and encourages her consumption of feminine fashions. Despite these differences, however, a naturalized link between femininity and bodily appearance has been a constant, though disguised, theme throughout the changing discourses of gender in China since the early 1950s. Jennifer Craik has argued that fashion, in its modern capitalist guise, is always linked with femaleness and femininity. In her view, this is in large part the effect of modern capitalism's links between men and production and between women and consumption (Craik 1994: 46). The effects of the internet and globalization on work practices is clearly challenging this argument, and in China as in the 'West' fashion is increasingly becoming a masculine domain as well. The link between femininity and appearance was obscured but not eradicated from Maoist imagery. A fundamental challenge to the link has yet to come.

China and the white West

Throughout the 1980s and the 1990s, if the fashionable feminine consumer of China's new modernity stood as a metaphor for the success of the market, she also signified the assertion of Chinese national identity at a time when consumption of the West was *de rigueur*. Louisa Schein (1994) has argued that the binary juxtaposition between the Chinese woman and the white Western woman during the 1980s and the 1990s commonly served to assert nationalist sentiments.[8] However, the use of the racialized 'motif of golden hair' (*jin toufa*), as Schein has put it, by no means conveyed a simple message. The image of the white woman simultaneously functioned as an emblem of national longing, lack and difference. This needs to be explained.

The white woman who dominated the outside covers of a number of women's journals between the early and mid-1990s appeared as the voluptuous embodiment of erotic desire, enjoying her own sensuality as well as being enjoyed by the male partner who frequently, though by no means always or even mostly, appeared at her side.[9] She signified liberation and individual self-realization through immersion in her own pleasure. Rigged out in jewellery, designer clothing and cosmetics, she was a symbol of consumer satisfaction and pleasure. Often in a state of relative undress, her beautiful hair and unblemished skin bespoke the bodily and aesthetic ideal of consumer desires.

While the white woman of these images was not unitary – she appeared in different poses and guises, and in different settings – the variations of her image came together as a symbolic representation of the West which was both desired and reviled. Marketization of the economy was bringing MTV into millions of homes, was flooding shops with more-or-less affordable Western goods, and was lifting many former restrictions on travel. The white woman represented what many consumers wanted, and what was no longer beyond their reach. She possessed symbolic authority as the attainment of consumer desire; her figure and face were appropriated to 'sell' the products which China still lacked, but on which China's market future depended. At the same time, however, her image represented the antithesis of Chinese values, of Chinese national identity. She rarely appeared with Chinese women or in settings that invoked the presence of China. Articles printed alongside her image in women's magazines of the early and mid-1990s repeatedly distanced her from what was desirable in the Chinese woman. In a series of articles on the question of 'modern feminine beauty', published in the journal *Zhongguo funü* (Women of China), readers suggested that the 'strong woman' (*qiang nüren*), the woman who had an independent career and position, was unfeminine.[10] In contrast with Western women, as one contributor intoned, 'Chinese women should preserve their Chinese characteristics and . . . should be more reserved and shy.' Surveys on what young people looked for in their selection of partner, or the kind of girl that appealed to the urban graduate, repeatedly suggested that the 'gentle and soft' (*wenrou*), unthreatening and servicing characteristics of the 'traditional oriental beauty' rated high on young men's lists. Along the same lines, Susan Brownell has pointed out that public discourse of the same period was careful to emphasize that sportswomen who might appear aggressive during competition were in fact gentle females. A judo player, for example, was described as a 'shy, demure-looking girl, but on the training mat she becomes as tough and aggressive as any tomboy' (Brownell 1998–1999: 42). The counter-positioning of images of the white/Western and Chinese woman thus on the one hand signified an affirmative message, ratifying the legitimacy of China's emerging consumer culture, into which the Western woman beckoned the Chinese into the delights of consumption. At the same time, the racialized dichotomy between the West and China affirmed China's claims to national and moral authority.

This value-laden juxtaposition of different images of femininity reminds us of arguments put forward by feminist scholars about the political uses of the female image. The trope of female bodily suffering and self-sacrifice has been widely deployed in literature, film and language as a signifier of a nationalism which was hurt and humiliated by the West and Japan (Liu 1994; Meng 1993). The central subject of this nationalism is male; women must suffer because men are too weak to reverse the injustices done to men through women (Donald 1998). A wave of cultural revivalism followed the national humiliation that fuelled so many political passions during the late 1980s, and by the mid-1990s symbolic assertions of male dominance were taking on other forms. The privileged position of an entrepreneurial masculinity has repeatedly been asserted through images of the 'traditional' Chinese woman who symbolizes China, but who has enough global appeal to be commercially viable on the international market. Her prevalent association with service and softness acknowledges her subordinate role in the male production of the consumer market. Portrayed as the consumer of what others produce, she reinforces male success in directing the market and asserts the moral superiority of Chinese values, even though this might be at the risk of her own self-erasure. In this context, Sheldon Lu's analysis of mainland TV soaps demonstrates that the fulfilment of male desire through possession of the white woman effectively erases the passive, 'traditional' wife, while simultaneously asserting her virtue (Lu 1998).

Recent shifts in the imaging of the beautiful Chinese woman show yet another meaning to her bodily appropriation as an emblem of consumer desire. Coinciding with what Chinese commentators dubbed the West's 'craze for China' (*Zhongguo re*), seen in recent 'oriental fashions' in Western markets, the image of the fashionable Chinese woman has increasingly appeared together with the Western woman in magazine advertisements and photographic illustrations. No longer is the white woman kept at a distance, different, desired, but also a source of danger to Chinese values. She is brought into contact with the Chinese woman through, for example, appearing in advertisements for local Chinese fashion products, or wearing 'traditional' Chinese clothes, notably the *qipao*. Schein has suggested that the diminished appearance of the white woman in Chinese commercial culture in the mid-1990s and the use of the minority woman as the emblematic 'other' to the Han, signified 'a turning away from the West in a fervent attempt to cast off the inferior position assigned to China in the dyadic relation with the West' (Schein 1994: 159). Here, in contrast, I would suggest that the assimilation of the feminine West into the fashions of China is a mode of presenting a newly confident nationalism to the world, which applauds Chinese and Asian values, through clothing Western women in them, while asserting China's capacity to contain, if not dominate, the West through the simultaneous appearance of the two.

On a slightly tangential note, this brief analysis also shows that, through the changing juxtapositions of the Chinese and white/Western woman, China and the West have not been locked into a simple opposition. Prasenjit Duara (1995) has argued for an approach to nationalism which is not premised on the awakening of a pristine national subject contesting the claims of the other, but on a relationship between self and other which takes different forms across time and place. Though my focus is very different, this analysis of changing representations, changing images and changing relationships between the white and the Chinese woman offers another lens on to the shifting forms that Chinese nationalism takes.

Hegemonic meanings?

Fashion is a domain of popular culture situated at a key point of intersection between local and global forces and interests. In urban Chinese fashion, the relationship between the local and the global is played out largely through the figure of the female body. The global joins the local in constituting discourses of gender. Here, therefore, the image of the local female consumer functions no longer as a marker of difference from the Maoist past, nor as an emblem of liberation from its constraints, but as a site where the hegemonic forces of global capital become part of the formation of gender identity. Her constitution becomes part of a global process blurring clear distinctions between the 'Chinese' and the 'West'. Does this mean, then, that the formation of gender – in this context of young femininities – is now part of a process in which the local is erased? If not, then where can we see markers in the Chinese world of fashion in which the ineluctable forces of 'Westernization' – often interchangeable in the Chinese media context for globalization – are not present?

There are, of course, many ways of responding to this question. An analysis of the financial interests behind contemporary fashion in China would be one. The links between these and editorial production of the images in fashion magazines is another. Indeed, editorial decisions in producing feminine images offer some interesting insights. Previous work I have done on these issues demonstrate that as producers of images to appeal to young Chinese consumers, editors appear as agents mediating images between global and local spheres (Evans 2001). Drawing on a global as well as a regional reservoir of images, editors of journals such as *Nüyou* (Woman friend) and *Ruili ke'ai xianfeng* (Cawaii and Boys Rush) seek to appeal to local readers within parameters established by the global market.[11] Editors consciously mould global designs in ways they deem to be acceptable for local consumption. Taking a style out of its Western/global context and representing it in a Chinese context may inscribe in it a 'look' that, for its consumers, is associated more with urban popular culture in China than with the high street fashions of the 'West'. And indeed, though often characterized as 'Western designs', they often come to Chinese magazines from Taiwanese, Japanese and Korean sources.

Another approach to the question is to look at local reception of magazine fashions. Shih Shu-mei, a US-based Taiwanese scholar who has written extensively about globalization and local identities, has analysed the different layers of nationalist and patriarchal meanings inscribed in media representations of the mainland 'sister' (Shih 1998). She suggests that the interweaving of political, economic and cultural anxieties in the figure of the Mainland woman as represented in the Taiwan and Hong Kong media consistently undermines the idea that her representation might mean the same thing across time and place. It also undercuts claims that there is a 'transnational' public sphere in which gender is produced in the same form across national and cultural boundaries. In the Taiwan media, the Mainland woman appears as the criminal, the deviant, the gender representative of the threat from across the Straits. In Hong Kong, she is represented as the prostitute and the mistress, a gendered embodiment of a fear, desire and destabilization that can be assimilated by Hong Kong business personified as the wealthy and successful entrepreneur. In Shih's analysis, woman neither appears as the 'third term' in the binary struggle between the colonizer and the colonized, nor as the gendered representation of a unitary Chinese identity. Though she may wear the same clothes and represent similar consumer desires, and though her appeal may be unproblematically characterized as 'Western' by Chinese and 'Western' observers alike, the different 'readings' of her image indicate the importance of the local in the construction of gendered meanings.

Appadurai (1990) has argued that the process of globalization of cultural forms and images is not simply one of homogenization. Repatriation of image and representation in local contexts produces diverse dialogues in local contexts that disturb the unitary force of the global. The differences and variations between the meanings given contemporary images of the Chinese beauty are, of course, significant, and have potentially immense political as well as economic impact, as Shih Shu-mei has shown. The centralizing tendencies in the production of many of these images do not, in themselves, direct readers' and spectators' responses to them. Indeed, local readers may indeed look on such images as potential spaces for experimentation with a range of subject positions associated with non-conformist versions of femininity, which those wedded to the notion of China's 'Westernization' do not see. For neither producers nor readers is there a neat distinction between the local and the global; rather, a negotiation between the two in which many interpretations and positions are possible. Hence, while young urban consumers in China clearly link contemporary fashions with 'the West' and 'the modern', the choices they make do not indicate a simple desire to 'look like' the quintessential 'Westerner'. A young woman may describe her use of makeup to make her eyes look bigger not as the desire to look more like Western/global women, but to give her a 'spirit' (*jingshen*) and 'liveliness' (*huoyue*) that, for her, is an important aspect of a 'modern' appearance. In the same way, the young beautician in a photography studio may describe the 'Western' images lining the walls of her studio as 'cool' (*kule*), 'alternative' (*lingwai*), 'independent' (*duli*), and even 'traditional oriental' (*chuantong dongfang*). She may discern in these images a range of differences corresponding with her local cultural and social context that those positioned outside that context would not be able to see. Fashion editors may be conscious in their selection of global images to appeal to their young consumers. Their consumers, however, are more concerned with the meaning of such images in their local and personal contexts. The attention they give to a particular 'look' is associated with its value in the local context.

Magazine editors I have interviewed in Beijing describe themselves as increasing the possibilities for individual expression in expanding consumer choice to their readers. 'Buying into' the discourse of individual choice and expression of consumer culture is thus an implicit acknowledgement of the function of market and global interests in the cultural production of social and gender identity. However, Chinese young women's interpretations of the different 'looks' on offer in fashion magazines demonstrate that there is no single 'femininity' associated with the image of the beautiful woman they so eagerly consume. Karen Hutchings (1996) has argued that the consumption of images and products manufactured by economic interests that demonstrate little commitment to challenging conventional gender hierarchies does not, in itself, mean a simple acceptance of the hierarchical gender relations inscribed in those images. Similarly, I would argue that what many may see as the pursuit of 'Westernized' gender meanings in contemporary feminine fashions in China may just as significantly be treated as a sign of challenge and difference by consumers within the local Chinese context. Indeed, young women commonly approach fashion as a performative means for the assertion of self-identity. For these young women, consumer capacity grants the possibility of affirming a series of desires that are much more linked to their search for independence within a patriarchal social and political environment than their conformity to the dictates of the market. Their mothers, now in their forties and fifties, may object to their appearance on the grounds that it signifies a kind of dependent femininity responsive to male expectations. Their daughters, however, argue that contemporary fashions signify recognition of a range of individual possibilities their parents did not have, including the affirmation of autonomy, pleasure, resistance and a desire for an 'alternative' lifestyle. As Jennifer Craik put it, 'It is as if the acquisition of a new visible identity worn on the body ensures the acquisition of a new "modern" cultural identity' (Craik 1994: 27). Within such a context, a young woman might well feel empowered by deciding to dress in a way that challenges her parents' tastes. In this sense, the particularities of her choices can be seen as an assertion of agency in the creation of new spaces of cultural and social practice, and not simply as pandering to consumer trends, or returning to some conventional notion of femininity.[12]

The female body thus emerges as a focal site where individual desires, local boundaries of gender and sexual politics, and global consumer capitalism are played out (Li 1998). From a meta-perspective, the gendered identifications of the female body through fashion are without doubt contained by the hegemonic power of the global. That hegemony, however, becomes 'conflicted', as Diane Crane put it, given that the images associated with it are given different 'readings' by different subjects (Crane 1999). From the perspective of the young woman, fashion may offer the opportunity to choose between different social and cultural meanings. The clothes and makeup the young woman wears become performative components of self-identification, even though at the same time they are indications of her integration into a social and cultural environment moulded by forces she cannot control.

Susan Brownell has argued that . . .

> the transformations in the configuration of gender, body and nation that have occurred over the last two decades are not innocent with respect to power; they moved away from the androgynous ideal, which many women experienced as liberating, and in fact masked the emergence of new forms of patriarchy
>
> (Brownell 1998–1999: 36)

These 'new forms of patriarchy' are widely manifest in the images of sweet femininity that continue to cover the pages of fashion magazines. The rhetoric of emancipation and self-expression that has accompanied the publication of these images over the past two decades cannot mask the evidence of the systematic subordination of the female to the powers and demands of the male. However, patriarchy is not carved in stone. These sweet images are juxtaposed with others, of the successful and fashionable university professor, the young businesswoman and mother, the international journalist, and so on, suggesting that the female is much more than a passive consumer of masculinist production. These images also offer subject positions to their targeted readers and consumers that detached commentators may miss, particularly those of the 'older generation'. Young women's insistence that consumer fashion represents one way to challenge the authority of the established order is another indication of new spaces and possibilities for negotiating gender meanings, even though their parameters are still set by the combined forces of global capital and patriarchy.

The femininities that are at the heart of consumer culture thus demonstrate a complex range of influences and meanings, reasserting hegemonic influences in the formation of gender at the same time as they contest them. Though driven by the partnership of global market and the Party-State, consumer culture opens up possibilities for individual agency that are not directly determined by either. In this sense, the agency shown by young women in making individual choices in dress can be seen as contributing to the formation of a public sphere in which local consumer desires are expressed in complex negotiation with global and state influences. The image of the fashionable female thus becomes much more than the emblem of consumer success. She offers a choice in the formation of new female subjectivities removed from the immediate arm of Party-State and parental authority. She also becomes a visual reminder of the way in which the cultural formation of gender is negotiated between the local Party-State and the global, in ways which offer many more possibilities for discovery and self-assertion than references to 'Westernization' and 'patriarchy' would imply.

Notes

1 I want to thank The Universities' China Committee in London for supporting the fieldwork contributing to this paper. I also want to thank Zhang Hui and Jing Jun for the assistance and advice they gave me in conducting this fieldwork.

2 It is worth pointing out that all publishing in the PRC remains under state ownership and control, even though there are currently moves to introduce private ownership into this sphere. Many women's magazines depend on considerable investment from private, including foreign, interests, yet all are formally owned by state institutions.

3 An interview I conducted early in 2001 with the chief editor of a woman's magazine that was affiliated to, though not owned by, the All China Women's Federation revealed that an issue of her magazine had been withdrawn from circulation, on the order of her immediate boss in the Women's Federation, after it published a two-page article on the lesbian and gay scene in Beijing. Her 'boss's' objection was not the public discussion of homosexuality, but rather discussion in which named individuals discussed their own experience as homosexuals.

4 I wish to thank Michael Curtin for making this very apt critical comment. It has given me much food for thought, not least as a reminder to think of different spectatorships in making conclusions about the interpretation of visual images.

5 The empirical data for the first draft of this chapter, presented to the SOAS seminar in 1999, came entirely from Mainland women's popular magazines. Since then, I have undertaken three periods of fieldwork, conducting often lengthy interviews with many different women in Beijing and the rural north-east, one theme of which has been to examine young women's views of beauty and its association with gender identity. My discussion in this paper draws on images and articles from women's magazines as well as the fieldwork interviews, all of which I have taped and transcribed.

6 Some of these major contributions are Bray 1997; Ko 1994; Mann 1997; Ebrey 1993.

7 The term 'socialist androgyny' is Marilyn Young's, but it is commonly rehearsed by other writers, Chinese as well as Anglophone, as 'gender neutrality', 'masculinization of women', 'gender erasure', 'defeminization', and so on.

8 Along similar lines, Dru Gladney (1994) has also argued that popular representations of minority sensuality and eroticism have served to delineate internal 'margins' or boundaries, to reshape and consolidate the 'centre' of Han nationalism. The saturation of women's print and advertising media by the beautiful white woman signified the use of the racialized emblem of 'golden hair', as Schein (1994) has put it, to gave way in the 1990s to a focus on the 'colour' of the ethnic woman. However, this did not simply replace one set of binaries with another. Indeed, I would argue that the use of visual and narrative hierarchies of

address that subordinated minorities, women and peasants in Chinese society operated alongside the image of the white woman to delineate internal and external boundaries along a grid of hierarchical meanings, and as Gladney (1994) said, to 'reshape and consolidate the "centre" of Han nationalism'.

9 For example, see issues of *Nüxing yanjiu* (Women's Studies), published between 1990 and 1994. This journal was renamed and 'refashioned' as *Nüxing yuekan* (Women) in early 1998, and as *Zhiye nüxing* (Career Woman) in 2001. As the editor of the journal told me in an interview with her in 2001, these changes were implemented in response to market demand, and to expand the magazine's appeal to professional women in general rather than to the academic invoked in the initial title.

10 The series was published in *Zhongguo funü* (Women of China) between 1991 and 1992 under the title 'Shenmo Shi Xiandai Nüxing Mei?' (What is Modern Feminine Beauty?).

11 These are the published translations of the Chinese titles of these two magazines. *Ruili ke'ai xianfeng* is a joint venture with Japan, published by China's Ministry of Light Industry.

12 In her analysis of a bride's involvement in her own wedding arrangements in the Hui quarter of Xi'an, Maris Gillette (2000) suggests that this agency may be contributing to the formation of a public sphere, in which consumer desires are expressed without the intervention of state interests.

References

Anonymous (1998) 'Shenmo Yang de Nüxing Zui Mei?' (What Is Feminine Beauty?), *Hunyin yu Jiating* (Marriage and Family), 6: 24–6.

Appadurai, A. (1990) 'Disjuncture and Difference in the Global Cultural Economy', *Public Culture*, (5) 3: 1–24.

Barlow, T. (1991) 'Theorizing Woman: *Funü, Guojia, Jiating* (Chinese Women, Chinese State, Chinese Family)', *Genders*, 10 (Spring): 132–60.

Baudrillard, J. (1976) *L'Echange symbolique et la mort*, Paris: Gallimard.

Bray, F. (1997) *Technology and Gender: Fabrics of Power in Late Imperial China*, Berkeley: University of California Press.

Brownell, S. (1998–1999) 'The Body and the Beautiful in Chinese Nationalism: Sportswomen and Fashion Models in the Reform Era', *China Information*, XIII (2–3): 36–58.

Chen, X. (1999) 'Growing up with posters in the Maoist era', in H. Evans and S. Donald (eds), *Picturing Power in the People's Republic of China: Posters of the Cultural Revolution*, Lanham: Rowman and Littlefield.

Craik, J. (1994) *The Face of Fashion: Cultural Studies in Fashion*, London and New York: Routledge.

Crane, D. (1999) 'Gender and Hegemony in Fashion Magazines: Women's Interpretations of Fashion Photographs', *The Sociological Quarterly*, 40 (4): 541–63.

Davis, D. S. (2000) 'Introduction: A Revolution in Consumption', in D. S. Davis (ed.), *The Consumer Revolution in Urban China*, Berkeley: University of California Press.

Donald, S. (1998) 'Symptoms of Alienation: the Female Body in Recent Chinese Film', *Continuum*, 12 (1): 91–103.

Duara, P. (1995) *Rescuing History from the Nation: Questioning Narratives of Modern China*, Chicago: University of Chicago Press.

Ebrey. P. B. (1993) *The Inner Quarters: Marriage and the Lives of Chinese Women in the Sung Period*, Berkeley: University of California Press.

Ervin, K. (1999) 'White Women, Male Desires: a Televisual Fantasy of the Transnational Chinese Family', in M. Yang (ed.), *Spaces of Their Own: Women's Public Sphere in Transnational China*. Minneapolis: University of Minnesota Press.
Evans, H. (1997) *Women and Sexuality in China: Dominant Discourses of Female Sexuality and Gender since 1949*, Cambridge: Polity Press.
—— (1999) '"Comrade Sisters": Gendered Bodies and Spaces', in H. Evans and S. Donald (eds), *Picturing Power in the People's Republic of China: Posters of the Cultural Revolution*, Lanham: Rowman and Littlefield.
—— (2000) 'Fashioning Identities, Consuming Passions: Public Images of Women in China', *New Formations*, 40: 113–27.
—— (2001) 'What Colour is Beautiful Hair? Subjective Interventions and Global Fashion in the Cultural Production of Gender in Urban China', *figurationen: gender, literature, kultur*, 2: 117–32.
Gane, M. (1991) *Baudrillard's Bestiary: Baudrillard and Culture*, London: Routledge.
Gillette, M. (2000) 'What's in a Dress? Brides in the Hui Quarter of Xi'an', in D. S. Davis (ed.), *The Consumer Revolution in Urban China*, Berkeley: University of California Press.
Gladney, D. C. (1994) 'Representing Nationality in China: Refiguring Majority/Minority Identities', *Journal of Asian Studies*, 53 (1): 92–123.
Hutchings, K. (1996) 'The Battle for Consumer Power: Post-War Women and Advertising', in G. Turner (ed.), *Fabrications: Journal of Australian Studies*, 51, St. Lucia: API Network and UQP.
Ko, D. (1994) *Teachers of the Inner Chambers: Women and Culture in Seventeenth Century China*, Stanford: Stanford University Press.
Larson, W. (1997) 'Women and the Discourse of Desire in Postrevolutionary China: the Awkward Postmodernism of Chen Ran', *boundary 2*, 24 (3): 201–23.
Li, X. (1998) 'Fashioning the Body in Post-Mao China', in A. Brydon and S. Niessen (eds), *Consuming Fashion: Adorning the Transnational Body*, Oxford: Berg.
Liu, L. (1994) 'The Female Body and Nationalist Discourse: Manchuria in Xiao Hong's *Field of Life and Death*', in A. Zito and T. Barlow (eds), *Body, Subject and Power in China*, Chicago, University of Chicago Press.
Lu, S. (1998) 'Chinese Soap Opera: The Transnational Politics of Visuality, Sexuality and Masculinity', paper presented to the Annual Meeting of the Association for Asian Studies, Washington, D.C., 26–28 March 1998.
Mann, S. (1997) *Precious Records: Women in China's Long Eighteenth Century*, Stanford: Stanford University Press.
Meng, Y. (1993) 'Female Images and National Myth', in T. Barlow (ed.), *Gender Politics in Modern China*, Durham, NC: Duke University Press.
Schein, L. (1994) 'The Consumption of Color and the Politics of White Skin in Post-Mao China', *Social Text*, 41: 141–64.
Shih, S. (1998) 'Gender and a New Geopolitics of Desire: The Seduction of Mainland Women in Taiwan and Hong Kong', *SIGNS*, 23 (2): 287–319.
Wang, Z. (2001) 'Gender, Employment and Women's Resistance', in E. J. Perry and M. Selden (eds), *Chinese Society: Change, Conflict and Resistance,* 2nd edn, London and New York: Routledge.
Yang, R. (1997) *Spider Eaters, A Memoir*, Berkeley and Los Angeles: University of California Press.
Young, M. (1989) 'Chicken Little in China: Some Reflections on Women', in A. Dirlik and M. Meisner (eds), *Marxism and the Chinese Experience: Issues in Contemporary Chinese Socialism,* Armonk, NY: M. E. Sharpe.
Zhong, X., Wang, Z. and Bai, D. (eds) (2001) *Some of Us: Chinese Women Growing up in the Mao Era.* New Brunswick and London: Rutgers University Press.

10 Wong Kar-wai's sensuous histories

Luke Robinson

Introduction: Hong Kong, handover and the problem of national allegory

In 1997, when *Happy Together* won the prize for Best Director at the Cannes Film Festival, Wong Kar-wai was still something of a niche interest outside (and arguably inside) his native Hong Kong. Marketed as an 'alternative' Asian director, his films received limited distribution and tended to play to audiences of enthusiasts in art-house cinemas. Although articles and interviews appeared in specialist magazines, academic studies of his work were limited. Three years later, when *In The Mood For Love* was awarded the Cannes Grand Prix de la Technique and its male lead the prize for Best Actor, the director was already a global name, and an industry of books, articles and websites dedicated to his cinema had begun to take shape. Yet despite such immense interest, this industry consistently displays a fascination with two particular aspects of Wong's work. The first is the characters that people his films, melancholic individuals incapable of forming lasting emotional bonds, doomed to a self-less anonymous existence defined only through commodities and [their] relationship to them (Marchetti 2000: 258). The second is the director's cinematic aesthetic, particularly his use of slow- and 'smudge'-motion.[1] These two techniques have consistently been characterized as a 'mark' of a Wong Kar-wai film, and their 'meaning' widely debated within the context of his oeuvre.

Academic criticism is no different in this regard. Broadly speaking, interpretations of Wong's films tend to cleave to one of three models: the post-colonial, the modernist, or the post-modernist. Although these approaches may appear quite distinct, the issue of the film-maker's aesthetic, and the relationships his characters have to each other and their environment, remains vital to their argument. Thus, critics as diverse as Ackbar Abbas (1997), Yau Ka-fai (2001) and Stephen Teo (1997) all cite Wong Kar-wai's visual style and characterization in defence of their respective readings of Hong Kong New Wave Cinema as post-colonial, modernist, or post-modernist.

Whilst these themes are amongst some of the most interesting and arresting in Wong Kar-wai's work, their academic appeal also reflects an element common to all three interpretative positions: the idea of literature or film as national allegory. This concept, most famously elaborated by Fredric Jameson (1986), relates changes in the form and content of a work of art to changes in its geopolitical environment. Abbas's concept of Hong Kong culture in the 1980s and 1990s as a 'space of disappearance' is most clearly indebted to this theory. If the emergence of such a space signifies the late flourishing of a new Hong Kong cultural subjectivity (Abbas 1997), this sudden interest in the particular nature of the Hong Kong experience is in fact the result of its imminent extinction, as embodied in the Handover of 1997: 'The anticipated end of Hong Kong as people knew it was the beginning of a profound concern with its historical and cultural specificity' (Abbas 1997: 7).

Ironically, then, then signing of the Joint Agreement in 1984 catalysed the emergence of a debate over 'national' identity and culture in a city-state which, until this point, had been considered devoid of either. Wong Kar-wai's films are seen as representative of this new culture, in terms of both style and content. The former in particular is highly important, for Abbas interprets the director's characteristically blurred visuals as a problematization of the very act of seeing; a problematization that posed a direct challenge to the colonial government, which depended culturally on the use of stable, simple images to 'disappear' the specific experience of Hong Kong's colonial history (Abbas 1997). The moment Wong Kar-wai's films become post-colonial is thus also the moment that they become national.

Yau Ka-fai (2001) also makes the connection between Handover and Hong Kong film in the 1980s and 1990s:

> The new Hong Kong cinema is a concept that dwells on the various responses to geohistorical situations from the early 1980s to around 1997, when the return of Hong Kong to China became (one of) the issue(s) of greatest concern to Hong Kong.
>
> (Yau 2001: 543)

The responses that he detects, however, are perhaps best described as simultaneously 'modern' and national. Hong Kong cinema becomes modern at this point because of its increasing interest in time. Following Deleuze's concept of the time-image, Yau sees this as the symptom of an emergent cinematic modernity. Yet he also posits the Hong Kong New Wave as a third, or minor, cinema. This, he maintains, is a cinema which seeks to address a people who as yet do not exist, and in the process to call them into being. This is how the 'national' is formed. Wong's *Ashes of Time* is cited as an example both of this modernity and of this 'thirdness'. Yau argues that the film takes a genre specific to Hong Kong (i.e., the kung-fu film) and renders it unrecognizable, blurring and fragmenting the visuals to the point where the 'action' becomes almost invisible to the naked eye. Traditional identification of and with a 'national' form thus become impossible. Simultaneously, the collapse of all chronological plot sequencing creates a sense of time that is rooted exclusively in the present. This is the quintessential moment of becoming, and Yau implies that it is in this moment, understood in relation to Deleuze's third time image, that a new Hong Kong subjectivity may be called into being.

The relationship between national allegory and the post-modernity of the Hong Kong New Wave is perhaps less obvious. Nevertheless, it is implicit in the relationship between the market, human relationships and the visual proposed in certain interpretations of Wong's films. The particular concern of these critics with the fetishized circulation of objects between characters unable to express or commit emotionally (see, e.g., Leong 1999) and with the free, decontextualized circulation of images within the films (see, e.g., Lalanne 1997), reflects a central tenet of post-modern theory: the domination of human relations and modes of communication by the market (see Harvey 1990; Jameson 1991). Yet, in the context of Hong Kong, such theorizing tends to become fatally tangled in speculation about the city's politics. Stephen Teo ascribes Hong Kong's obsession with consumerism in the 1980s and 1990s directly to a spirit of 'fin-de-siècle fatalism' engendered by the upcoming handover, and comments that 'The loss of a sense of the future together with the near-hysterical stress on the accumulation of and speculation in exchange values have triggered the current spirit of postmodernism [in the city]' (Teo 1997: 243).

Hong Kong's status as the post-modern society *par excellence*, a city in which the economic logic of commercial exchange has completely supplanted the social logic of human relationships, is thus predicated on its political position as a colony. Post-modernism and the national – or its lack – thus merge, and any film termed post-modern becomes a *de facto* allegory of its socio-political context.

This issue of lack, however, is key. Implicitly, all three models seem to centre Hong Kong subjectivity around a form of loss. For Abbas, and for Yau, this is the anticipated loss of the city as its inhabitants have known it until now, expressed most succinctly through the concept of the *déjà disparu*, the feeling and viewing of the 'space of disappearance' (Abbas 1997; Yau 2001). For the post-modernists, it is a loss of the political which expresses itself in constant consumption, a process of continual displacement in which one moment erases another, and one object the next. It is this sense of loss that is often invoked to explain the mood of nostalgia that permeates much of Wong Kar-wai's output, and his preoccupation with memories of the past. These themes are thus seen to represent an awareness that the present is always already ceasing to exist (Lalanne 1997), or as a way of coming to terms with, possibly even overcoming, Hong Kong's status as a 'disappearing' space (Tsui 1995). Remembrance, and the emotions it provokes, become ways in which an alternative history of the crown colony can be traced.

Whilst much has been written about the problem of 'national' cinema, Rey Chow (1995) provides the most succinct criticism of this concept apropos of Chinese language film. As Chow points out, 'national' readings of 'non-western' cinema tend to adopt a paradigm of either direct or indirect resistance to imperialism. Consequently all forms of 'non-western' culture are viewed as mere expressions of anti-colonial politics, in the process being condemned to an eternal and rather limited realism that denies any claim they may make on a more broadly interpretative aesthetic (Chow 1995). This, she stresses, is particularly problematic in relation to film. For Chow, film is a process of cultural translation that 'encompasses an entire range of activities, including the change from tradition to modernity, from literature to visuality, from elite scholastic culture to mass culture, from the native to the foreign and back and so forth' (Chow 1995: 192).

The national model thus reduces the highly complex cultural dynamics of the cinema to a simple, monological system. It is true that adjustments have been made to the concept of national allegory in the light of such criticism: Yau, for example, calls for its application not as a totalizing framework, but only to those works 'relevant' to its concerns (Yau 2001). Yet this merely raises further questions. What, in this context, does 'relevance' imply, and how does the critic determine it?

I do not wish to dismiss all such interpretations of Wong Kar-wai's films, nor do I intend to ignore the interest of critics in either Wong's style, or his characterization. However, given the problems discussed, Chow's formulation of the nature of cinema may prove a useful method of breaking a theoretical impasse. Put simply: if film is a project of cultural translation, what kind of project is the director – the translator, if you will – engaged in? And how does such a project relate to the issue that appears to have fascinated both amateur and professional critics of Wong's films, namely the relationship that they posit between cultural context, material practice, and visual subjectivity?

I would like to take two quotations from Wong Kar-wai himself as a point of entry to this problem. The first concerns the behaviour of Takeshi Kaneshiro's character, Cop 223, in the initial half of *Chunking Express*. When we initially encounter Cop 223, he has just been dumped by his girlfriend, a month before her birthday, which falls on 1 May. As a result, he spends the next month purchasing tins of pineapple, her favourite fruit, one tin a day, each with the expiry date of 1 May. If by the time he has collected all thirty tins she has yet to take him back, then he will give up on her. Asked what this behaviour is supposed to mean, Wong replies: 'That's simply his way of making every minute of his life count for something' (Rayns 1995: 14).

The second quotation comes from an article written by Wong for the magazine *Cahiers du cinéma*, and concerns his use of slow motion: 'The use I make of slow motion is a pragmatic one: it is an invitation to suspend the flow, a means of allowing characters and viewers to take pleasure in a look, a means of allowing us to dwell on a noise or an effect of light' (Wong Kar-wai 1999: 26, my translation).[2]

These quotations directly address the two issues that have dominated discussion of Wong's films. The scene from *Chunking Express* has been cited as a classic example of the commodity fetishism impeding the emotional development of Wong's characters (Marchetti 2000). The director's use of slow motion, as already noted, is central to Abbas's argument about the 'space of disappearance' and the post-colonial quality of these films. Yet Wong's own understanding of these moments is quite distinct from either of these interpretations. In his eyes, the objects which appear to circulate so freely between characters are not simply the fetishized, disposable products of an emotionally stunted universe. Rather than tracking the passing of time through capitalist space via displaced emotional affect, as one reviewer has implied (Gross 1996), their accumulation is actually a way of trying to slow it down. This is paralleled, quite explicitly, by Wong's statement about his cinematic technique. Rather than recording the 'disappearance' of Hong Kong, creating unstable subjectivities and challenging the visual status quo, his use of slow- and smudge-motion would appear to be about restabilizing that space, slowing it down so that people can absorb the cinematic not just visually but as a total sensuous experience. It is an experience in which the audience is expected actively to participate.

This point is significant. Whilst there is an indisputable correlation posited here, between the exchange and circulation of objects among characters within the film and Wong Kar-wai's conceptualization of the relationship between the cinema and its audience, neither this exchange, nor Wong's cinematography, can necessarily be deemed to result from any sense of 'loss' induced by Hong Kong's post-colonial or post-modern condition. Consequently, the recurrence of other themes within the films cannot simply be understood as a product of either of these states, even when such themes include disquisitions on the nature and quality of history and memory. So what is the relationship of objects, images and audiences in Wong Kar-wai's work? What role do themes such as memory, history and nostalgia play in this relationship? And what is the significance, if any, of what could be termed Wong's aesthetic of sensuous experience?

Object, subject, image

Arjun Appadurai defines the commodity stage of an object as being the period during which exchangeability is its most relevant social feature (Appadurai 1986). In this sense, many of the objects which feature in Wong Kar-wai's films are commodities, and the relationships which they negotiate are similarly commodified. This is noticeable as early as the first of the films, *As Tears Go By*. Ah Ngor (Maggie Cheung), a nice girl from Lantau, has gone to stay with her cousin Ah Wah (Andy Lau), a Mongkok gangster, whilst undergoing a hospital check-up. Although nothing happens, there is clear sexual tension between the two, and when Ah Ngor returns to Lantau, she leaves a new set of glasses for Ah Wah along with a note stating: 'I know they'll all get broken, so I hid one. One day, when you need this glass, call me and I'll tell you where it is'. It is through the giving of this set of glasses rather than words that she expresses her feelings for, and establishes a connection with, her cousin. This point is underlined when he finally travels to Lantau to find her, only to discover she has a boyfriend. As he leaves, Ah Wah turns to her and says 'Ah Ngor, I just wanted to tell you I've found that glass' – which, a little later on, he proceeds to throw overboard from the ferry. Seeming no longer to promise the possibility of emotional salvation through exchangeability, the glass loses its importance and becomes disposable. In this sense, it is a precursor of the earrings with which Yuddy (Leslie Cheung) entices Mimi (Carina Lau) into bed in *Days of Being Wild*. He throws her one whilst keeping the other for himself. Similarly, the significance of the eggs which Charlie Yeung seeks to trade in return for revenge on the men who killed her brother in *Ashes of Time* lies in their exchangeability (or in the latter case, their apparent lack of it).

In a Marxist sense these relationships are commodified, for the fundamental desires of those involved are alienated in their material surroundings, rather than expressed directly. The consequences are manifested in these characters' lack of awareness of their environment, their unwillingness to make decisions, and their tendency to treat other people as if they were as interchangeable as objects. Thus, Leon Lai's hit-man, at the beginning of *Fallen Angels*, says: 'I'm a lazy person – I like others to arrange things for me'. Michelle Li, his agent, then says of their potential victims: 'I don't know any of these people. They don't interest me either. Soon, they'll be history.' Tony Leung Chiu-wai's Cop 633 in *Chunking Express* is the apogee of this state of mind. Asked by waitress May (Faye Wong) whether he too wouldn't like to travel beyond the island, he simply shrugs and says: 'It's all the same to me.'

Yet whilst exchangeability and disposability may characterize certain objects, others display a far greater tenacity: they do not simply circulate within a single film, but travel between them. Clocks are a clear example. *Days of Being Wild* is full of shots of clocks, recording the passing of time. Indeed, the opening sequence of the film concerns clockwatching, with Yuddy attempting to inscribe his 'friendship' with Su Lizhen (Maggie Cheung) in the present: 'From now on we've been friends for one minute. You can't deny that.' Similarly, the first half of *Chunking Express* is measured out against shots of an electric clock in Hong Kong Airport, its changing face tracing how much longer Brigitte Lin's smuggler has left to catch her Indian drug mules, and how soon Cop 223 must give up on his departed girlfriend. *Happy Together* also references these moments, when Ho Po-wing (Leslie Cheung) returns, at the end of the film, to the flat that Lai Yiu-fai (Tony Leung Chiu-wai) has just vacated, finally breaking the vicious circle of their relationship. As Ho cleans, there is a shot of an electric twenty-four-hour clock flicking to midnight. The four zeroes it displays seem to mock his familiar refrain of 'Let's start over', the phrase that launches the film. Now he no longer has anything to start over from.

Important objects in these films, however cheap or ephemeral they may appear, are therefore far from disposable. Instead, they defy the flow of time, to return again and again at different points within Wong's oeuvre. Through their constant recurrence, an 'objective' history of the films is created, a process by which each film commemorates its predecessors via referents in the material world of its characters. As Wong says, this facilitates the merging of the films into 'different episodes of one movie' (Ngai 1997: 98). Unlike the standard commodity, they contain, rather than lose, time. Consequently, they do not simply mediate relationships, tracing the unstable spaces which short-circuit individual emotional contact; instead, as the different episodes progress, they increasingly become the means by which disaffected individuals come to rediscover their capacity to emote.

The most explicit exploration of this relationship can be found in the second half of *Chunking Express*. May, tired of waiting for Cop 633 to emerge from the cocoon-like environment he has created for himself following his girlfriend's departure, finally takes matters into her own hands. She repeatedly breaks into his apartment whilst he is absent, and 'looks after him' by proxy – via his belongings, and those of his ex-girlfriend, which he still hangs on to. She starts gently: cleaning, watering, tending. As she grows bolder, however, she begins to replace and eventually change things altogether, switching round the labels on cans of tinned fish, replacing the photos of his that adorn the living-room mirror with some of hers. The consequences are radical: gradually, Cop 633 returns to sentience. As he sits down to eat one day, he remarks: 'I've changed a lot lately. I've become more observant. I've begun to notice tiny things. Even sardines taste different.' On one level this is amusing: since May has switched the labels on the tins, the fish are clearly not sardines at all, so his apparent awareness is paralleled by an equally apparent lack of awareness. Yet, the fact remains that up until this point he has been completely oblivious to difference of any kind. Even when he catches May coming back to his apartment with goldfish, he still insists that the CD of 'California Dreaming' which she puts on belongs to his ex, when in fact it is one she has left there. However, the more his environment starts to metamorphose, its material components taking on a life of their own, the more he responds in kind. As he becomes more aware of it, and them, so he also becomes more aware of people as individuals. Inevitably, he begins to notice May, and ultimately he asks her out on a date. Change in his material environment has effected change in his way of life.

That this increased level of awareness may be considered a positive thing is attested to by those characters who fail to achieve it, often despite their better efforts. The hit-man in *Fallen Angels* is a case in point. He desperately wants to change, to escape his job, which involves wanting to end the transience of his present lifestyle: 'When you live out of a suitcase, you don't need a place of your own. Things have changed though. Got to start planning ahead.' As a result, after having supper in the restaurant where Takeshi Kaneshiro's Ho Chi-mo has started work, he enters into discussion with the owner about buying it. Yet, as they sit there talking, a song is put on the CD player, a song that, earlier in the film, he used to communicate to his agent via a bar jukebox the fact that he 'wanted out' of his job. We see his attention wander from the conversation, and in voiceover he states: 'I couldn't bear hearing that song. But some things you can't escape from. So, after that evening, I never went back'. Ironically, he tries to escape the inescapable; in doing so, he fails to engage the emotions stirred by the song, rejects the possibility of a life in a non-transient material environment, and instead returns to his old habits. People and objects disappear into the background of his awareness: he remarks of Karen Mok's character Punkie – after he has announced that he is leaving her and she has bitten his arm in an attempt to ensure a place in his memory – 'Will I remember her? Actually, it's not important.' It is in this state of abstraction that he dies carrying out his final hit. His last thoughts are, once again, of how he really should change his lifestyle.

It is the hit-man's failure to grapple with the pain of nostalgia, initiated by the song on the jukebox, which underlies his consequent inability to personalize his environment and make it less transient. In contrast, Cop 663 does precisely that: by turning his flat into a shrine to his departed girlfriend, he ironically allows himself to open up to his surroundings in a way that sows the seeds for future change. Essentially, he turns his ex-girlfriend's belongings into souvenirs of their relationship. In doing so he personalizes them, projecting his memories of what was between them into the objects, even to the point of holding conversations with them. This personalization via memory begins to rescue these objects from the commodity sphere, for commodification entails a certain homogenization of value which individuation necessarily reverses (Kopytoff 1986). Yet it also goes further. The souvenir, Susan Stewart (1993: 135) notes, 'is an object arising out of the necessarily insatiable demands of nostalgia', a word which quite literally derives from the Greek for 'I return' and 'I feel pain' (Serematakis 1996). As such, it sets up a relationship between subject and object that is highly sensitized, both emotionally and physically. At the same time, it allows the projection of the personal into the outside, material world, drawing the latter into the deeply subjective world of the former. The souvenir 'is a narrative which seeks to reconcile the disparity between interiority and exteriority, subject and object, signifier and signified' (Stewart 1993: 136–7). Through the nostalgia of its emotional associations, it attempts to open up the individual's body to the sensuous 'feeling' of the material world.

What this creates is a fetish, although not in the Marxist sense of the term. Peter Pels (1998) notes that the word was originally coined by seventeenth-century Dutch merchants trading on the West African coast as a name for goods that could not be understood in terms of rational, economic value: 'uncontrollable object[s] that burst the bounds of capitalist calculation'. The fetish represents the ability of material possessions to singularize themselves, to disrupt the circulation and commensurability of objects and values in a commercial system by taking on a life of their own beyond the boundaries of that system. It thereby questions humanity's ability to control and order the material world. This in turn throws into doubt the notion that materiality is enough to distinguish humans from things, or subjects from objects. Instead, it posits a world in which both are material. Old distinctions fall away and, in consequence, human beings may become subject to the actions of their possessions – or, as Pels puts it, 'the materiality of things can stand in the way of, and deflect, the course of human traffic' (1998: 95).

In fact, Pels makes a specific distinction between the fetish and the souvenir: the latter in his opinion is distinct from the former because its singularity has been projected from the outside, rather than being generated internally (Pels 1998). Yet in Wong Kar-wai's films, the creation of a souvenir acts as a catalyst for the emergence of the fetish. It initiates the breakdown of divisions between individual and object, reanimating both, before being taken to its full and logical extreme in the fetish relationship. One example would be the lamp bearing the image of Iguazu Falls in *Happy Together*. It is the first thing we see after the film's titles. Shot in colour, surrounded by material debris on an Argentinean hotel dresser, it glows with the image of the waterfall. A little later, Fai's voiceover explains its presence:

> Here [in Argentina] we had no idea where to go. Then Ho Po-wing bought a lamp. I really liked it. We wanted to find this waterfall; finally, we learned it was at Iguazu. We wanted to go home after it, but we lost our way.

The narrative segues into their failure to locate the Falls, and the consequent break-up of their relationship. Rather than quietly disappearing, however, the lamp remains an obstinate presence throughout the rest of the film, so much so that when Ho reunites with Fai on returning to the latter's apartment after been physically assaulted, he comments: 'You still have that lamp. Thought you'd have thrown it. . . . ' The point is that Fai cannot jettison it. Precisely because the lamp has become an object of nostalgia, indelibly associated with the abortive trip to the Falls and the collapse of their relationship in a country supposed to represent a new start, it has taken on an independent existence in relation to Fai's personal circumstances. Only by completing the journey which it represents, by merging himself as subject with the lamp as object and melding what might have been with what is, can Fai successfully reawaken himself to the world. Only then can he bring about change in his own life and leave Ho Po-wing once and for all. The lamp, as souvenir of their relationship, causes him the pain of nostalgia, initiating the process of feeling that opens him up to the lamp as object. As a result, it becomes a fetish, an independent thing defying the usual transience of the material under capitalism. In doing so, it completes the breakdown of subject–object division which was initiated via nostalgia, allowing itself to act upon Fai in such a way that he, too, becomes reanimated, and eventually takes circumstances into his own hands. The circle is complete.

Material objects in Wong's films are thus more than simply traces of a vanishing world. They are the means by which one learns to come alive to that world and fight against the artificial apathy that transience induces in the individual. What, then, is the relationship between the visual image and this material practice? If the recurrence of objects can be said to trace a material, or 'objective' history, across Wong Kar-wai's films, the world of images in them is perhaps more strongly linked to memory. The ending of *As Tears Go By* illustrates this nicely. Ah Wah's young accomplice, Fly (Jackie Cheung), has taken on an impossible hit: attempting to execute an informer who is in police custody. He knows he will die, but wishes to do so in order to prove his worthiness as a 'younger brother'. When Ah Wah finds this out, he rushes to save him, but is, inevitably, too late. Instead, he too is shot. We hear the gun report; there is a slow-motion image of the impact, with Ah Wah's head moving across screen right to left; and then we have a sudden flashback to an image we have seen earlier, a private one of Ah Wah and Ah Ngor embracing in a telephone booth. As quickly as this has come, it goes, to be replaced by a shot of Ah Wah collapsing to the ground, face-up, dying. The flashback is thus his final memory before death; memory, in its turn, is incarnated as pure image. Similar moments may be found in the later films, notably the extended quasi-hallucinatory sequence heralding Yuddy's demise on the train towards the end of *Days of Being Wild*.

This is not particularly unusual: as Maureen Turim (1989) notes, much early work on memory theory was stimulated by the emergence of film as a discipline, binding ideas about memory and the nature of images closely together. What is much stranger, however, is the way in which such memory images begin to detach themselves from these contexts in the later films, simultaneously suspending, and becoming suspended in, time. The flashback in *As Tears Go By* is neatly bounded, temporally and spatially: it is an image the characters have previously experienced, and the audience has already seen, which appears at a logical moment in the film's narrative. Yet one only has to look to *Days of Being Wild*, made only three years later, to find this expectation completely exploded. The initial encounter between Yuddy and Su Lizhen, at her kiosk, ends with the former saying to the latter: 'You'll see me tonight in your dreams.' We immediately cut to a full-screen, slow-motion pan of a jungle landscape, saturated in blue, backed by Latin music. It is clearly not Hong Kong, yet nor would it appear to be Su Lizhen's dream, since it is devoid of people, and we do not see her sleeping until after this shot is finished. In fact, it is not until Yuddy goes to the Philippines to find his mother that we realize that it is in all likelihood a shot of his parents' Filipino estate. A similar shot occurs as he is leaving the estate, later in the film, and the image from the beginning reappears in its entirety as he lies dying on the train at the end. But Yuddy, given up at birth, has never known his mother. This is not his memory: it is a free-floating image from the future, cut loose from its moorings and left swimming on the surface of the picture, languidly defying the traditional conventions of narrative and time.

There are equivalent moments in all the other films, although the most obvious is in *Happy Together*. Here an aerial image of Iguaza Falls, bathed in blue and backed again by Latin guitars, appears just after Ho and Fai's initial uncompleted journey. It returns throughout the film, despite the fact that none of the major characters manage to see the Falls until the very end. In *Ashes of Time*, Murong Yang (Brigitte Lin) drops a chopstick whilst in conversation with Huang Yaoshi (Tony Leung Kar-fai), yet we only see the image of the falling chopstick after it has already been picked up. The opening of *Fallen Angels* is a clip of Lai's and Li's meeting, something that the rest of the film then proceeds to work towards. The first narrative of *Chunking Express*, which chronologically precedes the second, is filled with shots of the characters from the later narrative. Thus, whilst Brigitte Lin's smuggler takes a cigarette break from her search for the missing Indians, May emerges from the shop behind her, carrying an oversized stuffed Garfield which we later see her place in Cop 633's apartment in the second storyline. Finally, there is the famous reference in *In the Mood for Love* to its sequel, *2046*, a fleeting close-up of hotel room number 2046 where Mr Chow (Tony Leung Chiu-wai) and Mrs Chan (Maggie Cheung) conduct their melancholy tryst. These images, independent of both the characters and the usual demands of linear time, operate rather like a form of collective memory for the film audience. Through their constant reiteration, however, they also form an alternative, visual history of the films, one that refuses the usual expectations that images should vanish in the flow of temporality. In fact, they upset the very notion of such a temporal flow. The relationship they construct between the audience and the passing of the film in 'real' time is thus very similar to that of the relationship between objects in the films and the passing of 'narrative' time for the characters. Like important artefacts, important images in the films become versions of Pels's (1998) fetishes, and, in doing so, they encourage the re-establishment of a direct affective relationship between themselves and the audience.

The breaking-up of time through the ordering of the image is fundamental to this process, but Wong also uses takes that unravel the very notion of time within a single frame, most notably in his 'smudge-motion' shots. One example would be the scene from *Chunking Express* in which Cop 663 sits at the Midnight Express food counter drinking coffee while May looks on adoringly. May does not move; the policeman sips his coffee in slow motion; yet the people passing around all move in double time. Although this image is probably the most of famous of these shots, Wong also makes extensive use of the technique in *Fallen Angels* and *Happy Together*. As Jean-Marc Lalanne (1997) points out, this style enables Wong to break with Bazin's notion that a film shot is not an image but a block of homogeneous time. On the one hand, the director inscribes his films with a sense of visual nostalgia, a feeling of temporality lost or misplaced. On the other hand, he directs the viewer to recapture that sense of time in the present. In freeing his images from the temporal context in which they are normally understood, Wong leaves the audience little choice but to appreciate them in the here and now. Without a sense of past or future movement to ground them, these are images from an extended present, a moment when we viewers are encouraged to feel what we see on screen. In this sense, the easy distinctions between viewing subject and viewed object are blurred. The more sensuous relationship with the screen that seems to be being explored here is similar to the one that Wong's characters are pushed into developing with the material world that surrounds them.

Consuming senses

What I am trying to suggest is that Wong Kar-wai's films are about more than a rendition of the postcolonial or postmodern experience. Rather, they are an attempt to explore the way in which we engage with both objects and images. Chris Doyle, Wong's long-time collaborator and regular cinematographer, once made this clear when he remarked that: 'You don't always need words to communicate an idea. The camera communicates visually and sensually . . . [Our films] speak to [Asian teenagers] at a more visceral level, a more physical, emotional, sensual level' (Vasuder 1997: 28).

Film, then, is about the production of both physical and emotional feeling through the use of the image. It should be appreciated not simply visually, fleetingly, but by deploying all the senses simultaneously, or, as Chang Chen's Taiwanese backpacker puts it in *Happy Together*: 'You see better with your ears.' As such, I would argue that Wong Kar-wai's project is loosely one of consumption, in Baudrillard's (1988) sense of the term as the systematic structuring of the consumer's relationship to signs and objects through the production of affect. In Baudrillard's theorization, pleasure – or its denial – is the affective key to consumption (Baudrillard 1988). For Wong, however, the key emotion is nostalgia. In pursuit of a fully sensual appreciation of the image, the distinctions between the viewer and the image on screen, between subject and object, have to be broken down in order that they may then mutually reanimate one another. On screen, this is achieved through the pain of nostalgia, and the independent meanings that it endows objects, which allows the reintegration of characters and their environment. At the same time, Wong positions the audience *vis-à-vis* certain images in a similar way. As his images take on a quasi-object status, Wong encourages a more sensual and active engagement between them and his audience. The director's style, his characters, the themes of history and memory in his work, can on some level all be related back to this project.

This sense of active engagement is crucial. Describing Wong's films as explorations in consumption does not imply that they are in any sense palliative. Cinema here is imagined not simply as a medium of entertainment, but as one of transformation. It has the capacity to reanimate our experience of a world to which we have perhaps become desensitized: the visual can inform our relationship to the material. This is articulated most clearly at the end of *Fallen Angels*, when Ho Chi-mo (Takeshi Kaneshiro) sits in his room in Chungking Mansions, reviewing images of his recently deceased father. The images are from a home video, deliberately amateurish in style, and they fill the screen. Initially in colour, they rapidly switch to black and white until we get to a sequence of his father cooking steak. At this point they switch back, and we hear Ho saying: ‘Watching dad cooking made me feel very happy. I know I’ll never taste his steaks again, but I’ll never forget just how they tasted.’ The home video has become a means by which the lost sensuous experience of vanished objects is recaptured, not merely in relation to one sense, sight, but also to a second, taste. Furthermore, by expanding these images to full-screen size and reducing Ho’s presence to voiceover, the relationship of character to video and audience to cinematic image is almost identical. If Ho can use film to channel his memories and re-stimulate his material sensibilities, so, it would appear to be suggested, can we.

From this angle, Wong seems to have much in common with early-twentieth-century critics such as Walter Benjamin, who viewed the cinema as a means for reconstructing the human capacity for bodily experience, a capacity they felt had been attenuated by industrialization (Buck-Morss 1991). His focus on everyday objects as the loci for communication between individuals, their elevation above the commodity stage as a result of these individuals’ engagement with their material or sensuous qualities, is also very close to Benjamin’s faith in the release of the ‘ur-phenomenon’ of ordinary things as the key to effecting social and material change. The ‘ur-phenomenon’ is the ideal essence of the object, captured in sensual form. On release, it generates a shock that jolts one out of the trance induced by rapid modernization, re-establishing the individual’s physical awareness, and ultimately self-control (Buck-Morss 1991). Such tendencies in Wong’s work have been the cause of criticism that the director harbours a romantic desire for emotional reunion with a real or natural presence that does not actually exist (Chow 1999).

If in this sense Wong could be said to be engaged in a modernist project, it is not a modernist project tied specifically to the emergence of a national space. Rather, it is a project tied to a process of global modernization, technologization and industrialization which has been going on for many years, and of which film has long been an integral part. This is particularly true in Hong Kong, where the film industry has always been international in outlook, a consequence of the need to negotiate between its Mainland roots, colonial production context, and a market concentrated mostly overseas (Lu 1997; Teo 2000). In other words, making films is a process of negotiating a position within a modern worldwide economy that links the global, the national and the individual. Film production and reception has therefore become a process of consumption that has its roots in inevitable contemporary mediations between local and international demands in the global marketplace.[3]

Unsurprisingly, Wong as a director is more than aware of these competing demands. He has talked on the record of the problems that independent film-makers face in Hong Kong, particularly issues of funding (Ngai 1997). He notes that budgets for production can only be obtained through securing guaranteed overseas sales before shooting has even begun, and such sales agreements can only be guaranteed by certain compromises. Whilst this is sometimes a question of packaging, as could be argued *vis-à-vis* the marketing of the director as a maker of 'Hong Kong art film' in North America and Europe (C. Wong 1999), sometimes such compromises are more concrete: the casting of stars who will be guaranteed to sell a product; borrowings from genres with tried and tested audience appeal (Ngai 1997). It is arguably these compromises that are reflected in, for example, the use of the Kung Fu movie as the basic form for *Ashes of Time*, or the presence of singer Faye Wong (Wang Fei) in *Chunking Express* and *2046*.

In light of the film industry's position in the global economy, and of my discussion of the relationship of images and objects in his oeuvre, it would be easy to assume that the politics of Wong Kar-wai's aesthetic could be aligned with the criticisms of capitalism along the lines of those Frankfurt School theorists with whom Benjamin was affiliated. Yet it would be entirely reasonable to argue that this relationship is in itself a product of capitalist relations, relations in which constant yet circular consumption – the pursuit of excitement, rather than the pursuit of pleasure – is the only way that the incomplete, irrational post-Enlightenment self may express itself (Ferguson 1990). Wong's films, with their incessant generation of a dispersed sense of personal identity and their emphasis on the sensuous as opposed to the reasoned, would seem a close fit for this model of capitalist subjectivity: one thinks immediately of the hit-man in *Fallen Angels* and his comment that 'We all need a partner. When will I find mine?' The point, I think, is that, precisely because these films attempt to mediate between so many different, sometimes conflicting, demands, it is difficult to talk about them as making unified statements about any single issue. Instead, what we can see is tensions between competing discourses that thread through the works, tensions that develop as a result of individual films being both a product and a reworking of the circumstances in which they have been generated. Ka-fai Yau's appreciation of *Ashes of Time* as a genre film that pushes the boundaries of its genre is an example of these tensions working at a formal level. The Kung Fu film may be the closest thing Hong Kong has to a 'national' cinema, but it is hard not to see *Ashes of Time* as an attempt to work between the vision of the individual film-maker and the pressure of the international market through a traditional genre which allows space for the interests of both. The result is a peculiar compromise between all these competing positions. Similarly, whilst the sense of incompleteness that characterizes Ferguson's modern self can be identified in many of Wong's characters, it is through coming to terms with the trappings of the contemporary world that these feelings may be addressed. The movement from commodity to fetish via souvenir allows for an opportunity to start again. The audience, encouraged to participate in the consumption of the visual image in a similar way, is thus provided with a similar mode of relating to our contemporary surroundings. Neither a confrontation nor a capitulation, we are given the option of coming to terms with a modernity that, like it or not, dominates everybody's lives. As the director says of the characters in *Chunking Express*, indubitably the most optimistic of his films: '[They] know how to entertain themselves, even if it's just by talking to a bar of soap. They know how to live in a city' (Rayns 1995: 14).

Perhaps the 'secret' of Wong Kar-wai's aesthetic project is as simple as that.

Conclusion

It seems ironic, if none the less essential, to attempt any conclusion of a chapter focused on a film-maker whose output strives to overcome the very kind of distancing that an academic project entails. I have suggested that most interpretations of Wong Kar-wai's films have tended to borrow explicitly or implicitly from the concept of national allegory, and that this has led to a particularly narrow understanding of what film is, and what it can achieve, in the Hong Kong context. It is true that there is a relationship between Wong's presentation of individuals' interaction with objects and the visual style of his cinema. That relationship, however, is not dictated by Hong Kong's political economy. Instead, it is both a product of, and a response on the part of the director to, an experience of modernity and the global market, an experience that in itself is not confined to Hong Kong. Wong's characters come to terms with their place in the modern environment by learning once more to appreciate it sensuously. The films provide their audiences with an opportunity to do the same, but through the medium of the visual. History, memory, loss, nostalgia: all these themes and emotions are part of the process of subject–object interpolation through which those in the films, and those watching the films, recover their ability to feel, and thus their capacity to anchor themselves in the contemporary urban environment.

However, the problems inherent in interpreting these films relate, also, to more general concerns about the interpretation of cinema in its contemporary context. Film is no longer simply an artistic medium, but big business. It can no longer be considered on a purely local level, but has to be placed within a global framework as well. Somehow, the analyst has to incorporate the director as artist, the audience as potential customer, and the market into an academic model that still allows room for an understanding of film as both art and industry. The fundamental problem with the national-allegorical model is its failure to account for the increasing complex mediations that are demanded of film today, or to recognize how these mediations may translate on a case-by-case basis. The question of which individual films or filmmakers are 'relevant' to the issue in hand assumes the fundamental unity of any given body of work which, in the current environment, is hard to justify. A more appropriate question might perhaps be which competing discourses within a film or films can be considered relevant to the variety of issues cinema addresses?

The concept of 'consuming' the film, imprecise as it is, could be seen as an acknowledgement of that complexity in its assumption of actual interaction between the diverse elements of the film production process. What is the director trying to communicate to those watching his work? How is the audience being encouraged to approach the images on screen? How does that relate to the status of both within the chain of economic command that constitutes the cinema industry? Wong Kar-wai's films, emerging as they do from an arena in which consumerism has already been the focus of considerable academic interest, might seem to be the perfect subject for such an investigation, and in many ways they are. The story that they tell is nevertheless distinct from the classic tale of contemporary consumerism, with its passion for consumption. Instead, they deal in the passions of consumption, the feelings that images and objects can evoke in their human counterparts when they come into contact with them, and the wider implications that these may have for the way we relate to the world around us. It is through these sensuous histories of things seen and exchanged that Wong Kar-wai evokes the broader complexity of life in contemporary Hong Kong.

Notes

1 'Smudge-motion' is a technique that blurs the background of a shot whilst keeping the foreground comparatively focused. It is also known as 'step-printing' (Tong 2003).

2 The French text reads: 'L'utilisation que je fais du ralenti [slow motion] est pragmatique: c'est un appel à une suspension du flux, une manière de laisser personnages et spectateurs jouir d'un regard, d'une attention à un bruit ou à une lumière.'

3 This point is indirectly supported by Peter Pels (1998), who notes that, since the emergence of the fetish as an object of consumption in European society was closely connected to the initial stages of market expansion, renewed interest in the term at the end of the millennium may reflect global changes that are breathing new life into the market and those modes of consumption implicated in it.

References

Abbas, A. (1997) *Hong Kong: Culture and the Politics of Disappearance*, Minneapolis: University of Minnesota Press.

Appadurai, A. (1986) 'Introduction: Commodities and the Politics of Value', in A. Appadurai (ed.), *The Social Life of Things: Commodities in Cultural Perspective*, Cambridge: Cambridge University Press.
Baudrillard, J. (1988) 'Consumer Society', in M. Poster (ed.), *Jean Baudrillard: Selected Writings*, Stanford: Stanford University Press.
Buck-Morss, S. (1991) *The Dialectics of Seeing: Walter Benjamin and the Arcades Project*, Cambridge, Mass.: MIT Press.
Chow, R. (1995) *Primitive Passions: Visuality, Sexuality, Ethnography and Contemporary Chinese Cinema*, New York: Columbia University Press.
—— (1999) 'Nostalgia of the New Wave: Structure in Wong Kar-wai's Happy Together', *Camera Obscura*, 42: 31–48.
Ferguson, H. (1990) *The Science of Pleasure: Cosmos and Psyche in the Bourgeois World View*, New York and London: Routledge.
Gross, L. (1996) 'Nonchalant Grace', *Sight and Sound*, 6 (9): 6–10.
Harvey, D. (1990) *The Condition of Postmodernity*, Cambridge, MA: Blackwell.
Jameson, F. (1986) 'Third World Literature in the Age of Multinational Capitalism', *Social Text*, 15: 65–88.
—— (1991) *Postmodernism, or the Cultural Logic of Late Capitalism*, London: Verso.
Kopytoff, I. (1986) 'The Cultural Biography of Things: Commoditization as Process', in A. Appadurai (ed.), *The Social Life of Things: Commodities in Cultural Perspective*, Cambridge: Cambridge University Press.
Lalanne, J.-M. (1997) 'Images from the Inside', trans. S. Wright, in J.-M. Lalanne *et al.* (eds), *Wong Kar-wai*, Paris: Dis voir.
Leong, A. (1999) 'Meditations on Loss: A Framework for the Films of Wong Kar-wai', *Asian Cult Cinema*, 22: 38–42.
Lu, S. (1997) 'Historical Introduction: Chinese Cinemas (1896–1996) and Transnational Film Studies', in S. Lu (ed.), *Transnational Chinese Cinemas: Identity, Nationhood, Gender*, Honolulu: University of Hawai'i Press.
Marchetti, G. (2000) 'Buying American, Consuming Hong Kong: Cultural Commerce, Fantasies of Identity, and the Cinema', in P. Fu and D. Desser (eds), *The Cinema of Hong Kong: History, Arts, Identity*, Cambridge and New York: Cambridge University Press.
Ngai, J. (1997) 'A Dialogue with Wong Kar-wai: Cutting Between Time and Two Cities', in J.-M. Lalanne *et al.* (eds), *Wong Kar-wai*, Paris: Dis voir.
Pels, P. (1998) 'The Spirit of Matter: On Fetish, Rarity, Fact and Fancy', in P. Spyer (ed.), *Border Fetishisms: Material Objects in Unstable Spaces*, New York and London: Routledge.
Rayns, T. (1995) 'Poet of Time', *Sight and Sound*, 5 (9): 12–16.
Seremetakis, C. N. (1996) 'The Memory of the Senses, Part I: Marks of the Transitory', in C. N. Seremetakis (ed.), *The Senses Still: Perception and Memory as Material Culture in Modernity*, Chicago: University of Chicago Press.
Stewart, S. (1993) *On Longing: Narratives of the Miniature, the Gigantic, the Souvenir and the Collection*, Durham, NC: Duke University Press.
Teo, S. (1997) *Hong Kong Cinema: The Extra Dimensions*, London: British Film Institute.
—— (2000) 'Local and Global Identity: Whither Hong Kong Cinema?', *Senses of Cinema*, 7. Available online at www.sensesofcinema.com/contents/00/7/hongkong.html (accessed 7 March 2006).
Tong, J. (2003) 'Chunking Express: Time and its Displacements', in C. Berry (ed.), *Chinese Films in Focus: 25 New Takes*, London: British Film Institute.
Tsui, C. K. (1995) 'Subjective Culture and History: The Ethnographic Cinema of Wong Kar-wai', *Asian Cinema*, 7 (2): 93–124.
Turim, M. (1989) *Flashbacks in Film: Memory and History*, New York and London: Routledge.

Vasuder, A. (1997) 'Interview: Chris Doyle – The Heart of the Matter', *Cinemaya*, 38: 23–8.
Wong, C. (1999) 'Cities, Cultures and Cassettes: Hong Kong Cinema and Transnational Audiences', *Post Script*, 19 (1): 87–106.
Wong, Kar-wai (1999) 'L'architecte et le vampire', *Cahiers du cinéma*, Numéro hors-séries 'Made in China', 26–9.
Yau, Ka-fai (2001) '3rdness: Filming, Changing, Thinking Hong Kong', *positions: east asia cultural critique*, 9 (3): 535–57.

Filmography

As Tears Go By (1988) Dir. Wong Kar-wai; Prod. Rover Tang; Cin. Andrew Lau.
Days of Being Wild (1991) Dir. Wong Kar-wai; Prod. Rover Tang; Cin. Chris Doyle.
Ashes of Time (1994) Dir. Wong Kar-wai; Prod. Tsai Mu-ho; Cin. Chris Doyle.
Chungking Express (1994) Dir. Wong Kar-wai; Prod. Chan Ye-cheng; Cin. Chris Doyle.
Fallen Angels (1995) Dir. Wong Kar-wai; Prod. Jeff Lau; Cin. Chris Doyle.
Happy Together (1997) Dir. Wong Kar-wai; Prod. Wong Kar-wai; Cin. Chris Doyle.
In The Mood For Love (2000) Dir. Wong Kar-wai; Prod. Chan Ye-cheng; Cin. Chris Doyle.
2046 (2004) Dir. Wong Kar-wai; Prod. Wong Kar-wai; Cin. Chris Doyle.

11 The consuming or the consumed?

Virtual Hmong in China

Nicholas Tapp

> Travel, indeed, struck him as being a waste of time, since he believed that the imagination could provide a more-than-adequate substitute for the vulgar reality of actual experience.
>
> J. K. Huysmans (1959)

Introduction

We're at the end of the economic process, as posited by us. We are consumers rather than producers – a kind of supplementary addition, an 'all or *sundry*' to a historical process in which man's interaction with her environment has been primary . . .

There is a kind of irony in thinking about consumption 'with Chinese characteristics', as if consumption with Chinese characteristics could not, somehow, properly be consumption as 'we' express and understand it in post-industrial societies, just as Chinese socialism could surely not be the real thing.[1]

But I should first introduce the Hmong people who are the subject of this paper. Traditionally shifting cultivators of dry rice, maize and, over the past century, opium, the Hmong make up about a third of the eight million southern minority people classified as 'Miao' by the Chinese. Over the past 150 years they have migrated out of southern China (particularly Guizhou, Sichuan, Yunnan and Guangxi) to North Vietnam, Laos and Thailand. In the 1960s they became involved in the conflicts of the Vietnam war in both Laos and Vietnam, and after 1975 those who had supported the American effort were resettled in refugee camps along the Thai border, from where some 140,000 have now been resettled in third countries like the US, France, Australia and Canada. The Hmong speak a quite distinctive language and have a strongly patrilineal lineage system, with many Chinese-type surnames like Lee, Wang and Xiong. I'm largely concerned with images and representations of the Hmong in this paper, and the extent to which the reception of these images constitutes a form of 'consumption' by particular audiences. In terms of images, we have gone from a situation where the popular image of the Hmong was one of shifting cultivators insatiably devouring their own environment, to one where American Hmong themselves are concerned with replicating these images of what for them has now become their history through various media including video and the internet.

Since Bourdieu's (1984) early work on symbolic and other forms of capital, Baudrillard has had much to answer for in the confusion about cultural and material consumption. Apart from his wonderful remark about 'the impossibility of determined discursive positions' (Baudrillard 1994), which I find refers particularly to China, there was very often in the Baudrillardian oeuvre an eliding of the difference between actual consumption (for example, of pork, however culturally informed) and mental consumption (for example, of movies, however expensive, or 'embodied'). Some of this confusion of levels and types of 'consumption' may have arisen from a general, post-modernist conflation of uses with values – effects with meanings – which we can trace directly back to Ricoeur's seminal paper on 'the text' (Ricoeur 1971).

The view that in 'late capitalist' society we consume signs or images of commodities, more than commodities as such, or that commodities are defined more by what they signify than by their use, has seemed to beg questions about the inherently symbolic nature of value. To use a tired example, the washing machine has a use, an end, for which it is sought (desired) and *valued*. Its possession may also express social values like status or taste, for which it may be sought (desired) and *valued*. Its value inheres then not only in the productive labour it encapsulates and represents (past), nor only in its current utility (present), but also in its potential (future) benefits which partly include what it may socially signify to ourselves and to others. All these meanings of value could be seen as symbolic,[2] and here I would like to emphasize the importance of time and temporality to considerations of value. I come back to considerations of value in the second part of this chapter.

But the resonances of our current uses of the term 'consumption' do also include the fact that consumption was actually a wasting disease, as Susan Sontag (1979) reminds us. It was a particular disease made fashionable by late-nineteenth-century intellectuals and artists, in the Decadent movement of the 'Yellow Nineties' led by Beardsley and Wilde. Although it referred specifically to tuberculosis, what is more interesting is that 'consumption' was a term used as a more general social category, applied to wasting and debilitating diseases for which there was no cure, except possibly Kafka's notorious sanatorium in the Alps.[3] Consumption came to be thought of as a disease particularly afflicting degenerate members of the elite, and the late nineteenth century was probably the first time that a fraction of the middle classes could afford to become merely consumers in the way idealized by writers and artists of the time. They consumed pipes of hashish and opium, rare wines and strange tastes; they consumed orchestras of scents, each of which was thought to evoke a particular emotion; and they also formed part of a class which could cross the world that imperial conquest, and new forms of transport and telecommunications, had recently compressed. The few first 'modern consumers', who devoted themselves to a life of consumption for its own sake, were the products of a society which was exploiting the natural environment, and the colonized territories, in order to thrive and prosper.

Yet the Orientalist worlds of Egypt and India[4] were known to them mostly only through fantasies such as 'Kubla Khan' or 'The Light of Asia'. Only a few of the nineteenth-century romantics, like Gauguin or (earlier) De Nerval, could actually explore the realities behind these representations. So it was largely a kind of imagery which these romantics fed upon, in their search to satiate jaded appetites through experiencing novel sensations. And inevitably one is aware, in considering the new realm of elite consumption which appeared at this time, of the parallel construction of a private, secret, late-Cartesian self which the romantics pioneered – the constitution of an inner self of emotion and sensation, where the dark satanic values of the materialist world of industrialism could be privately ignored, opposed or hopefully transcended. The ineffectual but significant rebellion – private and internalized as it was – of the romantics against the very social system which had made them possible, has not lost its relevance for us today, as I stress in the final section of this chapter.[5]

Sontag (1979) draws the metaphorical parallels between the understandings of cancer and of tuberculosis, showing how the pre-modern understanding of cancer (a canker; 'anything that frets, corrodes, corrupts or consumes slowly and secretly', quotes Sontag from the Oxford English Dictionary) also invoked the notion of consumption. Bumps and swellings, tumours, excrescences. But where cancer is seen as a disease of unnatural growth, tuberculosis was one of disintegration; cancer is middle-class, while tuberculosis was associated with poverty and deprivation. Both, as Sontag shows, have been understood as *diseases of passion* – insufficient passion in the case of cancer, excessive sensibility in that of tuberculosis. Consumption, the 'becoming frailty' suffered by Keats, Shelley, Chopin, Chekhov, Poe, Stevenson, Lawrence and many others, was associated with a fashionable paleness and thinness, the 'consuming passions' of romantic sensibility. These sickly, decadent resonances which we bring to our understandings of the term demand a consideration of consumption also in the context of other theories of the passions, in particular the consuming envies and gratitude spoken of by 'object-relations' psychoanalysts such as Melanie Klein. In Part III of this paper I attempt therefore to relate this more psychological sense of consumption to the lust and desire, passion and hatred for the Mother from whom one has separated – the desire to engulf, devour, to re-unite, to destroy, expressed in a Hmong culture hero in China called the Orphan.[6]

However, there are simpler senses of consumption which we should not lose sight of. The Hmong phrase *tsis txaus noj*, which is often encountered in villages in China, is easily translated as 'not enough to eat', and should remind us that the majority of Hmong in China are not in a position to purchase washing machines or TVs, although they may enjoy access to one local individual's TV and enjoy the images of consumption which are displayed there, or be consumed themselves by those images of consumption. It is the extent of and the interface between these different senses of the term which should concern us, and the fact that, while some may be in a position to gratify their more cultural appetites, others are hard put to it to eat at all.

Ethnography – Hmong identity and transnational change

Elisabeth Croll (1994) has drawn attention to how 'the desired for' in China – the heaven of currently rising aspirations – exemplifies a kind of new materialism replacing older moral values associated with the pre-reform period of socialism. There is now a multiplicity of ideas of Heaven, associated with the acquisition of material goods and often with the idea of 'the overseas'. If we were to translate this sociological language into a more aesthetic mode, we might find ourselves again talking about consuming passions, passions which devour an internal self as much as they may an external object of desire, envy, longing. But then we might also go on to think more about the construction of selfhood through those 'local structures of identity and desire' which Jonathan Friedman (1990) talks about. Of course, some Hmong partake in the general process of the acquisition or attempt to acquire material goods and services which represent a better life, as do other citizens of China – but does this desire for the signs of affluence tell us anything special about consumption 'with Chinese characteristics'? As a matter of fact (although this is largely accidental) I believe that it does.

At a recent workshop on Hmong Studies, it was very apparent that two quite different academic languages were being spoken.[7] One was an older language, concerned with problems of identification and classification, in which the loss of a 'Hmong culture' by the younger generation of Hmong-American settlers could be regretted; one was a newer language, spoken oddly enough by those who had worked with the refugee community in the US and with national minorities in China, which was more concerned with issues of cultural production and identity exchange (see Tapp 1998).

In the course of discussions, a senior Sinologist and specialist on the Hmong made the remark that the Hmong refugees now settled in Washington were still *tribal* – because as shifting cultivators they had always been used to taking their network of kinship relations with them and recreating them wherever they were. The assumption here seemed to be that no radical changes of social organization had marked the refugee diaspora because the Hmong, as shifting cultivators, had never known a fixed place from which they could feel dislocated. Yet the kind of nostalgia for a past life, or locality, expressed by many of the overseas Hmong refugees, would seem to argue against this view.[8]

Since the Hmong went to America, France and Australia, increasingly frequent visits of transnational Hmong to traditional Hmong communities in Thailand, Laos, Vietnam and southern China have taken place. Some of these have been private or tourist visits, others have been officially sponsored by local Hmong associations. In effect there have been some extraordinary encounters between Americanized Hmong, or 'Hmong-Americans', often business-suited and well educated, and Hmong villagers on the south Chinese borderlands at the brink of destitution. There has been a kind of sentimental nostalgia powering such visits, while there have of course also been instrumentalist commercial aspirations and even political motivations behind some of them.[9]

Both collective and individual visits of Hmong from the West have recently taken place to China, and a variety of academic and trading meetings in China have been organized at which Hmong originating from South East Asia, in expectation of meeting their long-lost cousins in their original homeland of China, have been dismayed to be confronted by welcoming parties of other groups classified together with the Hmong as 'Miao' by the Chinese, speaking entirely unknown languages and with utterly alien social practices.[10] There have been some real realignments (exchanges) of identity (or identification) as a result of this process of transnational contact. 'Miao' groups in China, for example, have begun politely referring to themselves as 'Hmong' in deference to their American guests, while some of the Hmong in the US have accepted that in China they might be referred to as 'Miao' (a term with only pejorative implications in South East Asia, of which the Hmong community outside China had largely succeeded in ridding themselves). And of course these processes of identity change do raise unresolved questions about how the category 'Hmong' has been essentialized, both by the Hmong themselves, and by those Western experts (missionaries, linguists, colonialists and anthropologists) working on the Hmong who saw in these mountaineering people an image of independence and egality they preferred to the hierarchic Asiatic despotisms which controlled them; past images of the Hmong which we find in a range of colonial and post-colonial literature.[11]

Some private-individual visits of Western Hmong to Chinese Hmong villages have also taken place, where the overseas Hmong can speak Hmong unproblematically and can sometimes trace relatives and acquaintances from Laos or Vietnam. Despite this, the tendency has been for the Western Hmong to extend 'Hmong' as a blanket term to cover the non-Hmong Miao they have also met, as if the latter were somehow proto-Hmong who had diverged from their proper paths. Since the overseas Hmong are often unable to distinguish the Chinese spoken by the Miao or Hmong they may meet from the other Miao languages they may speak, there has been a lack of recognition among the visiting Hmong of the existence in China of non-Hmong Miao languages, and an assumption that, where Chinese Miao are speaking languages other than Hmong, these people must really be Hmong who have somehow forgotten how to speak properly and have recourse to Chinese. This impression is furthered by the habit of non-Hmong Chinese Miao of referring to themselves as 'Hmong'!

The shifting processes of identity formation accomplished through these visits have been accompanied by new forms of cultural production. There is now a thriving Hmong video industry in the United States which includes not only love stories and martial arts dramas dubbed in Hmong, but also nostalgia: the Chinese village where our great-great-grandfathers *might* have come from, probably not Hmong but certainly Chinese and not unlike many Hmong villages in China . . . tombstones, pines, waterfalls and mountains, melodic Hmong love-songs and the joys of the itinerant . . . images of formal meetings in Jishou (Hunan) and Kaili (Guizhou); traditionally dressed Miao women welcoming the studious foreigners with libations at the gates of their villages . . . here too there is a kind of 'consumption' (in which we find an alliance between Miao cadres in China and well-funded Hmong from the US) of images *of those who lack an equivalent power to control/disseminate their own images*, that is, Miao villagers in China (some of whom may be Hmong). So there is a kind of exploitation of value here, through a process of powerful representation similar to that discussed by Baudrillard (1988). And there are essential issues of power, of control, over one's own self and its representations and reproduction by others, which are of concern here, in the emergence of new patterns of consumption within what may be a new 'micro public sphere' formed by the transnational Hmong/Miao community (Dayan 1998, following Dahlgren 1994).

Production and reception

In the Hmong case, this kind of inequity between levels and types of consumption is particularly apparent in Southeast Asia. American Hmong businessmen have taken to visiting North Thailand, at the Hmong New Year, to 'play' (*ua siv*) with local Hmong girls. New Year is traditionally a time when new couples can meet, but usually with a view to potential marriage. So the Thai Hmong girls have had great hopes of their American boyfriends – but for many of the American Hmong tourists this 'play' is just a 'sport', after which they return to their families in America. The Hmong in Thailand have (now) begun to see this as an exploitation of customary Hmong attitudes and expectations; and in addition HIV/AIDS has been rapidly spread through this – what is it? consumption of exotic images? exploitation of disadvantaged populations and bodies? resignification of cultural practices?[12] Internal relations within the same cultural group, in other words, are now beginning to adopt some of the forms of global and class inequality reflected in tourism and the sex trade, and are thereby beginning to challenge the ideology of equality and mutual help which crucially maintains the identity of the group. Yet it is that same ideology of fraternal egality which is overtly motivating the return visits of Western Hmong to Asia, and resulting in the individual clashes of interests which challenge it.

Some arranged marriages between young Miao brides from China and American Hmong men have taken place, and increasingly there are arrangements for joint-venture schemes in speciality Miao-area produce and investments in small manufacturing plants in Miao areas (see Schein 1998).

Louisa Schein has worked with the Hmu peoples of Southeast Guizhou who are also classified as 'Miao', and, with her long experience of the Hmong in the United States, has been primary in pointing attention to the kinds of identity transfer and new cultural production now taking place among the Hmong and related peoples. Such is the scale of the overseas Hmong nostalgia for a Chinese past that cottage industries have emerged in China producing 'Miao' costumes to be sold to the US for use at Hmong weddings, festive occasions and meetings (Schein 1998). Very often these 'Miao' costumes have very little to do with traditional Hmong costume, which has by-and-large been replaced in China by a kind of official minorities garb modelled on traditional Han peasant costumes.

There is an essential difference between this sort of productive process, which implies the symbolic consumption by relatively wealthy cosmopolitan Hmong in the States of commoditized forms of culture produced by their poorer 'brethren' in China (as in the invitation of Chinese Miao performing groups to events overseas), and the commercialization of Hmong tourist arts which has recently taken place in Thailand, although this too is an extraordinary process of aesthetic and productive transformation, and also one directly linked with the diaspora of refugee Hmong from Indochina.[13]

It was in the refugee camps along the Thai border that Hmong women from war-torn Laos began weaving concrete patterns illustrating their lives in Laos in a way which was entirely novel – since traditional art is entirely abstract – at about the same time that Western tourists visiting villages of the Thailand Hmong pioneered an interest in genuine, authentic 'hilltribe art'. The designs and patterns of refugee women, showing the planting of rice and the tapping of poppy-heads, bombs and 'yellow rain' falling from planes and helicopters,[14] proved a commercial success. An export trade in Hmong embroidery grew up, not only from the refugee camps to Thai villages and shops in urban Thai centres from where they could be sold to tourists, but also increasingly overseas for export, to shops like Liberty's in London and Bloomingdale's in New York. There soon followed the production of these new designs in Hmong villages in Thailand and the formation of needlework cooperatives by Hmong women in America.[15]

In the Hmong tourist arts one can see 'diasporic' Hmong producing commoditized images of their own culture for (consumption by) a largely non-Hmong clientele. This is a process somewhat different from the internal processes of consumption which have taken place between diasporic Hmong *themselves* which one can find in the Hmong American video market and the Hmong textiles businesses in China. And yet both these processes are importantly concerned with the production and presentation of particular images of the Hmong; one for a largely internal audience and clientele (videos of Chinese Miao bought by American Hmong), and one for an external audience (tourist-type ethnic art produced for sale to the general public). If (as Appadurai cites Simmel as saying) we call those objects valuable which resist our desire to possess them, it should be particularly important for future research to establish the extent to which the Chinese Hmong themselves are able to reappropriate their (newly revalued) images and representations, and the extent to which they have no choice but to comply with what is in fact a process of material and cultural domination.[16] And to understand the complexities of these processes, a kind of ethnographic 'audience research' is I think called for.[17]

Schein (1993) gives very telling instances of local Miao women confronted by visiting (Chinese) journalists and media people, and the issues of power and control which may ensue from this, with Miao women refusing to be photographed in certain postures, and the media people suggesting alternative representations which the Miao resist. She describes how a party of visiting journalists hired a 'bevy of local maidens' to brighten up the landscape, climbing with them up to a mountain pass above the village so they could be filmed along the way. Resting at the top of the pass, a photographer offered the girls some 'candy', but snatched it back before they could take it, demanding that they sing one more Miao song before they could have the candy. They stalled, however, and eventually got the candy without a song. Mary Rack, in her work in Hunan, also gives illuminating instances of how Miao images, together with other images of the local and the exotic, can be manipulated, in this ongoing process of cultural commodification *and* media representation (Rack 1999).

A techno-community

New technology has also enabled the production of new images of Hmong identity, for a variety of audiences, in which issues of power and control become particularly apparent.[18] Over the past six months I have been catching up with 'diasporic communications' through Hmong internet sites. Under the Hmong Electronic Resources Project based in Minnesota are listed the World Wide Web Hmong homepage, the Hmong-Australia homepage, Hmong Textiles, Samuel Neng Vang's homepage, Jeff Lindsay's homepage, the Lycos Search for Hmong, a Yamada Hmong World Wide Web Guide, the *Ywj Pheej* or Hmong Free Press, and cross-links to the University of Minnesota Refugee Studies Center, Lao group pages, US State Department reports on human rights abuses in Laos, and an extensive report called 'Hmong in the 90s: stepping towards the future' by the Hmong-American Partnership covering demography, immigration, secondary migration, country of origin, family, education, housing, income and employment among the Hmong of Minnesota, based on the 1990 US Census.

There are CDs for sale of traditional Hmong music, 'Hmong – Frequently Asked Questions', Job and Conference announcements, and a bookstore specializing in Hmong and related materials on China and Southeast Asia.

There are pages specially written outlining what is seen as Hmong culture and traditional custom – even a Hmong flag (with comments invited); Hmong 'creative work' including embroidery patterns and creative essays by students; a collection of extracts and snippets on 'Hmong history'; lists of publications on the Hmong; Hmong mailing lists and discussion forums; local Hmong TV and radio programmes and stations; and Hmong newspapers, journals and newsletters.

Some whole books are available online, like Barney's (1957) missionary thesis on Hmong messianism in Laos, and Hudspeth's (1937) *Stone Gateway and the Flowery Miao*.[19]

There have been at least three *Hmong Studies* journals online, with articles on adaptation, teenage truancy, shamanism, and many other subjects, and one Australian Hmong anthropologist and community leader recently directed me to a major article of his about Hmong identity which he now prefers to publish this way (Lee 1996). There are now several millions of Hmong words on the World Wide Web.

Despite a trend towards purely web-based research, there is a need for fieldwork of a fairly classic kind to supplement this. As other work has recently shown,[20] internet representations are open to analyses in terms of the same issues of representation, of identity, of political control and self-expression, and autonomy, which express themselves in other forms of cultural life, and may indeed be expressed even more clearly through what is said, and what is not, on the net – which I would see as a form of writing or inscription.

Some of the Hmong material on the net is in the nature of a public announcement of a distinctive minority identity and interests, a form of performative self-advertising directed at obtaining funding for community projects, or for political campaigns (like the one to have Hmong recognized as Vietnam veterans). A particular vision of Hmong history and identity is insisted on in this way, which is actually representative of only a minority of the range of Hmong overseas views on these issues. I have not so far found much representation of Hmong Christians, nor of explicit women's voices, on the Hmong-Net. Some of the material, on the other hand (a second type), seems to be genuinely educational in purpose, directing the inquiring surfer (or researcher) to publications and sources on the Hmong, with a more straightforwardly informational or propositional aim. The 'audience' here consists largely of those working directly with the Hmong in a variety of capacities – as researchers, as health workers or language teachers – and they are directed to information on the history, culture and background of the Hmong as a distinct and clearly articulated group.

Much of the 'public announcement' type of data is explicitly politically motivated, representing the views of the Vang Pao camp of extreme right-wing Hmong, although some representations of the more liberal Hmong tendency do also appear.[21] But the Hmong pages written in Hmong (a third type) are directed at a purely internal audience – computer-literate Hmong themselves. Entirely inwardly oriented, they range from discussions on aspects of traditional Hmong society and custom to exchanges of business information and constitutive debates or discussions and moral homily (quite a lot of this) directed at the younger generation about crises of cultural practice, centred around such issues as a recent series of teenage gang rapes.

It is not only Hmong who are addressing a wider public audience about Hmong identity and values; best-sellers like the journalist Jane Hamilton-Merritt's account of Hmong involvement in the secret wars in Laos, or Anne Fadiman's book on the collision of Hmong with American medical cultures, appeal to an even wider American public readership (Hamilton-Merritt 1993; Fadiman 1997). American Hmong voices on the net speak of a people with a highly articulate, sophisticated sense of their own identity, together with a shrewd knowledge of how to convey it, and for this reason the relationship between past and present images of the Hmong and Hmong culture, as propagated by particular groups with particular interests in the production of specific images for (consumption by) specific audiences, should have particular interest for us.

Some theory

The gradual shift of emphasis in theoretical preoccupation, from production towards consumption and expenditure, can to some extent be seen as a reflection of the preoccupations of a particular late phase of capitalism which some have called post-modern, in which the role of knowledge and communication is thought to adopt a special value, and cultural and symbolic capital may be fundamental.[22] The immediate products of labour have become less important, from the standpoint of a consideration of cultural consumption, than the products of new technologies and media; we ourselves live in a consumer-oriented society and most of us know more about consuming objects or images than we do about producing either. So that consumption-oriented analysis represents our own preoccupations, the particular phase of social development in which we find ourselves. We recognize that producers are consumers; but a relativist approach might query whether the emphasis on consumption relevant to a particular type of modern society has been appropriately applied to communities where production, and the relation of means to ends, is more immediate and direct, where access to basic information may be relatively unproblematic, or where consumption may not occupy the same stature as it does in our society, as may be the case in China.

Let us paint the socialist society of the pre-reform past in China as one in which conspicuous consumption, or consumption for the sake of consumption, was morally discouraged in a way comparable to the moral economy of peasant societies or a puritan ethos. As we know, a vase of flowers in the house during the Cultural Revolution was enough for one to be stigmatized as a decadent. And yes, flowers are not really necessary to the productive process, when that is taken as the overriding priority. They are symptoms of the 'sundry', rather than the 'all'. The weighing of consumptive against productive priorities, or values, raises the issue of the relationship of need and utility against the luxury which Bataille (1989) glosses as 'waste', the need *not* to use productively the 'fat' which is in fact essential to growth and development.[23] It is precisely this sort of weighing which is undertaken by the Chinese authorities in debates on the universality of human rights and their application in the 'special circumstances' of China.

'Socialism with Chinese characteristics', or 'market socialism', or the 'one country two systems' system, may perhaps be characterized as the growing acceptance, and recognition, of consumption as a part of the economy. Croll's (1994) work on the collapse of older collective ideas of heaven was particularly important in calling attention to this sociological shift.

If we can characterize the post-reform epoch in China in such terms, then the encounter between American Hmong and Chinese 'Miao' should be particularly important in illustrating the extremes of the transfer of new consumptive orientations which may be definitive of novel types of identity, or even in contributing to our understanding of how those magical signs and significations which may dominate both production and consumption are historically produced (Baudrillard 1988).

Yet there are worryingly evolutionistic implications to this line of argument. We know too that China has been rather good at consumption in the past, and the example of Shanghai in the 1930s is often cited. No such simple transition has in fact occurred in China as a whole, and perhaps not anywhere else. There have always been societies where consumption and extravagance, expenditure and the role of information, have been highly valued and enjoyed by sections of the society – where, to use Baudrillard's early (1988) terms, the magic of symbolic exchange prior to the industrial dominance of use-values and exchange-values eerily prefigured the magic of advertising, the reign of connotation. Anthropological re-thinkings of the role of ideology in 'simple' societies started in the late 1950s, and for perhaps half a century theory has tried to integrate an understanding of the role of culture, knowledge and information into analyses which were originally too narrowly economistically (production) focused. There is now a temptation to indulge in a new version of (culturalist) dogmatic evolutionism, in which it is perhaps too easy to talk about living in a special phase of consumer capitalism or modernity, a 'society of the spectacle' where the role of consumption has become central. Then as good moralists we can of course regret this state of affairs, and trace its invasion into more purely organized societies.

But we should beware of assuming that the interest in consumption inevitably reflected or somehow identified a particular phase of social development. While clearly provoked by current crises and conditions, the emphasis which there was on consumption merely went some way towards rectifying a previous imbalance in the general understanding of theories of economy, which are in this sense crucially linked with (shifting) theories of meaning.

Productive authors

The emergence of an interest in consumption in the early 1980s was paralleled by an equivalent interest in reception theory or reader response theory.[24] The problem in literary terms has been where to locate the meaning of a text: solely in the intention of the author, as the (very) old school had it; somehow inherent in the text, as in the 'New Criticism'; or in some kind of dialogic encounter of text with reader who annotates and interprets it – a more recent approach. The shift from author to text to reader has really paralleled the shift from production to exchange to consumption of goods and services in analyses of value. In semiotic terms, this latter shift was resisted by a residual fear about the loss of *authorial responsibility*, a deeply ego-rooted fear that, if interpretations could be endlessly differently made by endless future readers and receivers, no determinate meaning could ever be fixed (for instance, in the texts literature professors teach). It was easy to leap from such analyses to comparisons with consumer insatiability, and the (inherently) unlimited nature of wants.

Eco (1992) has paradoxically taken this fear of what he calls an 'unlimited semiosis'[25] (which Michaels (1980) had argued was due to the erroneous assumption of an isolated Cartesian self who interacts with an entirely autonomous text) rather seriously, arguing for a re-location of textual meaning somewhere between the text and its author, in that space, he says, where Mr. Wordsworth has not yet quite become his work; in what he calls an *intentio operis* or 'intention of the work'. Might it be possible to examine this space between author and work, between sender and message, and how might this compare to the hiatus between the producer and the product?[26]

If Ricoeur (1971) were taken at face value, and a complete conflation of consequences with significances insisted on, then the reader must precisely be seen as the consumer of texts, in this symbolic sense of consumption. And to privilege the reader would then be inevitably to privilege the consumer. It may be argued that we live in a society where readers are more important than authors – particularly since the challenges to traditional notions of authorship posed by mass electronic communications including the internet – and the many consumers more primary than the few producers.[27] But (to pursue the parallel) without any originary authors, what would readers (who may themselves be authors) read? And similarly (but not identically), without producers, what would consumers (who may themselves be producers) consume? The flaws in (the strong sense of) the argument only become apparent when we try to push it to its logical and extreme conclusions. First, to argue for the primacy of the producer's viewpoint over that of the consumer might be then taken as equivalent to a semiotic argument for the dominance of the authorial self and its ultimate dictatorial right to determine all future meanings (and uses) of the text. Second, and conversely, to *attack* the autonomy of the authorial (or Cartesian) self, and argue instead for a completely unlimited semiosis, might also be taken as equivalent to an attack on the primacy, importance or value of the producer; an argument that, while the producer may produce goods, what is done to them after that is anyone's business but the producer's own![28]

The potential conflations and confusions we have instanced between economic and semiotic domains are related, and not helped by the basic ambiguity of the term 'consumption' and the assumption that audiences must invariably be clienteles. In an age of mass consumption, important efforts have been made to establish authorship as distinct from consumption; hence the widespread concern with intellectual property rights, with copyrights and patents to protect the author and trademarks to protect the consumer. Notions of authorship and intellectual 'property' specific to Chinese political culture have been well examined by Alford (1995).[29]

It may be that 'late capitalist' society is marked by a greater and wider separation of production from consumption, and similarly of reader from author – and more than this, of consumer from consumer, as of the privileged reader from the not so privileged reader or those unable to read.[30] In examining how relations to consumption may define social classes and differentiations, Bourdieu (1984) was also intending to throw light on the limitations and constraints on actual polysemy. But how far could one go in taking the sign as a site of class struggle? In theoretical terms there has been a need for a more dialogic approach towards considerations both of value and of meaning, an approach which would be able to move back or forwards to the essential unity and inter-dependence of production with consumption, producer with consumer, (and again) of author with reader. Critical theory may require a closer relationship between the two divorced ends of this economic–semiotic spectrum, while practice increasingly demonstrates their artificial social separation.

Loss of the real?

For producers to be theoretically identified with consumers in this way may seem a kind of William Morris-like idyll of the industrial artisan, a Pre-Raphaelite dream of the ideal-archaic state of affairs, although it is precisely this unification of production with consumption which some have found in the internet.[31] As the power of the consumer grows and technical knowledge becomes more widely available, it has been argued, it may be the case that some consumers do indeed become producers again.

What is remarkable is that it is precisely this long-standing dream of the identity of consumer with producer which has informed the past painting of images of the Hmong by romantic Western ethnographers, and which may furthermore now lie at the source of the nostalgia of the American-Hmong themselves for their Chinese homeland. As Geddes (1976) put it in a striking quotation from Savina (1924):

> From time immemorial there has existed in China a race of men whose origins we do not know. Living continuously on the heights, away from all other Asiatics, these men speak a particular language unknown to all those who surround them, and wear a special dress which is seen nowhere else.

The image of isolation and noble self-sufficiency so often applied to the Hmong, the ability to provide for all one's needs so often attributed to them, points to and implies a sense of the unity of production with consumption which is always dreamed of as in the past.

At the same time, a related image of the Hmong as rapacious consumers of their natural environment has also haunted the traditional literature. It is only now we are beginning to realize what a false image the representation of Hmong as inveterate shifting cultivators throughout history has presented – both of the Hmong, who were not always shifting cultivators, and of shifting cultivation, where for example it was combined with various forms of forest management. Yet it is not these new realizations of the complexity of the Hmong past which Hmong from France and the United States carry with them when they return to Asia to visit relatives in Laos or Vietnam, or search out ancestral roots in southern China. Largely it is an image of a pastoral and idyllic past, derived in part from Western writings, often themselves based on the accounts of particular Hmong informants, in which the production and consumption of goods were more nearly aligned with each other, less stridently opposed.

It has to be seen as extraordinary that cultural capital can be so easily transformed into material capital in the way typified by the encounters and emerging economic relations between the American Hmong and the Chinese Miao, if we can accept an analysis in these sorts of terms. Romantic and sentimental images of the Hmong as having once had a homeland in China (really largely irrelevant to the material experiences of most Hmong from South East Asia whose families may have left China a hundred or more years ago) have somehow combined with the agony and anxiety of a displaced community, in bringing about new forms of political and academic association and new forms of economic enterprise. In this movement of return and realignment towards both Han Chinese culture and the state, a renewed sense of cultural identity expressing itself in a concern with the replication of authorized images has proved crucial. An authorized version of Hmong history has emerged among some of the overseas Hmong, for instance, which bears only an incidental relationship to reality, and an ancestral Hmong kingdom located variously in Sichuan and Mongolia (see Tapp 2004).

In this unequal process of the transnational production of particular images of the Hmong for (consumption by) particular audiences, the state plays an uncertain role, authorizing some forms of intervention (economic investment in Miao regions by overseas Hmong, such as was occurring in Sichuan with Taiwanese capital, as I show in the next section) and outlawing others (such as international Miao and Yao associations).[32] Louisa Schein (1998) suggests that the consumption of romanticized Miao images from China by wealthy American Hmong may be seen 'almost as "traditional" palliatives for the experience of "discomforting" modernity'. Indeed, this may be so, yet, as her own analysis shows, the situation is both more complex and more theoretically important than this, and the materials considered here merit further investigation.

Inscriptions of loss

We should remember that the Hmong have always had a particular relation to writing, of which the internet is perhaps one form.[33] While not claiming any traditional literacy – either in their own or in others' languages (unlike the related Yao peoples)[34] – Hmong have always shown a keen awareness of the *power* of the literacy which both expressed and enabled the might of neighbouring civilizations such as the Chinese, and they even have a series of narrative tales and legends which account for their original loss of writing, usually attributed to the actions of the avenging Chinese (Tapp 1989).

While differentiating themselves from the neighbouring Han Chinese civilization through a series of sharp contrasts in which images of loss and deprivation (of writing, of the state, of a king) figure strongly, at the same time the Hmong have arrested the attention of all the states they have inhabited (China, Vietnam, Laos and Thailand) through a series of resistances to state authority, which have often adopted a messianic form. In these messianic uprisings, a form of writing specific to the unwritten Hmong language, usually revealed to a prophet who leads the movement, validates the prophet's status. The most well-known of these messianic scripts is currently in some use by the overseas Hmong and in Southeast Asia, and has been introduced to the Hmong of China. It was invented (or discovered) by a man from Laos in a refugee resettlement area within Laos, and is one of the very few examples in history of a complete form of alphabetic writing for a language being discovered by a single individual (Smalley *et al.* 1994).

The legendary character who inspires these messianic movements centred on writing, through prophets who announce his birth, is a Hmong 'Emperor of China' who is always described as an *orphan* who has lost his father, and the Hmong of China have a series of fables about Laus Ntsuag, the 'Old

Orphan' who is without a father. In a patrilineal descent system such as that of the Hmong, to be without a father is effectively to be deprived of social status; without the clan affiliation bestowed by paternity, marriage (which cannot take place within the same paternal surname) is impossible.[35] The Hmong Orphan tales in China, therefore, focus on the marriage of the Orphan to a mystical maiden who is sometimes a spirit, sometimes a magic animal, after which a life of wealth and prosperity ensues.

In some ways the figure of the Orphan, so important in Hmong legendary lore, represents a sense of the sort of boundless potentiality which Steiner (1975) argued was inherent in the nature of language, through its capacity for fiction, counter-factual statements and conditionality. By being fatherless, clanless, and without therefore any social context or embeddedness, the Orphan is seen as effectively unmarked by the rich web of linguistic and kinship significations which inform the fabric of social life. The Orphan is posited as prior to these social and linguistic differentiations, and yet he is thought of as being able to overcome them, able to overturn the poverty and destitution of what should be his normal lot, precisely because of the formlessness and potentiality attributed to him, his capacity to avoid being caught within the mesh of social distinctions.

At the same time, however, the fact that the Orphan should be gendered as *male* shows how it is the very rhetoric of kinship and linguistic distinctions he is conceived of as overcoming which in fact posits him as prior (see Butler 1993). And throughout Hmong depictions of the Orphan there is a complete absence of the marking of maternity, a disavowal of the significance of motherhood and maternal descent (often the Orphan has a mother, and is yet seen as kinless) which seems to reflect the effective invisibility of Hmong women in everyday social life. While it is the absence of the father which is spoken of, the real absence in these stories is of any significance attached to the mother. It may, therefore, be possible to see the figure of this culture hero as expressing a kind of historic rage and envy, directed at the maternal image of the Han Chinese, in opposition to which Hmong historical identity has been constructed.

This would then show a desire, on the part of the historically constituted Hmong subject, to *consume Chineseness*, together with a fierce rage at the initial rejection of the 'Miao' by their Chinese mother-culture, and a desire to reject that culture in turn, and to establish a clearly defined separate identity; the mixture of frustration and gratification of which Klein (1957) first spoke.[36] The probability of such a fundamental ambivalence (the love for an object, and the desire to destroy it through consuming it), expressed in a simultaneous desire to be reunited with the mainstream of Han culture and yet to establish an autonomous identity clearly independent of it, is supported by historical data recording strong divisions in the Ming and the Qing between the more acculturated, Sinified Hmong (successful consumers of Chinese culture), and those who stayed up on the mountain tops and undertook messianic rebellions against it.

The sense of bereavement, of loss and regret towards the past – which we find not only in these Orphan tales but also in other Hmong tales such as those about the loss of writing and territory – may then be traced to the sense of an original differentiation of cultural identities between the Han and the Miao, the taking of different paths, the diversion from a common ancestral origin (cf. Ebrey 1996). This sense of both a lost and a regretted past should also be understood in terms of a messianic movement of history which points towards an always yet-to-be realized *future* of plenitude and accomplishment. Clearly any attempt to account for the pervading sense of loss which permeates Hmong cultural productions should also take into account the historic relations between Miao and Han. Such a culturally grounded account may also contribute to an understanding of some of the nostalgia experienced by Hmong refugees overseas. For there has been a duplication or even triplication of nostalgic regret, first for an immediate past in Southeast Asia which the first generation Hmong immigrants may have personal recollections of; and then for a more distant, mythologized past, in the foothills of southern China, which is leading directly to the re-encounters I have described; and finally for an even more antique time, in which distinctions between the Miao and Han were unknown or irrelevant. This past bereavement, and bereavement of the past, cannot be wholly attributed to a sense of the 'loss of the real' associated with the 'anachronistic' structure of consumption, as Baudrillard (1988, 1994) suggested, and it is something more than Jameson's (1985) endless imitation of dead styles.[37]

Virtual ambivalence

Certainly there was a kind of nostalgia, but for a real rather than an imagined past, in the reasons for the oldest of four Hmong brothers to revisit his home village in Sichuan where I undertook fieldwork.[38] The oldest brother had been with the Kuomintang shortly before Liberation, and was transported to Taiwan where he took a Chinese wife (giving his children Hmong generational names) and worked in the Post Office. Of his three younger brothers, two had remained in the village as farmers (one had been with the People's Liberation Army in Korea but had then retired back to the village), the other brother had risen to become a central-level cadre in the Minorities Affairs administrative hierarchy in Beijing. After economic reform the brothers had been able to make contact again, through intermediaries in Hong Kong, and the oldest brother's return, as a visiting Taiwanese, in 1988 and thereafter, was treated with great panoply by the local government. He had contributed to a local road-building project, and established scholarships at primary and secondary level for Hmong and other students. There were plans to establish a local hospital, and he had helped his youngest brother (in fact a half-brother) in the management of a local construction company which had formerly been a commune enterprise, to the extent that the manager had become a successful local entrepreneur in his own right, with no time for his fields. This is a common enough kind of story regarding transnational Chinese investments in China; not so common in the case of a widely distributed national minority like the Miao, whose formal association with members of the same group overseas is otherwise quite strictly controlled.[39]

What I found remarkable in Sichuan was the extent to which a kind of local cultural revival of interest in Hmong culture, associated with the patronage of the Taiwanese brother, was adopting some very *un*-Hmong, Han Chinese forms: the writing down of a genealogy (the Hmong traditionally have had no writing); and plans for the establishment of an ancestral hall in memory of the four brothers' paternal grandfather (the Hmong have no such institutions). This is not an essentialist argument; the absence of writing, and of temples or ancestral halls, are often taken as almost emblematic of Hmong identity by contrast with that of the Han Chinese.

So there was some 'recycling of cultural fragments' (Siu 1989) taking place in Sichuan, some 'resignification' of cultural practices, coalescing around Objects of Aspiration (dreams, Heaven?) which really were more important for what they signified (the Hmong ability to participate in Han Chinese status) than for what they were in themselves (ancestral hall, written genealogy).

There was then also a deep ambivalence here, a desire to consume Chineseness yet nevertheless not be consumed by it, since cultural revival was also adopting the form of tape-recording Hmong songs and printing Hmong legends and transcribing Hmong rituals; an almost ethnographic endeavour, then, in its production of images of exotic culture for consumption by whom? for posterity? (the ravages of the Cultural Revolution were frequently referred to, the 'forgetting' this has resulted in) or for a wider Chinese public? And we might compare or contrast this kind of production of cultural goods to the 'consumption' by American Hmong of exotic Miao images from China. But the nature of the audiences in question here is entirely different; the Sichuan movement was largely local, partly directed at local Hmong consumption while also for display to a wider Chinese public, but the videos and costumes bought by American Hmong point to more global processes, involving solely the Hmong community, yet a community divided by the same sorts of inequities which characterize relations between the Han and minorities within China. The emergence of new patterns of consumption in China is thus a multi-faceted process, involving considerations of value, desire and need.

At the minority folk village constructed as a presentation of national minority culture across the Hong Kong border in Shenzhen, brochures admit that they are not intended to reproduce the real conditions of minority life, because the principle has been followed of 'originating from real life but rising above it, discarding the dross and selecting only the essential' (see Tapp 1993). Here, idealized minority images (signs) are employed as icons of national identity, yet the kind of idealization which takes place in these images has much in common with the images produced by transnational members of those minorities themselves. We do need to consider the transnational exchanges which have occurred in the context of a kind of elite cultural production, both in the US and in China, which may largely exclude and misrepresent the majority of Hmong on state benefits in the US, or in more remote villages in China. There is a sense in which the excluded either become the objects of elite cultural representation or the unwitting consumers of images controlled and manipulated by others.

Consumption in the more literary sense evokes images of ungratified desires, of desires for unattainable objects which internally consume the desirer, of desires which, once satisfied, inevitably lead to further desires and are therefore truly insatiable and endlessly devouring both of the self and of its objects of desire. There is a passage in *A Rebours* (Huysmans 1959) where the dandy hero, Des Esseintes, undertakes 'foreign travel'; he has an entire room resembling a ship's cabin fitted inside an aquarium where he can admire clockwork fish entangled in artificial seaweed through port-holes let into the side of the room, which he has furnished with sextants and binoculars, charts and ships' timetables, and pictures of seascapes and the smell of tar – so that he enjoys all the anxiety and delights of travel without ever having actually to leave his house.[40] This is virtual enjoyment and virtual reality as it was discovered by the late-nineteenth-century romantics. The American Hmong may now be constructing this sort of virtual reality for themselves through the internet and videos and other images of an imagined life in China, and perhaps what is most interesting is how this kind of cultural consumption may feed into and impact the aspirations of the Hmong in China for a more prosperous and abundant future and the material goods they need.

Notes

1 This chapter was originally given as a paper at the London China Seminar at the School of Oriental and African Studies, London, 18 February 1999, on the theme of 'Consumption with Chinese characteristics'. I would like to thank all those at the seminar who commented on my paper, and in particular Stephan Feuchtwang, Michael Palmer, Stuart Thompson and Harriet Evans for their helpful suggestions. The chapter refers to work in progress, and to research which is largely still to be undertaken.

2 The transformation of use into exchange value is a signification or semiotic process, as Eco (1976) noted. See also Stewart (1993).

3 Thomas Mann describes such a sanatorium in *The Magic Mountain*, first published in 1924, the year Kafka died in one.

4 Like the medieval world of the Pre-Raphaelites.

5 As Jameson (1985) pointed out, the 'older or classical modernism' was oppositional and subversive to the established order. Both Bell (1976) and Campbell (1987) explored the relationship of romanticism to consumerism. Here, however, I consider in particular the 1890s aesthetes Campbell thought unimportant to modern consumerism.

6 I have a much expanded consideration of this elsewhere (Tapp 2001).

7 The First International Conference on the Hmong/Miao in Asia, Aix-en-Provence, 11–13 September 1998.
8 Dealing with similar materials, I have argued more extensively about the role of nostalgia elsewhere (Tapp 2003).
9 There have been political intents in the form of an American-Hmong nationalist movement which has sought to establish an anti-communist Hmong state in North Laos and Vietnam with Chinese assistance.
10 For a fuller account of these meetings, see Tapp (2003).
11 See in particular Savina (1924) and Bernatzik (1970).
12 See Patricia Symonds (1996) on the spread of AIDS in North Thailand through practices such as these.
13 Erik Cohen (2000) looks at some aspects of this process (within Thailand alone).
14 Yellow rain' is the name the Hmong gave to the spraying of chemicals on Hmong villages and forests in Laos.
15 See Nancy Donnelly's (1994) ethnography of the history of a Seattle needlework cooperative.
16 Simmel (1978) in Appadurai (1986: 3). See also Miller (1987).
17 This has not so far been undertaken with regard to minorities in China.
18 Soon after their arrival in the US, the Hmong showed a particular propensity for telephone communications (Tapp 1982).
19 Hudspeth (1937) actually writes about a non-Hmong group in Yunnan, the A Hmao, although this is not generally recognized.
20 Penny Harvey and Sarah Greene, 'Social Context of Virtual Manchester', talk given at Department of Anthropology, London School of Economics, 18 September 1998 (also the title of their ESRC project).
21 I understand some of the latter may have been deliberately bugged by the former.
22 In their different ways, Lyotard (1979), Habermas (1988) and Bourdieu (1984) agree on the central role of knowledge and communication in modern society.
23 Baudrillard (1988) also talked about the 'something more', the productive waste which defines affluence, the creation of value through destruction, as expenditure takes precedence over accumulation and appropriation.
24 This is well described by Terry Eagleton (1991); see also Tompkins (1980).
25 Hall (1997) and others prefer the term 'polysemy'.
26 Eco's words mark a partial return to a pre-Bakhtinian author.
27 Benjamin (1969) originally drew attention to how mechanical reproduction must jeopardize the authority of the original.
28 Bourdieu (1984) deals with this point in passing, in the opening pages of Distinction, when he discusses pure production and artistic autonomy, comparing the 'pure intention' of the artist in creating an open, polysemic work to that of a producer who aims to be autonomous, showing how the artist's intention is also determined by the structures of taste.
29 My thanks to Michael Palmer for these important points.
30 This should also be considered in the light of a growing complexification of the relation between means and ends.
31 See Richard D. Coyne (1999). See also Sadie Plant (1997) on cyberspace and the apparent realm of freedom promised by the internet.
32 For example, in the International Association of Yao Studies with which I was involved in Hong Kong, citizens of China were not permitted to join on an individual basis; separate associations had to be founded for each province, which were then separately affiliated to the international organization.
33 With thanks to Stuart Thompson for his remarks on the 'weaverless web'. The internet may be heteroglottic in challenging accepted notions of individual authorship.

34 The Yao have always aspired to Chinese literacy, have ritual texts written in Chinese, and wherever possible would invite itinerant Han teachers to their villages to teach the children characters (Lemoine 1982).
35 Of course there are pragmatic strategies for avoiding this situation. A child can be adopted into his or her mother's clan, or the clan of a mother's second husband, for example.
36 For example, her 'Envy and Gratitude' (Klein 1957) and other works.
37 Something more, too, than Stewart's 'nostalgic's utopia . . . where authenticity suffuses both word and world' (Stewart 1993). When we have said this, what have we explained?
38 I have described this more fully in Tapp (2001).
39 For example, Ong's (1999) discussion of philanthropy, Anagnost (1997) on constructions of civility.
40 Huysmans (1959), which is regarded as 'The Bible' of the Decadent movement.

References

Alford, W. (1995) *To Steal a Book is an Elegant Offence: Intellectual Property Law in Chinese Civilization*, Stanford: Stanford University Press.
Anagnost, A. (1997) *National Past-Times: Narrative, Representation, and Power in Modern China*, Durham, NC: Duke University Press.
Appadurai, A. (1986) 'Introduction: Commodities and the Politics of Value', in A. Appadurai (ed.), *The Social Life of Things: Commodities in Cultural Perspective*, Cambridge: Cambridge University Press.
Barney, G. (1957) 'Christianity and Innovation in Meo Culture: A Case Study in Missionization', unpublished MA thesis, University of Minnesota.
Bataille, G. (1989) *The Accursed Share*, vol. I, trans. R. Hurley, New York: Zone Books.
Baudrillard, J. (1988) *The Consumer Society: Myths and Structures*, London: Sage.
—— (1994) *Simulacra and Simulation*, Ann Arbor: University of Michigan.
Bell, D. (1976) *The Cultural Contradictions of Capitalism*, New York: Basic Books.
Benjamin, W. (1969) *Illuminations*, ed. H. Arendt, New York: Schocken.
Bernatzik, H. A. (1970) *Akha and Miao: Problems of Applied Ethnography in Further India*, New Haven: Human Relations Area Files.
Bourdieu, P. (1984) *Distinction: A Social Critique of the Judgement of Taste*, trans. R. Nice, London: Routledge and Kegan Paul.
Butler, J. (1993) *Bodies that Matter: On the Discursive Limits of 'Sex'*, London: Routledge.
Campbell, C. (1987) *The Romantic Ethic and the Spirit of Modern Consumerism*, Oxford: Basil Blackwell.
Cohen, E. (2000) *The Commercialized Crafts of Thailand: Hill Tribes and Lowland Villages*, Honolulu: University of Hawai'i Press.
Coyne, R. (1999) *Technoromanticism: Digital Narrative, Holism, the Romance of the Real*, Cambridge, MA: MIT Press.
Croll, E. (1994) *From Heaven to Earth: Images and Experiences of Development in China*, London: Routledge.
Dahlgren, P. (1994) 'La sphere publique a l'age des nouveaux medias', in D. Dayan and I. Veyrat-Masson (eds), *Espaces publics en image*, Hermes series, vols 13 and 14, Paris: CNRS.
Dayan, D. (1998) 'Particularistic Media and Diasporic Communications', in T. Liebes and J. Curran (eds), *Media, Ritual and Identity*, London: Routledge.
Donnelly, N. (1994) *Changing Lives of Refugee Hmong Women*, Seattle: University of Washington Press.

Eagleton, T. (1991) *Ideology: An Introduction*, London: Verso.
Ebrey, P. (1996) 'Surnames and Han Chinese Identity', in M. Brown (ed.), *Negotiating Ethnicities in China and Taiwan*, Berkeley: Institute of East Asian Studies, University of California.
Eco, U. (1976) *A Theory of Semiotics*, Bloomington: Indiana University Press.
—— (1992) *Interpretation and Overinterpretation*, Cambridge: Cambridge University Press.
Fadiman, A. (1997) *The Spirit Catches You and You Fall Down: A Hmong Child, Her American Doctors, and the Collision of Two Cultures*, New York: Farrar, Straus and Giroux.
Friedman, J. (1990) 'Being in the World: Globalization and Localization', in M. Featherstone (ed.), *Global Culture: Nationalism, Globalization and Modernity*, London: Sage.
Geddes, W. (1976) *Migrants of the Mountains: The Cultural Ecology of the Blue Miao (Hmong Njua) of Thailand*, Oxford: Clarendon Press.
Habermas, J. (1988) *Legitimation Crisis*, Cambridge: Polity Press.
Hall, S. (ed.) (1997) *Representations: Cultural Representations and Signifying Practices*, London: Sage.
Hamilton-Merritt, J. (1993) *Tragic Mountains: The Hmong, the Americans, and the Secret Wars for Laos, 1942–1992*, Bloomington: Indiana University Press.
Hudspeth, W. (1937) *Stone Gateway and the Flowery Miao*, London: The Cargate Press.
Huysmans, J. K. (1888) *A rebours*, trans. Robert Baldick (1959) as *Against Nature*, Harmondsworth: Penguin Classics.
Jameson, F. (1985) 'Postmodernism and Consumer Society', in H. Foster (ed.), *Postmodern Culture*, London: Pluto Press.
Klein, M. (1957) *The Writings of Melanie Klein*, London: Tavistock.
Lee, Gary Yia (1996) 'Cultural Identity in Post-Modern Society: Reflections on What is a Hmong?', in *Hmong Studies Journal* 1 (1). Available online at http://members.aol.com/hmongstudies/hsj.html (accessed 7 April 2005).
Lemoine, J. (1982) *Yao Ceremonial Paintings*, Bangkok: White Lotus Press.
Lyotard, J.-F. (1979) *The Postmodern Condition: A Report on Knowledge*, Manchester: Manchester University Press.
Mann, T. (1924) *Der Zauerberg*, trans. John E. Woods (1995) as *The Magic Mountain*, New York: Alfred A. Knopf.
Michaels, W. (1980) 'The Interpreter's Self: Peirce on the Cartesian Subject', in J. Tomkins (ed.), *Reader-Response Criticism*, Baltimore: Johns Hopkins University Press.
Miller, D. (1987) *Material Culture and Mass Consumption*, Oxford: Basil Blackwell.
Ong, A. (1999) *Flexible Citizenship: The Cultural Logics of Transnationality*, Durham, NC: Duke University Press.
Plant, S. (1997) *Zeros + Ones: Digital Women + the New Technoculture*, New York: Doubleday.
Rack, M. (1999) 'Images of Minorities, Memories of Bandits: Negotiating Local Identities in Lowland West Hunan', unpublished PhD thesis, University of Edinburgh.
Ricoeur, P. (1971) 'The Model of the Text: Meaningful Action Considered as Text', *Social Research*, 38: 529–62.
Savina, F. M. (1924) *Histoire des Miao*, Hong Kong: Société des Missions-Étrangères de Paris.
Schein, L. (1993) 'Popular Culture and the Production of Difference: the Miao and China', unpublished PhD thesis, University of California, Berkeley.

—— (1998) 'Importing Hmong Brethren to Hmong America: A Not-So-Stateless Transnationalism', in Pheng Cheah and B. Robbins (eds), *Cosmopolitics: Thinking and Feeling Beyond the Nation*, Minneapolis: University of Minnesota Press.

Simmel, G. (1978) *The Philosophy of Money*, London: Routledge.

Siu, H. (1989) 'Recycling Rituals: Politics and Popular Culture in Contemporary Rural China', in P. Link, R. Madsen and P. Pickowicz (eds), *Unofficial China: Popular Culture and Thought in the People's Republic*, Boulder: Westview Press.

Smalley, W., Chia Koua Vang and Gnia Yee Yang (1994) *Mother of Writing: The Origin and Development of a Hmong Messianic Script*, Chicago: The University of Chicago Press.

Sontag, S. (1979) *Illness as Metaphor*, London: Allen Lane.

Steiner, G. (1975) *After Babel: Aspects of Language and Translation*, Oxford: Oxford University Press.

Stewart, S. (1993) *On Longing: Narratives of the Miniature, the Gigantic, the Souvenir, the Collection*, Durham, NC: Duke University Press.

Symonds, P. (1996) 'Empowerment and Participation: Prevention in the AIDS era', paper presented at the Sixth International Conference on Thai Studies, University of Chiang Mai, 14–17 October 1996.

Tapp, N. (1982) 'The Relevance of Telephone Directories to a Lineage-Based Society: A Consideration of Some Messianic Myths among the Hmong', *Journal of the Siam Society*, 70 (1 and 2): 114–27.

—— (1989) *Sovereignty and Rebellion: The White Hmong of Northern Thailand*, New York, Singapore and Oxford: Oxford University Press.

—— (1993) 'Folk Culture Villages in Shenzhen', *Anthropology Today*, 9 (3): 23, 25.

—— (1998) 'The Hmong/Miao in Asia', *Anthropology Today*, 14 (6): 23.

—— (2001) *The Hmong of China: Context, Agency and the Imaginary*, Leiden: Brill.

—— (2003) 'Exiles and Reunion: Nostalgia among Overseas Hmong (Miao)', in C. Stafford (ed.), *Living with Separation in China: Anthropological Accounts*, London and New York: RoutledgeCurzon.

—— (2004) 'The State of Hmong Studies (An Essay on Bibliography)', in N. Tapp, J. Michaud, C. Culas and G. Y. Lee (eds), *Hmong/Miao in Asia*, Chiang Mai: Silkworm Books.

Tompkins, J. (ed.) (1980) *Reader-Response Criticism*, Baltimore: Johns Hopkins University Press.

12 Afterword

Reflections upon China, consumption and cultural change

Kevin Latham

The chapters in this volume cover a wide range of issues related to consumption in contemporary China. They do not by any means, and nor are they intended to, offer a comprehensive overview of the broad spectrum of diverse consumer practices in China. However, they do offer food for thought about the diverse ways in which consumption in Chinese contexts needs to be considered. From the examples discussed in the different chapters here we can see that understanding consumption in China requires attention to more than just consumerism, and consumption is not simply a manifestation or epiphenomenon of economic reform in the PRC and the emergence and transformation of contemporary Chinese capitalism. Rather, consumption has to be seen as a fundamental component of contemporary Chinese cultural practices, taking into account both the continuities and the ruptures between different contexts in Greater China and beyond.

The chapters in this volume also warn against unnecessary and misplaced essentialism. Many of the chapters here emerged from the question of what consumption with Chinese characteristics is, and the answers that they offer confirm the importance of acknowledging the specificities of Chinese contexts. They also reveal common themes and issues that cut across different examples. However, at the same time they suggest that the identification of common elements that run through or underpin them all would be contrived. Indeed, the combination of particular historically situated examples, such as Bayne's photography in Hangzhou or Klein's ethnic foodways in Guangzhou, combined with the broader historical perspectives, such as Croll's, Stafford's or Thompson's, that identify both changes over time and continuities traceable to previous generations and other contexts within Greater China, suggest that consumption in China entails constantly shifting, overlapping, diverging and interconnecting sets of practices.

In contrast to previous studies of Chinese consumption, this volume has shown the importance of understanding consumption in China not solely as a phenomenon characteristic of the post-Mao reform period in the PRC. Indeed, this has been an eye-catching feature of Chinese consumption in recent years. However, the chapters here have suggested that additional perspectives on Chinese consumption are to be obtained through consideration of more broadly defined Chinese cultural contexts.

At the same time we have seen how consumption in China is both constantly changing itself and also constantly participating in other areas of cultural change. Hence, we have seen how Chinese consumption is continually taking on new forms, whether it be through changing restaurant fashions, media imagery, or its relation to resurrected Confucianism. Yet consumption also plays a crucial part in fundamental social and cultural changes with a broader significance for understandings of Chinese society. In this respect there is little more fundamental than the way that the Chinese authorities, social and commercial organizations and individual Chinese people conceptualize themselves. In this volume, for instance, Palmer, Klein and Latham have all plotted the emergence of new legal and social figures in the contemporary PRC through the concept of 'the consumer'. This change, and all the consequent changes in social practices that it sets in motion, marks a significant re-imagining of the populace and a movement away from notions of 'the masses' – with all the political and historical baggage that comes with that term in China – to something quite different. Past conceptualizations of the Chinese populace as in need of mass political education, which still circulate, now contend with increasingly strong notions of individual – or in some cases collective – consumer rights, decision-making powers, volition, tastes, spending power and personality. Through new forms of consumption in the PRC, Chinese people are coming to re-imagine themselves and others in previously unthinkable ways.

However, despite the important relation between consumption and change, the chapters in this volume have also revealed how consumption in the present is strongly linked to the past (see e.g., Evans) and to so-called traditional aspects of Chinese social interaction such as eating and food habits (Klein, Thompson), death rites (Thompson), interpersonal relations, Confucianism and religion (Croll, Stafford, Thompson). Evans, for instance, showed that although there are clear changes in the relation between gender and consumption in the contemporary PRC – particularly considering what is consumed and how – there are all the same less immediately striking, but just as important, continuities to be found between the very different consumer practices of reform- and Mao-period China. Meanwhile Croll and Stafford both demonstrated the importance of broader cultural practices of *guanxi* relations and networking that at least cross the Taiwan Straits and point to even broader Chinese cultural contexts. Indeed, consumption, seen through the diverse perspectives of this volume, proves to be a useful vehicle for plotting similarities and partial connections (cf. Strathern 1991) between different parts of Greater China. The different papers suggest ways in which consumer cultures in the region are moving closer together in terms of products, methods, marketing and experiences (see also Gold 1993; Barme 1999). At the same time we have seen how consumption understood more broadly than simply consumerism to include cultural practices such as ritual, eating, religion and social networking, also increasingly reveals cross-regional similarities, even if it is important to note the distinctive contexts of Hong Kong, Taiwan and the PRC.

Several of the chapters in this volume have further established the importance of considering China's consumption in increasingly transnational and global contexts (e.g. Robinson, Tapp, Stafford, Croll). China is being rapidly incorporated into global systems of communications, finance, leisure, entertainment, scholarship and much more. Hence, what is going on in China in terms of consumption clearly has to be seen in the context of globalization and transnational cultural interaction. However, understanding globalization from a Chinese perspective is not a matter of imposing a global formula of post-modernity or consumer behaviour but requires attention to the particular characteristics of each case. Klein's ethnic food consumption in Guangzhou is set against a backdrop of global fast food chains (cf. Watson 1999), but the changing dynamics of Guangzhou's restaurants and food journalism are totally bound up with the specificities of Guangzhou, China, the role of the Party and the State in society and attitudes and understandings of Cantonese diners and connoisseurs. Similarly, the emergence of the consumer as an important figure in media production is not by any means unique to China, but the specific situation that the newspaper discussed by Latham finds itself in is inexplicable without reference to China's particular state media system, the political demands on Chinese journalists and so on. In the same vein, Evans shows how understanding contemporary Chinese media images of women requires careful attention less to similar international examples than to conceptualizations of gender dating back to the Mao period. Similarly, Bayne's account of photography in Hangzhou shows that, although this was an example of Chinese consumers increasingly taking up a global leisure and consumer practice, they were none the less very much caught up in a moment of transition quite particular to China's historical, political, economic and social development.

The focus on media and new technologies in various chapters of this volume (Tapp, Robinson, Latham, Klein, Evans) has shown their importance for understanding contemporary Chinese consumption. The media are a fundamental part of contemporary Chinese consumption. In relation to the PRC, Klein, Evans and Latham all point to the range of roles that media take whether themselves as objects of consumption or in controlling or promoting it. But the importance of media clearly extends beyond the context of the PRC. Robinson's chapter on the films of Wong Kar-wai reveals a similar complex configuration of roles and relationships between media and consumption in which film is consumed and becomes a vehicle of consumption itself, while at the same time offering a means for viewers to contemplate notions of identity in Hong Kong. By Robinson's account we come to see both how consumption features prominently in contemporary Chinese society and how, through the consumption of Wong's films about consumption, people may also revisit their relationship with modernity, global and Chinese consumerism and personal practices of identification. In a very different context, we have seen with Tapp's account of Hmong identities other ways in which the consumption of identities is inseparable, if not enabled, by the emergence of new media technologies.

A recurring issue throughout the volume has been that of the relation between consumption, identities and practices of identification. In fact, considering the themes of all the chapters from Confucianism and *guanxi* through to eating, the cultural recognition of deceased kin, representations of gender and the transnational mediated consumption of ethnicity, the theme of identification figures as one of the most common links between chapters in this volume. However, the diversity of the practices and contexts that are dealt with warns against looking for simple formulations of the relationship between identity and consumption. There are connections between these practices and contexts, but they are more often than not what Marilyn Strathern has called 'partial connections' (1991) – partial in the senses of both being incomplete and pertaining to particular perspectives. This therefore leads us to look for and acknowledge connections where they exist and analytically to make connections between diverse contexts. However, as Strathern points out, a key issue to pay attention to in anthropological comparison is that of purpose, and in making connections between practices of identification we are not looking for the building blocks of an essential identity so much as seeking to understand the particular kinds of connections that we and others are making. There is no essence to the relationship between Chinese identities and consumption: one does not 'become' (or for that matter 'deny being') Chinese through consumption, and we must avoid simple formulae that would suggest one creates, selects or produces one's identity through buying or choosing consumer goods, eating, reading a newspaper or engaging in other forms of consumption. Yet clearly, as we have seen, one does participate in and contribute to the manifestation, maintenance and transformation of contemporary Chinese culture through these diverse practices of consumption.

This is a conclusion which, slightly surprisingly perhaps, stands opposed to many previous considerations of Chinese consumption in which consumption has in fact commonly been segregated in one way or another from Chinese culture. For instance, for some the rise of contemporary consumerism in the PRC is positioned as a threat to Chinese culture, conceived in terms of traditional high culture (e.g. Meng 1997: 67). Another version of this position, which tends to decentre consumption as a Chinese cultural practice, is to categorize it as one aspect of Chinese '*popular* culture' rather than Chinese culture as such (e.g. Gold 1993; Barme 1999; cf. also Johnson, Nathan and Rawski 1985). Alternatively, consumption is categorized as economic, rather than cultural, activity (e.g. Chao and Myers 1998; Wu 1999) or as a political challenge to party hegemony (Davis 2000; Madsen 2000). In other accounts Chinese culture is considered to impact upon consumer activity (Li 1998; Yau 1994) rather than to constitute it.

Viewed collectively, the chapters in this volume, by contrast, suggest that consumption should be considered an important constitutive part of Chinese culture as much as kinship, lineages and religion – on an anthropological understanding of culture – or alternatively art, literature, music or other features of so-called 'High Culture'. Thompson's chapter clearly illustrates, for example, how the conceptualization of food and consumption can play a crucial role in the performance of death rites – considered by Watson (1988) to be a fundamental feature of Chinese culture and being Chinese – and highlights the cultural importance of understanding consumption in terms much more broadly than simply consumerism. At the same time, we have seen consumption related to a range of other fundamental Chinese cultural practices, including the conduct of interpersonal relations, the appeal to Confucianism, media use and production, legal statutes, food and gender relations. Indeed, the recurring theme of identity that we have noted also reinforces the vision of consumption's central role in understanding Chinese culture. From this perspective, the partial connections we have identified point to ways of navigating one's way through contemporary Chinese culture that do not assume or look for an underlying essence but do recognize the importance, the significance, the usefulness and the analytical and critical value of drawing attention to overlaps, patterns, continuities and connections across different areas of Chinese cultural practice.

References

Barme, G. R. (1999) *In the Red: On Contemporary Chinese Culture*, New York: Columbia University Press.

Chao, L. and Myers, R. H. (1998) 'China's consumer revolution: the 1990s and beyond', *Journal of Contemporary China*, 7 (18), 351–68.

Davis, D. S. (2000) 'Introduction: a Revolution in Consumption', in D. S. Davis (ed.), *The Consumer Revolution in Urban China*, Berkeley: University of California Press.

Gold, T. (1993) 'Go with your feelings: Hong Kong and Taiwan popular culture in Greater China', *China Quarterly*, 136, December.

Johnson, D., Nathan, A. J. and Rawski, E. S. (eds) (1985) *Popular Culture in Late Imperial China*, Berkeley: University of California Press.

Li Conghua (1998) *China: the Consumer Revolution*, Singapore: John Wiley and Sons (Asia) Pte Ltd.

Madsen, R. (2000) 'Epilogue: The Second Liberation', in D. S. Davis (ed.), *The Consumer Revolution in Urban China*, Berkeley: University of California Press.

Meng, F. H. (1997) *Madness and Joy of the Spirit of the People: the problem of cultural conflict in contemporary China* (Zhongshen kuangxi: dangdai zhongguo de wenhua chongtu wenti), China's Problems series, Beijing: Jinri zhongguo chubanshe.

Strathern, M. (1991) *Partial Connections*, Lanham: Rowman and Littlefield.

Watson, J. L. (1988) 'The Structure of Chinese Funerary Rites: Elementary Forms, Ritual Sequence, and the Primacy of Performance', in J. L. Watson and E. S. Rawski (eds), *Death Ritual in Late Imperial and Modern China*, Berkeley: University of California Press.

—— (ed.) (1999) *Golden Arches East: McDonald's in East Asia*, Stanford: Stanford University Press.

Wu Yanrui (1999) *China's Consumer Revolution: the emerging patterns of wealth and expenditure*, Cheltenham: Edward Elgar.

Yau, O. H. M. (1994) *Consumer Behaviour in China: customer satisfaction and cultural values*, London: Routledge.

Index

For Product Safety Concerns and Information please contact our EU
representative GPSR@taylorandfrancis.com
Taylor & Francis Verlag GmbH, Kaufingerstraße 24, 80331 München, Germany

www.ingramcontent.com/pod-product-compliance
Ingram Content Group UK Ltd.
Pitfield, Milton Keynes, MK11 3LW, UK
UKHW021722240926
475702UK00029BA/1808
* 9 7 8 0 4 1 5 5 4 6 8 6 7 *